Istvan Kecskes (Ed.)

Common Ground in First Language and Intercultural Interaction

Mouton Series in Pragmatics

Volume 26

Common Ground in First Language and Intercultural Interaction

Edited by
Istvan Kecskes

DE GRUYTER
MOUTON

ISBN 978-3-11-161962-0
e-ISBN (PDF) 978-3-11-076675-2
e-ISBN (EPUB) 978-3-11-076677-6
ISSN 1864-6409

Library of Congress Control Number: 2022946791

Bibliographic information published by the Deutsche Nationalbibliothek
The Deutsche Nationalbibliothek lists this publication in the Deutsche Nationalbibliografie; detailed bibliographic data are available on the internet at http://dnb.dnb.de.

This volume is text- and page-identical with the hardback published in 2023.
Typesetting: Integra Software Services Pvt. Ltd.

www.degruyter.com

Contents

Istvan Kecskes

Introduction

In classic pragmatic models interlocutors can successfully communicate intended meanings by taking common ground into account. This common ground in interactions is typically taken to be a body of information that is in a sense assumed to be shared between participants. Duranti (1997) argued that even comparatively simple exchanges such as greeting are organized according to complex socio-historic cultural knowledge and are dependent for their interactional accomplishment on participants "sharing" that knowledge, having it as part of common ground. Where this knowledge is not shared, one might expect breaches to these taken for granted linguistic forms, with all kinds of interactional consequences. The more common ground we share with another person, the less effort and time we need to convey and interpret information. Enfield (2008: 223) uses the term, "economy of expression" for this phenomenon.

In recent years the traditional approach to common ground (e.g. Stalnaker 1978, 2002; Clark and Brennan 1991; Clark 1996) has been challenged from different perspectives. Taking into account not only L1 but also intercultural interactions and attempting to bring together the traditional view with the egocentrism-based view of cognitive psychologists (Barr 2004; Barr and Keysar 2005; Colston and Katz 2005), Kecskes and Zhang (2009) argued that construction of common ground is a flexible and dynamic process. It is the convergence of the mental representation of shared knowledge that we activate, assumed mutual knowledge that we seek, and rapport as well as knowledge that we co-construct in the communicative process. Based on this approach Kecskes and Zhang (2009) made a difference between core common ground and emergent common ground. The former is knowledge we assume to share at the time of conversation and the later is knowledge that is generated and shared in the process of interaction.

People usually infer this "core common ground" from their past conversations, their immediate surroundings, and their shared cultural background and experience. We can distinguish between three components of core common ground: information that the participants share, understanding the situational context, and relationships between the participants – knowledge about each other and trust and their mutual experience of the interaction. According to current research if people have common or similar prior experience, participate in similar actions and events, they know each other and have been in similar situations before, all that will result in core common ground. Similar prior contexts, prior experience and similar understanding of the actual situational context will build common ground. This is all the result of a longer, diachronic process, so

https://doi.org/10.1515/9783110766752-001

what is happening in intercultural interactions where we have temporary speech communities? Of course, interlocutors there also share some core common ground, but it is usually quite limited. Understanding between interlocutors with similar histories, experiences and world knowledge is believed to be much easier than between those who lack or have limited common backgrounds (Gumperz 1982; Scollon and Scollon 2001; Tannen 2005; Kecskes 2021).

Communication conventions are usually acquired through a long-lasting history of socialization and usage in the first language. They are generally processed unconsciously during interaction, thus, not easily subject to repair procedures. However, participants of intercultural communication do not share much of that type of common ground, which has led to a "problem approach" in second language and intercultural communication research. Gass and Varonis (1985: 340) summed up the various issues associated with "shared background" and described in their study what can be termed a problem approach to the study of cross-cultural, cross-linguistic communication: ". . . NSs [native speakers] and NNSs [nonnative speakers] are multiply handicapped in conversations with one another. Often, they may not share a world view or cultural assumptions, one or both of which may lead to misunderstanding. In addition, they may not share common background . . . that would permit them to converse with shared beliefs about what Gumperz and Tannen (1979) call the "semantic content" of the conversation. Furthermore, they may have difficulty with speaking and interpreting an interlocutor's discourse as a result of a linguistic deficit."

The main problem in intercultural interactions is that interlocutors do not and cannot have that type of core common ground that L1 speakers have because of limited common prior experience. Consequently, since they have little shared knowledge to activate and seek, they have to co-construct common ground in the course of conversation. Generally, there is more reliance on core common ground in L1, while in intercultural interaction we see the priority of emergent common ground. This dynamic understanding of common ground has been applied in many research projects addressing both L1 and intercultural interactions in recent years. As a result, several new elements, aspects and interpretations of common ground have been identified. Some researchers (e.g. Roberts 2012; Garcia-Carpintero 2015) came to view the common ground as one component in a complex contextual information structure. Others analyzing intercultural interactions pointed out dynamism of the interplay of core common ground and emergent common ground (e.g. Ladilova and Schröder 2022; Macagno 2018; Diedrichsen and Nolan 2019; Ping 2018). The volume aims to present current research from different angles of pragmatics and communication to examine 1) what adjustments to the notion of common ground based on L1 communication should be made in the light of research in intercultural communication, 2) What the relationship is between context, situation and common ground, and 3) how relevant knowledge and content get selected for inclusion into core and emergent common ground.

The volume consists of five parts. After this introduction the second part contains chapters about general issues of common ground such as the relationship of common ground and context (Keith Alan), cognitive character of common ground (Brian Nolan), obstacles in common ground building (Arto Mustajoki) and negotiation of common ground (Fabricio Macagno). The third part focuses on emergent common ground in online discussions (Elke Diedrichsen) and in classroom interactions (Adriana Merino and Eunhee Kim). The fourth section looks at common ground building from different perspectives. Karsten Senkbeil's chapter discusses mutual knowledge and hidden common ground. Olga Obdalova, Ludmila Minakova and Alexandra Soboleva argued that the linguistic code functions as common ground in English as a Foreign Language communication. Qing Yang's chapter treats disagreement as interactional resource for developing interculturality. The last part explores common ground in different discourses such as written discourse (Ivana Trbojevic), business communication (Liu Ping) and aikido training (Greet Angèle De Baets, and Ellen Van Praet).

References

Barr, Dale J. 2004. Establishing conventional communication systems: Is common knowledge necessary? *Cognitive Science* 28(6). 937–962.

Barr, Dale J. and Boaz, Keysar. 2005. Making sense of how we make sense: The paradox of egocentrism in language use. In Colston Herbert L. and Albert N. Katz (eds.), *Figurative Language Comprehension: Social and cultural influences*, 21–43. Mahwah, N. J.: Lawrence Erlbaum.

Clark, Herbert H. 1996. *Using Language*. Cambridge: Cambridge University Press.

Clark, Herbert H. and Susan E. Brennan. 1991. Grounding in communication. In Resnick Lauren B., Levine John M. and Stephanie D. Teasley (eds.), *Perspectives on Socially Shared Cognition*, 127–149. Washington, DC: American Psychological Association.

Colston, Herbert L. and Albert N. Katz (eds.). 2005. *Figurative Language Comprehension: Social and cultural influences*. Hillsdale, NJ: Erlbaum.

Duranti, Alessandro. 1997. Universal and cultural-specific properties of greetings. *Journal of Linguistic Anthropology* 7(1). 63–97.

Diedrichsen E and Nolan B (eds.) 2019. *Linguistic perspectives on the construction of meaning and knowledge*. Cambridge: Cambridge Scholars Publishing.

Enfield, Nicholas J. 2008. Common ground as a resource for social affiliation. In Kecskés István and Jacob Mey (eds.), *Intention, Common Ground and the Egocentric Speaker-Hearer*, 223–254. Berlin/New York: Mouton de Gruyter.

García-Carpintero, M. 2015. Accommodating presupposition. *Topoi*. doi: 10.1007/s11245-014-9264-5.

Gass, Susan M. and Evangeline Marlos, Varonis. 1985. Miscommunication in native/nonnative conversation. *Language in Society* 14(3). 327–343.
Gumperz, John J. 1982. *Discourse Strategies.* Cambridge: Cambridge University Press.
Gumperz, John J. and Deborah, Tannen. 1979. Individual and social differences in language use. In Fillmore Charles J., Kempler Daniel and William S.-Y. Wang (eds.), *Individual Differences in Language Ability and Language Behavior*, 305–325. New York: Academic Press.
Kecskes, I. 2021. Processing implicatures in English as a Lingua Franca communication. *LINGUA*254.
Kecskes, Istvan and Fenghui, Zhang. 2009. Activating, seeking and creating common ground: A socio-cognitive approach. *Pragmatics and Cognition* 17(2). 331–355.
Ladilova, Anna and Ulrike Schröder. 2022. Humor in intercultural interaction: A source for misunderstanding or a common ground builder? A multimodal analysis. *Intercultural Pragmatics* 19(1). 71–101.
Liu, Huiying and Ping Liu. 2019. Common ground and metapragmatic expressions in BELF meetings: A response to Zhang and Wu. *Journal of Pragmatics* 148, July 2019. 118–121.
Macagno, F. 2018. Assessing relevance. *LINGUA* April 2018.
Roberts, C. 2012. Information structure in discourse: towards an integrated formal theory of pragmatics. *Semantics. Pragmatics* 49. 1–69. [Originally published in OSU Working Papers in Linguistics, 1998, vol. 49 (eds. J. Yoon and A. Kathol).]
Scollon, Ron and Suzanne Wong, Scollon. 2001. *Intercultural Communication: A discourse approach* (2nd edn.) Cambridge: Blackwell.
Stalnaker, Robert C. 1978. Assertion. In Cole Peter (ed.), *Syntax and Semantics 9: Pragmatics*, 315–332. New York: Academic Press.
Stalnaker, Robert C. 2002. Common ground. *Linguistics and Philosophy* 25. 701–721.
Tannen, Deborah. 2005. Interactional sociolinguistics as a resource for intercultural pragmatics. *Intercultural Pragmatics* 2(2). 205–208.

1 Understanding common ground

Keith Allan

The interdependence of common ground and context

Abstract: The aim of this essay is to argue that common ground is context shared between S (speaker, writer, signer) and H (audience) under the following conditions: S utters υ, evoking context C1 (the 'world and time spoken of') so as to bring about in C3 (the 'situation of interpretation' from H's point of view) H's understanding υ in terms of the relevant beliefs that S holds or purports to hold in respect of uttering υ (i.e. speaking of C1) in C2 – the 'world and time spoken in' – which is the situation of utterance from S's point of view. If C3 is very different from C2 such that H does not share some of S's system of beliefs and assumptions, H may be well able to understand what S intended to mean; nevertheless, υ can have reduced comprehensibility and its psycho-social appropriateness may be differently evaluated from the way S expected to be understood: examples would be when a 21st century H reads a sonnet by William Shakespeare or, for another instance, reacts to Jeannie Gunn referring in 1908 to Indigenous Australians as *niggers* (despite her showing greater respect for their culture and land rights than most of her white contemporaries).

1 Overview

Common ground (CG) exists between members of community K who mutually know or believe some possibly singleton set of (purported) facts F. A purported fact can be expressed as a proposition φ believed to be true within K (that is, by at least some members of K). When a member μ of K applies knowledge of F (that is, belief in the truth/existence of F) in order to interpret state of affairs, a possibly singleton set of propositions Φ, μ_K can presume that others in the community will also be able to apply knowledge of F (belief in the truth/existence of F) in order to interpret Φ (cf. Garfinkel 1964: 33). The existence of F, Φ, and the application of knowledge of F to interpreting Φ is what constitutes common ground for members of the community K. Once attended to, Φ becomes part of F, incrementing the common ground. When S, the speaker, writer, signer, is a member of K ($\mu_S \in K$), S's utterance υ pragmatically entails that S presupposes that Φ is already part of the conversational context at t (in other words, it is in the CG), or that H ($\mu_H \in K$) is prepared to add Φ, without objection, to the context against which υ is evaluated, such that the CG is extended. Pragmatic entailment

https://doi.org/10.1515/9783110766752-002

can be characterized as follows: when A pragmatically entails B, B cannot – given A – be denied without creating a paradox, absurdity, or contradiction. Pragmatic entailment gives rise to Moore's paradox: *I went to the pictures last Tuesday, but I don't believe that I did* (Moore 1952: 543); more generally, *p and I don't believe that p* and *p and I believe that not-p*.[1]

In saying that both S and H are members of K ($\mu_S \in K$ and $\mu_H \in K$) I invoke the normal situation in which S and H are members of same community and, broadly speaking, share knowledge of a common language and knowledge of a common culture. This default is the basis for real world variations, where S and H do not share knowledge of a common language and/or knowledge of a common cultural heritage. In such statistically unusual cases, S and H negotiate CG on the basis of common humanity. Speakers also address animals (which may seem to react appropriately) and inanimate or metaphysical objects (which don't react[2]) in which cases 'H' is anthropomorphized. I assume that when S utters υ, there is always an actual or presumed H. Typically, in conversation S perceives an actual H (seen and/or heard); but a writer presumes a reader (H); the farewell video of a suicide bomber presumes a viewing listener (H); persons (including writers of secret diaries) may on rare occasions talk to themselves (S=H).

The context of a language expression ε, a constituent of utterance υ, such that $\varepsilon \subseteq \upsilon$, comprises C1, C2, and C3. C1, 'the world (and time) spoken of' by S, is a mental model of an actual or recalled or imagined world. C1 captures what is said about what at some world – a possible world accessible from C2.[3] A model of the world (and time) spoken of is the content of a mental space which can be readily associated in a variety of ways with other worlds (and times) occupying other mental spaces. C1 is largely identified from co-text:

(i) via the semantic frames and scripts (Bartlett 1932; Fillmore 1982; Marslen-Wilson, Levy and Tyler 1982; Mazzone 2011; Minsky 1977; Prince 1981; Sanford and Garrod 1981; Schank 1984; Schank and Abelson 1977) evoked by the various constituents ($\varepsilon_{1...n}$) of υ – given their structure within υ; and

---

1 There is similarity between my 'pragmatic entailment' and 'explicature' in Relevance Theory (Sperber and Wilson 1995; Carston 2002; Capone 2013) but the definitions are not the same. An explicature is a proposition communicated by an utterance if and only if it is a development of a logical form encoded by the utterance (Sperber and Wilson 1995: 182). Nonetheless, it is possible that my 'pragmatic entailment' may indeed be what, in RT, is an 'explicature'.

2 Ignoring inanimates programmed to react to recognized speech through artificial intelligence and prayers imagined to be answered by gods.

3 Although some of the worlds described in Douglas Adams *Hitchhiker's Guide to the Galaxy* (Adams 1992) are subject to different natural laws than the world of its readers, they are 'accessible' worlds in my use of the term because we can understand them in the sense that we can follow the action in the way the author seems to have intended.

(ii) S's attitude to what is spoken of or to the persons addressed as this is revealed by the locution.

(i) and (ii) contribute to identifying what S's purpose might be in making the utterance, which is the effective meaning of ε⊆υ.

C2, 'the world spoken in', is the situation in which υ is expressed from S's point of view (POV), where the POV derives from S's weltanschauung. C2 captures who does the saying to whom, and where and when this takes place. C2 normally determines the social relationships and conventions that S is expected to follow and, in consequence, sets the standard for the psycho-social appropriateness of what is said. C2 is what governs, for instance, whether such terms as *bitch, cunt,* or *nigger* are used as a slur or as an expression of (?bantering) camaraderie and whether or not a particular form of words is polite (or not).

C3 is a corresponding situation of interpretation in which H seeks to understand ε⊆υ, i.e. the meaning of ε in the context (C1 + C2) of the utterance υ in which it occurs (the interpretation from H's POV/weltanschauung). In face-to-face interaction, C3 is approximately identical with C2 but they are perceived from different points of view. So far as possible, S predicts common ground with H in order to shape utterance υ for maximum comprehensibility. Where C3 is very different from C2 such that H does not share many of S's system of beliefs and assumptions, the context is disparate from S's presumed common ground. Although H may be well able to understand what S intended to mean, ε⊆υ can have reduced comprehensibility and its psycho-social appropriateness may be differently evaluated from the way S expected to be understood, as when a 21st century H reads a sonnet by William Shakespeare (S).

Ideally, CG is context mutually believed to be shared between S and H where S attempts to present C1 in uttering ε⊆υ so as to achieve the relevant beliefs in C3 that S holds or purports to hold in C2; concomitantly, in C3 H seeks to interpret C1 in the light of H's assumptions about C2.

For the remainder of this essay: §2 elaborates CG; §3 elaborates context; and §4 demonstrates the interdependence of common ground and context.

2 More on common ground

I assume, contrary to Chomsky (1975: 56f, 1980: 229f, 239), that human language is characteristically a form of social interactive behaviour (Allan 1986/2014; 2003; 2010; 2020a). This is the motivation for its coming into existence (Dunbar 1996) and by far the majority of its usage is when S addresses utterance υ to audience H for an unbounded number of perlocutionary and illocutionary purposes such as to establish or maintain a social relationship, to inform, question, demand, warn, apologize, and so forth. S and H are mutually aware that, normally, their interlocutor is an intelligent being, that is, a person capable of rational behaviour.[4] S does not need to spell out those things which are obvious to the sensory receptors of H, or such that H can very easily reason them out on the basis of communicative competence – knowing the language and the conventions for its use that each of us develops from birth as we experience the world around us. These assumptions about the interlocutor's abilities with respect to what is presented in υ constitute CG. So, for instance, when S points to something visible in the situation of utterance and says *Isn't that nice?* there is an assumption that H understands English and can also perceive whatever 'that' refers to; or, saying *Let's go to Uluru* assumes that 'Uluru' will be understood as referring to a certain place (https://en.wikipedia.org/wiki/Uluru). Some CG is universal, for example, knowledge of the sun as a heavenly body that is a source of light and warmth, rain as a source of fresh water replenishing the earth, the physiological and socio-cultural differences between the sexes. Some CG is very restricted, for example, between a couple who use *the Hobgoblin* to refer to the man's first wife. Normally, S can readily assess the probable CG with H, and chooses his or her words accordingly. S must make assumptions about H's capacity to understand υ well enough that S's expressed intention in the message is going to be, in S's opinion, more or less correctly interpreted by H (Allan 1986/2014; Clark, Schreuder and Butterick 1983; Colston 2008). Because addressing a neophyte or a child must be differently handled from addressing a group of experts, assumed CG is based on an assessment of H's competence to understand υ, and it motivates such things as choice of language and language variety, style and level of presentation. CG allows meaning to be underspecified by S, so that language understanding is a constructive process in which a lot of inferencing[5] is expected from H.

In addition to these linguistic aspects of CG there are assumptions about what H may know of the world, which can affect the choice of utterance topic, and even whether or not S should address H at all. H also makes assumptions about the CG with S, basing it on H's assessment of υ in the context of utterance and of S as a person. S's assessment of CG with H and H's assessment of CG with S are unlikely to be identical: as I have just said, all that is required is that the overlap in S's and H's assessments of mutual CG enables S to be satisfied that H understands

4 And not (or not necessarily) a person of above average IQ.

5 Inferencing, which may arise from spreading activation within an associative network, includes enrichment of implicitures and implicatures, disambiguation, and the like.

υ well enough for S's communicative purpose to, in S's judgment, succeed. This will apply to each utterance in a discourse such that the relevant CG is dynamic and accretes. As conversation proceeds, the CG develops (Stalnaker 2002: 701): if, where X, Y, and Z are interlocutors, X says φ and Y says χ then, normally all of X, Y and Z (keeping score in terms of Lewis 1979) will know that X either subscribes to or purports to subscribe to φ and Y to χ, whether or not the other interlocutors also subscribe to φ and χ. Furthermore, in a talk exchange, the roles of S and H will alternate among interlocutors. The situation is again complicated by the fact that, when uttering υ, S will often address more than one person and so is required to assess CG with an audience of any number of people.

It is, of course, possible that individual μ_i does not know/believe F, permitting miscommunication to arise. For instance, if X says *I've just been talking to Louise* and Y responds *Louise who?* then X is expected to explain who 'Louise' is. Sometimes S assumes something is not in CG with H, when in fact it is; in which case, H will often correct S (Horton and Gerrig 2005: 24).

It is necessarily the case that what S utters is based on S's own knowledge and perspectives, which may not match H's even though S is desirous of communicating with H. Such egocentrism is a function of what is severally salient to S and H; to seek CG with another person[6] is an effortful process employing cognitive resources to incorporate beliefs about the knowledge and perspectives of other interlocutors. Thus, I assume a conscious effort on S's or H's part but nonetheless predict that, given the near constant exposure to language interchange during the waking hours of most human beings, under most circumstances S and H automatically assume that for S to get a message across in υ, and for H to understand υ, one has to put oneself into the interlocutor's shoes. For instance, this enables us to correctly interpret utterances in unfamiliar accents or dialects through a sort of analysis-by-synthesis: 'It seems as if listeners sometimes perceive an utterance by reference to their own motor activities. When we listen to speech, we may be considering, in some way, what we would have to do in order to make similar sounds' (Ladefoged 1982: 104).[7] Linguistic communication in general is a matter of putting oneself into the interlocutor's shoes and, because this behaviour is the norm, it very quickly becomes automatic except perhaps in people with autism spectrum disorders, or those who are severely narcissistic or very deeply depressed. Otherwise, neither S nor H needs to consciously accommodate

---

6 People occasionally address animals or inanimate objects, but these are effectively anthropomorphized.

7 I see this as altruism rather than egocentricism. The reader of this essay will probably be faced with the task of trying to interpret utterances in an unfamiliar dialect when reading example (17) below.

themselves to the needs of an interlocutor; such behaviour has become automatic and takes no noticeable processing effort. In the words of Horton (2008: 202): 'automatic commonality assessment provides one possible basis upon which language users may generate inferences about common ground.'

Generalizing, CG is achieved under the following circumstances:

(1) X saying φ to Y pragmatically entails (a) X believes that φ and (b) Y has reason to believe that X believes that φ.

(2) If in saying φ to Y, X refers to α, this act of referring to α pragmatically entails that (a) X believes Y can identify α (knows who or what α is) and (b) Y recognizes that X believes Y can identify α. Typically, when Y cannot identify α, Y asks X for further information.

(3) X asking Y φ pragmatically entails (a) X believes Y may be able to do φ and expects Y to accede or refuse to do φ; (b) Y recognizes that X believes Y may be able to do φ and Y needs to decide whether to accede or refuse.

It seems probable that other illocutionary types will give rise to additional patterns corresponding to the preconditions of those illocutions, but I do not have space to offer a complete account of CG here.

3 More on context

A competent S supplies sufficient context for the anticipated audience that a competent H can recreate the world and time being spoken of (C1); consequently, Aristotle recommended: 'Your language will be appropriate if it expresses emotion and character, and if it corresponds to its subject' (*Rhet.* 1408^{a}10, Aristotle 1984: 2245). Aristotle is talking about S's style and manner of presentation, which a competent S knows will normally be evaluated by a competent H; typically this is part of the CG. In a similar vein, Quintilian approved language expression that is 'adapted to the matter and the persons concerned' (Quintilian 1920–22, XI.i.2). And three centuries later, Augustine used the word *contextio*, e.g 'caetera contextio sermonis' "the general drift of the passage" and 'contextio Scripturae' "the purport of Scripture".[8] *Contextio* derives from the verb *contextare* denoting the

8 Quotes from Augustine are found in *De genesi ad litteram* I.xix.38 (Augustine 1836); Taylor SJ 1982: 66.

weaving together of words, which is not quite equivalent to English *context* – for which Augustine used 'circumstantiae' "what stands around, context, circumstances". Until modern times, when context was discussed it was usually referred to as *circumstantiae* or *circumstances*. Indeed, the context of expression $\varepsilon \subseteq \upsilon$ could alternatively be described as the circumstances in which $\varepsilon \subseteq \upsilon$ occurs.

Saying that a competent S supplies sufficient context that the anticipated audience can recreate the world and time being spoken of places more focus on the establishment of CG than was usual before the late 20th century. Stalnaker 2014 treats context as CG (p. 3 and passim): 'context [is] a body of available information: the common ground' (Stalnaker 2014: 24, an idea already in Stalnaker 1978). Stalnaker also believes that common ground is something that speakers typically presuppose (Stalnaker 2014: 25). So, what is 'presupposition'? Scott Soames' defines 'utterance presupposition' as follows:

> An utterance U presupposes P (at t) iff one can reasonably infer from U that the speaker S accepts P and regards it as uncontroversial, either because
> a. S thinks that it is already part of the conversational context at t, or because
> b. S thinks that the audience is prepared to add it, without objection, to the context against which U is evaluated. (Soames 1982: 486, (13))

My notion of pragmatic entailment corresponds to Soames' notion of what H, and a bystander, or an overhearer can reasonably infer from the utterance; and I prefer to say that S does the presupposing which sanctions S's utterance, υ, which in turn induces the pragmatic entailment. Consequently, rewriting Soames' definition in my terms gives (4).

(4) S's utterance υ pragmatically entails that S presupposes that φ is already part of the conversational context at t (i.e. it is in the CG), or that the audience (primarily H) is prepared to add φ, without objection, to the context against which υ is evaluated (thus extending the CG).

CG may be established by introducing someone or something in what is often called a 'presupposition' but is in fact pragmatic entailment. Consider (5):

(5) I'm going to a wedding next week. My ex-wife's cousin is marrying a grandson of one of the Rolling Stones.

S does presuppose the future factuality of φ, viz. the ex-wife's cousin marrying a grandson of one of the Rolling Stones; but S does not presuppose that H knows any of this already because, if S did, the second sentence would be something like *Remember my ex-wife's cousin . . .*. Instead H infers φ from what (5) pragmatically entails (Grice 1981; Abbott 2008). Thus (5) contains a counterexample to Stalnaker's claim that S 'presupposes that φ if and only if [S] accepts (for the purposes of the conversation) that it is common ground that φ' (Stalnaker 2014: 25). S may presuppose that the utterance carries one or more pragmatic entailments that H will accept as an extension to the common ground. Lewis 1979: 340 spoke of H 'accommodating' to such introductions: in (5) it is a predictable part of a personal relations frame or schema. In (5), although the Rolling Stones can be assumed to be in the CG, the actual individuals to be married and S's ex-wife – even that S had an ex-wife – need no more be known to H such that they can be named and/or picked out in a crowd than they are known to readers of this essay. It is conceivable that the people to be married are unknown except as hearsay to S. The descriptions are adequate to the purpose of the communication because the principal focus is in the first sentence of (5); the second sentence is an elaboration of it and rhetorically subordinate (Mann, Matthiessen and Thompson 1992; Mann and Thompson 1987).

Allan 1980; 1981; 2011 (see also Copestake and Briscoe 1992) drew attention to the significance of identifying C1, the world spoken of, in making the different interpretations of the animal nouns in sentences (2)–(7).

(6) It's because Nellie likes rabbits that she won't eat rabbit.

(7) The girl holding the plate was wearing rabbit.

(8) The girl who wore mink was eating rabbit.

(9) Because she decided she preferred the lamb, Hetty put back the pigskin coat.

(10) The butcher has some impala right now.

(11) The tannery has loads of impala right now.

(6) refers to live rabbits and then rabbit-meat, (7) to rabbit pelt, (8) to mink pelt and rabbit meat, (9) to lamb pelt, (10) to impala meat, and (11) to impala pelts. In (6)–(11) the different interpretations are derived from the semantics and pragmatics of the co-text (utterance internal CG) rather than knowledge of human behaviour that is a part of utterance external CG, but the oddity of (13) in contrast to (12) is custom/ situation-based and more obviously derives from utterance external CG.

(12) A. Have some more oysters.
B. Have some more lamb [with those potatoes].

(13) ?* Have some more lambs [with those potatoes].

The CG relevant to evaluating (12)–(13) is that, where one or more ingesta are normally eaten at a sitting, a countable NP is used when speaking English felicitously; where only a part is normally eaten at one sitting, the uncountable (bare) form is used except in generics like *Hindus don't eat cows, and Muslims don't eat pigs*. From this follows the difference between *Have a coffee* [cup of coffee] and *Have some coffee* [from this pot]. I would speculate that a non-native speaker of English who uttered (13) might be offering more pieces of lamb rather than more whole lambs.

A rather similar kind of contextual influence, based on CG, affects the differing interpretations of 'old' in (14)–(15). The different interpretations of 'old' in (14) and (15) arise from the effect of C2 (essentially, the situation of utterance) on C1, what is spoken of: α_i in (14) vs α_j in (15).

(14) Queen Elizabeth II is old [uttered in 2021].

(15) Little Moreton Hall is old [uttered in 2021].

Both utterances of (14)–(15) are true as uttered in 2021, which is part of C2: Her Majesty was born in 1926, so in 2021 she was 95 years old, which counts as old for a human; Little Moreton Hall (https://en.wikipedia.org/wiki/Little_Moreton_Hall) was built very early in the 16th century, so it is approximately 500 years old, which counts as old for a building. Our knowledge of the differing life-spans of things is called upon when evaluating the particular meaning of *old* and the truth of such utterances.[9] The time of utterance is relevant: in 1520 (14) would have been nonsense and (15) false ('truth-or-falsity [is characteristic] of *a use* of a sentence' (Strawson 1950: 326)).

And, now consider (16), from Smith 2012: 5.

(16) Doorbell! She stumbles through the grass barefoot, sun-huddled, drowsy. The back door leads to a poky kitchen, tiled brightly in the taste of the previous tenant.

---

9 This parallels the different interpretations of *cut* given in Searle 1980.

The H anticipated by S (Zadie Smith) is a reader of her novel *NW* which in itself arouses certain expectations. (16) evokes a world from the text in which 'She' was barefoot outside in the back yard drowsing in the sun. The very mention of 'She' being barefoot implicates that it is not her normal state – a conclusion surely confirmed from CG, given that the novel is about a locality of early 21st century London centred on NW10. There is a CG based implicature that the doorbell rang and 'She' went through the cramped kitchen, with its tiles 'She' probably doesn't like, to find out who is ringing the doorbell. As already said, the time is early 21st century as determined by additional co-text, which will also most probably offer more information about the identity of 'She' and the location (to which the book's title, *NW*, is already a clue[10]). These expectations arise from CG, namely, the reader's experience of novels. Although 'She' could be a girl-child, the second sentence quoted evokes attitudes to her environment that are more typical of an adult than a child. The reference to a previous tenant makes it most likely that the property is rented not owned – which hints at her socioeconomic status. These are all things cued by the semantics of the language used to evoke C1 but fleshed out by the pragmatic modulation of C1 in the CG that Zadie Smith (in C2) shares with her readers (in C3).

It is widely acknowledged that *cunt* is the most offensive word in English. Although French *con* and Spanish *coño* have the same origin (Latin *cunnus* "cunt, promiscuous woman") their extended uses are far less dysphemistic. For instance, French *Vieux con* (literally, "old cunt") is more likely to be jocular than insulting – comparable with British *old bugger*.[11] So, generally speaking, *cunt* is strongly tabooed. However, like *silly ass, idiot, bastard,* and *fucker,* it can be used as an expression of bantering camaraderie or to show camaraderie and empathy[12] as in (17) from *Trainspotting* (Welsh 2001: 99–100) – which is in the Leith dialect of Edinburgh (Scotland).

(17) – Granty . . . ye didnae hear? . . . Coke looked straight at Lenny.
– Naw. Wha . . .
– Deid. Potted heid.
– Yir jokin! Eh? Gies a fuckin brek ya cunt . . .
– Gen up. Last night, likes.
– Whit the fuck happened . . .

10 Try Googling 'nw10'.
11 On Spanish *coño* see Allan and Burridge 2006: 52.
12 See Allan 2015; 2020b; Cepollaro and Zeman 2020; Hornsby 2001; Jeshion 2013.

– Ticker. Boom. Coke snapped his fingers. – Dodgy hert, apparently. Nae cunt kent aboot it. Perr Granty wis workin wi Pete Gilleghan, oan the side likesay. It wis aboot five, n Granty wis helpin Pete tidy up, ready to shoot the craw n that likes, whin he jist hauds his chist n cowps ower. Gilly gits an ambulance, n they take the perr cunt tae the hospital, but he dies a couple of ooirs later. Perr Granty. Good cunt n aw. You play cairds wi the guy, eh?
– Eh . . . aye . . . one ay the nicest cunts ye could hope tae meet. That's gutted us, that hus.[13]

A newspaper report of 'the perr cunt' Phil Grant's fatal heart attack, even if equally sympathetic, would necessarily use very different language – as a matter of social appropriateness. In other words, a different C2 would likely lead S to present the C1 of (17) using different locutions.

The phenomenon of subversion/reclamation of slurs is not so outlandish when we compare it with the existence of contronyms[14] in the vocabulary of English, e.g. *bound* "fastened to a spot" vs "heading for somewhere"; *cleave* "adhere to" vs "separate"; *consult* "offer advice" vs "seek advice"; *dust* "remove fine particles" vs "cover with fine particles"; *fast* "moving quickly" vs "fixed, unable to move"; *give out* "provide, supply" vs "stop for lack of supply"; *hold up* "support" vs "impede"; *overlook* "supervise" vs "neglect"; *sanction* "approve" vs "boycott"; *trim* "decorate" vs "remove excess from"; etc. Some are controversial, for instance *infer* is used to mean both "imply by saying" and "understand from what is said"; *rent* and *let*[15] can both be ambiguous between "allow the use of something in return for being paid" and "use something in return for payment to the owner". What contronyms show is that speakers and writers and their audiences can happily operate using a word or phrase with contrary meanings

---

13 A translation for those who need it. 'Granty [Phil Grant] . . . did you not hear?' Coke looked straight at Lenny. 'No. What?' 'Dead. Stone dead.' [*Potted head* is rhyming slang for "dead", its literal meaning is "brawn".] 'You're joking! Eh? Give us a fucking break, you cunt . . .' 'Honestly. Last night.' ['Likes' = *like I say* approximately "I'm telling you".] 'What the fuck happened?' 'Ticker [heart]. Boom.' Coke snapped his fingers. 'Dodgy heart, apparently. No cunt knew about it. Poor Granty was working with Pete Gilleghan on the side [illegally]. It was about five and Granty was helping Pete tidy up, ready to go [*shoot the craw/crow* is rhyming slang for "go"] and that, when he just holds his chest and keels over. Gilly [Gilleghan] gets an ambulance, and they take the poor cunt to hospital, but he dies a couple of hours later. Poor Granty. Good cunt and all. You play[ed] cards with guy, didn't you?' 'Eh . . . Yes . . . One of the nicest cunts you could hope to meet. That's gutted me, that has.'

14 Also called *contranyms* and *autoantonyms*, among other things.

15 There are also the verb *let* "allow" as in *Let me pay* and the noun *let* "hindrance" as in tennis (when during service a ball is hindered by the net cord).

because they rely on C1 and C2 to disambiguate – which is exactly what normally applies with terms of abuse and their contronymic subversions (Allan 2020b).

Consider the effects of C3 on interpretations of C1 as presented in C2. In the later 19th century white people were regarded as superior to non-whites even by enlightened scholars such as Charles Darwin.

> At some future period, not very distant as measured by centuries, the civilised races of man will almost certainly exterminate, and replace, the savage races throughout the world. At the same time the anthropomorphous apes [. . .] will no doubt be exterminated. The break between man and his nearest allies will then be wider, for it will intervene between man in a more civilised state, as we may hope, even than the Caucasian, and some ape as low as a baboon, instead of as now between the negro or Australian and the gorilla. (Darwin 1871: 201)

Today Darwin's view seems racist: the lesson is that what was not intended as a slur by S at the time of utterance C2, can be perceived as a slur by a reader today (H at C3) because beliefs have changed over time (a shift in weltanschauung). Asim 2007 criticizes dysphemistic uses of *nigger* by a number of white authors but forgives its use in Mark Twain's *The Adventures of Huckleberry Finn* (Twain 1884) because use of terms like *Injun* and *nigger* are unequivocally suited to the context of the book. In 1885 *Huckleberry Finn* was not deprecated for the use of racial slurs but because the humour and language used is 'of a very coarse type [. . .] more suited to the slums than to intelligent, respectable people' (*Boston Evening Transcript* March 17, 1885, p. 6). *Nigger, nigra* and *nigga* are colloquial counterparts to *Negro*: compare similar colloquial–formal correspondences such as *bubby–baby, bust–burst, crick–creek, critter–creature, cuss–curse, gal–girl, hoss–horse, sassy–saucy, tit–teat.* Colloquial language uses informal and intimate styles (cf. Joos 1961); it includes, but is not identical with, slang (see Allan and Burridge 2006). The term *African-American* did not exist in the 1880s and, given the deliberate use of colloquial language in *The Adventures of Huckleberry Finn*, the term *nigger* was an appropriate alternative. By all accounts, Samuel Clemens had African-American friends and thought highly of them (Fishkin 1993); he was no racist (cf. Kennedy 2003: 109f; Asim 2007: 107; McWhorter 2011). Although some of the characters in the book are racist, so was much of white America, and for them (as for too many people today) *nigger* is an expression of disparagement that discredits, slights, smears, stains, and besmirches African-Americans (and other dark-skinned people). But whereas some of the characters created by author Mark Twain employed *nigger* as a slur, his alter ego Samuel Clemens deplored such practice. Today, the text of *Huckleberry Finn* has been censored, for instance, with *slave* substituted for *nigger* and *Injun* omitted (Twain 2011a) and with *nigger* replaced by *hipster* but *Injun* retained (Twain

2011b).[16] Enlightened people such as Asim, Kennedy, and McWhorter condemn such bowdlerisation in C3, recognising that in the context in which Twain wrote (the world spoken in, C2) the terms he used – that in other contexts might be slurs – in *The Adventures of Huckleberry Finn* are not. Their use in the book is socially appropriate, though perhaps their use by certain fictional characters may nonetheless be slurs within the world of the book, C1.

In §3 of this essay, I have demonstrated the importance of distinguishing between those different aspects of context that I have named C1, C2, and C3. I have also given a sketchy account of the interplay between context and CG. In the next, and final section, I elucidate the interdependence of CG and context.

4 The interdependence of CG and context

The interdependence of CG and context is shown in (18).

(18) (a) Common ground (CG) for any community K of two or more people is that every member, or almost every member, of K believes some fact or set of facts F.

(b) F can be expressed as a proposition or set of propositions Φ believed to be true (or purported to be true) within K.

(c) A member μ of K (μ_K) is presumed to know or believe Φ (F) by (almost) every other member of K.

(d) μ_K knows/believes that (a), (b), and (c) are purported to be true.

(e) Both S and H are members of K, $\{\mu_S, \mu_H\} \subseteq K$.

(f) S utters υ to H in context C2. υ expresses a state of affairs, a possibly singleton set of propositions, Φ_υ.

(g) When μ_K applies knowledge of F (that is, belief in the truth/existence of F) in order to interpret υ, i.e. the state of affairs expressed in Φ_υ, μ_K can presume that others in the community will also be able to apply knowledge of F (belief in the truth/existence of F) in order to interpret Φ_υ.

(h) The existence of F, Φ_υ, and the application of knowledge of F to interpreting Φ_υ is what constitutes CG for members of the community K. Once attended to, Φ_υ becomes part of F, incrementing the common ground. In other words, S's (μ_S's) utterance υ pragmatically entails that S presupposes that Φ_υ is already part of the conversational context

16 See McWhorter 2011.

(C1 + C2) at time of utterance (in other words, it is in the CG), or that the audience (primarily H, μ_H) is prepared to add Φ_υ, without objection, to the context against which υ is evaluated, the CG is extended.

(i) If language expression ε is a constituent of utterance υ, such that $\varepsilon \subseteq \upsilon$, then part of the context C_ε of ε, namely $C_\varepsilon 1$, is the world (and time) spoken of, constituted by the topic of discourse revealed by expression ε's co-text, namely, what has been said and what is said, including text that follows ε. This is effected (i) via the semantic frames and scripts evoked by the various constituents ($\varepsilon_{1...n}$) of υ – identified through ε and its co-text; and (ii) S's attitude to what is spoken of or the persons addressed as this is revealed by the locution. (i) and (ii) contribute to identifying what S's purpose might be in making the utterance, which is the effective meaning of $\varepsilon \subseteq \upsilon$.

(j) Part of C_ε, $C_\varepsilon 2$, is, from S's point of view (deriving from S's weltanschauung), the situation in which $\varepsilon \subseteq \upsilon$ is expressed. C2 captures who does the saying to whom, and where and when this takes place. C2 normally determines the social relationships and conventions that S is expected to follow and, in consequence, sets the standard for the psycho-social appropriateness of what is said. Together with C1, C2 is what governs whether such terms as *bitch*, *cunt*, or *nigger* are, from S's POV, used as a slur or an expression of camaraderie and whether or not a particular form of words is polite (or not). In other words, C2 includes what is known about S and the perlocutionary effect of this and similar uses of ε.

(k) Finally, part of C_ε, $C_\varepsilon 3$, is a corresponding situation of interpretation in which H seeks to understand $\varepsilon \subseteq \upsilon$, viz. the meaning of ε in the context C1 + C2 of the utterance υ in which it occurs – the interpretation from H's POV, deriving from H's weltanschauung. In face-to-face interaction, C3 is closely similar to C2, though they differ in POV. So far as possible, S predicts CG with H in order to shape utterance υ for maximum comprehensibility. Where C3 is very different from C2 such that H does not share many of S's system of beliefs and assumptions, the context is disparate from S's presumed common ground. Although H may be well able to understand what S intended to mean, $\varepsilon \subseteq \upsilon$ can have reduced comprehensibility and its psycho-social appropriateness may be differently evaluated from the way S expected to be understood, as when as when a 21st century H reads a sonnet by William Shakespeare (S).

(18)(a)–(d) define the basis for CG. (e) establishes the basis for initiating an occurrence of CG within some particular context of utterance wherein S utters υ to H, see (f). (g) initiates the evocation of CG relevant to υ. (h) explains how Φ_υ, what is said in υ, increments the CG. (i) elaborates the world (and time) spoken of in υ, identifying it as C1, part of the context which establishes the co-text. (j) establishes C2 as the situation of utterance from S's POV. In face-to-face interactions C2 is effectively simultaneous with C3. But C3, as established in (k), is the context from H's POV. C3 may be simultaneous with C2 but they may be in different locations (as with a telephone conversation or video conference), or they may be at different time points in which case it is likely the locations will also be different, though this is not necessarily the case. These differences potentially lead to H misinterpreting S's intended meaning.

It has long been accepted that CG and context are closely related. In the course of this essay I have established that they are separate entities, but interdependent. CG is invariably partially dependent on context and context is partially dependent on CG when S utters υ to H.

References

Abbott, Barbara. 2008. Presuppositions and common ground. *Linguistics and Philosophy* 21: 523–538.

Adams, Douglas. 1992. *The Hitchhiker's Guide to the Galaxy: A Trilogy in Four Parts*. London: Pan Books.

Allan, Keith. 1980. Nouns and countability. *Language* 56: 541–567.

Allan, Keith. 1981. Interpreting from context. *Lingua* 53: 151–173.

Allan, Keith. 1986/2014. *Linguistic Meaning*. 2 vols. London: Routledge and Kegan Paul. (Reprint edn, Beijing: World Publishing Corporation, 1991. Reissued in one volume as Routledge Library Editions: Linguistics Volume 8, 2014.).

Allan, Keith. 2003. Linguistic metatheory. *Language Sciences* 25: 533-560.

Allan, Keith. 2010. *The Western Classical Tradition in Linguistics (Second expanded edition)*. London: Equinox. [First edn 2007.].

Allan, Keith. 2011. Graded salience: probabilistic meanings in the lexicon. In by Kasia M. Jaszczolt and Keith Allan (eds.) *Salience and Defaults in Utterance Processing*, 165–187. Berlin/Boston: Walter de Gruyter.

Allan, Keith. 2015. When is a slur not a slur? The use of *nigger* in 'Pulp Fiction'. *Language Sciences* 52: 187–199.

Allan, Keith. 2020a. Linguistics and communication. *Intercultural Pragmatics* 17(3): 293–313.

Allan, Keith. 2020b. The semantics and pragmatics of three potential slurring terms. In Kerry Mullan, Bert Peeters and Lauren Sadow (eds.), *Studies in Ethnopragmatics, Cultural Semantics, and Intercultural Communication: Ethnopragmatics and Semantic Analysis*, 163–183. Singapore: Springer.

Allan, Keith and Kate Burridge. 2006. *Forbidden Words: Taboo and the Censoring of Language*. Cambridge: Cambridge University Press.

Aristotle. 1984. *The Complete Works of Aristotle. The Revised Oxford Translation*. Ed. by Jonathan Barnes. Bollingen Series 71. Princeton: Princeton University Press.

Asim, Jabari. 2007. *The N Word: Who Can Say It, Who Shouldn't, and Why*. New York: Houghton Mifflin.

Augustine. 1836. *Sancti Aurelii Augustini Hipponensis Episcopi Opera Omnia. Tomus Tertius.* Parisiis: Gaume Fratres.

Bartlett, Frederic C. 1932. *Remembering: An Experimental and Social Study*. Cambridge: Cambridge University Press.

Capone, Alessandro. 2013. Explicatures are NOT cancellable. In Alessandro Capone, Franco Lo Piparo and Marco Carapezza (eds.), *Perspectives on Linguistic Pragmatics*, 131–151. Chaim: Springer.

Carston, Robyn. 2002. *Thoughts and Utterances: The Pragmatics of Explicit Communication*. Oxford & Malden MA: Blackwell.

Cepollaro, Bianca and Dan Zeman, (eds.). 2020. *Grazer Philosophische Studien. Special Issue: Non-Derogatory Uses of Slurs.*

Chomsky, Noam. 1975. *Reflections on Language*. New York: Pantheon Books.

Chomsky, Noam. 1980. *Rules and Representations*. New York: Columbia University Press.

Clark, Herbert H., Robert Schreuder and Samuel Butterick. 1983. Common ground and the understanding of demonstrative reference. *Journal of Verbal Learning and Verbal Behavior* 22: 245–258.

Colston, Herbert L. 2008. A new look at common ground: memory, egocentrism, and joint meaning. In Istvan Kecskes and Jacob L. Mey (eds.), *Intention, Common Ground and the Egocentric Speaker-Hearer*, 151–187. Berlin/New York: Mouton de Gruyter.

Copestake, Ann and Ted Briscoe. 1992. Lexical operations in a unification-based framework. In James Pustejovsky and Sabine Bergler (eds.), *Lexical Semantics and Knowledge Representation: Proceedings of ACL SIGLEX Workshop on Lexical Semantics and Knowledge Representation, Berkeley, California.*, 101–119. Berlin: Springer.

Darwin, Charles. 1871. *The Descent of Man, and Selection in Relation to Sex*. London: John Murray.

Dunbar, Robin I.M. 1996. *Grooming, Gossip and the Evolution of Language*. London: Faber and Faber.

Fillmore, Charles J. 1982. Frame semantics. In Linguistic Society of Korea (ed.), *Linguistics in the Morning Calm*, 111–138. Seoul: Hanshin.

Fishkin, Shelley F. 1993. *Was Huck Black?: Mark Twain and African-American Voices*. New York: Oxford University Press.

Garfinkel, Harold. 1964. Studies of the routine rounds of everyday activities. *Social Problems* 11: 225–250.

Grice, H. Paul. 1981. Presupposition and conversational implicature. In Peter Cole (ed.), *Radical Pragmatics*, 183–198. New York: Academic Press. [Reprinted in H. Paul Grice. 1989. *Studies in the Way of Words*, 269–282. Cambridge MA: Harvard University Press.]

Hornsby, Jennifer. 2001. Meaning and uselessness: how to think about derogatory words. *Midwest Studies in Philosophy* 25: 128–141.

Horton, William S. 2008. A memory-based approach to common ground and audience design. In Istvan Kecskes and Jacob L. Mey (eds.), *Intention, common ground, and the egocentric speaker-hearer*, 189–222. Berlin/New York: Mouton de Gruyter.

Horton, William S. and Richard J. Gerrig. 2005. Conversational common ground and memory processses in language production. *Discourse Processes* 40: 1–35.

Jeshion, Robin. 2013. Expressivism and the offensiveness of slurs. *Philosohical Perspectives* 27: 232–259.

Joos, Martin. 1961. *The Five Clocks*. New York: Harcourt, Brace & World.

Kennedy, Randall L. 2003. *Nigger: The Strange Career of a Troublesome Word*. [First published 2002]. New York: Vintage Books.

Ladefoged, Peter. 1982. *A Course in Phonetics*. 2nd edn. New York: Harcourt Brace Jovanovich.

Lewis, David. 1979. Scorekeeping in a language game. *Journal of Philosophical Logic* 8: 339–359.

Mann, William C., Christian M.I.M. Matthiessen and Sandra A. Thompson. 1992. Rhetorical Structure Theory and text analysis. In William C. Mann and Sandra A. Thompson (eds.), *Discourse Description: Diverse Linguistic Analyses of a Fund-Raising Text*, 39–76. Amsterdam/Philadelphia: John Benjamins.

Mann, William C. and Sandra A. Thompson. 1987. *Rhetorical Structure Theory: A Theory of Text Organization*. Information Sciences Institute, 4676 Admiralty Way, Marina Del Rey, CA 90292–6695.

Marslen-Wilson, William, Elena Levy and Lorraine Komisarjevksy Tyler. 1982. Producing interpretable discourse: The establishment and maintenance of reference. In Robert J. Jarvella and Wolfgang Klein (eds.), *Studies in Deixis and Related Topics*, 339–378. Chichester: John Wiley.

Mazzone, Marco. 2011. Schemata and associative processes in pragmatics. *Journal of Pragmatics* 43: 2148–2159.

McWhorter, John. 2011. Who are we protecting by censoring 'Huck Finn'? *The Root*. Available online: https://www.theroot.com/who-are-we-protecting-by-censoring-huck-finn-1790862356

Minsky, Marvin. 1977. Frame-system theory. In Philip N Johnson-Laird and P.C. Wason (eds.), *Thinking: Readings in Cognitive Science*, 355–376. Cambridge: Cambridge University Press.

Moore, George E. 1952. A reply to my critics. In Paul A. Schilpp (ed.), *The Philosophy of G.E. Moore*, 533–687. 2nd edn. New York: Tudor Publ. Corp.

Prince, Ellen. 1981. Toward a taxonomy of given-new information. In Peter Cole (ed.), *Radical Pragmatics*, 223–256. New York: Academic Press.

Quintilian. 1920–22. *The Institutio Oratoria of Quintilian*. Transl. by Harold E. Butler. Loeb Classical Library. 4 vols. London: William Heinemann.

Sanford, Anthony J. and Simon C. Garrod. 1981. *Understanding Written Language*. Chichester: John Wiley.

Schank, Roger. 1984. *The Cognitive Computer*. Reading MA: Addison-Wesley.

Schank, Roger and Robert C. Abelson. 1977. *Scripts, Plans, Goals and Understanding: An Inquiry into Human Knowledge Structures*. Hillsdale NJ: Lawrence Erlbaum.

Searle, John R. 1980. The background of meaning. In John R. Searle, Ferenc Kiefer and Manfred Bierwisch (eds.), *Speech Act Theory and Pragmatics*, 221–232. Dordrecht: Reidel.

Smith, Zadie. 2012. *NW*. New York: Penguin Press.

Soames, Scott. 1982. How presuppositions are inherited: a solution to the projection problem. *Linguistic Inquiry* 13: 483–545.

Sperber, Dan and Deirdre Wilson. 1995. *Relevance: Communication and Cognition*. 2nd edn. Oxford: Basil Blackwell. [First edn. 1986].

Stalnaker, Robert C. 1978. On the representation of context. *Journal of Logic, Language and Information* 7: 3–19. [Reprinted in Robert C. Stalnaker. *Context and Content*, 96–113. Oxford: Oxford University Press.]

Stalnaker, Robert C. 2002. Common ground. *Linguistics and Philosophy* 25: 701–21.

Stalnaker, Robert C. 2014. *Context*. Oxford: Oxford University Press.

Strawson, Peter F. 1950. On referring. *Mind* 59: 320–344. [Reprinted in Jay Rosenberg and Charles Travis (eds.). 1971. *Readings in the Philosophy of Language*, 175–195. Englewood Cliffs: Prentice-Hall.]

Taylor S.J., John H. 1982. *St Augustine, Vol.1. The Literal Meaning of Genesis*. Ancient Christian Writers. New York: Paulist Press.

Twain, Mark (Samuel Clemens). 1884. *The Adventures of Huckleberry Finn: (Tom Sawyer's comrade): Scene, the Mississippi Valley: Time, forty to fifty years ago*. London: Chatto & Windus.

Twain, Mark (Samuel Clemens). 2011a. *The Adventures of Tom Sawyer and Huckleberry Finn*. Ed. by Alan Gribben. Montgomery, AL: NewSouth Books.

Twain, Mark (Samuel Clemens). 2011b. *The Hipster Huckleberry Finn*. Ed. by Richard Grayson. Brooklyn: Dumbo Books.

Welsh, Irvine. 2001. *Trainspotting*. London: Vintage Books. First published 1993.

Brian Nolan

Understanding common ground as a cognitive object

Abstract: At first glance, the idea of common ground seems a simple notion. In fact, nothing could be further from the truth. Common ground is actually very nuanced and complicated, with a dynamic connection to knowledge, context and situation. Common ground has been characterised to date as joint action, dynamic, and containing shared knowledge of various kinds. In this paper we propose a view of common ground as a type of cognitive object. We argue that common ground, the informational contents of common ground, and the operations that act on it in its construction and maintenance (grounding, verification, repair, accommodation, etc.), can be considered as contributing to the emergent common ground, while distributed across the minds of the discourse interlocutors. We argue for a view of common ground as distributed, complex, and adaptive across discourse agents. In motivating this view, we show how knowledge, context and situation intersect to help delineate the scope boundaries of the common ground informational content, and act as cognitive framing devices. We propose a formalisation of this model of common ground that can i) resolve diverse kinds of linguistic ambiguity found in discourse, and ii) be utilised in the characterisation of, for example, speech acts such as the assertive and declarative, along with indirect requests. The formalisation exemplifies elements of the interfaces between knowledge, context, situation, and both core and emergent common ground. The important questions we consider are therefore:

1. What is the relationship between context, situation and common ground?
2. What is the relationship between core and emergent common ground?
3. How does relevant knowledge and content get selected for inclusion into core and emergent common ground?
4. Considered as a cognitive object, what operations are used to manage the informational content of common ground?

1 Introduction

There has been much discussion in the literature as to the nature of common ground, but a complete understanding has evaded our grasp (Clark, E. V. 2015; Clark, H. 1996; Kecskes 2003, 2010, 2013a, b, 2015; Kecskes and Zhang 2009; Kecskes and Mey 2008; Stalnaker 2014). The reason is that common ground is actu-

https://doi.org/10.1515/9783110766752-003

ally rather complicated, and it has a dynamic connection to knowledge, context and situation. We propose here a view of common ground as a type of cognitive object that is distributed, complex, and adaptive across human discourse agents. In motivating this view, we show how knowledge, context and situation intersect to delineate the scope boundaries of the common ground informational content, and act as cognitive framing devices to support the discourse agents. We propose a formalisation of this model of common ground that can i) resolve diverse kinds of linguistic ambiguity found in discourse, and ii) be utilised in the characterisation of, for example, speech acts[1] such as the assertive and declarative, along with indirect requests. The formalisation exemplifies elements of the interfaces between knowledge, context, situation, and core and emergent common ground. In considering common ground as a cognitive object, we argue that the informational contents of common ground, and the operations that act on it in its construction and maintenance (grounding, verification, repair, accommodation, etc.), can be considered as contributing to the emergent common ground, while distributed across the minds of the discourse interlocutors. The important questions we address are therefore:

Question 1 What is the relationship between a) context, situation and common ground, and b) core and emergent common ground?
Question 2 What operations manage the informational content of common ground?
Question 3 As a cognitive object, how does contextually relevant knowledge and informational content get selected for inclusion into core and emergent common ground?

This chapter is organised as follows. In Section 2, *Common ground as a distributed, complex, and adaptive cognitive object*, we motivate a view of common ground as a cognitive object that has complex adaptive systematic behaviours which are distributed over the dialogue interlocutors in real-time. Section 3, *Context, common ground, and knowledge*, addresses the issue of what guides the selection of contextual knowledge into core and emergent common ground. In an ongoing dialogue, the contributions are intrinsically dependent on a context. Discourse participants rely on context to advance a conversation, and assume that context is dynamically framed to include the set of propositions and beliefs that form part of common ground. A speaker makes an assessment about packaging information in a particular way to promote clarity and understanding within the hearer. This assessment includes the kind of background information presupposed. In

1 Searle's (1979) taxonomy of speech acts includes the assertive, directive, commissive, expressive, and declarative.

Section 4, *The importance of a situation as a cognitive framing mechanism*, we argue that utterances must be interpreted in the context of a given situation. A situation is meaningful for the interpretation of an utterance. Speakers recognise and use situations to make sense of what they encounter on the basis of their respective personal, social, and socio-cultural knowledge. A situation frames a relevant subset of contextual knowledge within common ground. Section 5, *Application of common ground as a cognitive object in language use*, examines how we use our common ground to help resolve many different kinds of ambiguity commonly found in conversation. Common ground is also utilised in the retrieval of meaning from speech acts. As a cognitive object, common ground is an essential component of advancing a dialogue between interlocutors. In Section 6, *Operations – the construction and maintenance of common ground*, we set out the operations used to establish and maintain the initial core common ground and subsequent emergent common ground. In all of our communicative interactions, common ground plays a central role in the way that we process and accumulate information. In Section 7, Egocentrism, cooperation, game theory, and emergent common ground, we motivate a connection between egocentrism as a rational human behaviour and Game Theory, where egocentrism contributes to the emergent common ground. Finally, within Section 8, *Discussion*, we discuss the key points in our argumentation for considering common ground as a cognitive object. As a cognitive object, we view common ground as having the primary characteristics of being distributed, complex and adaptive with the major function of managing shared knowledge and information between discourse interlocutors. Also, as a cognitive object, common ground is necessary for advancing a dialogue, and framing a relevant subset of the knowledge from the broad context. As such, processing core and emergent common ground is a natural part of our cognitive capability for the management of information and knowledge.

2 Common ground as a distributed, complex adaptive cognitive object

We advance here a view of common ground as a complex adaptive cognitive object that is distributed over the dialogue interlocutors in real-time. One of the interesting things about humans who form dynamic relationships in discourse is that they engage in a collective behaviour across a group. This complex adaptive behaviour functions is intrinsic to common ground as a cognitive object.

A cognitive object is a construct of the human mind that has a purpose, function, and a set of behaviours. It has access to various kinds of knowledge stored in our long term memory. The cognitive object has the means, its maintenance operations, to manage and update this knowledge. Long-term memories are often outside our awareness but can be called into working memory when needed. Long-term memory encompasses: a) Episodic memory which contains our memory of specific past events and personal experiences; b) Semantic memory which stores our knowledge about the world including facts, information, concepts, rules, and principles; and c) Procedural memory which involves memories of body movement, how to engage a strategy, or use artefacts and objects in the physical environment.

This distributed complex adaptive object works with a number of human actors, people in a discourse acting as free agents, that: i) Utilise feedback (i.e., common ground operations like repair, accommodation, echo questions for confirmation), ii) Exhibit emergent properties and self-organisation (emergent common ground), and iii) Produce unpredictable dynamic behaviour which converges on an equilibrium of emergent shared knowledge in the common ground.

Human cognition includes complex operations that support functions ranging over the areas of perception, knowledge acquisition, information management, memory, learning, attention, problem solving, decision-making, reasoning over information and knowledge, intelligence, and language use. We make the assumption that the language faculty operates under a framework of conceptual principles that handle all human cognitive abilities.

As free agents, humans act autonomously to accomplish their objectives. A goal directed, knowledgeable person therefore has the properties of autonomy, reactivity, proactiveness, and social ability (1). People cooperate to achieve common goals, and adapt to their environment.

(1) Properties of free human agents

Autonomy:	People are potentially egocentric in their behaviour, and encapsulate some state that is not directly accessible to other people. They make decisions about what to do based on this state, without the direct intervention of other people.
Reactivity:	People are situated in an environment, are able to perceive it, and can respond in a timely fashion to changes that occur.
Proactiveness:	People do not simply react to their environment. They can take the initiative using goal-directed behaviour.
Social ability:	People interact with other people via language. They engage socially in order to achieve their goals.

People engage in speech acts that are reliant on knowledge and language use. We can describe proactiveness and goal-directed behaviour in terms of the assumptions on which they rely (pre-conditions), and the effects that a speech act may have (post-conditions).

In a usage-based approach to linguistics (Beckner et al. 2009: 2), language itself is often regarded as a complex adaptive system that emerges from the linguistic interactions of multiple agents, based on past experiences of use, while subject to many general cognitive and socio-cognitive processes. Furthermore, in this approach, language structures are not considered fixed entities but rather a series of processes that advance in actual speech communication.

> In general terms, a 'complex system' is any system consisting of a large number of heterogeneous entities that, interacting with each other and with their environment, generate multiple layers of collective structure exhibiting hierarchical self-organization without centralized control. (Baicchi 2015: 10)

This perspective enables us to see language as distributed, complex and adaptive over multiple human actors. It thereby contributes to our understanding of the emergent nature of language, with common ground as a distributed repository of shared knowledge. Each discourse actor has the means to process and utilise that knowledge. Common ground, as a complex adaptive object, emerges from the interactions between members of a speech community across time and location.

As an emergent complex adaptive cognitive object, common ground is continuously and dynamically negotiated. As a cognitive object, common ground is argued to be actually composed of diverse autonomous parts that are interrelated and interdependent. We denote the interlocutors in dialogue as agents interacting in a communicative environment where human cognition and language interact. Common ground is dynamic and the agents in which it resides interact such that their behaviours give rise to hierarchical self-organisation and emergence. Agents interactively use language in their communities such that their communicative exchanges produce emergent changes at many different levels, in common ground. Essentially, as a cognitive object, common ground is distributed over a set of human agents that interact together in such a way as to form a connected whole, with the whole being part of a larger environment. They are distinguished within the environment by means of a framing boundary.

The human agents individually represent the common ground cognitive object and its structures. From the interactions, the agents exhibit an emergent behaviour. By this we mean the range of actions and processes carried out in response to a range of inputs, both internal and external to the agent's boundaries, in combination with the environment, the context, in which the agents are embedded. These actions and processes are the pragmatic operations for the construction and maintenance of core and emergent common ground. The resulting common ground is the outcome of the particular assessments made by individual agents, which behave (possibly in an egocentric manner) based on information drawn from context.

The agents make their decisions, actions, and choices simultaneously and in parallel, with the consequential result that they influence each other's behaviours. Agents' behaviours follow common decision-making rules based on their dynamic beliefs, desires and intentions (BDI) states. From these rules and the BDI states a coherence emerges, and it is significant that this is not the outcome of predetermined strategy or centralised control. It just emerges! As a cognitive object, common ground is open, complex, and non-linear, whereby speakers behave in such a way as to assess, reassess, and influence each other's behaviour. As a cognitive object, common ground operates within a 'society' of agents that interact in ways that are unpredictable. These interactions influence the common ground such that it evolves over time according to the general principles of its operations.

As a cognitive object, common ground can be *structurally* divided into individual components, its knowledge sets and its operations. Its function is to manage and represent shared knowledge to advance a dialogue between discourse interlocutors. Common ground has functional components (memory, knowledge representation, situational awareness, reasoning, operations) whose combined power working together is greater than that achieved by working separately. These functional components contribute naturally to the common ground cognitive object, and draw directly from context to inform it, via situations that frame the context into common ground.

Self-organisation in common ground is via the spontaneous emergence of order and coherence, which means that no single agent constructs and maintains it, but it emerges spontaneously from the interactions. Therefore, there is a continual dynamic flux between the agents in discourse. Order is not prearranged but is emergent, such that the state of the common ground advances across a dialogue between the agents / interlocutors. Common ground is thereby constructed and maintained and its contents can be adjusted, updated and repaired as needed. Common ground fluctuates between *stability* which enhances the storage of shared information, and *chaos*, where (emergent) common ground can rapidly receive information and knowledge updates to advance communication. As a cognitive object, common ground has variables that are constantly being updated, with one variable potentially affecting other variables contained within it, and therefore state conditions. The human agents in a dialogue, holding dynamic communicative interactions, will affect one another as well as the common ground. That is, common ground will be initially constructed, then maintained as needed, with this mutually shared knowledge. These discourse interactions will cause the common ground to advance through a spontaneous self-organisation leading to an emergent common ground.

Knowledge representation is important for common ground. As humans, we exhibit our intelligence via manipulation of our belief state space about the surrounding world and our knowledge through reasoning processes. A *state space* is a space of possible courses of inference when combining actual beliefs about the current world, the various kinds of knowledge, and rules of inference. The two fundamental knowledge related issues are: i) How to represent knowledge, and ii) how to characterise the processes managing knowledge through reasoning.

We differentiate between knowledge, information and data. Data are the primitive verifiable facts of any representation (Nolan 2022a). Data reflects simple facts about the current world and it is often quite voluminous while frequently changing. Information, then, can be simply understood as interpreted data. However, knowledge is not the same as information. The acquisition of knowledge is based on accumulation of information. Information is simply data that has been interpreted while knowledge is information that is modelled in order to be useful. Knowledge results from the modelling of patterns within a given set of information, and it enables us to draw conclusions in certain contexts. Knowledge, then, is the relation among sets of information, which are very often used for further information deduction. Additionally, knowledge is general (unlike data), and contains information about the behaviours of abstract models of the world.

Language derives from the need of humans to communicate. Communication is a shared activity in which people cooperatively behave according to the set of linguistic and pragmatic conventions grounded in their speech community (Clark H. 1996). Speakers engage in joint communicative actions which depend on 'shared cognition', and the awareness that beliefs, desires and intentions can be shared with other agents via language. As a cognitive object, common ground facilitates this communication. We consider common ground as a cognitive object encompassing: 1) knowledge, and 2) management operations (Table 1) on the knowledge.

Common ground mediates the multifaceted relationship between context and language in communicative interaction, across the interfaces between knowledge, language, and culture. As mentioned earlier, the function of common ground is to manage a shared knowledge state. The idea is that the knowledge in the presumed common background is shared by the participants in a conversation (Stalnaker 2014: 45). This knowledge provides a resource that speakers exploit in determining how to say what they want to say, thereby facilitating the characterisation of speech acts in terms of the way the act is intended to change the context. An utterance is context-dependent, context constrains content, and content may, in turn, affect subsequent context. Common ground knowledge is highly context-dependent, and discourse is produced and interpreted under the guidance of our mental context models.

In discourse, shared knowledge need not be expressed, and may remain implicit. Once knowledge is communicated to a hearer, this knowledge becomes

Table 1: Common ground as a cognitive object.

Common ground	
Knowledge	**Informally:** *Local dialogue* knowledge *Language* knowledge *Environment* knowledge *Recent events* knowledge *Historical* knowledge *Common sense* knowledge *Cultural* knowledge **More formally:** 1) Declarative, descriptive, or propositional knowledge 2) Competence, procedural, or ability knowledge 3) Acquaintance knowledge 4) Empirical/a posteriori knowledge 5) A priori knowledge 6) Heuristic/tacit 7) Testimonial knowledge 8) Meta knowledge 9) Structural knowledge
Operations	**FUNCTION: OPERATION** **GET**: Attention and salience **ADD**: Grounding **CHECK**: Tracking **CHECK**: Verification **FIX**: Repair **UPDATE**: Accommodation

part of the common ground pertaining to that discourse, and can be presupposed in all further communication between the speaker and hearer. Such shared knowledge is the common ground of the speakers and hearers.

The role of knowledge has consequences in the production and comprehension of discourse. The management of knowledge guides the production of speech acts such as assertions. The same is true for questions, where the speaker assumes the hearer has some knowledge that (s)he wishes to acquire. Many elements of discourse are shaped by the ways that participants represent and manage mutual knowledge. Mutual knowledge[2] is a fundamental concept about information found in the domains of game theory, epistemic logic, and epistemology. An event is mutual knowledge if all agents know that the event occurred. However, mutual

2 https://en.wikipedia.org/wiki/Mutual_knowledge_(logic).

knowledge by itself implies nothing about what agents know about other agents' knowledge. In this regard, it is possible that an event is mutual knowledge but that each agent is unaware that the other agents know it has occurred. Common knowledge is a stronger related notion and any event that is common knowledge is also mutual knowledge. Knowledge management strategies for most discourse is based on the shared nature of the interlocutors' knowledge in the same cultural community. Clearly, knowledge of various kinds is of central importance to common ground. Indeed, common ground makes contextually relevant knowledge available to the discourse interlocutors.

We look next at context, common ground, and knowledge.

3 Context, common ground, and knowledge

We now examine the factors that guide the selection of contextual knowledge into core and emergent common ground, and what context contributes to pragmatic meaning. In an ongoing dialogue, contributions are intrinsically attached to, and dependent on, a context. Context is dynamically framed within some situation giving a subset of relevant contextual information, including the set of propositions and beliefs that form part of common ground. In a discourse, a speaker makes an assessment about their need to package information in a particular way to aid hearer clarity and understanding. This assessment includes the kind of background information presupposed.

A function of context is to constrain a communicative situation and influence language use, with the most relevant contexts being the social and the linguistic environments. In turn, it is recognised that context informs pragmatic meaning and assists in the construction and maintenance of common ground. Yet, context is quite difficult to define. Nevertheless, discourse interlocutors are naturally adept at understanding the relevant features of context to apply to make their utterances relevant and meaningful. People have arrays of linguistic, cognitive, social, cultural, resources, and knowledge to use for retrieving meaning from an utterance.

A worthwhile approach is to consider context in relation to a situational frame. Framing is the technique through which certain features of the situation are made salient. This places boundaries on the extent of the context, such that the frame contains a relevant subset of the context, facilitating the interpretation of the situation. Frames are basic cognitive constructs which guide our perception of reality:

> I assume that definitions of a situation are built up in accordance with principles of organization which govern events . . . and our subjective involvement in them; frame is the word I use to refer to such of these basic elements as I am able to identify. (Goffman 1974: 10f)

A context evolves in the course of a conversational exchange, and is used by the participants to help them achieve their communicative goals. What interlocutors say or mean depends on features of the context, as long as the contextually relevant knowledge is available to the hearer of an utterance. A speech act exploits the subset of context contained in common ground including the beliefs, desires and intentions of the participants. The illocutionary point of an utterance is to change certain features of the context. If communication is to be successful, the contextual knowledge on which the content of a speech act depends must be available to the hearer. Linguistic accounts appeal to context to add meaning to underspecified content in the computation of the meaning of an utterance. However, context remains a fuzzy concept and heretofore it has seemed difficult to provide a characterisation that connects with language, linguistics and culture (Serangi 2009; Sharifian 2011, 2015abc, 2017ab; Goodwin and Duranti 1992; Diedrichsen 2019).

How can the structure of context and common ground, and the representation of actions in context, be characterised in a model, that draws on our ontological knowledge of the world, while using inferences about beliefs, desires, intentions, and goals? Such a representation of context and common ground must be available to language. The characteristics of context are that, in our cognition of it, it acts as a knowledge repository with knowledge appropriately represented, to assist in building the situation model. It is updated across a discourse interaction, and plays a role in the activation of knowledge. It informs part of the *core* common ground between the interlocutors framed by a discourse situation, and is activated in the ongoing interaction as it becomes relevant, and eventually shared to an appropriate extent in the *emergent* common ground.

Context contains the set of knowledge modified and updated during the discourse, and cannot be separated from the knowledge it organises (Table 2). It frames our knowledge of the things and events in the world, and includes various kinds of knowledge, some of which are process oriented and dynamic. Other kinds

Table 2: Generalised contents of common ground.

Structure of common ground	Volatility / Dynamicity
Local dialogue knowledge	More volatile / dynamic
Language knowledge	↑
Environment knowledge	│
Recent events knowledge	│
Historical knowledge	│
Common sense knowledge	↓
Cultural knowledge	Less volatile / dynamic

are less volatile and can include, for example, concepts, propositions, properties of entities in the world. Specifically, context includes cultural and, general knowledge and shared beliefs, and the experiential and societal knowledge that arises from the interplay of culture and social community. Context may also include location and environment.

Context constrains our interpretation of a situation and guides the determination of relevant meaning from a discourse with respect to an utterance. People interpret what happens around them and build a mental representation that reflects their conceptualisation and understanding of a specific situation. Knowledge plays a role in models of context and common ground. The types of knowledge characterised and found in common ground relate to declarative, procedural, heuristic, meta and structural knowledge, amongst others (Nolan 2022b). The representation of knowledge enables us to capture the essential features of a class of entities in a domain area and to make that information available for use.

There are different kinds of knowledge (Nolan 2022b):

1) Declarative,[3] descriptive, or propositional knowledge (knowledge-*that*) is where a person *knows that p* (where p is a proposition).
2) Competence, procedural, or ability knowledge is where a person knows how to do something requiring a skill. This knowledge-*how* involves an ability to perform a skill (consciously or unconsciously) and is concerned with rules, strategies, and procedures.
3) Acquaintance knowledge is where a person knows something or someone, via direct experience with people, objects and artefacts within the world.
4) Empirical/a posteriori knowledge proceeds from observations or experiences to the deduction of probable causes. Scientific inquiry is a way of acquiring world knowledge.
5) A priori knowledge is gained independently of investigation.

---

3 The term declarative as a term has a number of different uses that are potentially confusing. Firstly, it is one of the speech act types denoted in Searle's (1979) taxonomy of speech acts, These declarative acts bring about a corresponding change in the world and depend on an appropriate context. For example, in the appropriate context and on the assumption that the speaker has the authority to make the declaration 'I declare X to be Y', such that X will now be known as Y. The second use of the term declarative is to denote a knowledge type. Declarative knowledge describes what is known about concepts, facts, and objects, via a matrix of attributes and their values so that an entity or concept may be fully described. Thirdly, the term declarative is sometimes used to denote an instance of the mood structure of a clause. We would call this the indicative mood of a clause, rather than the declarative mood. The set of moods include the indicative mood, the imperative mood, the interrogative mood, the conditional mood, and the subjunctive mood. The mood structure of the clause refers to the organisation of the constituents.

6) Heuristic/tacit knowledge is amassed through the experience of solving past problems and describes a rule-of-thumb to guide the reasoning process.
7) Testimonial knowledge is gained either directly through someone telling us what they know, or indirectly from the testimony of others.
8) Meta knowledge is knowledge about the other kinds of knowledge and how to use them. It guides our reasoning processes.
9) Structural knowledge describes our overall mental model of concepts and objects. It is concerned with ordered sets of rules, relations between concepts, and relations between concept and object.
10) Linguistic knowledge is knowledge of our language(s), lexicon, syntax and grammar.

The role of knowledge in models of context and common ground has consequences for the production and comprehension of discourse (Figure 1). The management of knowledge guides the production of speech acts and many elements of discourse are shaped by the ways that participants represent and manage (mutual) knowledge (Nolan 2014). Common ground contains the subset of context compatible with our knowledge, and it emerges through communicative interaction where assessments are made of the extent of the shared knowledge between interlocutors, such that the common ground is constructed and maintained, appropriate to the context of a situation in which the discourse unfolds.

In Figure 1, we represent context, knowledge, core common ground for the interlocutors ‘a’ and ‘b’, their emergent common ground, and the knowledge base for both (as **k**.a and **k**.b, respectively), in a Venn diagram where the various sets of knowledge overlap. We indicate that ‘a’ and ‘b’ have their respective beliefs, desires, intentions (BDI) and plans. We also suggest in this diagram that the discourse is guided by, for example, Gricean principles (Grice 1967) for interlocutor ‘a’ (= speaker S), while meaning is retrieved from the utterance by interlocutor ‘b’ (= hearer H) via, for example, principles of relevance. Points of agreement and complementarity between the Gricean, Relevance Theory (RT) and Horn’s neo-Gricean frameworks have been critically examined by Carston (2006: 303) and it is worth mentioning some of these points here to get a sense of their complexity and richness.. According to Carston, RT is concerned with speaker meaning, both what it is and how the hearer attempts to recover it. For Horn, a primary goal of RT pragmatics is to provide an account of utterance comprehension.

> ‘Grice’s goal of developing an account of speaker meaning (of which implicature constitutes a proper subpart) is distinct from Relevance theorists’ goal of developing a cognitive psychological model of utterance interpretation, which does not address the question of how and why the speaker, given what she wants to convey, utters what she utters. (Horn 2005: 194)

The RT framework offers a view of human cognitive processing, including what it is that causes us to focus on certain information sources, but not others, and to process certain inputs while excluding others (Carston 2006: 304). The claim of RT is that human cognition is oriented to selecting and processing relevant inputs that are potentially beneficial to the ongoing functioning of the cognitive system and whose processing costs to the system are relatively low (Sperber and Wilson 1995, 2002). A rich source of information is attention pre-empting linguistic utterances which carry a presumption that they will achieve a certain level of relevance, and a satisfactory cognitive benefit for minimal processing effort. This kind of stimulus is considered to be ostensive. That is, it is produced by an intentional agent who makes fully overt (mutually manifest, in RT terms) an intention to provide relevant information. In turn, the cognitive system of the hearer is attuned to look for a certain degree and quality of relevance from ostensive stimuli and to then process them on this basis. Central to RT is the Communicative Principle of Relevance, under which utterances (ostensive stimuli) convey a presumption of their own optimal relevance. This presumes that any given utterance is: (a) relevant enough to warrant the hearer's processing effort, and (b) the most relevant one compatible with the speaker's current state of knowledge, personal preferences, and goals. The process that the hearer follows in comprehending an utterance to recovering the speaker's meaning is to test possible interpretations in their order of accessibility, stopping once the expectation of (optimal) relevance is satisfied. Neither Grice nor Horn were much interested in this cognitively-oriented approach of RT. However, both offer principles and maxims that influence the speaker's choice of utterance to communicate meaning and on how it is understood by the hearer (Carston 2006: 305). According to the processing within Grice's framework, a literal interpretation is always retrieved initially, tested for adherence with the maxims. If this is found to be unsatisfactory, blatantly false or trivially true, then a non-literal interpretation is accessed. The aims of Grice's philosophy of language therefore includes at least the following:

(1) to distinguish between what an expression e means, what speaker S said in a given situation by uttering e, and what S meant by uttering e in that situation;

(2) to elucidate the nature of non-natural meaning by providing analyses of speaker's meaning, sentence meaning, and what is said;

(3) to provide an account of how it is possible for what S says and what S means to diverge;

(4) to distinguish between semantic content and pragmatic implications and so clarify the relationship between classical logic, natural language semantics and ordinary language use.

Horn (2005: 19) argues that the Gricean maxims should be reduced to two general principles. These are the Q-Principle, oriented to the interests of the hearer, and the R-Principle, which is oriented to the interests of the speaker (Carston 2006: 312). The hearer-based Q-Principle and the speaker-based R-Principle are both presented (like the Gricean maxims) as injunctions to the speaker, and each has its hearer's corollary since '*The speaker and hearer are aware of their own and each other's desiderata [that is, the economies of both parties], and this awareness generates a variety of effects . . .*'. While Horn claims RT to be a hearer-based account, considerations of speaker effort do play a role (Carston 2006: 317). What a hearer is entitled to expect from an utterance is that it will be the most relevant one (have the most cognitive effects for the least cognitive expenses), taking into account the speaker's abilities and preferences or goals. It is the case that speakers often prefer to not exert any significant mental or physical effort on their part, though this will usually be guided by overall speaker goals. For example, the speaker may prefer to not risk offending the hearer and so speak in an indirect way. The speaker may prefer to not disclose some relevant but incriminating information. The speaker may want to impress or alternatively, may want her speaking to distract the hearer's attention from something. These possible preferences affect the degree of effort that a speaker is willing to expend in encoding and articulating linguistic forms. So, for the hearer, following the relevance-based comprehension procedure, the speaker's effort is one of many factors that may affect a specific expectation of relevance of an utterance.

Common ground knowledge is context-dependent, and discourse is produced and interpreted under the guidance of our mental context models. Once knowledge is communicated to a hearer, it becomes part of the common ground of the discourse, and can be presupposed in further communication between the speaker and hearer.

In Figure 2, we show the interlocutors 'a' and 'b' in a dialogue, and schematically represent the knowledge in the knowledge base as KBa and KBb.

The conversational exchanges are represented by arrows, and the knowledge bases updated at each conversational turn (numbered +0 to +n and shown as KBa+n and KBb+n). Emergent common ground is schematically represented at the end of the dialogue fragment with the knowledge base for 'a' (KBa+n) being broadly equivalent to the knowledge base for 'b' (KBb+n) within the confines of this dialogue interaction.

In this view, a speech act is necessarily interpreted in the context of a given situation, a structured object that acts as a framing device linking semantics to events, through to syntax, and onwards to utterance meaning via common ground. People deduce what happens around them and, consequently, build mental rep-

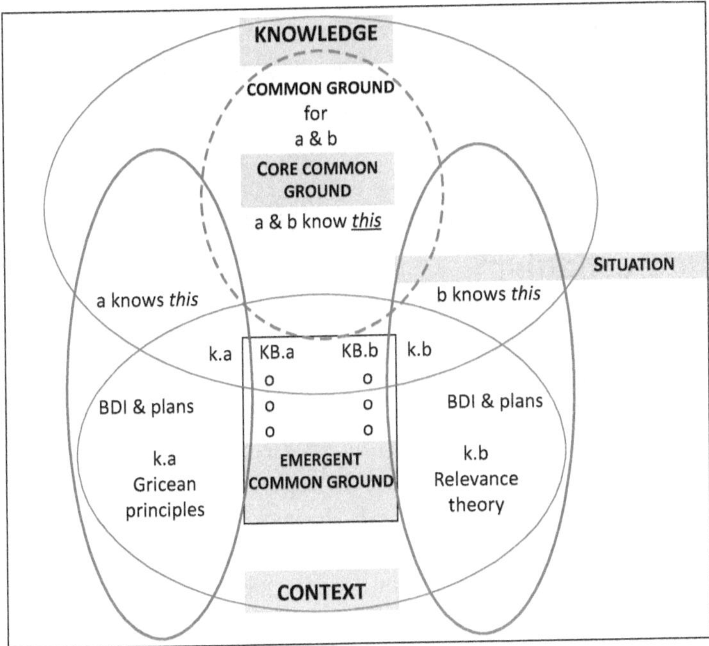

Figure 1: Core and emergent common ground with shared knowledge.

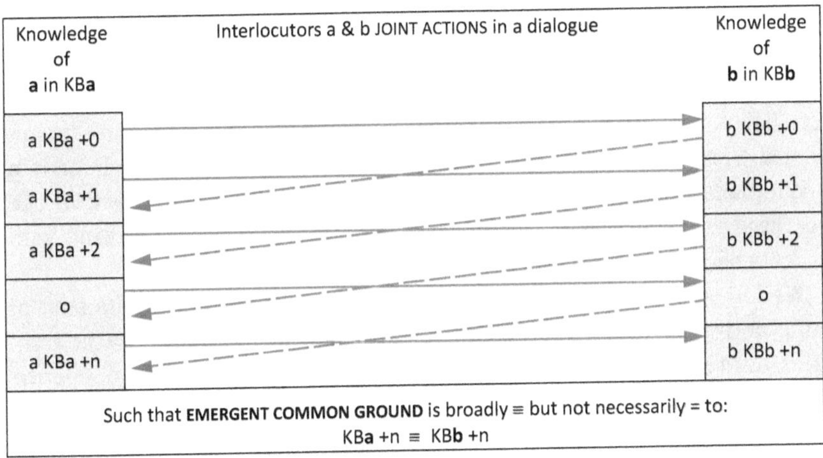

Figure 2: Construction of core and emergent common ground.

resentations which reflect their conceptualisation and construal of a specific situation. This interpretation is constrained by the knowledge framed in the situation. We examine the situation next.

4 The importance of a situation as a cognitive framing mechanism

We argue that utterances must be interpreted in the local context of a given situation. Speakers categorise situations on the basis of their previous experience, and they make sense of what they encounter on the basis of their respective personal, social, and socio-cultural knowledge. For an utterance to be interpretable, speakers frame their understanding of the situation (Fetzer and Fischer 2007: 59) and the situational context needs to be established. The idea of a situation as meaningful for the interpretation of an utterance is not new (Austin 1950; Barwise 1981, 1988; Barwise and Perry 1983; Sag, Wasow and Bender 2003).

A situation is a structured entity with important characteristics that acts as a unifying means to connect semantics through to utterance meaning. The schematic structure of a situation (2) includes its constructional signature (the clausal syntactic pattern that carries the utterance), illocutionary force, the initial context at the time of the utterance, the initial common ground of the speaker S and hearer H, preconditions that may exist, the proposition, the Belief, Desire and Intention (BDI) states of the speaker, and the post-context '*as it is*' after the utterance (Nolan 2017, 2022ab). The events and arguments of the situation are represented. The situational preconditions constrain as necessary. As well, certain preconditions hold for the successful performance of an illocutionary act. We can view these preconditions as ranging over the cognitive state of the agent, with respect to belief, desire and intention.

We formalise the representation of a situation to include the framing of context and common ground, for both speaker S and hearer H, showing the associations and links between the situation, context and common ground. Cooperative behaviour across a dialogue is characterised by the partners in the interaction taking the cognitive states of their interlocutor into account, following their goals, having the intention to achieve their desired goals, and both expecting and believing that the partners in the interaction will adhere to rational behaviours of dialogue. We can represent the cognitive states of an interlocutor agent in a dialogue in our model, where several predicates have a reserved meaning (3). Therefore, we represent a) the set of *beliefs* that the agent S has at any given time, b) the *goals* that speaker / agent S will try to achieve, c) the *actions* that agent S performs, d) the *knowledge of the effects* of these actions, and e) the *contextual knowledge* of the agent S, along with preconditions and postconditions. An important dimension of this model is the representation of contextual knowledge at the interface between knowledge and language, mediated by the speech act.

(2) Schema of a situation including context and common ground

SITUATION	*sit*
SIGNATURE	Utterance syntactic pattern
Event(s)	< v_1 (. . . v_n) . . . >
Verbal arguments	< ARG1, (ARG2, . . ., ARG_n) . . . >
Event participants	< ARG1, (ARG2, . . ., ARG_n) . . . >
Location.time	(time)
Location.space	(place – may be unspecified)
ILLOCFORCE	IL
INITIAL CONTEXT → CORE COMMON GROUND	
	InitialCG.S
	InitialCG.H
Precondition(s)	
PROPOSITION	P
BELIEF	KB.S = speaker knowledge base set of Bs KB.H = hearer knowledge base – unspecified
DESIRE	KB.S set of Ds KB.H – unspecified
INTENTION	KB.S set of Is KB.H – unspecified
POST CONTEXT → EMERGED COMMON GROUND	
Postconditions	
	PostCG.S
	PostCG.H

(3) Cognitive states for an agent in a dialogue
  a. **BEL'** (Agent, P): the agent *believes* that P is true, where P is a proposition.
  b. **KNOW'** (Agent, P): expresses a *knowledge state* of the agent with respect to P.
  c. **WANT'** (Agent, P): the agent *desires* the event or state implied by P to occur.
  d. **INTEND'** (Agent, P): the agent *intends* to do P.

A proposition has a truth-evaluable content derived from the interpretation of an utterance of an expression. The linguistic meaning of an expression, the encoded meaning, fundamentally under-determines the proposition that is intentionally communicated by S even when this is explicitly expressed. The propositional content expressed is derived taking into account the context of utterance. As we have argued, an utterance must be interpreted in the context of a given situation, where a situation serves as a framing mechanism to link semantics to events through to syntax, and through to utterance meaning.

5 Application of common ground as a cognitive object in language use

While an essential component of advancing a dialogue between interlocutors, as a cognitive object common ground also serves to resolve different kinds of ambiguity commonly found in conversation, such as lexical or structural ambiguity. Additionally, common ground is also necessary for the appropriate retrieval of meaning from a speech act.

Lexical ambiguity can be common in conversation but we typically resolve this very quickly by appealing to context to contribute necessary information. One example is shown in (4). This presents the problem that, without additional information in our common ground, we don't actually know what this utterance means. We don't have an appropriate single interpretation. In fact, the problem lies with the word *duck*. Is this [duck:N] or [duck:V]? If the [duck:N] is correct, then we interpret as [3SGF possesses a duck:N]. Otherwise, we resolve with a meaning of [1SG.ACTOR DO-ACTION$_{\text{duck}}$ with causal effect on 3SGF.UNDERGOER 'avoiding a projectile']. We can only resolve this with contextual information from our common ground. Once we accept the N or V distinction, we update emergent common ground. Specifically, H processes the utterance. In doing this, H checks common ground first then context as to what information can contribute to the relevant meaning, to resolve the ambiguity. Once this is achieved, the emergent common ground is updated.

(4) Lexical ambiguity
Speaker: 'I made her duck'.
a) CONTEXT-1: [3SGF *possesses* a duck:N]
b) CONTEXT-2: [1SG.$_{ACTOR}$ DO-ACTION$_{duck}$ with causal effect on 3SGF.$_{UNDERGOER}$]
Hearer processes the utterance:
- We are informed by consulting context that one of the possible interpretations is true.
- Hearer accepts the assertion, once the lexical ambiguity is resolved.
- Therefore, emergent common ground is now updated with the new information.

Another example of lexical ambiguity is given in (5). Here, the ambiguity resides in whether we can interpret *visiting* as [visiting:V] or [visiting:ADJ]. Again, we cannot interpret this utterance without the appropriate contextual knowledge from common ground. If the appropriate selection is [visiting:V] then [I *visit* relatives] is the retrieved meaning. Otherwise, with the [visiting:ADJ] interpretation, then a meaning such as [relatives *visiting* me is annoying]. Once we accept the V vs. ADJ distinction based on information in common ground, we update emergent common ground.

(5) Lexical ambiguity
Speaker: 'Visiting relatives can be annoying'.
a) CONTEXT-1: [I visit relatives] → [visit:V] with 1SG.ACTOR
b) CONTEXT-2: [relatives visiting me (=visiting-relatives)] → [visiting:ADJ] and 1SG.UNDERGOER
Hearer processes the utterance:
- The hearer needs to adopt the appropriate *construal* of the situation to enable the correct interpretations: Do I.$_{ACTOR}$ visit relatives, or do relatives visit me.$_{UNDERGOER}$?
- From consulting common ground, we are informed that one of the possible interpretations is true.
- Hearer accepts the assertion, once the lexical ambiguity is resolved via the appropriate situation construal.
- Emergent common ground is updated with the new information.

As well as lexical ambiguity, common ground also plays a role in the resolution of the structural ambiguity in an utterance. The classic example of structural ambiguity is that given in (6). Here, we cannot resolve the actual meaning without the contribution of solid and robust information from that part of context in common ground. There are two possible interpretations, due to the clausal structure. The first interpretation, [The man *possesses* a telescope], yields 'I saw the man who had the telescope'. In the second possible interpretation, the telescope is an INSTRUMENT to aid the viewing, giving [1SG uses the telescope as an INSTRUMENT to see the man]. Once common ground informs us as to which interpretation is correct, we resolve the meaning of the utterance and update emergent common ground.

(6) Structural ambiguity
Speaker: 'I saw the man with the telescope'.
 a) CONTEXT-1: [The man possesses a telescope]
 b) CONTEXT-2: [1SG uses INSTRUMENT.telescope to see the man]
Hearer processes the utterance:
 - From consulting common ground, we are informed that one of the possible interpretations is true.
 - Hearer accepts the assertion, once the structural ambiguity is resolved.
 - Emergent common ground is updated with the new information.

We next look at an example of an assertive speech act, followed by an example of an indirect request, where context plays a role in the construction of the emergent common ground. In example (7), the speaker asserts 'Aifric broke the wine glass', but the hearer does not know whether this is true or false. The hearer needs to be guided by context and common ground knowledge as to its appropriate interpretation. Is the wine glass actually broken or not? A precondition of accepting the utterance as true is the contextual evidence, that knowledge in common ground, which will reveal, say, that the wine glass is indeed broken. Once this is accepted from context, the assertion can be accepted as a true fact. Once this happens, emergent common ground is updated with this new information fact.

(7) Speech act: assertion
Speaker: 'Aifric broke the wine glass'
From CONTEXT:
 a. The wine glass is broken or
 b. The wine glass is not broken

Hearer processes the utterance:

- Assume that a. holds. Therefore from common ground, we are informed that the proposition is TRUE in a. The hearer accepts the assertion.
- Emergent common ground now contains:

  BEL' [**do'**(Aifric) CAUSE BECOME **broken'**(the wine glass)]
- Consequently, speaker and hearer now believe that 'Aifric broke the wine glass'.

As regards the speech act of indirect request in (8), the speaker utters what looks at first glance like an assertion 'It is very cold in here!' However, the speaker can get information from context to guide the interpretation: *Is it actually cold? Is the window open?* In this context, the hearer can see that the window is open (and not closed) and therefore interprets the utterance as an indirect request by the speaker for the window to be closed such that the coldness will be removed. The hearer reasons that 'It is very cold in here' + window open → speaker makes a REQUEST to 'close window'. Emergent common ground is now updated.

(8) Speech act: indirect request

Speaker: 'It is very cold in here!'.

From CONTEXT:

a. The window is open or

b. The window is closed

Hearer processes the utterance:

- From consulting context, we are informed that proposition a. is TRUE.
- The hearer reasons with the speaker's utterance, while informed by context.
- The hearer infers the speaker's indirect REQUEST to 'close the window'.
- The hearer can decide whether to act on the indirect request from the speaker.
- In any event, emergent common ground now contains the following information:

  It is very cold in here + The window is open

  $\rightarrow_{\textbf{hearer reasoning}}$ = speaker makes REQUEST to 'close the window'

In the next section, we examine the operations for the construction and maintenance of common ground.

6 Operations – the construction and maintenance of common ground

As an abstraction, a communicative interaction between two interlocutors might, for example, require that a dialogue along the following lines be exchanged, and which can be diagrammed over a state space (see Figure 3). Essentially, discourse interlocutors, A and B, can:

i. Propose '*something*' : a fact/piece of knowledge/event/course of action
ii. Accept
iii. Reject
iv. Retract
v. Disagree
vi. Counter propose '*something else*'

In our communicative interactions, common ground plays a central role in the way that we process and accumulate information (Clark E.V. 2015: 328). Various operations are employed to update common ground as appropriate to the flow of discourse. A set of operations establish common ground, maintain the initial core, and also emergent, common ground. In conjunction with the general cognitive operation of: i) salience and attention, which functions to identify candidates for inclusion into common ground, the construction and ongoing maintenance of common ground makes use of several critical operations, including ii) grounding, iii) tracking, iv) verification, v) repair, and vi) accommodation.

The information in common ground, and the operations (Table 3) that act on it in its construction and maintenance actively contribute to the interlocutors' emergent common ground.

6.1 Attention and salience

A process associated with salience is the allocation of attention. In a discourse, the hearer's attention is guided by the speaker to establish a salient profile of foregrounded and backgrounded information in their discourse model (Falk 2014: 4). Foregrounding functions to indicate the salience of discourse parts in relation to imminent discourse. Here, speakers convey the importance of an entity in the mental model to the hearer, relative to the continuing discourse that is to follow, such that the referent is then expected to play a role. Attention tends to go to items that are informationally rich, given a particular context. Our experience of reality evolves across a number of domains simultaneously, with perception across the

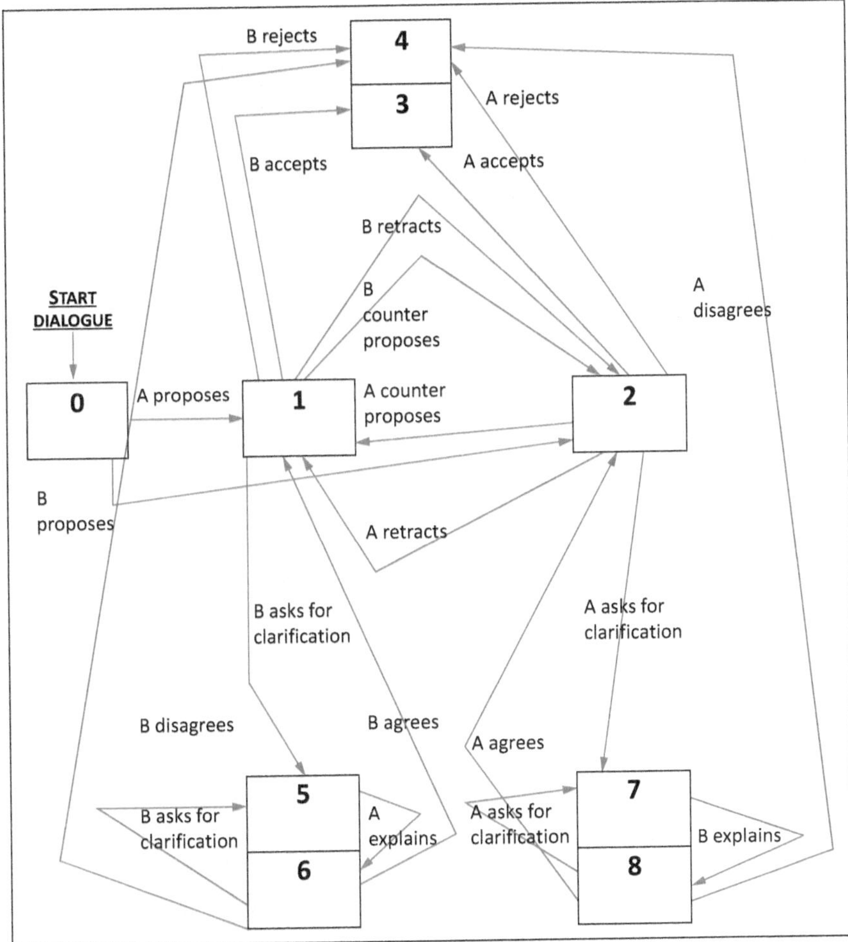

Figure 3: State space for communicative interaction.

Table 3: The operations on common ground.

Operations on common ground	
FUNCTION	OPERATION
GET:	Attention and salience
ADD:	Ground
CHECK:	Track
CHECK:	Verify
FIX:	Repair
UPDATE:	Accommodate

visual, auditory and tactile domains. We cannot attend in equal measure to all input channels to our experience. Instead, we concentrate on a small number of areas and give these our attention. According to Langacker (1987: 115), in virtue of this focus of attention, inputs from this small number of areas are perceived as being more prominent or salient. The cognitive ability of focusing attention is relevant from a linguistic point of view. Indeed, Langacker's notion of 'construal' covers the relationship between the speaker and hearer and the situation represented, and embodies the role that attention plays in language. Construal reflects the user's ability to adjust the focus of attention by altering the mental imagery representing a situation. Salience detection via cues is considered a key attentional mechanism, as it enables us to focus our perceptual and cognitive resources on the most relevant subset of available data. Humans have trouble giving attention to more than one item simultaneously, and we have the challenge of continuously prioritising and coherently integrating different influences.

According to Baicchi (2015: 23), our attention is naturally drawn to ontologically salient entities. Baicchi defines the notion of salience in two different but closely related ways. The first usage, cognitive salience, is where the activation of concepts occurs in actual speech events. This may result from the activation of a concept via conscious selection, whereby the concept enters our focus of attention and is processed in current working memory. In spreading activation, the activation of one concept causes the activation of others. Once a concept has been activated, it is said to be salient when it becomes part of a person's centre of attention. The second usage is ontological salience, which relates to the stable properties of entities in the world. Some entities are better at attracting our attention than others and are more salient in this sense. The notion of salience may denote both a temporary activation state of mental concepts (cognitive salience) and an inherent, more permanent, property of entities in the real world (ontological salience).

6.2 Grounding additions to common ground

Additions to common ground take place in communicative exchanges through the grounding of new information (Clark E.V. 2015: 328). With grounding, information known to the speaker becomes accepted and known to the hearer. As a common ground operation, grounding is intrinsically connected with the participants' management of common ground (Fetzer and Fischer 2007: 18). To ground new information, interlocutors rely on a variety of strategies, using both linguistic and non-linguistic devices, to mark new information as new, and to indicate that that information has been grounded (Clark E. V. 2015: 329–330). The methods that the dialogue participants use for grounding include: acknowledgment by the hearer of new information, repeating information, providing a simple confirmation or minimal acknowledgement, and continuation to next turn.

Grounding operation method 1. An acknowledgment by the hearer of the new information from the original speaker, using a demonstrative or pronominal reference as in (9) and (10). These assertions rely on an understanding of pronominal reference and determiners to identify the relevant antecedent.

(9) Speaker: I just got back from Dublin.
Hearer: *That* must have been a fascinating trip.

(10) Speaker: Did you talk to Aisling yet?
Hearer: Yes, I told *her* about Tara's wedding plans.

Grounding operation method 2. Repeating the information is a transparent way to ground it, by incorporating it into a continuation assertion (11).

(11) Speaker: Aisling said she would be in Dublin in December.
Hearer: Great, so we meet next in Dublin.

Grounding operation method 3. A simple confirmation (*yes*, *yeah*, *yup*, *uh-huh*) from the hearer combined with further information from the hearer (12), possibly to do with time or location.

(12) Speaker: Will you be going to see Tara and Marcus soon?
Hearer: Yeah, on our next visit to Dublin.

Grounding operation method 4. The hearer provides a minimal acknowledgement (13).

(13) Speaker: Is Joyce's *Ulysses* the book you were talking about?
Hearer: uh-huh / yup.

Grounding operation method 5. The hearer presupposes understanding of the speaker's contribution in the continuation of the next turn (14).

(14) Speaker: We're hoping to leave for Carlingford on the 1st May.
Hearer: So, we should bring all our beach stuff then?

Grounding operation method 6. The hearer uses gestural indications of understanding that imply acknowledgement, such as a *head-nod, thumbs-up* gesture. Some combination of gestures (15) may be used with verbal acknowledgments.

(15) Speaker: Have you heard that our restaurant meet-up has been postponed due to COVID-19 restrictions?
Hearer: < *thumbs-up*> yup.

These different ways of grounding new information are naturally interwoven into our interactions. They acknowledge new information introduced by the speaker to the hearer, and advance the construction and maintenance of common ground.

6.3 Tracking information

Core common ground contains already known information. Emergent common builds on core common ground to accommodate new information in a dynamic emergent manner, via an update mechanism. The maintenance of common ground requires that we track what is already in common ground. We know, by representing in our mental models of SELF and OTHER, what the other knows, and track this in detail (Clark E.V 2015: 339). This tracking operation is essential for using a given–new strategy in managing information, where given information is already grounded and new information is not yet grounded. In language, speakers tends to place given information before new. The given information is grounded and therefore known to both speaker and hearer. The new information is being added by the speaker and therefore not yet known to the hearer. The hearer must acknowledge this information before grounding and adding it to common ground. This flow of new information is important for effective discourse (Clark E.V 2015: 346). The given-before-new order is coherent with our understanding that each interlocutor first grounds new information from the preceding speaker, and then, by return, may add something new.

6.4 Verification

Verification of common ground updates occur each time that a conversational partner responds to a contribution, without taking the opportunity to repair perceived misunderstandings, such that it can be reasonably inferred that no misunderstandings are evident. In this, participants can assume understanding as long as they satisfy each other's expectations for the current state of the interaction.

With this default verification, affirmations of understanding occur when conversational participants use acknowledging indicators such as *yeah*, *uh huh*, *yup*, *I see*, and so on. These verifications allow the conversation to continue.

6.5 Repair

Sometimes, of course, the grounding operation fails and repair is necessary (Clark E.V 2015: 330). The interlocutors can activate several different strategies for dealing with errors and their repair. These include: a general clarification request, full repeat, rejection and restart, or quick feedback with the correct form.

Repair Operation method 1. This repair operation may involve a general request for clarification (16). Alternatively, it may involve a more specific request, with a partial repeat of the problematic utterance (17). Part of the uttered clause can be selected for clarification (underlined here for emphasis). These examples pick out the leaving date for clarification.

(16) Speaker: We're leaving on the twenty-seventh.
Hearer: What?

(17) Speaker: We are leaving on the 1st of the month.
Hearer: We're leaving on the *what*?

Repair Operation method 2. This repair operation may consist of a full repeat (Clark E.V 2015: 331), to check on what the prior speaker actually said, followed by confirmation and continuation (18). Alternatively, this may involve rejection and restart (19).

(18) Speaker: We heading to Sliabh Gullion Forest Park on Sunday.
Hearer: You're going to *Sliabh Gullion* Forest Park on Sunday?
Speaker: Yes.

(19) Speaker: We're going to Sliabh Gullion Forest Park on Sunday.
Hearer: You're going to Sliabh Feá Forest Park on Sunday?
Speaker: *No*! We're going to Sliabh *Gullion* Forest Park!

Lexical repair operation. Lexical repairs are evident when the wrong word for something (20) is used (Clark E.V 2015: 338).

(20) a. *It* got . . . the *wheel* got out
b. Straight on *red*, . . . sorry, straight on *black*
c. And I know the peasants were all *depressed* → *oppressed.*

With the lexical repair operation, the speaker usually provides immediate feedback to the hearer with the correct lexical item.

6.6 Accommodation

Context and common ground are essential in advancing a dialogue, while accommodation is a process that a hearer engages in to adjust to the flow of dialogue. Once the hearer recognises that something is wrong in a dialogue, an accommodation is needed to add a missing presupposition in a common ground update. An utterance then is an augmentation to a context that satisfies some presupposition(s).

> Ordinary conversation does not always proceed in the ideal orderly fashion described earlier. People do make leaps and shortcuts by using sentences whose presuppositions are not satisfied in the conversational context. This is the rule rather than the exception [. . .] I think we can maintain that a sentence is always taken to be an increment to a context that satisfies its presuppositions. If the current conversational context does not suffice, the listener is entitled and expected to extend it as required. (Karttunen 1974: 191)

Accommodation is an inferential process which operates on presuppositions. It is an adjustment to common ground necessary in the case when a speaker uses an expression which requires that context be updated with some previously unmentioned information (Beaver and Zeevat 2012; Thomason 1992). What is accommodated is the presupposition triggered by some reference in an utterance.

7 Egocentrism, cooperation, game theory, and emergent common ground

We need to make some comments on egocentrism. In the writing of Kecskes, the idea of egocentrism as a human behaviour is interesting for many reasons. One of these reasons is that it correlates with some important ideas in Game Theory as applied to language use. Like cooperation, egocentrism is very much a part of human rationality, and people are inherently cooperative and inherently egocentric (Kecskes 2019: 407). Consequently, egocentrism and cooperation are not mutually exclusive phenomena. In turn, egocentrism is not a negative behaviour but is instead rooted in the interlocutors' greater reliance on their own knowledge instead of knowledge that may be mutual. Kecskes argues that in the first phase of the communicative process, instead of looking for any significant common ground, speakers articulate their own thoughts with whatever linguistic means they could use easily. As prior experience strongly impacts how we operate, people are inevitably influenced by what they have done before and how they have achieved this, and this including communication. Egocentrism is therefore quite natural and to be expected.

The sociocognitive approach to intercultural pragmatics (Kecskes 2010, 2013a and Kecskes and Zhang 2009) emphasises the role of co-construction along with the importance of all kinds of prior knowledge in a dialogue. This prior knowledge includes cultural models and private mental models. In meaning construction there is also a reliance on pre-existing encyclopaedic knowledge, based on prior experience, and current knowledge created in the process of interaction. Kecskes (2019: 409) writes: 'communication is driven by the interplay of cooperation required by societal conditions and egocentrism rooted in prior experience of the individual'. As it turns out, Kecskes' idea of egocentrism is very similar to the notions of rationality and enlightened self-interest found in Game Theory.

Game Theory models the interaction between two or more participants in a situation. In a dialogue these participants are the interlocutors. Applied to language use, the theory attempts to create a model and predict the outcome of a dialogue between rational individuals, often with uncertainty and an unevenness of shared information in the initial core common ground. Language is first and foremost a means for communication. As a side effect of communication, knowledge of various kinds is transmitted between the communicators. Core common ground is established and emergent common ground develops as the dialogue advances. In Game Theory, a game is a sequence of decision problems, involving two or more agents, where the outcome depends on the way the actions of different agents interact. One or more game agents have to choose between several actions. Therefore, at the core of every game theoretic situation there is a decision to be made. In this, agents have to decide between available actions, and based on their own preferences given the expected or resulting outcomes so far. For example, if someone is offered an apple or a banana but can only take one of them, and if the apple is preferred over the banana, then the choice will be for an apple as a clear preference and the outcome is known. That choice to select an apple is the decision made.

Game Theory can be classified as either cooperative or non-cooperative. In pragmatics, it is usual to assume that interlocutors in their use of language conform with Grice's (1967) cooperative principle that assumes speakers to be rational and cooperative language users. This suggests that the model of a discourse situation is typically one of cooperative information exchange.

With a cooperative situation, the interlocutors are in a situation where there is an implicit agreement between the interlocutors for cooperation adhering to Grice's cooperative principle. In a non-cooperative situation, there is no binding agreement for cooperation between the interlocutors. Typically, then, in a non-cooperative situation, the speaker desires all the relevant and reliable information. However, the hearer may not wish to cooperate and instead choose to not reveal all of the information they possess, for whatever reason. Both interlocutors are aware of the other's strategies and possible reactions. Consequently, the Gricean maxims of cooperation do not seem to apply in a non-cooperative[4] situation where an egocentric approach is predominant. The interlocutors then act in their own enlightened self-interest.

A given assumption, of course, is that the interlocutors, being rational, want to maximise their own expected effectiveness and benefit. That is, they exhibit egocentrism as a rational behaviour. Each interlocutor has to rely on the rationality of the others, without any doubt, and in turn depends on the other interlocutors relying on their own rationality. Each individual knows the discourse communicative strategies available, but they do not know the other interlocutor's strategy choices. The outcome of one interlocutor's choices affects all the other interlocutors, the way in which the dialogue advances, and the emergent common ground.

8 Discussion

We have promoted the idea of common ground as a distributed, complex, adaptive cognitive object. A major function of common ground is to manage shared knowledge and information between discourse interlocutors so as to advance a dialogue, framing a relevant subset of knowledge and information. As knowledge and information in the broader context is so large as to be unmanageable by any individual, common ground crucially acts as a framing mechanism over a situation to delineate that knowledge needed for a dialogue. It is a natural part of our cognitive endowment and tasked with information and knowledge management.

4 Of course, it is the case that actually flouting of the maxims can be conversationally cooperative once all the participants in the conversation can see that a maxim has been broken on purpose by S in order to create an extra layer of meaning that is accessible through inference.

The establishment and maintenance of common ground, as a cognitive object, avails of several operations in a sequence guided by the particular discourse. Salience and attention identify candidates for inclusion into common ground. We initially establish what is in our common ground. We ground information. We track what is going on in the dialogue and respond appropriately, perhaps via a repair of some kind. We ratify the new information in the speaker's utterance, and add it to the current common ground. In turn we accommodate new information and adjust common ground in response to evidence that becomes available to us.

The complexity in common ground comes from language interactions and cognitive functions. The cognitive object viewpoint allows us to gain some understanding of the nature of the behaviours pertaining to common ground, especially seemingly unpredicted behaviour. Through self-organisation, common ground is seen to be more structured than heretofore. As a distributed, complex, adaptive cognitive object, common ground never 'settles down' but is continually operational. It has a continuous feedback ability. Feedback within common ground means that its outputs at time T affect the inputs at time T+1. Following from this, as the discourse interlocutors interact, the results of some of their interactions influence future interactions. As a cognitive object, common ground creates feedback through its operations, exhibits emergent properties and self-organisation, and produces non-linear dynamic behaviour. The outputs from common ground are not proportional to the set of inputs and cannot be predicted by separately understanding its parts, and combining them additively. Common ground can be studied more holistically as a cognitive object.

We have outlined, in a formalised manner, the relationship between context, situation and core and emergent common ground. We showed how contextually relevant knowledge and content get selected for inclusion into core and emergent common ground, along with the operations used to manage the informational content of common ground, considered as a cognitive object.

This cognitive object viewpoint has many advantages and benefits, and allows us to treat common ground within a functional-cognitive perspective. We get an understanding of the functions of common ground and its operations, as a cognitive object with its behaviours, tasked with managing a subset of contextual information and knowledge to advance a discourse. It allows us some understanding of the dynamics of common ground in language in interaction, and the central importance of emergent common ground. We gain insights into how adaptiveness supports the phenomenon of emergent common ground. We make these insights by considering common ground as a cognitive object.

References

Anderson, John R. 1980. Concepts, propositions, and schemata: what are the cognitive units? *Nebr Symp Motiv.* 1980; 28. 121–162. PMID: 7242754.

Austin, John L. 1950. *Truth. Philosophical Papers* (3rd edn. 1979). Oxford: Oxford University Press. 117–133.

Baicchi, Annalisa. 2015. *Construction Learning as a Complex Adaptive System Psycholinguistic Evidence from L2 Learners of English.* Springer Briefs in Education. Cham / Heidelberg / New York / Dordrecht / London: Springer.

Barwise, Jon. 1981. Scenes and Other Situations. *The Journal of Philosophy* 78. 369–397.

Barwise, Jon. 1988. *The Situation in Logic.* Stanford: CSLI.

Barwise, Jon. & Perry, John. 1983. *Situations and Attitudes.* Cambridge, MA: The MIT Press.

Beaver, David & Zeevat, Henk. 2012. Accommodation. In Gillian Ramchand & Charles Reiss (eds.), *The Oxford Handbook of Linguistic Interfaces*, 503–538. Oxford: Oxford University Press.- DOI: 10.1093/oxfordhb/9780199247455.013.0017.

Beckner, Clay, Blythe, Richard, Bybee, Joan, Christiansen, Morten, Croft, William, Ellis, Nick, Holland, John, Ke, Jinyun, Larsen-Freeman, Diane, & Schoenemann, Tom. 2009. Language is a complex adaptive system. *Language Learning* 59(s1). 1–26. Available (25th Sept. 2021) online: https://www.santafe.edu/research/results/working-papers/language-is-a-complex-adaptive-system. DOI:10.1111/j.1467-9922.2009. 00533.x.

Carston, Robyn. 2005. Relevance Theory, Grice, and the neo-Griceans: A response to Laurence Horn's "Current issues in neo-Gricean pragmatics". *Intercultural Pragmatics* 2(3). 303–319.

Clark, Eve V. 2015. Common Ground. In B. MacWhinney & W. O'Grady (eds.), *The Handbook of Language Emergence*, 328–353. West Sussex, UK: John Wiley & Sons Ltd.

Clark, Herbert H. 1996. Using Language. Cambridge: Cambridge University Press.

Diedrichsen, Elke. 2019. On the Interaction of Core and Emergent Common Ground in Internet Memes. *Internet Pragmatics.* Special issue on the Pragmatics of Internet Memes. [Online first]. Amsterdam: Benjamins. DOI: https://doi.org/10.1075/ip.00033.die.

Falk, Simone. 2014. On the notion of salience in spoken discourse: Prominence cues shaping discourse structure and comprehension. *TIPA. Travaux interdisciplinaires sur la parole et le langage.* http://journals.openedition.org/tipa/1303; DOI:10.4000/tipa.1303.

Fetzer, Anita & Fischer, Kirsten. (eds.). 2007. *Lexical Markers of Common Grounds* (Studies in Pragmatics, Vol, 3). Leiden, The Netherlands: Brill.

Goffman Erving. 1974. *Frame analysis.* Cambridge: Harvard University Press.

Goodwin, Charles & Duranti, Alessandro. 1992. Rethinking context: An introduction. In Alessandro Duranti & Charles Goodwin (eds.), *Rethinking Context: Language as an Interactive Phenomenon*, 1–42. Cambridge: Cambridge University Press.

Grice, Herbert Paul. 1967/1989. Logic and conversation. In Herbert Paul Grice (ed.), *Studies in the Way of Words*, 22–40. Cambridge, MA: Harvard University Press.

Holland, John Henry. 1995. *Hidden order: How adaptation builds complexi*ty. Boston, CA, USA: Addison Wesley.

Horn, Laurence. 2005. Current issues in neo-Gricean pragmatics. *Intercultural Pragmatics* 2(2). 191–204.

Karttunen, Lauri. 1974. Presuppositions and Linguistic Context. Theoretical Linguistics 1. 181–194.

Kecskes, Istvan. 2003. *Situation-based utterances in L1 and L2.* Berlin: Mouton de Gruyter.

Kecskes, Istvan. 2010. Situation-bound utterances as pragmatic acts. *Journal of Pragmatics* 42(11). 2889–2897.

Kecskes, Istvan. 2013a. Intercultural Pragmatics. In Farzad Sharifian & Maryam Jamarani (eds.), *Language and intercultural communication in the New Era*, 39–59. London: Routledge.

Kecskes, Istvan. 2013b. Intercultural encyclopedic knowledge, and cultural models. In Farzad Sharifian & Maryam Jamarani (eds.), *Language and intercultural communication in the New Era*, 39–59. London: Routledge.

Kecskes, Istvan. 2015. Language, culture, and context. In Farzad Sharifian (ed.), *The Routledge Handbook of Language and Culture*, 113–128. Oxon / New York: Routledge.

Kecskes, Istvan. 2019. Cross-Cultural and Intercultural Pragmatics. In Yan Huang (ed.), *The Oxford Handbook of Pragmatics* (Oxford Handbooks), 400–415. Oxford University Press: Oxford.

Kecskes, Istvan & Zhang, Fenghui. 2009. Activating, seeking, and creating common ground: A socio-cognitive approach. *Pragmatics & Cognition* 17(2), 2009. 331–355. DOI:10.1075/p&c.17.2.06kec.

Kecskes, Istvan & Mey, Jacob. (eds.). 2008. *Intention, Common Ground and the Egocentric Speaker-Hearer*. Berlin / New York: Mouton de Gruyter.

Langacker, Ronald. W. 1987. *Foundations of cognitive grammar*. Vol. 1, *Theoretical prerequisites*. Stanford, CA: Stanford University Press.

Nolan, Brian. 2014. Extending a lexicalist functional grammar through speech acts, constructions and conversational software agents. In Brian Nolan & Carlos Periñán (eds.), *Language processing and grammars: The role of functionally oriented computational models*, 143–164. Amsterdam and New York: John Benjamins Publishing Company.

Nolan, Brian. 2017. The syntactic realisation of complex events and complex predicates in situations of Irish. In Brian Nolan & Elke Diedrichsen (eds.), *Argument realisation in complex predicates and complex events*, 14–42. Amsterdam and New York: John Benjamins Publishing Company.

Nolan, Brian. 2022a. *Language, culture, and knowledge in context: A functional-cognitive approach*. Sheffield: Equinox Publishing Company.

Nolan, Brian. 2022b. The cultural, contextual and computational dimensions of common ground. In Istvan Kecskes (ed.), *Handbook of Intercultural pragmatics*, Chapter 5, 107–138. Cambridge: Cambridge University Press.

Sag, Ivan. A., Wasow, Thomas, & Bender, Emily. 2003. *Syntactic Theory: A formal introduction*. 2nd edn. Stanford: CSLI Publications.

Searle, John R. 1979. *Expression and Meaning: Studies in the Theory of Speech Acts*. Cambridge: Cambridge University Press.

Serangi, Srikant. 2009. Culture. In Gunter Senft, Jan-Ola Östman & Jef Verschueren (eds.), *Culture and language use*, 81–104. Amsterdam / Philadelphia: Benjamins Publishing Company.

Sharifian, Farzad. 2011. *Cultural Conceptualisations and Language: Theoretical framework and applications*. Amsterdam/Philadelphia: John Benjamins Publishing Company.

Sharifian, Farzad. 2015a. Cultural Linguistics. In Farzad Sharifian (ed.), *The Routledge Handbook of Language and Culture*, 473–492. Oxon/New York: Routledge.

Sharifian, Farzad. 2015b. Language and culture: overview. In Farzad Sharifian (ed.), The *Routledge Handbook of Language and Culture*, 3–18. Oxon/New York: Routledge.

Sharifian, Farzad (ed.). 2015c. *The Routledge Handbook of Language and Culture*. New York/London: Routledge/Taylor and Francis.

Sharifian, Farzad. 2017a. *Cultural Linguistics: Cultural conceptualisations and language.* Amsterdam/Philadelphia: John Benjamins.
Sharifian, Farzad (ed.). 2017b. *Advances in Cultural Linguistics*. Singapore: Springer Nature.
Sharifian, Farzad & Palmer, Gary. B. 2007. *Applied Cultural Linguistics: Implications for second language learning and intercultural communication*. Amsterdam/Philadelphia: John Benjamins Publishing Company.
Sperber, Dan & Wilson, Deirdre. 1995. Postface. *Relevance: Communication and Cognition*. 2nd edn. Oxford: Blackwell; Cambridge, MA: Harvard University Press.
Sperber, Dan & Wilson, Deirdre. 2002. Pragmatics, modularity and mind-reading. *Mind and Language* 17. 3–23.
Stalnaker, Robert C. 2014. *Context*. Oxford: Oxford University Press.
Thomason, Richmond. H. 1992. Accommodation, meaning, and implicature: Interdisciplinary foundations for pragmatics. In Phillip R. Cohen, Jerry Morgan, & Martha. E. Pollack (eds.), *Intentions in Communication*, 325–363. Cambridge, MA: Bradford Book, MIT Press.

Arto Mustajoki

From laboratory to real life: Obstacles in common ground building

Abstract: Common ground is one of the key terms in communication research. The term is also widely used in many other research fields, for example in politology, history and ethics. In communication research, common ground building is regarded as a permanent feature of interaction. However, in real life communicative encounters, this is true only for harmonious goal-oriented interaction (e.g. team meeting). The situation is very different in interaction which is non goal-oriented (small talk) or non-harmonious (hate speech, occasional negative comments). In actual communication, there are also persistent obstacles which complicate common ground building. The communicants may not recognise the need for it because of common ground fallacy. Ecocentrism, being an unavoidable feature of humans, hinders us from taking others' perspective into full consideration. Cognitive biases complicate mutual understanding. False beliefs concerning other communicants' opinions and knowledge make communicants put into the mental worlds of others things which are not there. In everyday communication, there are also situational factors which reduce our capacity to common ground building, such as tiredness, emotional overload and need to think of something which is more important than the current interaction.

1 Introduction

Common ground is one of the key terms in communication research (Clark 1996; Horton and Keysar 1996; Stalnaker 2002; Kecskes and Zhang 2009; Rączaszek-Leonardi 2014; Mazzarella and Domaneschi 2018; Ladilova and Schröder 2022). Some other related terms are also in use, such as 'mutual knowledge', 'socially distributed knowledge', 'shared knowledge', 'shared reality', 'shared belief', 'assumed familiarity', 'presumed background information', and 'embodied synchrony' (Echterhoff et al. 2009; Allan 2013).

Communication researchers tend to think that common ground is their own concept, but in reality, the term is also widely used in many other research fields, for example in politology (e.g. Morrissey and Boswell 2020) and history (e.g. Okihiro 2001). In fact, political discourse gives people good reason to think that building common ground is not the aim of communication. There are many other spheres where common ground is mentioned as a prerequisite or goal of com-

https://doi.org/10.1515/9783110766752-004

munication, one of them being inter- and transdisciplinary research. In recent years, we have witnessed an intensifying discussion of its significance in making ground-breaking findings in research. At the same time researchers report how difficult it is to achieve common ground due to differences in terminology and ways of thinking (Morgenstern 2000; Repko 2007). When one aims at a guided dialogue on research ethics, a necessary starting point is building a common ground (Mustajoki and Mustajoki 2017: 9).

According to Zapf (2008: 171–172), the concept of common ground has a long history before it emerged in communication studies and other contemporary fields of research. He argues that the first usage of the term arose from trading practices in the Mediterranean area over a thousand years ago when travelling traders raised feelings of suspicion, mistrust and fear among local people.

Consequently, 'common ground' is a widespread and flexible concept. Therefore, it is of little surprise that it has several definitions even in communication research. Despite this (or because of this), the term is very practical: everyone roughly understands what it means but at the same time it gives much space for interpretations by individual researchers.

The aim of this article is to bring new insights to the discussion of the nature and significance of common ground in human interaction. As pointed out by many researchers (Weigand 1999; Kecskes 2014), intercultural interaction (in the traditional sense) does not principally differ from monocultural encounters, because cultural behavioural patterns and language are often connected not to ethnic or country-wise background, but are based on religion, political or ideological confection, profession, hobby, age, family or other factors which collect and unify people. A Russian fisherman easily understands a Finnish fisherman. A German mathematician understands a French mathematician better than a German historian. Hence, in using the concept of common ground in this article, all types of interaction are taken into consideration. If special attention to the language question is required, I will do so.

In their very critical article *The illusion of common ground* Stephen Cowley and Matthew Harvey (2016) challenge the meaningfulness of common ground as a technical term. My approach is less dramatic. I do not deny the concept as such but wish to give it a more precise place in analysing people's communicative behaviour outside laboratories. I have a means to real-life interaction the material produced in Saint Petersburg University's "One Speech Day" project, which is based on whole-day recordings of informants (Sherstinova 2009; Mustajoki and Sherstinova 2017). Instead of homogenous communicants concentrating on solving joint tasks in a laboratory, people's normal mundane life opens up to a researcher a quite different world where interlocutors with various backgrounds and language command meet in changing conditions and do not always aim at a specific goal.

In Section 1, I will expand the definition of common ground with some additional elements which, to my mind, are important in real-life interaction. Section 2 presents four types of interaction regarding whether it is harmonious or not and goal-oriented or not. Section 3 is dedicated to obstacles in common ground building in harmonious goal-oriented interaction. Several underlying factors, for example egocentrism and cognitive biases, will be discussed. The conclusion provides a summary of obstacles in common ground building.

2 Common ground as a prerequisite for starting an interaction

The term 'common ground' is used in literature in two meanings: 1) an a priori assumed state, a starting point for interaction and 2) an aim for interaction, its final target which is achieved through a dynamic process of interlocutors (Kecskes and Zhang 2009; cf. Gibbs and Colston 2017).[1] As will be discussed in more detail later, common ground is not always a goal of communication, while as a prerequisite for starting an interaction it is always present. More concretely, entering an interaction is based on the assumption that interlocutors have *at least something* in common for making an attempt at conducting a conversation reasonable.

According to a regular definition, common ground is a set of mutual knowledge and beliefs shared among communicants; it is formed on the basis of membership of a certain community, linguistic interactions and physical environments (Clark 1996). When considering people's prerequisites and obstacles in interaction, I use the term 'mental world'. It covers everything people bring to the communicative situation (Mustajoki 2012, 2021). If we consider elements which are relevant especially as prerequisites for successful interaction, besides knowledge, beliefs, attitudes and values, four more important (and rather obvious) factors should be added: language command, cognitive styles, emotional and physiological state as well as intentions.

In fact, *language command* is the most important part of things interlocutors bring to communicative encounters. With its help, it is possible to fill gaps in other parts of common ground. Languages like English, Russian or Finnish, naturally, are cornerstones of language command at a general level but the ability to use a sublanguage of a certain profession or hobby and speak and understand

1 Edda Weigand (1999) speaks in this connection of 'harmony' that can be 'pre-established' or 'dialogically achieved'.

the (social) dialect or slang in hand is equally important. Language command is not only about lexicon and grammar as interactional skills are equally important. Language command varies. You may be capable of conducting effective trade negotiations, but this does not guarantee that you can maintain everyday chat in a pub. You may be good at giving talks, but you may be hopeless at small talk.

Choice of a common language in regular interaction between friends and acquaintances is simple and automatic. In institutional and other public settings, the language question is also rather clear, albeit there can be some alternation in applied registers. The situation is different in encounters with strangers who do not have the same mother tongue. In this case, the interlocutors have first to decide the language of conversation. This may be the native language of one of them or a third language as a lingua franca. Sometimes, speakers of neighbouring languages understand each other by speaking in their mother tongues. If no lingual common language is available and there is an urgent need for interaction, communicants may use gestures and drawings or call for an interpreter (Mustajoki 2010). When interacting with a certain person is not obligatory and lingual common ground is not possible, people can just stay away from such company.

A relevant feature people bring to interaction is their *cognitive styles* (Stanovich and West 2000; Nisbett et al. 2001). Different learning styles have been a topic of lively discussion in pedagogy. However, small-scale learning sessions occur in our daily life all the time when we try to understand where to buy a needed piece of clothing, how to use a new device or how to cook a particular soup. People sometimes think that problems professionals meet in explaining something to laypersons come from vocabulary. An equally relevant factor is a possible discrepancy of cognitive styles of interlocutors; if they are completely different, it is troublesome to close the gap in common ground.

Physiological and emotional states, present in a certain communication situation, make common ground building more complex. It is hard for a tired, depressed, frightened or seriously ill person to concentrate on his/her own or another interlocutor's speech. When interlocutors' minds are filled with extra worries, it causes an additional cognitive load that increases people's egocentrism and weakens their ability to conduct recipient design (Roßnagel 2000; Vogels et al. 2020). Tiredness and other psychological or physiological factors reduce people's willingness and capability to avoid automatic stereotypical thinking and speaking (Bodenhausen 1990) – a further reason for failures in common ground building.

It is difficult to change the factors mentioned above during interaction, but in successful common ground building these factors have to be considered. The last factor to be raised is more changeable. If communicants' *intentions* differ in the beginning, they must be somehow unified during interaction, otherwise it is hard to reach common ground because the general frame of communication collapses. This issue does not emerge in laboratory conditions where test subjects are given a joint task beforehand. The situation is very different in everyday interactional encounters. The aim of an interaction is seldom determined by other people, instead it is a matter of negotiation of interlocutors themselves. If intentions differ, interlocutors may come to a unified understanding about the purpose of interaction – but only if they first recognise the difference and are then willing and able to come to a joint resolution. If the intention of a teacher or speaker is to transfer some knowledge and skills to the listeners, but the audience has no intention to listen, there is no hope of common ground. Similar situations are seen in official and non-official questionings and interviews if the other party has no motivation to participate in common ground building.

Two more examples about differences in intentions can be given by way of illustration. If a person says something in an emotion mode, she will not be happy with a reaction in a matter-of-fact mode. If John vents his anger after a working day by making critical comments about his boss (so called ‘unburden speech’, Mustajoki 2017: 63), he will not like it if instead of consolation he receives as a reaction the piece of advice that *You should change your work*. Even in goal-oriented settings, discrepancies may occur in the participants’ comprehension of the exact goal of the discussion. For example, if some of them think that they are preparing a final version of a proposal, while others consider that this is just a preliminary brainstorming session.

3 Harmonious and non-harmonious, goal-oriented and non goal-oriented interaction

It is reasonable to assume that when interlocutors meet, they tend to achieve common ground, because it belongs to the normal rules of communication. Following Weigand (1999), I call such an interaction harmonious. As we all know, this is not always the case in real life. We see non-harmonious scenes in parliaments, pubs and homes, in fact everywhere. Even when interlocutors seem to be polite, they may not be aiming at common ground. It is characteristic for non-harmonious interaction that its participants do not even try to understand each other; in fact, they refuse to listen and concentrate on expressing their own views (cf. Ladegaard 2008; Zhang and Pitts 2019). Conflict talk and hate speech are extreme forms of such non-harmonious goal-oriented interaction.

If interlocutors know beforehand that they have opposite opinions about politics, covid-19 vaccination or human rights, they may apply different conversational strategies. One option is just to avoid these dangerous topics in conversation with such a person. Where these issues have come up, interlocutors may choose a benign convergent or unfriendly divergent strategy (Gasiorek 2017; Zhang and Pitts 2019).[2] The first choice leads to a manageable conversation and does not alienate interlocutors, the latter may cause an unpleasant debate with unfavourable consequences. An alternative is to try to be as neutral as possible, but if the other party wishes to promote his or her extreme opinions, it is hard to avoid confrontation.

Different conversational strategies (harmonious/convergent vs. non-harmonious/divergent) also emerge in everyday micro-dialogues. If Mary says to her spouse John *I have flu*, she probably seeks consolation for her unpleasant state of health. There are various options for John's reaction. If he says *I'm sorry, I hope it will soon be over*, he applies a convergent strategy by taking into consideration Mary's emotional state. The phrase *Indeed, I know many people who have flu right now* demonstrates a neutral attitude towards the situation. A convergent form of the perspective of Mary's aim strategy is applied in *It's your own fault, you never wear a hat in winter*. The example shows that common ground is not always about the factual content of the interaction but about the intentions of the interlocutors, in this case about seeking for understanding for emotions and feelings. John's negative attitude from the point of view of the speaker's intention may be regarded as a manifestation of an occasional non-harmonious attitude towards the speaker.

Most of everyday interaction between people is harmonious but not goal-oriented. Typically, it is everyday chat about this and that with family members and friends. Similar conversations can be heard in pubs and staff rooms at work places. Small talk at receptions belongs to this category of interaction as well, although the register used is more official. Most interaction that is not goal-oriented is rather egocentric: the speaker wants to say something rather than listen. Of course, listening satisfies one's curiosity but it also occurs for reasons of politeness.

Everyday interaction also includes moments of harmonious goal-oriented interaction when communicants want to agree on something: what to eat for dinner, where to go for a holiday, whether to buy or not buy a new TV set. Harmonious goal-oriented interaction is, by definition, the mode applied in team meetings and more or less official discussions at work places. Sometimes such gatherings take on a very structured form. This happens when parties having opposite opinions on a complex problem are called upon to resolve it. There are several techniques that are available for the process (Franco 2008). The procedure towards a common

---

2 In operational research these terms are used to describe different phases of a process aiming at common ground. First, applying divergent thinking the participants explicitly explore their different perspectives of the problem. Then, convergent thinking helps them to form a new consolidated angle of view (see e.g. Franco and Montibeller 2010).

understanding usually begins with a phase where actors make their own unshared private knowledge explicit and tangible to others (Beers et al. 2006), which is rarely the case in other types of communication.

A harmonious goal-oriented interaction is meant to lead to a satisfactory common ground. However, two reservations have to be made. First, this is not about common ground in general but about the current practical issue (Garfinkel 1967; Linell 2009; Gander 2018). Second, it is hard to imagine that complete common ground can be reached even concerning one single thing. It is often the case that participants afterwards disagree about their final resolution. This concerns both official negotiations and occasional everyday agreements.

In the context of common ground building, interaction can be divided into four main categories, see Figure 1.

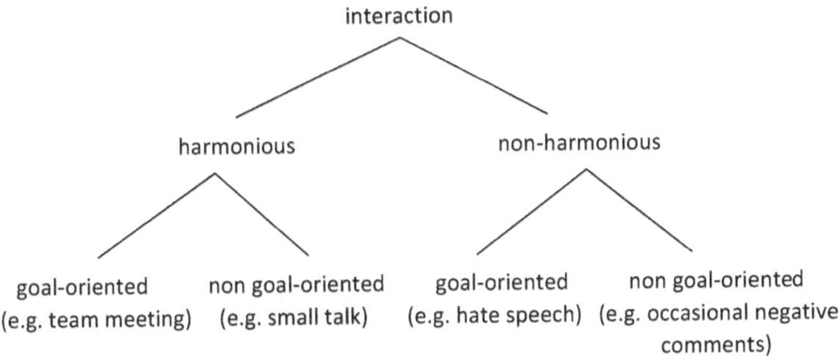

Figure 1: Different types of interaction concerning harmony and orientation.

In the next section, I will discuss the obstacles hindering common ground building in goal-oriented harmonious interaction. In other types of interaction, the question of common ground building is not relevant because interlocutors are not aiming at it.

4 Obstacles in building common ground in harmonious goal-oriented interaction

A note about the factors influencing common ground building discussed in this section: they reflect communicants' actions during interaction regardless of whether they are aware of them or not.

4.1 Egocentrism

Egocentrism is a basic feature of humans.[3] It helps people to survive and succeed in their lives. Egocentrism emerges, among other things, in the way people see and experience their surroundings (Keysar 2008; Kecskes and Zhang 2009; Todd et al. 2011; Eyal et al. 2018). At the same time, it is also true that people possess an ability to adopt – to a certain degree – other people's perspective.[4] This phenomenon has been widely studied within the theory of mind, mentalising and mindreading (Brown-Schmidt and Hanna 2011; Sanders et al. 2013; Apperly 2018).[5] Recent research has shown the connection of perspective-taking to the mechanism of neural mirroring (Mahy et al. 2014).

Most people are capable of feeling empathy (see e.g. Voutilainen et al. 2014). However we cannot, on this basis, make the conclusion that people are able to know what other people know and think. At a general level, what helps us in perspective-taking is that people's mental worlds partly overlap. We also have an overall impression of potential differences between our mental worlds and those of others. Nevertheless, we can never be sure about the recipient's knowledge of the question at hand and what he or she is thinking of at the current moment.

There are good reasons to assume that people are even more egocentric than research shows. Our evidence-based understanding of perspective-taking mainly originates from results of laboratory experiments. However, laboratory conditions can never fully correspond to real-life settings. A permanent problem in authentic interaction is non-concentration due to mind-wandering: people are not present in the current situation and are thinking of something else.[6] Additionally, people have to avoid unnecessary energy consumption (Mustajoki 2012, 2021 and the literature there). All these factors open up more space for egocentrism and reduce the possibility of proper perspective-taking.

---

3 In many (probably most) situations, cooperation is a behavioural norm and therefore is applied during interaction, but as argued by Kecskes and Zwang (2009: 332–333; cf. Gibbs and Colston 2017), it can exist as a driving force for interaction along with egocentrism.

4 For an overview of discussion on the role of mindreading, see Westra and Nagel 2021.

5 Perspective-taking has been regarded as a feature of the human race but similar processes have been recognised among other animals (Krupenye and Call 2019). At the same time, one can see a paradox in perspective-taking as to humans and animals: although people do not always ascribe a state of mind to other people, they are able to do so to non-humans such as plants, gods or computers (Waytz et al. 2010).

6 Killingworth and Gilbert (2010) argue that the mind wanders on average 46.9% of the time people are awake. In the role of the recipient, mind-wandering is probably more likely than in other activities.

A further factor is the quick tempo of a normal interaction. This means that, in standard situations, communicants work with information which is only available at the forefront of their brains for a second. Participants in meetings have a little more time for comprehending each other's speech, but they often do not use this option because they fill that time-window with planning their own contributions to the discussion. This results in improper listening to others' speech.

Egocentrism occurs in differences in interpretations of words and concepts. Each of us has our own understanding for words like *democracy, freedom* and *progress*. Even tangible words, such as *stone, house* and *car,* provoke different personal associations in us. Many researchers (e.g. Gauker 1992; Bergman 2001) claim that complete understanding is an unreachable goal in interaction because people place different meanings on words and phrases. Therefore, the communicants have to resign themselves to sufficient understanding (Allwood 1986; Deppermann 2015; Gander and Gander 2020). This is one reason why complete common ground is also impossible.

4.2 Recipient design fails

Recipient design[7] (Sacks et al. 1974; Newman-Norlund et al. 2009; Mustajoki 2012; Deppermann 2018) is the main tool that leads interaction towards (sufficient) understanding and common ground (Bremer and Simonot 1996). The ability to conduct recipient design develops in the early years of childhood. Although adults are better at this, no one can reach full mastery in this ability. There are some regular obstacles which hinder proper recipient design.

Avoidance of unnecessary energy consumption causes problems in recipient design. For the speaker, the easiest way to save energy is to avoid individualisation of speech without thinking of the communication situation or the audience at hand (Kecskes 2017). A possible consequence of this is that the speaker thinks that common ground is already there and no recipient design is needed, in other words the speaker falls into the trap of the common ground fallacy (Keysar and

7 Besides recipient design, there are other terms that describe approximately the same thing. The term 'audience design' (Sacks and Schegloff 1979; Horton and Gerrig 2002) emphasises a wider group of recipients. 'Accommodation', the basic term of the Communication Accommodation Theory, may refer to the same phenomenon, but may also take into account a broader characteristic of speech, for example when the speaker adjusts his or her speech to the dialect or register used by the recipient (Dragojevic and Giles 2014; Palomares et al. 2016). A general term used in this connection is 'tailoring' (Pierce-Grove 2016; Leskelä et al. 2022).

Henly 2002; Mustajoki 2012, 2021).[8] This is also a manifestation of egocentrism. The common ground fallacy rarely happens when it is evident from the very beginning that the interlocutors' mental worlds are far from each other, for example, in encounters with children or strangers of foreign appearance. In contrast to those situations, the common ground fallacy is more likely in encounters with people we know best, for instance with family members and friends. We share a substantial part of knowledge with them and may be aware of gaps in common ground generally, but it is often impossible to know exactly what happened in their lives before we met them (Mustajoki 2017).

An overall factor increasing the probability of common ground fallacy is the ordinariness of the topic and situation in hand. If a person is involved in an interaction on a certain theme with the same persons all the time, he or she gradually starts thinking that these issues are also self-evident for people outside that community. This fallacy is common when researchers of one field meet colleagues from other fields (Choi and Richards 2017) and when a specialist writes for the general public (Leskelä et al. 2022).

Conducting recipient design consumes energy especially if the situation is new for the speaker (Mustajoki 2021; Mustajoki and Baikulova 2022 and the literature there). The speaker must find a reasonable balance between energy consumption and the risk that the recipient does not comprehend his or her speech (cf. Sperber and Wilson 1986; Do et al. 2020; Mustajoki and Baikulova 2022). However, a speaker may save cognitive effort in the wrong place.

Non-listening and half-listening caused by mind-wandering and non-concentration are common phenomena in interaction. They take place even in laboratory conditions.[9] Concentration on one's own speaking means that monitoring of others' reactions does not work, and this may be fatal for perspective-taking and recipient design (Clark and Krych 2004; Ferreira et al. 2005). In addition, the work of memory is crucial (McKinley et al. 2017). It is difficult to build common ground if we do not remember what other communicants have said.

A frequent problem in building common ground derives from an unreliable source of knowledge. The speaker may rely on sketchy data regarding others' mental worlds. This concerns both knowledge and culture factors, but it is especially relevant regarding opinions and views. When x says something to y about a matter z, it may be just a quick intuitive reaction or a preparatory standpoint

8 Another term used approximately in the same sense is 'false consensus effect' (Ross et al. 1977; Clarke 1996; Nickerson 1999).

9 Laboratory experiments show that people are often inattentive listeners even when they try to concentrate (Galantucci and Gareth 2014; Roberts et al. 2016).

without serious reasoning. When x and y, after some weeks or months, meet again, y may take it for granted that x still thinks in that way. In reality, x has meanwhile thought of z more thoroughly and arrived at a completely different conclusion. X's new point of view may gradually become apparent during the discussion but for y it may be difficult to realise it because y remains stuck to the first impression about x's view on this matter.

A persistent characteristic of speech production is people's unawareness of the way in which they speak. Speakers tend to overestimate how effectively they communicate (Keysar 2008: 277). They are often less clear than they assume themselves to be (Mazzarella and Pouscoulous 2020). As a result of this, they do not realise the problems the recipient has in comprehending their speech. An additional risk derives from vague and cryptic speech (Alkhatnai 2017). For a wise use of underdeterminacy it helps to keep things short and avoid saying anything that is not needed for understanding, though on the other hand it can also be a risk for common ground building (Schoybye and Stokke 2016). Various forms of indirect implicit speech are regular phenomena in everyday interaction as well. They are mostly a deliberate tactic of speech production but when over-used, may endanger mutual understanding (for more detail, see Mustajoki and Baikulova 2022).

4.3 Cognitive biases

We humans tend to think that we are, in comparison to other species, the rational race. In order to emphasise this, we call ourselves *homo sapiens* (Stanovich 2018). It is true that all people are capable of using reasoning and judgment, but it is equally true that very often we do not apply this competence and instead resort to quick intuitive decision making. Recent brain research has shown that people tend to rely on implicit, automatic and unconscious System 1 instead of using System 2, which enables explicit, controlled and conscious processes (for over-views, see Bargh and Chartrand 1999; Kahneman 2003). These systems work in close connection with each other and mostly as a joint device, but in order to understand the process of interaction, it is reasonable to see them as separate devices. The usage of System 1 is reasonable because System 2 takes approxi-mately three times more cognitive energy than actions based on System 1 (Gilbert et al. 1988). Naturally, the work of the two systems also influences the way people interact (Mustajoki 2021).

A manifestation of the usage of System 1 rather than System 2 is people's inclination to fall into the trap of cognitive biases. There are dozens of cognitive biases (Kahneman 2003, 2011; Friedman 2017). Let us take a look at some of them that are linked to self-perception and the perception of fellow creatures and are, therefore, relevant obstacles in common ground building (cf. Nickerson 1999).

- We tend to think that we can read rather well the minds of other people while the opposite is not true: other people are not able to read what is going on in our minds.
- If you know little about a particular matter you are more confident of your knowledge than if you know more about it.
- We are prone to presume that other people think more negatively of us than they do in reality.
- People attribute their own negative actions and actions of their own group to external causes, while in the evaluation of other people's behaviour they refer to internal causes (the qualities of these people).
- People are usually highly hesitant to change their opinions even if they receive facts that contradict them.
- Similarly, people tend to listen to information that supports their preconceptions, stereotypes and attitudes.
- We tend to presume that other people do and like the same things as we do more often than they do in reality (e.g. read the same books, have the same hobbies, do the same things during the holiday, eat similar food).
- If a person has a positive feature we value, we tend to forgive him or her for negative features in other issues; the person may be a leader of a country, an organisation or a team or, e.g. a husband (the so called halo effect).

Cognitive biases are, as a rule, linked to self-deception and egocentrism. Many of them are well-known but are, nevertheless, often forgotten when people, including researchers, consider obstacles to common ground building. In reality, cognitive biases cause unsettled situations in interaction when people try in vain to understand each other.

A further hindrance in reaching common ground are defects in the work of memory and the senses. This is a common problem in courtrooms when parties try to create a common understanding of the scene in hand on the basis of the eyewitnesses' accounts. Similar negotiations take place in everyday life. They may concern little 'crimes' at home or, for example, what happened at a recent wedding or at a football match. Descriptions of such events are never identical not only due to the poor working of the memory but also because every person selects merely a tiny fraction from the huge amount of information perceived by their senses (Dijsterhuis 2004).

4.4 Recipient pretends to understand

Alan Firth (1996) denotes by the term 'let it pass' a situation where the recipient does not indicate that he did not understand what the speaker said.[10] When Per Linell (1995: 187) examined the cases of non-understanding, he differentiated three types: latent (no traces of miscommunication in the data), covert (trace or indirect reflections in the data) and overt (clear reflections in the data). Volker Hinnenkamp (2003) differentiates seven types of misunderstandings but only concentrates in his studies on overt and covert misunderstandings. He considers that as "empirical linguists, we have no access to completely covert misunderstandings because they do not show up on the linguistic surface" (Hinnenkamp 2003: 60). Indeed, conventional methods used in interactional research do not reveal 'let it pass' cases which do not leave traces in research data.

In Mustajoki and Sherstinova (2017) we present a new "Retrospective Commenting Method" which tries to tackle the problem that Hinnekamp raises. The method is realised in the context of the "One Speech Day" project, which is being pursued at Saint Petersburg University (Sherstinova 2009). Informants carry a type recorder with a microphone and record all their speech during a single day. In that way, we obtain the most authentic material but when studying it one faces the same problem as any researcher examining linguistic corpora: we see only the text of the recording but not what is happening in the interlocutor's mind. In the new methodological extension, the recorded material is afterwards analysed with the informant. The method is quite laborious but it enables one to get information on what really took place in a conversation. In the pilot study, 19 cases of miscommunication were detected during a day. In total, 61% of them were resolved during interaction and 33% were unsolved; two cases remained ambiguous (Mustajoki et al. 2021). The method still needs further improvement, but the received results show that latent, completely covert cases of misunderstanding are possible and not very rare.

When the recipient does not react to non-understanding, he violates the cooperation principle and complicates common ground building. Therefore, it makes sense to examine what circumstances further such behaviour.

There are some factors which increase the possibility of not revealing non-understanding.[11] One of them is the size of the audience. The larger the audience is, the higher the threshold of interrupting the speaker. In a school class or

10 According to Firth (1996: 243) the idea for the term was adopted from Cicourel (1973).

11 In Mustajoki (2006: 61–65) I found plenty of examples of metalinguistic commenting on causes of pretending to understand or not understand.

big lecture hall, listeners are very hesitant to ask for clarification, but in say a group of three interlocutors, it is less probable than in dyadic conversation that all non-understandings will lead to a request for clarification (Cooney et al. 2020). Such behaviour may be caused by unwillingness to interfere in a speaker's torrent of words. The recipient may also think that others have understood everything and does not want to show his or her ignorance.[12]

Let us consider a meeting where the leader of a team tells about a new project with the University of Ljubljana. He expects that everyone knows that Ljubljana is the capital of Slovenia. What really happens is the following. Participant A does not concentrate on listening and hears that the partner university is Lisbon. B is not sure whether Ljubljana is the capital of Slovakia or Slovenia. C has no idea which country the chair is speaking of. Factors which increase the option of not asking for clarification include listeners who think that everything will be clear when the interaction continues or they may think that the whole project does not concern them. An important factor is fear of revealing one's ignorance: such participants may think that everyone else knows the university and the city.

In a dyadic face-to-face interaction, pretence of understanding is more difficult due to monitoring by the speaker, but if the topic is not interesting or there is something else that is important to think of, pretence of understanding does take place. In changing everyday circumstances, where people are doing something else when they are speaking, the recipient often pretends to hear and listen – and the speaker does not notice this (Mustajoki and Baikulova 2020). Sometimes the recipient may think that he will understand the passage which remained unclear later or he just assumes that the piece of information is not relevant. In fact, aiming at common ground consists of small steps, some of which may be omitted for various reasons.

In the case above, the use of the 'let it pass' strategy was connected with a geographical name. Similar situations occur when the speaker wants to show his or her knowledge, intelligence or wit by using unusual metaphors, figurative expressions, aesthetically elegant expressions or fashionable new words. In doing so, speakers put more weight on their own personal goals than on common ground building (cf. Montminy 2010; Mustajoki 2021).

12 Andrea Golato (2010) shows that in German the particle *achso* indicates understanding, but *ach* only marks the receipt of information without explicitly denoting understanding.

5 Conclusion

People bring to communication situations their language command, knowledge, culture, beliefs, attitudes, stereotypes, values, intentions, cognitive styles and physiological and emotional states, in other words, their whole mental worlds. In normal everyday interactional encounters outside laboratories, all these elements both hinder and help communicants to conduct a reasonable conversation. The part of their mental worlds they share in the beginning comprises the common ground for the current interaction. Then, if interaction is harmonious and goal-oriented, the interlocutors try to expand their common ground and, with its help reach the goal that has been set. In a harmonious non goal-oriented interaction, communicants do not build a common ground in order to reach a goal, but they learn from each other new things which may be useful in future encounters.

There are two general prerequisites for common ground building. First, the communicants have to recognise the gaps in common ground which derive from differences in their mental worlds. The gaps may concern language command, intentions for that communication situation, schemes or scenarios relevant for the current issue, opinions on matters of principle or any other elements of the mental world. The means for recognition are concentration (avoidance of mind-wandering), monitoring and perspective-taking. The second prerequisite is consideration of the differences in the mental worlds in action through recipient design (accommodation of speech to the recipient). In order to do this, some skills are needed, as well as a willingness to put in some cognitive energy.

Even if the participants of a conversation are willing to put effort into common ground building, there are some obstacles which make it more difficult. Ecocentrism, being an unavoidable feature of humans, hinders us from taking others' perspective into full consideration. Cognitive biases complicate mutual understanding. False beliefs concerning other communicants' opinions and knowledge make communicants put into the mental worlds of others things which are not there. False beliefs may be caused by previous experiences or they are the result of a 'let it pass' strategy of communicants when they have not understood what others have said. Finally, an obstacle in common ground building may be derived from deficiencies in expressing oneself and unawareness of the way one speaks.

In non-harmonious interaction the question of common ground building is not relevant, because such a goal has not been set for communication.

References

Alkhatnai, Mubarak. 2017. Vague language and its social role. *Theory and Practice in Language Studies* 7(2). 122–127.

Allan, Keith. 2013. Common ground – aka "common knowledge", "mutual knowledge*", "shared knowledge", "assumed familiarity", "presumed background information". In Jan-Ola Östman & Jef Verschueren (eds.), *Handbook of Pragmatics*, 1–26. Amsterdam/ Philadelphia: John Benjamins.

Allwood Jens. 1986. Some perspectives on understanding in spoken interaction. In Mats Furberg, Thomas Wetterström & Claes Åberg (eds.), *Logic and Abstraction* (Acta Philosophica Gothoburgensia 1), 1–30. Gothenburg: Gothenburg University.

Apperly, Ian. 2018. Mindreading and psycholinguistic approaches to perspective taking: Establishing common ground. *Topics in Cognitive Science.* 1–7. DOI: 10.1111/tops.12308

Bargh, John A. & Tanya L. Chartrand. 1999. The unbearable automaticity of being. *American Psychologist* 54. 462–476.

Beers, Peter J., Henny P. A. Boshuizen, Paul A. Kirschner & Wim H. Gijselaers. 2006. Common ground, complex problems and decision making. *Group Decision and Negotiation* 15. 529–556.

Bergman, Mats. 2001. Misunderstanding, and successful communication. *Acta Philosophica Fennica* 69. 67–89.

Bodenhausen, Galen V. 1990. Stereotypes as judgmental heuristics: Evidence of circadian variations in discrimination. *Psychological Science* 1(5). 319–322.

Bremer, Katrina & Margaret Simonot. 1996. Preventing problems of understanding. In Katharina Bremer, Peter Broeder, Celia Roberts, Margaret Simonot & Marie-Thérèse Vasseur (eds.), *Achieving understanding: Discourse in intercultural encounters*, 159–180. London, New York: Longman.

Brown-Schmidt, Sarah & Joy E. Hanna. 2011. Talking in another person's shoes: Incremental perspective-taking in language processing. *Dialogue & Discourse* 2(1). 11–33.

Choi, Seongsook & Keith Richards. 2017. *Interdisciplinary discourse: Communication across disciplines*. London, UK: Palgrave Macmillan.

Cicourel, Aaron V. 1973. *Cognitive sociology: Language and meaning in social interaction.* London: Macmillan.

Clark, Herbert H. 1996. *Using Language.* Cambridge: Cambridge University Press.

Clark, Herbert H. & Meredyth A. Krych. 2004. Speaking while monitoring addressees for understanding. *Journal of Memory and Language* 50. 62–81.

Cooney, Gus, Adam M. Mastroianni, Nicole Abi-Esber & Alison Wood Brooks. 2020. The many minds problem: Disclosure in dyadic versus group conversation. *Current Opinion in Psychology* 31. 22–27.

Cowley, Stephen & Matthew Harvey. 2016. The illusion of common ground. *New Ideas in Psychology* 42. 56–63.

Deppermann, Arnulf. 2015. When recipient design fails: Egocentric turn-design of instructions in driving school lessons leading to breakdowns of intersubjectivity. *Gesprächsforschung. Online-Zeitschrift zur verbalen Interaktion Ausgabe* 16. 63–101.

Deppermann, Arnulf. 2018. Changes in turn-design over interactional histories – the case of instructions in driving school lessons. In Arnulf Deppermann & Jürgen Streeck (eds.), *Time in embodied interaction. Synchronicity and sequentiality of multimodal resources*, 293–324. Amsterdam [et al.]: Benjamins.

Dijksterhuis, Ap. 2004. Think different: The merits of unconscious thought in preference development and decision making. *Journal of Personality and Social Psychology* 87. 586–598.

Do, Monica L., Anna Papafragou & John Trueswell. 2020. Cognitive and pragmatic factors in language production: Evidence from source-goal motion events. *Cognitio* 205. 10477.

Dragojevic, Marko & Howard Giles. 2014. Language and interpersonal communication: Their intergroup dynamics. In Charles R. Berger (ed.), *Interpersonal communication*, 29–51. Berlin: De Gruyter.

Echterhoff, Gerald, E. Tory Higgins & John M. Levine. 2009. Shared reality: Experiencing commonality with others' inner states about the world. *Perspectives on Psychological Science* 4. 496–521.

Eyal, Tal, Mary Steffe & Nicholas Epley. 2018. Perspective mistaking: Accurately understanding the mind of another requires getting perspective, not taking perspective. *Journal of Personality and Social Psychology* 114(4). 547–571.

Ferreira, Victor S., L. Robert Slevc & Erin S. Rogers. 2005. How do speakers avoid ambiguous linguistic expressions? *Cognition* 96. 263–284.

Firth, Alan. 1996. The discursive accomplishment of normality: On 'lingua franca' English and conversation analysis. *Journal of Pragmatics* 26. 237–259.

Franco, L. Alberto. 2008. Facilitating collaboration with problem structuring methods: A case of an inter-organisational construction partnership. *Group Decision and Negotiation* 17(4). 267–286.

Franco, L. Alberto & Gilberto Montibeller. 2010. Facilitated modelling in operational research. *European Journal of Operational Research* 205(3). 489–500.

Friedman, Hershey H. 2017. *Cognitive Biases that Interfere with Critical Thinking and Scientific Reasoning: A Course Module*, June 30, 2017. www.researchgate.net/profile/Hershey-Friedman/publication/316486755_Cognitive_Biases_that_Interfere_with_Critical_Thinking_and_Scientific_Reasoning_A_Course_Module/links/5a08ee0aaca272ed279ff7e6/Cognitive-Biases-that-Interfere-with-Critical-Thinking-and-Scientific-Reasoning-A-Course-Module.pdf

Galantucci, Bruno & Gareth Roberts. 2014. Do we notice when communication goes awry? An investigation of people's sensitivity to coherence in spontaneous conversation. *PLoS ONE* 9(7): e103182. https://doi.org/10.1371/journal.pone.0103182

Gander, Anna Jia. 2018. *Understanding in Real-Time Communication: Micro-Feedback and Meaning Repair in Face-to-Face and Video-Mediated Intercultural Interactions. Studies in Applied Information Technology*. Gothenburg: Gothenburg University.

Gander, Anna Jia & Pierre Gander. Micro-feedback as cues to understanding in communication. In Christine Howes, Simon Dobnik & Ellen Breitholtz (eds.), *Dialogue and perception. Extended papers from DaP2018*, 1–11. Gothenburg: Gothenburg University.

Garfinkel, Harold. 1967. *Studies in ethnomethodology*. Englewood Cliffs: Prentice Hall.

Gasiorek, Jessica. 2017. Nonaccommodation. In Howard Giles & Jake Harwood (eds.), *Oxford Encyclopedia of intergroup communication*. New York, NY: Oxford University Press. doi:10.1093/acrefore/9780190228613.013.440

Gauker, Christopher. 1992. The Lockean theory of communication. *Noûs* 26(3). 303–324.

Gibbs Jr, Raymond W. & Herbert L. Colston. 2017. The emergence of common ground. In Rachel Giora & Michael Haugh (eds.), *Doing pragmatics interculturally: Cognitive, philosophical, and sociopragmatic perspectives* (Trends in linguistics. Studies and monographs 312), 13–28. Berlin & New York: Mouton de Gruyter.

Gilbert, Daniel T., Brett W. Pelham & Douglas S. Krull. 1988. On cognitive busyness: When person perceivers meet persons perceived. *Journal of Personality and Social Psychology* 54(5). 733–740.

Golato, Andrea. 2010. Marking understanding versus receipting information in talk: *Achso* and *ach* in German Interaction. *Discourse Studies* 12(2). 147–176.

Hinnenkamp, Volker. 2003. Misunderstandings: Interactional structure and strategic resources. In Juliane House, Gabrielle Kasper & Steven Ross (eds.), *Misunderstandings in social life: Discourse approaches to problematic talk*, 57–81. London etc.: Longman.

Horton, William S & Richard J. Gerrig. 2002. Speakers' experiences and audience design: Knowing *when* and knowing *how* to adjust utterances to addressees. *Journal of Memory and Language* 47(4). 589–606.

Horton, William S. & Boaz Keysar. 1996. When do speakers take into account common ground? *Cognition* 59. 91–117.

Kahneman, Daniel. 2003. Maps of bounded rationality: Psychology for behavioral economics. *American Economic Review* 93(5). 1449–1475.

Kahneman, Daniel. 2011. *Thinking, Fast and Slow.* New York: Farrar, Straus and Giroux.

Kecskes, Istvan. 2014. *Intercultural Pragmatics.* Oxford: Oxford University Press.

Kecskes, Istvan. 2017. Implicitness in the use of situation-bound utterances: From lexis to discourse. In Piotr Cap & Marta Dynel (eds.), *Implicitness: From lexis to discourse*, 201–215. Amsterdam & Philadelphia: Benjamins.

Kecskes, Istvan & Fenghui Zhang. 2009. Activating, seeking, and creating common ground: A socio-cognitive approach. *Pragmatics & Cognition* 17(2). 331–355.

Keysar, Boaz. 2008. Egocentric processes in communication and miscommunication. In Istvan Kecskes & Jacob Mey (eds.), *Intention, common ground and the egocentric speaker-hearer*, 277–296. Berlin: Mouton de Gruyter.

Keysar, Boaz & Anne S. Henly. 2002. Speakers' overestimation of their effectiveness. *Psychological Science* 13. 207–212.

Killingsworth, Matthew & Daniel T. Gilbert. 2010. A wandering mind is an unhappy mind. *Science* 330. 932.

Krupenye, Christopher & Josep Call. 2019. Theory of mind in animals: Current and future directions. *Wiley Interdisciplinary Reviews. Cognitive Sciences* 10. e1503.

Ladegaard, Hans J. 2008. Pragmatic cooperation revisited: Resistance and non-cooperation as a discursive strategy in asymmetrical discourse. *Journal of Pragmatics* 41(4). 649–665.

Ladilova, Anna and Ulrike Schröder. 2022. Humor in intercultural interaction: A source for misunderstanding or a common ground builder? A multimodal analysis. *Intercultural Pragmatics* 19(1). 71–101.

Leskelä, Leealaura, Arto Mustajoki & Aino Piehl. 2022. Easy and plain languages as special cases of linguistic tailoring and standard language varieties. *Nordic Journal of Linguistics* 45. 194–213.

Linell, Per. 1995. Troubles with mutualities: Towards a dialogical theory of misunderstanding and miscommunication. In Ivana Marková, Carl Graumann & Klaus Foppa (eds.), *Mutualities in dialogue*, 176–213. Cambridge: Cambridge University Press.

Linell, Per. 2009. *Rethinking language, mind and world dialogically: Interactional and contextual theories of human sense-making*. Charlotte, NC: Information Age Publishing.

Mahy, Caitlin E.V., Louis J. Moses & Jennifer H. Pfeifer. 2014. How and where: Theory-of-mind in the brain. *Developmental Cognitive Neuroscience* 9. 68–81.

Mazzarella, Diana & Filippo Domaneschi. 2018. Presuppositional effects and ostensive-inferential communication. *Journal of Pragmatics* 138. 17–29.
Mazzarella, Diana & Nausicaa Pouscoulous. 2020. Pragmatics and epistemic vigilance: A developmental perspective. *Mind & Language* 24(2). 263–296.
McKinley, Geoffrey L., Sarah Brown-Schmidt & Aaron S. Benjamin. 2017. Memory for conversation and the development of common ground. *Memory & Cognition* 45. 1281–1294.
Montminy, Martin. 2010. Two contextualist fallacies. *Synthese* 173. 317–333.
Morgenstern, Norbert R. 2000. Common ground. In *GeoEng2000: An International Conference on Geotechnical and Geological Engineering*, 1–20. Lancaster, PA: Technomic Publishing Co.
Morrissey, Lochlan & John Boswell. 2020. Finding common ground. *European journal of political theory.* 1–20.
Mustajoki, Arto. 2006. The Integrum Database as a powerful tool in research on contemporary Russian. In Galina Nikiporets-Takigawa (ed.), *Integrum: tochnye metody i gumanitarnye nauki*, 50–75. Moscow: Letnii sad.
Mustajoki, Arto. 2010. Types of non-standard communication encounters with special reference to Russian. In Mika Lähteenmäki & Marjatta Vanhala-Aniszewski (eds.), *Language ideologies in transition multilingualism in Russia and Finland*, 35–55. Frankfurt am Main etc: Peter Lang.
Mustajoki, Arto. 2012. A speaker-oriented multidimensional approach to risks and causes of miscommunication. *Language and Dialogue* 2. 216–242.
Mustajoki, Arto. 2017. Why is miscommunication more common in everyday life than in lingua franca conversation? In Istvan Kecskes & Stavros Assimakopoulos (eds.), *Current issues in intercultural pragmatics*, 55–74. Amsterdam & Philadelphia: John Benjamins.
Mustajoki, Arto. 2021. A multidimensional model of interaction as a framework for a phenomenon-driven approach to communication. *Russian Journal of Linguistics* 25(2). 369–390.
Mustajoki, Arto & Alla Baikulova. 2020. The risks of misunderstandings in family discourse: Home as a special space of interaction. *Language and Dialogue* 10(3). 340–368.
Mustajoki, Arto & Alla Baikulova. 2022. Avoidance of cognitive efforts as a risk factor in interaction. *Discourse Studies* 24(3). 269–290.
Mustajoki, Arto, Natalia Cherkunova & Tatiana Sherstinova. 2021. Communication failures in everyday conversations: A case study based on the "Retrospective Commenting Method". *Computational linguistics and intellectual technologies: Papers from the International Conference "Dialogue 2021"*, 514–523. Moscow. Available online: https://helda.helsinki.fi//bitstream/handle/10138/333972/_dialog2021scopus_524.pdf?sequence=1
Mustajoki Arto & Tatiana Sherstinova. 2017. The "Retrospective Commenting" Method for longitudinal recordings of everyday speech. In Alexey Karpov, Rodmonga Potapova & Iosif Mporas (eds.), *SPECOM 2017, Lecture notes in artificial intelligence*, vol. 10458, 1–9. New York: Springer. https://link.springer.com/chapter/10.1007/978-3-319-66429-3_71
Mustajoki, Henriikka & Arto Mustajoki. 2017. *A new approach to research ethics: Using guided dialogue to strengthen research communities*. London & New York: Routledge.
Newman-Norlund, Sarah E., Matthijs L. Noordzij, Roger D., Inge A.C. Volman, Jan Peter de Ruiter, Peter Hagoort & Ivan Toni. 2009. Recipient design in tacit communication. *Cognition* 111. 46–54.
Nickerson, Raymond S. 1999. How we know and sometimes misjudge what others know: Imputing one's own knowledge to others. *Psychological Bulletin* 126. 737–759.
Nisbett, Richard E., Kaiping Peng, Incheol Choi & Ara Norezayan. 2001. Culture and systems of thought. Holistic versus analytic cognition. *Psychological Review* 108(2). 291–316.

Okihiro, Gary. 2001. *Common ground: Reimaging American history*. Princeton, NJ: Princeton University Press.

Palomares, Nicholas A., Howard Giles, Jordan Soliz & Cindy Gallois. 2016. Intergroup accommodation, social categories, and identities. In Howard Giles (ed.), *Communication accommodation theory: Negotiating personal relationships and social identities across contexts*, 123–151. Cambridge: Cambridge University Press.

Pierce-Grove, Ri. 2016. Conclusion: Making the new status quo: Social media in education. In Christine Greenhow, Julia Sonnevend & Colin Agur (eds.), *Education and social media: Toward a digital future*, 239–246. Cambridge, MA & London: The MIT Press.

Rączaszek-Leonardi, Joanna, Agnieszka Dębska & Adam Sochanowicz. 2014. Pooling the ground: Understanding and coordination in collective sense making. *Frontiers in Psychology* 5 (1233). 1–13.

Repko, Allen F. 2007. Integrating interdisciplinarity: How the theories of common ground and cognitive interdisciplinarity are informing the debate on interdisciplinary integration. *Issues in Integrative Studies* 25. 1–31.

Roberts, Gareth, Benjamin Langstein & Brunno Galantucci. 2016. (In)sensitivity to incoherence in human communication. *Language & Communication* 47. 15–22.

Roßnagel, Christian. 2000. Cognitive load and perspective-taking: Applying the automatic controlled distinction to verbal communication. *European Journal of Social Psychology* 30(3). 429–445.

Ross, Lee, David Greene & Pamela House. 1977. The "false consensus effect": An egocentric bias in social perception and attribution processes. *Journal of Experimental Social Psychology* 13, 1977, 13. 279–301.

Sacks, Harvey & Emmanuel A. Schegloff. 1979. Two preferences in the organization of reference to persons in conversation and their interaction. In George Psathas (ed.), *Everyday language*, 15–21. New York: Irvington.

Sacks, Harvey, Emmanuel A. Schegloff & Gail Jefferson. 1974. A simplest systematics for the organization of turn-taking for conversation. *Language* 50(4). 696–735.

Sanders, Robert E. Yaxin Wu & Joseph A. Bonito. 2013. The calculability of communicative intentions through pragmatic reasoning. *Pragmatics & Cognition* 21(1). 1–34.

Schoubye Anders J. & Andreas Stokke. 2016. What is said? *Noûs* 50. 759–793.

Sherstinova, Tatiana. 2009. The structure of the ORD speech corpus of Russian everyday communication. In Václav Matoušek & Pavel Mautner (eds.), *TSD 2009. LNAI*, vol. 5729, 258–265. Berlin-Heidelberg: Springer.

Sperber, Dan & Deirdre Wilson. 1986 (1995). *Relevance: Communication and Cognition*. Oxford: Blackwell.

Stalnaker, Robert. 2002. Common ground. *Linguistics and Philosophy* 25. 701–721.

Stanovich, Keith E. 2018. Miserliness in human cognition. The interaction of detection, override and mindware. *Thinking & Reasoning* 24(3). 423–444. Available online: https://doi.org/10.1080/13546783.2018.1459314

Stanovich, Keith E. & Richard F. West. 2000. Individual differences in reasoning: Implications for the rationality debate? *Behavioral and Brain Sciences* 23. 645–726.

Todd, Andrew R., Karlene Hanko, Adam D. Galinsky, & Thomas Mussweiler. 2011. When focusing on differences leads to similar perspectives. *Psychological Science* 22(1). 134–141.

Vogels, Jorrig, David M. Howcroft, Elli Tourtouri & Vera Demberg. 2020. How speakers adapt object descriptions to listeners under load. *Language, Cognition and Neuroscience* 35(1). 78–92.

Voutilainen, Liisa, Pentti Henttonen, Mikko Kahri, Maari Kivioja, Niklas Ravaja, Mikko Sams & Anssi Peräkylä. 2014. Affective stance, ambivalence, and psychophysiological responses during conversational storytelling. *Journal of Pragmatics* 68. 1–24.

Waytz, Adam, Kurt Gray, Nicholas Epley & Daniel M. Wegner. 2010. Causes and consequences of mind perception. *Trends in Cognitive Sciences* 14. 383–388.

Weigand, Edda. 1999. Misunderstanding: The standard Case. *Journal of Pragmatics* 31. 763–785.

Westra, Evan & Jennifer Nagel. 2021. Mindreading in conversation. *Cognition* 210. 104618. Available online: https://doi.org/10.1016/j.cognition.2021.104618

Zapf, Michael Kim. 2008. Transforming social work's understanding of person and environment: Spirituality and the "common ground". *Journal of Religion & Spirituality in Social Work: Social Thought* 27(1–2). 171–181. DOI: 10.1080/15426430802114200

Zhang, Yan Bing, & Margaret Jane Pitts. 2019. Interpersonal accommodation. In Jake Harwood, Jessica Gasiorek, Herbert Pierson, Jon F. NussBaum & Cindy Gallois (eds.), *Language, communication and intergroup relations*, 192–216. New York & London: Routledge.

Fabrizio Macagno

Presupposition failures and the negotiation of the common ground

Abstract: In pragmatics, it is a commonly accepted view that the cooperative activity of conversation is based on the "common ground" between the interlocutors – a concept that only apparently is uncontroversial. Described in cognitive terms as "knowledge of each other's beliefs and attitudes" (Gibbs 1987) (or "shared knowledge", see Kecskes and Zhang 2009) and at a logical level as a set of propositions whose truth is taken for granted and not subject to further discussion (Stalnaker 1974; von Fintel 2008), common ground is a challenge to any theory of presupposition or even implicatures. Despite its importance, very few studies have proposed alternatives to the cognitive or logical approaches, considering not only the relationship between an utterance and the granted information, but more importantly its dialogical and dialectical nature, which emerges when the ground is in fact not completely common. This paper intends to present an approach to common ground based on the notions of presumption and commitment: common ground is defined as a commitment that is presumed by the speaker to be held also by the interlocutor. However, presumptions are the result of a presumptive reasoning based on evidence of different types and resulting in different degrees of defeasibility – and thus "commonality." Moreover, two different types of "grounds" presumed to be common can be distinguished, which are named "Shared" and "Communal" grounds. This approach can explain the conditions under which a proposition can be reasonably treated as part of the interlocutors' commitments, and how this presumptive attribution can go wrong and needs to be explicitly discussed. Building on a corpus of intercultural dialogues among 8–10-year-old students, it will be shown how common ground is based on and results from a dialectical process through which the status of the interlocutors' commitments are brought to light and negotiated.

1 Introduction

Presupposition is one of the most controversial topics in pragmatics, semantics, and logic (for a review, see Schwarz 2015). Strawson (Strawson 1964; Strawson

Acknowledgment: The author would like to thank the Fundação para a Ciência e a Tecnologia for the research grants PTDC/FER-FIL/28278/2017 and UIDB/00183/2020.

https://doi.org/10.1515/9783110766752-005

1950) defined presupposition as a relation between statements, namely the use of a sentence in a specific context: a statement *A* presupposes another statement *B* if and only if *B* is true both in case *A* is true and in case *A* is false. In this view, presuppositions are statements (Atlas 2020) – and thus they have a pragmatic dimension in the sense that they can be asserted, and more importantly accepted or rejected (Black 1962: 53). A crucial problem arises when a statement has a false presupposition (see Capone 2020). For example, the sentence

a. "The King of France is magnificent"

uttered when there is no king of France results in a statement that cannot be verified. However, it still counts as a statement. As Ducrot noticed, imagine this sentence uttered by an enemy of Napoleon to a supporter of him during the French Republic (Ducrot 1966: 42): the presupposition is false, but the statement would cause serious problems to the speaker. Thus, a statement with a false presupposition is still a statement, even though it cannot be verified (Donnellan 1966).

The relationship between a statement and its presupposition has been explained in terms of pragmatic constraints on the use of sentences (Levinson 1983: 205). To presuppose a proposition is "to take its truth for granted, and to assume that others involved in the context do the same" (Stalnaker 1974: 472). The speaker is subordinating the felicity (or appropriateness) of an utterance to the truth of its presuppositions – or the acceptance thereof (Stalnaker 1974; Stalnaker 2002; Allan 2013). A presupposition is thus an implication that its truth is "somehow taken for granted, treated as uncontroversial," backgrounded (Chierchia and McConnell-Ginet 1990: 23).

The pragmatic approach to presupposition crucially depends on the notion of common ground, namely what all the conversational participants accept, believe, know, or hold as true (depending on the different theories) (Reimer and Bezuidenhout 2004: 308). On Stalnaker's perspective, the common ground corresponds to what the speaker represents as common knowledge by his speech act – it is an act by the speaker, an attitude to treat certain information necessary for the interpretation of his speech act as granted (Stalnaker 1973; Stalnaker 1998). Thus, common ground is the field on which the language game is played, the potentially defective context that makes an utterance acceptable, and which can correspond to the interlocutors' common beliefs (Stalnaker 2002; Stalnaker 1998).

The linguistic and philosophical perspectives on presupposition and common ground focus mostly on the problems of the presupposition triggers and their defeasibility, the update of the context by a presupposition (Schlenker 2010), and the relationship and difference between presupposition and other aspects of meaning (Schwarz 2015). These dominating views have almost obscured an essential dimension of these phenomena, namely their conversational and dialogical aspect, which raises distinct questions and distinct types of explanations. Why are some presuppositions successful in a dialogue while others are disputed, rejected, or argued against? How can an interlocutor reject a presupposition? How are presuppositions related to the common ground?

To address these questions, a pragmatic perspective focused only on the speaker's presuppositional acts (Ducrot 1972; Ducrot 1966) or representations (Stalnaker 1974) is not sufficient. It is necessary to analyze how presuppositions modify the dialogical context, and how they can be instruments from developing the common ground.

2 Presuppositions and common ground

The notions of common ground and presupposition are essentially intertwined, but the nature and possibility of this relation has led to several controversies in the literature. A pragmatic presupposition is a condition that a speaker poses for his or her utterance to be acceptable; it is what is taken for granted, what is normally expected to hold in the common ground between the participants (Beaver 1997: 2439). Thus, a speaker who sincerely asserts that "The king of France is magnificent" assumes that it is common ground that France has a king (von Fintel 2008: 138). However, what does it mean?

Classically, common ground is defined as common or mutual belief, namely the beliefs that the participants to a conversation share and recognizes that they share (Stalnaker 2002: 704). Thus, common ground corresponds to an iterated belief (or knowledge): *p* is common belief (or knowledge, in Schiffer's view, within a group, see Schiffer 1972: 30–36) if an only if all believe that *p*, and all believe that all believe that *p*, etc., in an infinite regress (Clark 1996: 99). On this account, what the speaker presupposes corresponds to what s/he believes to be common belief (or ground) (Stalnaker 2002: 707). An alternative perspective depicts the common ground in terms of assumptions, namely propositions that a speaker supposes that are shared with the hearer (Gauker 1998: 155; Von Fintel 2000). In both cases, the correspondence between presupposition and common ground involves the issue of unshared presuppositions that do not result in the unacceptability of the utterance (Gauker 1998). Speakers sometimes presuppose without believing that the presupposition is common ground – whether considered as a prior assumption or a prior belief (Burton-Roberts 1989: 26). For example, informative presuppositions (Abbott 2008) such as

b. "I am moving with my fiancé to Seattle" (told by a daughter to her father without having informed him that she got engaged, see Von Fintel 2000; Stalnaker 1974; von Fintel 2008)

are based on a divergence between what the speaker displaces as a condition for the acceptability of his or her utterance and what can be believed or assumed to be already shared.

The phenomenon of accommodation (Lewis 1979) was developed to address this imperfect correspondence between presupposition and common ground. Accommodation is a process in which a proposition *p* becomes common ground by the hearer recognizing that the speaker takes *p* as common ground. Thus, in the aforementioned case of the daughter moving to Seattle, the father adjusts his beliefs and includes the unshared presupposed content in the common ground. In this sense, the presupposition is added to the common ground prior to the acceptance of the utterance – it does not need to be part of the *prior* assumptions or beliefs (von Fintel 2008: 143). Accommodation is a charitable adjustment of the common ground relevant to the conversation.

Presupposition and common ground can be thus distinguished. Presuppositions are conditions set out by an utterance for its acceptability: "language-based practice or convention of interpretation [. . .] allows certain bits of language, such as singular terms, charitably to have a taken-for-granted semantic evaluation in the course of making and understanding assertions" (Atlas 2005: 144). Presupposition is matter of interpretation – it is an inference (a presumptive one, see Donnellan 1966) that is drawn from the sentence or the utterance (depending on the theory), and leads to the retrieval of a content. However, this inferred content has specific pragmatic effects and constraints. These presuppositional inferences are backgrounded – they are treated as not subject to discussion – and they bound the speaker to a commitment different from assertion. As Black pointed out, the use of presuppositions commits the speaker to their truth based on conventions – and more precisely conventional rules for implication, resulting from semantic or syntactic constraints, definitions, or pragmatic conventions (felicity conditions of speech acts. . .) (Black 1962: 61–62).

In this picture, common ground is a limitation of presuppositions, or more precisely a dialogical constraint on these inferences. The speaker may trigger specific background authorized inferences (Clark 1977; Just and Carpenter 1978), namely imply directly a specific content that is necessary for the understanding of the utterance. However, the possibility of an inference needs to be distinguished from its acceptability and – more importantly – its reasonableness. The first and most basic condition of acceptability consists in the possibility of accessing (identifying) the presupposed information. For example, an utterance like

c. "John lived in New York too" (in a context in which the other places in which John lived were not mentioned before)

triggers a presupposition that does not allow any kind of accommodation (Asher and Lascarides 1998: 247; von Fintel 2008: 154). Thus, the hearer needs to be able to draw the presuppositional inference so that s/he connect it with his knowledge or the context (Asher and Lascarides 1998: 277). If accommodation is possible, the acceptance of the presupposed inference (Black 1962: 55–56) has been classically analyzed as constrained by two conditions (von Fintel 2008: 145):

(i) the listeners may be genuinely agnostic as to the truth of the relevant proposition, assume that the speaker knows about its truth, and trust the speaker not to speak inappropriately or falsely;
(ii) the listeners may not want to challenge the speaker about the presupposed proposition, because it is irrelevant to their concerns and because the smoothness of the conversation is important enough to them to warrant a little leeway.

The two conditions can easily explain the accommodation of presuppositions triggered by utterances like the following:

d. "I am sorry that I am late. I had to take my daughter to the doctor" (Von Fintel 2000; see also Stalnaker 1974).

Here, the presupposition in not known to be false, and is irrelevant to the conversation at hand. For this reason, it can be accommodated – namely taken (provisionally) as common ground.

The phenomenon of accommodation explains one aspect of the relationship between presupposition and common ground, namely why a presupposition can be integrated in the common ground. However, if we look at the cases of accommodation failures, we notice that this relationship is much more complex. First, the notion of accommodation and the conditions thereof do not fully explain the effects of a case like (*a*) above, in which the speaker presupposes that Napoleon is the king of France. This presupposition conflicts with what the hearers know and accept (and is relevant to their concerns) and, for this reason, it cannot be accommodated by them. However, whether or not the interlocutors accommodate the controversial proposition, they infer it as part of the common ground. In this sense, the presuppositional inference produces a clear conversational effect: the hearers need to reject a proposition allegedly, or presented as, part of the communal commitments. This effect is triggered also by some newspaper titles, such as the following drawn from The New York Times:[1]

e. "Another Failed Presidency at Hand."

Clearly, the presuppositions in (*e*) ("the present presidency failed;" "other presidencies failed") cannot be considered as common ground by the audience – at least a part of it. However, it is treated as such, and the reader is invited to understand why by reading the article. This effect is different from the one elicited by the use of (*a*) in different contexts, such as the present times (*a'*), or to refer to current British politics (*a''*). In uttering that "The King of France is magnificent" in a political setting in which no French politician can be presumed to have excessive authoritarian ambitions, or in a situation, such as a dialogue about British politics, in which the referent cannot be presumed to be shared, the speaker cannot even presume that someone is disposed to accept the presupposition. In contrast, in (*e*) the presupposed content is presumed to be not accommodable by at least a part of the readers, but the presuppositional inference still produces a clear effect – assuming for the sake of the argument that the presupposed content can be possibly accepted if reasons are given.

Thus, the relationship between presupposition (*pp*) and common ground leads to different scenarios:

i) The hearer draws a presuppositional inference, but s/he cannot evaluate it (cannot determine whether *pp* is acceptable or not) (case *c*);
ii) *pp* can be accepted by the hearer as a background assumption (case *d*);
iii) *pp* can be accepted by the hearer as a background assumption *provisionally* (waiting for further information) (case *b*);
iv) *pp* cannot be accepted by the hearer as it conflicts with other commitments – in some circumstances, it can be *assumed* provisionally for the sake of the argument (case *e*);
v) *pp* cannot be accepted by the hearer as the hearer cannot be presumed to accept *pp* (case *a*).
vi) *pp* cannot be accepted by the hearer as not presumably acceptable in general (case *a'*, *a''*).

Thus, presupposition needs to be distinguished from both common ground and the hearer's ground, and the hearer's acceptance and rejection of *pp* is not only a matter of personal knowledge, but reasonableness.

1 https://www.nytimes.com/2021/09/07/opinion/biden-failed-afghanistan.html

The second dimension of this relationship is that it is not univocal, as the contrast between the following utterances illustrates (Levinson 1983: 204):

f. Sue cried before she finished her thesis.
f'. Sue died before she finished her thesis.

As Levinson pointed out, while (*f*) presupposes that Sue finished her thesis, (*f'*) does not. However, this difference is due to the fact that in this latter case, the presuppositional inference triggered by 'before' would be unreasonable. In this sense, presuppositional inferences are not independent of the common ground – rather, they are commonly triggered defaultively, unless contrary evidence is provided (Donnellan 1966: 293).

However, if a proposition can be treated as common ground even though it is not accommodated, and if presuppositions are not independent of the common ground, how is it possible to represent this relationship?

3 Presupposition, common ground, and presumptive reasoning

The aforementioned aspects of the relationship between presupposition and common ground show its complexity, and its impossibility to reduce it to a mechanic process. Instead, it needs to be addressed considering two fundamental dimensions of "pragmatic" inferences (Harris and Monaco 1978), namely their presumptive nature and their defeasibility. On this perspective, both the common ground and presupposition can be conceived as defeasible inferences, which can be evaluated, accepted, rejected, and most importantly backed or undermined by reasons.

Common ground cannot be conceived as knowledge of what the other *knows* or *believes*, as it would imply the impossible – and in many cases unreasonable – knowledge of another's (and even *the* others') mind (García-Carpintero 2016). Moreover, treating it in terms of belief would not explain the differences between the types of accommodation failures. In line with Donnellan's approach to presupposition (Donnellan 1966: 190–192), Bublitz and Clark instead suggested to regard it in terms of reasoning. For Bublitz, the "common" nature of the ground is an assumption: the speaker and hearer "operate on the assumption that their respective grounds are congruent enough to arrive at equally congruent coherence interpretations" (Bublitz 2011: 370). Thus, the common ground is conceived as an "empathetic process" of making assumptions about what is acceptable by our interlocutor – a dynamic (Kecskes and Zhang 2009) and presumptive process. These assumptions need to be justified, in the sense that what is conceived as "common ground" by a speaker needs to be grounded on reasons: "people take a proposition to be common ground in a community only when they believe they have a proper shared basis for the proposition in that community" (Clark 1996: 96). Thus, common ground is inferred based on evidence, which can result from direct, personal experiences with the interlocutor (personal common ground), or be drawn from what the speaker holds to be true or acceptable about a community to which the interlocutor belongs (communal common ground) (Clark 1996: 100). Common ground is thus a conversational record – what can be taken as accepted by the participants in a given stage of a conversation – and is based on presumptions, i.e., defeasible conclusions that can hold until contrary evidence is provided (Thomason 1990: 337–338). In this framework, presuppositions trigger background inferences that activate, amend, or modify what is presumed to be accepted.

Thomason's idea of conceiving the common ground in terms of presumptive conversational record provides an explanation of the relationship between presupposition and common ground in terms of defeasible reasoning. The conversational record – or rather the commitment store (Hamblin 1970: 257) – is constituted by propositions accepted explicitly by a participant to a dialogue (light-side commitments) or only presumed to be such, based on different reasons (dark-side commitments) (Walton and Krabbe 1995: 124–126). Thus, the commitment store can be updated in different ways (Ginzburg 1994; Ginzburg 1996; Walton and Krabbe 1995: 23–24) – directly, by proposing the acceptance of new commitment, or indirectly, by presuming it as already accepted. However, a presumption is not simply an assertion – it is the result of an inference grounded on presumptive rules (Ullman-Margalit 1983; Macagno and Walton 2012), i.e., defeasible generalizations. The structure of this type of defeasible reasoning (Walton, Reed and Macagno 2008) can be described as follows (Rescher 2006: 33):

Premise 1:	*P* (the proposition representing the presumption) obtains whenever the condition *C* obtains unless and until the standard default proviso *D* (to the effect that countervailing evidence is at hand) obtains (Rule).
Premise 2:	Condition *C* obtains (Fact).
Premise 3:	Proviso *D* does not obtain (Exception).
Conclusion:	*P* obtains.

On this dialectical perspective, Thomason's intuition is developed by considering not only the conclusion of presumptive inferences, but their grounds (the rules).

Presuppositions can be conceived as presumptive, tentative conclusions that can be accepted until contrary evidence is provided. Presuppositions result in commitments that the speaker presumptively attributes to the hearer (mutual ground) and/or a community (common ground) (Geurts 1999: 4; Geurts 2017; Macagno 2012; Macagno 2015; Macagno and Walton 2014:chap. 5). Clearly, such commitments can be retracted or denied by providing reasons (Von Fintel 2004); however, this involves a shifting of the burden of proving (and disproving) a commitment.

By distinguishing between presumptive rules and presumptive conclusions, it is possible to describe the nature of the presupposed propositions, namely the possible reasonable grounds on which they are based. Such grounds (rules) can be classified according to their subject matter, and can include the following categories (Macagno 2018; Macagno 2019):

PR_0. Pragmatic presumptions (relationships between a speech act and the speaker's intentions).
PR_1. Linguistic presumptions (commonly accepted meaning of lexical items; definitions: rules of language. . .).
PR_2. Encyclopedic presumptions (information that considered to be shared because it concerns individuals, facts, events, and descriptions of the world as socially conceived).
PR_3. Behavioral presumptions (habits).
PR_4. Value presumptions (expectations about preferences).

These categories can be more or less specific, or rather, include defeasible generalizations directly or indirectly related to the participant to the concerned dialogue (Clark 1996: 113–115; Kecskes 2013: 4; Kecskes and Zhang 2013). For example, the speaker may draw a presumptive conclusion about the common ground based on the generic presumptive generalization that usually Italians read football news, or on the specific one that the hearer does. While the latter is related to the speaker's evidence on the hearer's behavior, the former defines an aspect of the "culture" of a community (Kecskes 2015; Macagno and Bigi 2017). More importantly, the two types of presumptive conclusions are grounded on different types of evidence, and thus their defeasibility conditions are different. While presumptions directly related to interlocutors are grounded on available evidence (for example, previous conversations, direct common experience), indirect presumptions are more complex patterns of reasoning, as the presumption that a commitment is shared by the interlocutor rests on the presumptions that a given community is committed to it, and that the speaker belongs to such a community. For this reason, these two types of presumptive conclusions activate two different types of grounds that are presumed to be common – the Shared Ground (what is shared by the interlocutor based on the evidence from the interaction) (see Clark 1996: 112) and the Communal Ground (what is shared by the interlocutor based on his or her belonging to a community) (see Clark 1996:96–100). The Shared Ground results from the interaction and defines what is accepted therein (see the notion of "temporarily shared social reality" in Rommetveit 1974: 25). The Communal Ground results from a "culture" and defines what is commonly accepted therein.

4 The reasonableness of presuppositions

The relationship between presupposition and presumptive reasoning needs to be analyzed considering the two reasoners involved in the interaction (Atlas and Levinson 1981: 40). The two agents act based on symmetrical presumptive inferences – one predictive, as aimed at "discovering" a commitment that has not been made manifest, and one interpretative, as aimed at retrieving the meaning of an utterance and its grounds. The two inferences can be represented as follows:

Speaker	Hearer
– The Speaker *S* belongs to (knows) community (culture) *C* or discourse *D* to which the Hearer *H* belongs. – Proposition P_A is normally accepted by (a commitment of) the members of *C* / *D*. – Therefore, *H* should accept or be committed to P_A.	– The Speaker *S* said *A*, presupposing P_A. – Speakers normally take for granted something only when they have reasons (*G*) to hold P_A as a shared commitment (If P_A, then $G \rightarrow CP_A$). – There are no reasons to believe that *S* has no reasons to take P_A as a shared commitment. – Therefore, *G* (there are reasons to hold P_A as a generally shared commitment in *C* / *D*). – Therefore, CP_A (P_A is presumably a shared commitment in *C* / *D*).

This mirroring presumptive reasoning has the advantage of revealing how the grounds are coordinated (Bublitz 2011: 382) also when what is taken for granted by the speaker is not a commitment of the hearer. More importantly, it reveals how the common ground is projected by the speaker – thus linking a linguistic phenomenon to an inference about the speaker's perspective on what should be shared by the community or by the interlocutor.

The dialectical mechanism of presumptive reasoning can explain the complex relationship between presupposition and common ground. First, it distinguishes the grounds for presupposing from what is presupposed, including the dimension of reasonableness of presuppositions (the presupposition can be identified or reconstructed but the hearer cannot be presumed to be committed to the presupposed content). Second, it distinguishes the hearer's commitments from the (presumed) commitments of a community. Thus, a presupposition can "fail" not only because it cannot be reconstructed and evaluated, but also because it is unreasonable. Moreover, also in case the hearer is not committed to a presupposition, the reason is acceptable. On this perspective, we can have four different scenarios in which a renegotiation of the implicit commitments can occur (the presupposed content is referred as P_A):

1. P_A is an implicit commitment of the Hearer, but the grounds on which the Speaker bases his or her presumptive conclusion are not acceptable (ex.: "How is your love story going?" told by the mother to her son who never revealed to have a girlfriend). The Hearer can reject P_A or question the grounds in case P_A is incoherent with other *H*'s explicit commitments.
2. P_A is not a commitment of the Hearer and P_A is incoherent with other *H*'s commitments, but *H* has not reasons to hold that P_A is not grounded on reasons (ex.: "How is your nice girlfriend?" told by the mother to her son after seeing him with a lady). The Hearer can reject P_A by questioning the presumable grounds of P_A.
3. P_A is not a commitment of the Hearer and P_A is incoherent with other *H*'s commitments, but *H* has not reasons to hold that P_A is not a commitment of the community to which *H* belongs (examples *a*, *e*).
4. P_A is not a commitment of the Hearer and P_A is incoherent with other *H*'s commitments, and *H* has reasons to hold that P_A is not a commitment of the community to which *H* belongs (example *a'*, *a''*).

These scenarios can explain the different ways the common ground is negotiated, and more importantly the different dialectical effects of a presupposition. The first two scenarios represent the possible failures of the attribution of a commitment based on specific, direct presumptions, whether unreasonable (1) or reasonable (2). The last two scenarios mirror cases in which the speaker draws a presumptive conclusion about the Hearer's commitments based on an acceptable (3) or unacceptable (4) cultural presumption. These scenarios depict the possibilities of common ground negotiation, which range from denial (1) to a discussion that may concern the culture of a community (4).

5 Presuppositional inferences and the development of common ground

The complex relationship between presuppositions and a community's culture, mediated by the presumptive reasoning – which mirrors the "egocentric" (Kecskes and Zhang 2009; Mustajoki 2012) speaker's view of what counts as "shared" or part of the culture, can be illustrated through some examples from a corpus of students' interactions within the European Project DIALLS. These data were collected in five European countries (England, Lithuania, Germany, Portugal and Spain) plus Israel within a European project aimed at developing a Cultural Literacy Learning Program (CLLP) focused on the development of dialogue and argumentation skills in pre-primary, primary and secondary students for improving communication and understanding each other's views and cultures. Student-student and student-teacher interactions stimulated by text and film materials on social and cultural topics were videotaped and transcribed after obtaining the informed consent of the students' parents.[2]

The following examples were drawn from discussions between 8–9 years old students on a movie entitled Papa's Boy,[3] telling the story of a little mouse (coded as a boy) who is interested only in ballet dancing and dances around in a tutu – not meeting the expectations of his father, a famous boxer. However, the father's attitude changes when he is attacked by a cat, and the boy manages to escape the clutches of the cat and save his father by dancing. This short film was used in the program to elicit a debate on equality and living together.

In the discussions that followed the projection of the movies, the students addressed the problem of how to interpret the story, and how to evaluate the characters' behavior. More importantly, they explicitly and implicitly tackled some crucial gender-related cultural issues, such as the definition of masculinity, the value of respect, and the notion of conformity. These dialogues can be defined "intercultural" for two distinct reasons. First, the students participating belong to different cultures as classically defined (Sarangi 2017; Noels, Yashima and Zhang 2011; Kecskes 2013) to different extents, ranging from 1% (as in the case of Spain) to 10% (Cyprus) and even more than 30% (Germany) of students with migratory background or classified as an ethnic minority. Second, in a communicative perspective these dialogues are intercultural in the sense that they bring to light potential cultural differences that characterize each individual (Auer and Kern 2001). On this view, the various cultural values or beliefs that define an individual become cultural differences when they conflict with the ones with which the hearers indentify themselves in the dynamic construction of the interaction (Sousa and Bradley 2006).

In these dialogical exchanges, presuppositions play a crucial role for developing the common ground between the interlocutors, both at the level of the spe-

---

2 Full description of the anonymization procedure can be found at (Rapanta *et al.* 2020).
3 https://dialls2020.eu/library/papas-boy/

cific ground made coherent for the purposes of the specific interaction (Shared Ground or SG), and the Communal Ground (CG). Through presuppositions, students define the background on which they can develop their interpretations and discussions. For example, we consider the following example, drawn from the Cypriot corpus (CY_10_B_KL1_C10_GR&EN, lines 3940–3952):[4]

Case 1: Developing a new Shared Ground

1. S5. A difference is that the little mouse is a girl and **her** dad is a boy and it's normal not to have the same taste, that's it.
2. T. Right. Is it natural? Yes. [. . .]
3. S7. The little mouse could fly because **she** knew ballet and the dad didn't know ballet. [. . .]
4. S8. Err then the first time she danced ballet, **her** dad realized that he thought he should teach **her** boxing like kick-boxing, I remember.
5. T. Uh-huh. That's what he thought.
6. S8. And she didn't like because **she was not**, girls don't learn boxing easily.
7. T. Indeed.

Here, the students (S7 and S8) use presuppositions for both developing a Shared Ground concerning the interpretation of the text, and activating the Communal Ground needed for interpreting it. The first use emerges when both students use pronouns and possessives presupposing that the mouse is a girl, and when at 3 S7 takes for granted information that can be directly presumed based on the evidence (the mouse knows ballet; the dad does not; ballet allows the mouse to fly). Here, the students place in the commitment store propositions that constitute the SG needed for the interaction. The second use emerges at 6, when, through the causal clause (Konig and Siemund 2009), S8 presupposes the generalization that "girls do not learn boxing easily," and the causal relation that "difficulty in learning diminishes the enjoyment of an activity." Here, implicit commitments resulting from the interlocutors' "communal" ground are activated, namely become part of the commitments relevant to the discussion.

The role of presuppositions for the development of the common ground (both shared for the purposes of the dialogue and the communal one) becomes clear when the interlocutors dispute what is taken for granted, such as in the following case from the Lithuanian corpus (LT_5_B_KL1_C5_LT&EN, lines 1499–1509):

4 In all the examples, presuppositions are indicated in bold and negotiations (rejections and counterarguments) in italics.

Case 2: Negotiating a Shared Ground

1. S1. Have you noticed anything special **about the boy**? because **a boy normally doesn't wear skirts.**
2. S3. He also doesn't wear ballet shoes.
3. S2. *I also thought it was a girl.*
4. S4. *Me too, I thought it was a girl.*
5. S1. I don't think it should be like that, because **a boy couldn't really wear a skirt.**
6. S3. Because a boy is not a girl.
7. S2. Maybe in other countries it could be [. . .]

Unlike case 1, in this excerpt the interlocutors do simply take for granted information and build thereon the further interactions. Rather, they negotiate it. In 1, S1 displays and activates the SG commitments derived from the video that the mouse is a boy, and that he wears a skirt, and the communal commitment (CG) that wearing in a not normal way can be judged as special. However, the SG commitment about the gender of the mouse is challenged at 3 and 4, leading to a revision of the SG commitment at 5, based on newly activated CG commitments, i.e., that "boys cannot wear skirts" and that "if it someone behaves differently, then he is not a boy." This latter CG commitment is disputed at 7, thus reopening the negotiation of the SG commitment about the gender of the mouse. The presuppositions play a crucial role in this case, as they propose a coordination between the speaker's and the interlocutors' grounds, which are rejected, discussed, and negotiated. In this sense, presuppositions work as instruments for implicitly proposing a ground, and presuppositional failures (whether accommodated or rejected) represent simply one of the dynamics of communication.

The common ground can be also developed by brining to the light side the commitments that are taken for granted by a speaker – without necessarily disputing them. This dynamic is alternative to the implicit acceptance of the contents taken for granted (case 1) or their rejection (case 2), and can be illustrated in the following excerpt from the German corpus (DE_3_B_KL1_C3_DE&EN, lines 1203–1210):

Case 3: Coordinating the Shared Grounds

1. T. Right. The dad felt weird at the start because hi **his boy danced**. BUT WHY?
2. S1. Um, uh, because **he that dad was a boxer**.
3. S2. *And if the dad is a boxer the boy isn't allowed to dance?*
4. S1. Nope.
5. T. *Why not?*
6. S1. No, he is allowed to dance.
7. S4. *Because he should actually be a boxer too.*
8. S1. *The dad wanted the son to be a boxer.*

The presuppositions in 1 and 2 are related to the interpretation of the evidence (the short movie), and thus are presented as part of the Shared Ground. However, in 3, S2 brings an implicit commitment to the light side, simply making it explicit. This move is a request of clarification, which does not result in any rebuttal or negotiation. Instead, at 5, 7, and 8, reasons are asked and provided in support of this – now explicit – proposal of a shared ground. This dynamic illustrates another characteristic of commitments, namely their interrelation – a feature that defines the Communal Ground and becomes crucial in cases involving it (see case 6 below).

The dynamic of the coordination of the common ground becomes more complex when a commitment is proposed as part of the Communal Ground, but the interlocutors disagree. An example is case 4 below, drawn from the Spanish corpus (ES_6_B_KL1_C6_CA&EN, lines 1619–1628):

Case 4: Negotiating the Shared and Communal grounds

1. S1. Oh, well, the father, at first the father feels sad because **her daughter** is not a boxer . . . and. . .
2. S2. *Is it a he-mouse or a she-mouse, what do you think?*
3. S1. It's a she-mouse, the girl [What are you saying!]
4. S3. Why? What makes us think that?
5. S1. Well, because **she dances ballet.**
6. S4. *What's that, a boy can not dance ballet? Go ahead.*
7. S1. Well, it's just that . . . she also **had a girl's face** . . . and **it's dressed like a girl.**
8. S4. *Oh, so boy-mice and gir-mice have different faces? Can you tell?*

The Shared Ground proposed by S1 at 1 is disputed at move 2, which leads to a metadialogical discussion that involves bringing to light the bases of the presupposition. In particular, at 5 and 7, S1 defends his proposed SG commitment by invoking an apparently deeper one, a Communal Ground commitment (if a person dances ballet, then she is a girl; if someone has a girl's face then she is a girl; if someone is dressed like a girl, then she is a girl) triggered justificatory clauses (Charnavel 2017; Konig and Siemund 2009). These Communal Ground commitments are disputed by S4, who provides reasons against these generalizations. This example shows an interesting dialectical difference between the rejection of a Shared Ground commitment and a Communal Ground one. In the first case, the interlocutors (S2 and S3) ask the speaker (S1) for the reasons in support of his proposal. In the second case, S4 provides the reasons for refusing the commitment – he has to argue against a ground proposed as communal.

The same dialectical mechanism emerges in the continuation of the dialogue when the teacher joins the discussion (ES_6_B_KL1_C6_CA&EN, lines 1657–1664):

Case 5: Negotiating the Communal Grounds

1. S5. No, because **she's** free
2. T. Who is free?
3. S5. The **she-mouse**, because the father can't tell them . . .
4. T. *The he-mouse. Here they continue to think that, S5 says it's a she-mouse . . .*
5. S5. *She-mouse.*
6. T. *But why can't a he-mouse dance?*
7. S5. Because **the face** . . . and **the clothes** and everything, SHE HAS A **SHE-MOUSE FACE**!
8. T. *But is there such a thing as boy or girl clothing?*

At 1, S5 ignores the previous discussion and displays a Shared Ground commitment that has already been disputed (the mouse is a girl). However, the presupposition used to propose this implicit commitment fails, and cannot be reconstructed by the teacher (2), which results in S5's clarification. However, at 4, the teacher corrects the SG commitment, and then addresses the Communal Ground commitments that S5 used to draw it using rhetorical questions as arguments against them.

Negotiations of the Communal Ground are more complex, as they represent deeper commitments (Kecskes and Zhang 2009) that are often related to and grounded in others – in a network that defines a "cultural" difference. An example is the following, drawn from the Israeli corpus (IL_10_B_KL1_C10_HE&EN, lines 2564–2570):

Case 6: Negotiating the networks of Communal Grounds

1. S1. In question two I think the mouse like [..] can't all the time **deal with girly stuff** because **he has like a whole world ahead of him** and **he's supposed to like deal with for example basketball, football, {boys'} [stuff]** [. . .] and he **can't just be a girl all the time** [. . .]
2. S8. I think thaaaat. . . that why you say is wrong because [..] *any boy can do whatever a girl can do and[..] any girl can play whatever a boy does, and any girl can play football and any boy can play*, uh, dunno with dolls or such things. Because it's about what everyone loves, whatever they love they'll do and persist with it. *Like in the, in class, we have it in class we always play ball. Girls and boys as well, and you can see it just in front of your eyes.*
3. S1. *Yes I know but, I didn't mean that. I meant, he can play whatever he feels like but, like, he ca-, he can do whatever he feels like but, like-*
4. S28. I actually differ from you in opinion S1 because, for example, for example there are boys who actually like, actually the boys in class have like always with ball like if they forget what was last time, dodgeball or football, so *there are some that the boys are saying football and the girls are saying dodgeball.* So there are also boys. For instance, like S9. Like S9 he sometimes also says dodgeball. And also for instance in my summer camp, can't remember for example a year or two years ago for instance *there was a girl who really loved playing football there really* {unclear}

At 1, S1 presupposes that a boy doing "girly stuff" is wasting his time, is somehow acting wrong, and is trying to be a girl. Unlike case 3, in which the speakers tried to bring to light what the characters of the story were thinking (thus coordinating the Shared Ground), here the presumptions used for developing the Shared Ground are based on commitments belonging to a deeper, Communal Ground. These deeper commitments become the target of the negotiations advanced by S8 and S28, who dispute the value judgment on who plays or acts in a non-stereotypical way (at 2) and the presumed association between a child's gender and specific activities (at 3). These challenges, supported by reasons, bring to light what is "presupposed" by the presuppositions used by S1, namely the underlying network of presumed communal commitments.

6 Conclusion

The relationship between common ground and presupposition (Kecskes and Zhang 2013) and the very notion of common ground has been a philosophical and linguistic challenge. This paper intended to build on the philosophical and linguistic insights to propose a dialectical perspective on how presuppositions are used for displaying, coordinating, and negotiating the common ground (see also Ortaçtepe Hart and Okkalı 2021). Presuppositions are regarded as backward inferences drawn from the utterances – and like all inferences they can be analyzed as dialectical patterns of reasoning, resulting in interlocutors' commitments. Like generalized implicatures, such inferences are defeasible, tentative, and can hold until contrary evidence is provided. More importantly, they are based on presumptive rules and evidence that can be drawn from the immediate, direct context of the interaction, or the speaker's evidence on the community the interlocutor is presumed to belong to. These different types of evidence and thus presumptive reasoning define different types of grounds that are presumed to be common – a Shared Ground (a kind of volatile ground for the purposes of the interaction), and a Communal Ground, a deeper and more stable set of commitments that are presumed to define a "culture," and thus can be activated in different types of interactions.

The coordination of these two grounds is a complex phenomenon, where the (implicit and explicit) acceptance, questioning, rejection, and countering of the presuppositions plays a crucial role. Presuppositions activate implicit commitments that define the ground that is presumed to be common. They display a proposed Shared Ground or activate presumed Communal commitments. However, presuppositions are only the first step in the coordination of the grounds. The presupposed propositions are presumed to be part of what the interlocutor, or the community to which s/he belongs, is implicitly committed to. But the tacit acceptance of this presupposition is only the most frequent dynamic of ground coordination. As shown in the examples from classroom dialogues, presuppositions can be made explicit, confirmed, contested, and discussed to different extents and with different strategies. While the propositions presumed to be part of the Shared Ground are easily and directly contested or rejected, the negotiation of the Communal Ground is normally more complex: Communal Ground presumptions shift the burden of proof, as the hearer needs to provide reasons not to accept these deeper commitments.

References

Abbott, Barbara. 2008. Presuppositions and common ground. *Linguistics and Philosophy* 31(5). 523–538. doi:10.1007/s10988-008-9048-8.

Allan, Keith. 2013. What is common ground? In Alessandro Capone, Franco Lo Piparo & Marco Carapezza (eds.), *Perspectives in pragmatics, philosophy & psychology. Volume 2*, 285–310. Cham, Switzerland: Springer.

Asher, Nicholas & Alex Lascarides. 1998. The semantics and pragmatics of presupposition. *Journal of Semantics* 15(3). 239–300. doi:10.1093/jos/15.3.239.

Atlas, Jay David. 2005. *Logic, meaning, and conversation*. Oxford, UK: Oxford University Press.

Atlas, Jay David. 2020. Negative existence statements: Kripke, Strawson, and topic noun phrases. *Intercultural Pragmatics* 17(3). 315–333. doi:10.1515/ip-2020-3003.

Atlas, Jay David & Stephen Levinson. 1981. It-clefts, informativeness and logical form: Radical pragmatics (revised standard version). In Peter Cole (ed.), *Radical pragmatics*, 1–62. New York, NY: Academic Press.

Auer, Peter & Friederike Kern. 2001. Three ways of analysing communication between East and West Germans as intercultural communication. In Aldo Di Luzio, Susanne Günthner & Franca Orletti (eds.), *Culture in Communication: Analyses of intercultural situations*, 89–116. Amsterdam, Netherlands-Philadelphia, PA: John Benjamins.

Beaver, David. 1997. Presupposition. In Johan van Benthem & Alice ter Meulen (eds.), *The handbook of logic and language*, 939–1008. Amsterdam, Netherlands: Elsevier.

Black, Max. 1962. *Models and metaphors: Studies in language and philosophy*. Ithaca, IL: Cornell University Press.

Bublitz, Wolfram. 2011. It utterly boggles the mind: knowledge, common ground and coherence. In Hanna Pishwa (ed.), *Language and Memory*, 359–386. Berlin, Germany, and New York, NY: De Gruyter Mouton.

Burton-Roberts, Noel. 1989. *The limits to debate: A revised theory of semantic presupposition*. Cambridge, UK: Cambridge University Press.

Capone, Alessandro. 2020. Presuppositions as pragmemes: The case of exemplification acts. *Intercultural Pragmatics* 17(1). 53–75. doi:10.1515/ip-2020-0003.

Charnavel, Isabelle. 2017. Non-at-issueness of since-clauses. In Dan Burgdorf, Jacob Collard, Sireemas Maspong & Brynhildur Stefánsdóttir (eds.), *Semantics and Linguistic Theory*, vol. 27, 43–58. Washington, DC: Linguistic Society of America. doi:10.3765/salt.v27i0.4127.

Chierchia, Gennaro & Sally McConnell-Ginet. 1990. *Meaning and grammar: An introduction to semantics*. Cambridge, MA: MIT press.

Clark, Herbert. 1977. Inferences in comprehension. In David LaBerge & Jay Samuels (eds.), *Basic processes in reading: Perception and comprehension*, 243–263. Hillsdale, NJ: Erlbaum.

Clark, Herbert. 1996. *Using language*. Cambridge, UK: Cambridge University Press.

Donnellan, Keith. 1966. Reference and definite descriptions. *The philosophical review* 75(3). 281–304.

Ducrot, Oswald. 1966. "Le roi de France est sage". Implication logique et Présupposition linguistique. *Etudes de linguistique appliquée* 4. 39–47.

Ducrot, Oswald. 1972. *Dire et ne pas dire*. Paris, France: Hermann.

Fintel, Kai von. 2008. What is Presupposition Accommodation, Again? *Philosophical Perspectives* 22(1). 137–170. doi:10.1111/j.1520-8583.2008.00144.x.

Fintel, Kai Von. 2000. *What is presupposition accommodation?* Manuscript, Massachusetts Institute of Technology.

Fintel, Kai Von. 2004. Would you believe it? The King of France is back! (Presuppositions and truth-value intuitions). In Marga Reimer & Anne Bezuidenhout (eds.), *Descriptions and Beyond*, 315–341. Oxford, UK: Oxford University Press.

García-Carpintero, Manuel. 2016. Accommodating Presuppositions. *Topoi* 35(1). 37–44. doi:10.1007/s11245-014-9264-5.

Gauker, Christopher. 1998. What Is a Context of Utterance? *Philosophical Studies* 91(2). 149–172. doi:10.1023/A:1004247202476.

Geurts, Bart. 1999. *Presuppositions and Pronouns*. Oxford, UK: Elsevier.

Geurts, Bart. 2017. Presupposition and givenness. In Yan Huang (ed.), *Oxford handbook of pragmatics*, 180–198. Oxford, UK: Oxford University Press.

Gibbs, Raymond. 1987. Mutual knowledge and the psychology of conversational inference. *Journal of pragmatics* 11(5). 561–588. doi:10.1016/0378-2166(87)90180-9.

Ginzburg, Jonathan. 1994. An Update Semantics for Dialogue. In Harry Bunt, Reinhard Muskens & Gerrit Rentier (eds.), *Proceedings of the 1st International Workshop on Computational Semantics*, 111–120. Tilburg Netherlands: Institute for language technology and artificial intelligence.

Ginzburg, Jonathan. 1996. Dynamics and the semantics of dialogue. In Jerry Seligman & Dag Westerstahl (eds.), *Logic, language and computation 1*, 221–237. Stanford, CA: CSLI publications.

Hamblin, Charles Leonard. 1970. *Fallacies*. London, UK: Methuen.

Harris, Richard & Gregory Monaco. 1978. Psychology of pragmatic implication: Information processing between the lines. *Journal of Experimental Psychology: General* 107(1). 1–22. doi:10.1037/0096-3445.107.1.1.

Just, Marcel Adam & Patricia Carpenter. 1978. Inference processes during reading: Reflections from eye fixations. In John Senders, Dennis Fisher & Richard Monty (eds.), *Eye movements and the higher psychological functions*, 157–174. Hillsdale, NJ: Erlbaum.

Kecskes, Istvan. 2013. *Intercultural pragmatics*. Oxford, UK: Oxford University Press.

Kecskes, Istvan. 2015. Intracultural communication and intercultural communication: Are they different? *International Review of Pragmatics* 7. 171–194. doi:10.1163/18773109-00702002.
Kecskes, Istvan & Fenghui Zhang. 2009. Activating, seeking, and creating common ground: A socio-cognitive approach. *Pragmatics & Cognition* 17(2). 331–355. doi:10.1075/pc.17.2.06kec.
Kecskes, Istvan & Fenghui Zhang. 2013. On the dynamic relations between common ground and presupposition. In Alessandro Capone, Franco Lo Piparo & Marco Carapezza (eds.), *Perspectives in pragmatics, philosophy & psychology*, 375–395. Cham, Switzerland: Springer.
Konig, Ekkehard & Peter Siemund. 2009. Causal and concessive clauses: Formal and semantic relations. In Elizabeth Couper-Kuhlen & Bernd Kortmann (eds.), *Cause – Condition – Concession – Contrast. Cognitive and Discourse Perspectives*, 341–60. Berlin, Germany: Mouton de Gruyter.
Levinson, Stephen. 1983. *Pragmatics*. Cambridge, UK: Cambridge University Press.
Lewis, David. 1979. Scorekeeping in a language game. *Journal of Philosophical Logic* 8(1). 339–359. doi:10.1007/BF00258436.
Macagno, Fabrizio. 2012. Reconstructing and assessing the conditions of meaningfulness: An argumentative approach to presupposition. In Henrique Ribeiro (ed.), *Inside arguments: Logic and the study of argumentation*, 247–268. Newcastle upon Tyne, UK: Cambridge Scholars Publishing.
Macagno, Fabrizio. 2015. Presupposition as argumentative reasoning. In Alessandro Capone & Jacob Mey (eds.), *Interdisciplinary studies in pragmatics, culture and society*, 465–487. Cham, Switzerland: Springer.
Macagno, Fabrizio. 2018. A dialectical approach to presupposition. *Intercultural Pragmatics* 15(2). 291–313. doi:10.1515/ip-2018-0008.
Macagno, Fabrizio. 2019. Presupposition triggers and presumptive interpretation. In Alessandro Capone, Marco Carapezza, and Franco Lo Piparo (eds.), *Further Advances in Pragmatics and Philosophy: Part 2 Theories and Applications*, 155–79. Cham, Switzerland: Springer
Macagno, Fabrizio & Sarah Bigi. 2017. Understanding misunderstandings. Presuppositions and presumptions in doctor-patient chronic care consultations. *Intercultural Pragmatics* 14(1). 49–75. doi:10.1515/ip-2017-0003.
Macagno, Fabrizio & Douglas Walton. 2012. Presumptions in Legal Argumentation. *Ratio Juris* 25(3). 271–300. doi:10.1111/j.1467-9337.2012.00514.x.
Macagno, Fabrizio & Douglas Walton. 2014. *Emotive language in argumentation*. New York, NY: Cambridge University Press.
Mustajoki, Arto. 2012. A speaker-oriented multidimensional approach to risks and causes of miscommunication. *Language and Dialogue* 2(2). 216–243. doi:10.1075/ld.2.2.03mus.
Noels, Kimberly A., Tomoko Yashima & Rui Zhang. 2011. Language, Identity and Intercultural Communication. In Jane Jackson (ed.), *The Routledge Handbook of Language and Intercultural Communication*, 52–66. London, UK: Routledge.
Ortaçtepe Hart, Deniz & Seçil Okkalı. 2021. Common ground and positioning in teacher-student interactions: Second language socialization in EFL classrooms. *Intercultural Pragmatics* 18(1). 53–82. doi:10.1515/ip-2021-0003.
Rapanta, Chrysi, Dilar Cascalheira, Beatriz Gil, Cláudia Gonçalves, D'Jamila Garcia, Rita Morais, João Rui Pereira, et al. 2020. Dialogue and Argumentation for Cultural Literacy Learning in

Schools: Multilingual Data Corpus. doi:10.5281/ZENODO.4058183. https://zenodo.org/record/4058183 (13 April, 2021).
Reimer, Marga & Anne Bezuidenhout (eds.). 2004. *Descriptions and beyond*. Oxford, UK: Oxford University Press.
Rescher, Nicholas. 2006. *Presumption and the Practices of Tentative Cognition*. Cambridge, UK: Cambridge University Press.
Rommetveit, Ragnar. 1974. *On Message Structure: A Framework for the Study of Language and Communication*. London, UK: John Wiley & Sons, Ltd.
Sarangi, Srikant. 2017. Mind the gap: 'Communicative vulnerability' and the mediation of linguistic/cultural diversity in healthcare settings. In Hywel Coleman (ed.), *Multilingualisms and development*, 239–258. Amsterdam Netherlands: John Benjamins.
Schiffer, Stephen. 1972. *Meaning*. Oxford, UK: Oxford University Press.
Schlenker, Philippe. 2010. Presuppositions and Local Contexts. *Mind* 119(474). 377–391. doi:10.1093/mind/fzq032.
Schwarz, Florian. 2015. Introduction: Presuppositions in Context – Theoretical Issues and Experimental Perspectives. In Florian Schwarz (ed.), *Experimental Perspectives on Presuppositions*, 1–38. Cham, Switzerland: Springer.
Sousa, Carlos M P & Frank Bradley. 2006. Cultural distance and psychic distance: two peas in a pod? *Journal of international marketing* 14(1). 49–70. doi:10.1509/jimk.14.1.49.
Stalnaker, Robert. 1973. Presuppositions. *Journal of philosophical logic* 2(4). 447–457. doi:10.1007/bf00262951.
Stalnaker, Robert. 1974. Pragmatic presuppositions. In Milton Munitz & Peter Unger (eds.), *Semantics and philosophy*, 197–214. New York, NY: New York University Press.
Stalnaker, Robert. 1998. On the representation of context. *Journal of Logic, Language and Information* 7(1). 3–19. doi:10.1023/A:1008254815298.
Stalnaker, Robert. 2002. Common ground. *Linguistics and Philosophy* 25. 701–721. doi:10.1023/A:1020867916902.
Strawson, Peter. 1950. On referring. *Mind* 59(235). 320–344.
Strawson, Peter. 1964. Identifying reference and truth-values. *Theoria* 30(2). 96–118. doi:10.1111/j.1755-2567.1964.tb00404.x.
Thomason, Richmond. 1990. Accommodation, meaning, and implicature: Interdisciplinary foundations for pragmatics. In Philip Cohen, Jerry Morgan & Martha Pollack (eds.), *Intentions in communication*, 325–364. Cambridge, UK: MIT Press.
Ullman-Margalit, Edna. 1983. On Presumption. *The Journal of Philosophy* 80(3). 143–163. doi:10.2307/2026132.
Walton, Douglas & Erik Krabbe. 1995. *Commitment in dialogue*. Albany, NY: State University of New York Press.
Walton, Douglas, Christopher Reed & Fabrizio Macagno. 2008. *Argumentation schemes*. New York, NY: Cambridge University Press.

2 Emergent common ground

Elke Diedrichsen

Grounding emergent common ground: Detecting markers of emergent common ground in a YouTube discussion thread

Abstract: The socio-cognitive approach (Kecskes and Zhang 2009; Kecskes 2014) integrates two approaches to common ground by considering its two dimensions: Core common ground is the portion of knowledge and intention shared among interlocutors and acting as a basis for the interaction, whereas emergent common ground is dynamically built out of knowledge and intention portions that the interacting parties bring into the ongoing conversation. These portions may be divergent and contradictory, as they originate from each interlocutor's own background, and they may be influenced by the current situation.

In this chapter, I will explore how emergent common ground in particular is handled in online interactions. The hypothesis is that grounding in terms of the establishment and markup of common ground applies to the dynamic concept of emergent common ground as well. Grounding entails formal markers that show addressees that there is a mismatch in beliefs or knowledge bases between interactants, and to alert them that unknown or unexpected information is to be expected. In order to obtain a database that is rich in emergent common ground, I chose online interactions that deal with a particular culture-specific phenomenon. The empirical, data-driven study identifies and describes emergent common ground in an online discussion thread in YouTube, that is associated with a short documentary on Hikikomori in Japan. Following a discussion of the theoretical background of the analysis, and in particular the general pragmatic conditions in online interactions, a number of sources of emergent common ground in online discussions will be discussed and identified in the material. These are collapsing contexts, coherence/adjacency, stance, and uncommon ground, which deals with the role of presumptions and dark-side commitments. As a fifth source of emergent common ground, updates on a participant's self-identification and role intentions can be added.

The study will identify markers of emergent common ground in the selected discussion thread. While the demarcation of emergent common ground for the addressees can be seen as a cooperative move, there are reasons to assume a more general egocentric attitude among the interactants in this online discussion. It can be shown that people have a tendency to discuss and evaluate a culturally sensitive topic from the perspective of their own culture, even if there is information available that teaches them where and how the topic under discussion is different from their own culture.

https://doi.org/10.1515/9783110766752-006

1 Introduction

Common ground is premised on the belief shared between interactants in a conversation that certain portions of knowledge are common to them and do not need any introduction or explanation. Many theories of pragmatics regard common ground as a prerequisite for the production and comprehension of utterances in conversation (H. H. Clark and Marshall 1981; H. H. Clark 1996; Tomasello 2008; Levinson 2006; Enfield 2008; E.V. Clark 2015, Kecskes 2014; Ladilova and Schröder 2022). People establish their joint actions and communicated contents as part of their common ground in a process called *grounding* (H. H. Clark 1996).

Communicative contributions create common ground (Lambrecht 1994), but they also indicate how they are attributed to common ground. The act of grounding is intrinsically connected with information management. Lexical markers, including discourse markers, temporal connectives, and modal particles, contribute directly to the grounding of the conversational record. They can activate and impose common ground, and keep track of the common ground reached during a conversation (Fetzer and Fischer 2007; Pittner 2007; Tenbrink 2007).

Kecskes and Zhang (2009) introduce the socio-cognitive approach to communication. It is based on the observation that interaction is much more egocentric, dynamic and chaotic than it is assumed by pragmatic theories that base their approach to information management in human interaction mainly on the concept of common ground as an a priori given knowledge resource.

Cognitive psychology studies (Barr and Keysar 2005; Keysar 2008; Colston 2008; Gibbs and Colston 2019) attest that interactants show egocentric behaviour in conversations. This is due to attention biases or deficits, distraction, or general egocentric predisposition. The authors maintain that spontaneous interaction should not be considered as an endeavour that is carefully crafted around the participants' a priori shared knowledge. Rather, it is a trial-and-error process that requires constant engagement from both parties in order to create and maintain common ground. Within a culture of speakers, understanding is generally enabled because interactions are embedded in a sociocultural background of linguistic and extralinguistic knowledge. In cases where there is not enough shared background, like in Lingua Franca interactions (Kecskes 2014), speakers will have to engage more, for example adjust the way they express themselves in order to ensure understanding. In such encounters, intercultures emerge. An interculture is a spontaneous, interactively co-constructed set-up of shared ideas and knowledge bases, which emerges *in situ* from interactants' respective cultural backgrounds, their shared knowledge, and anything that is contributed by the shared situation (Kecskes 2014: 15; see also Koole and ten Thije 1994: 69; Nolan, this volume).

The socio-cognitive approach works on the basis of the insight that in human interaction, cooperation and egocentrism are not antagonistic phenomena. Two kinds of common ground are suggested, which are potentially part of any interaction in variable degrees: Core and emergent common ground (Kecskes and Zhang 2009; Kecskes 2014).

Core common ground is generalised common knowledge that belongs to a speech community as a result of prior interactions and experiences. This knowledge is shared before and independent of the actual situational context. Emergent common ground is contingent on the actual situation. It is defined as dynamic, particularised knowledge, interactively created in the ongoing communication, and triggered by the actual situational context. It complements the knowledge shared by interactants prior to the communication.

Common ground is an assumption that speakers make in the course of actual communication. Core and emergent common ground are different components of assumed common ground, and they are “interconnected and inseparable” (Kecskes and Zhang 2013: 381). Core common ground can affect the formation of emergent common ground, as it restricts its occurrence. Emergent common ground may originate from parts of the core common ground. Emergent common ground can contribute to core common ground, as it may become ritualised and part of the common ground over time (Kecskes and Zhang 2013: 380–381).

In this article, I will focus on emergent common ground and explore how it is introduced and handled in online interactions. My claim is that grounding in terms of the establishment and markup of common ground applies to the dynamic concept of emergent common ground as well. The traditional notion of grounding entails formal demarcation for and hints towards established common ground. I will show that there are also markers to make addressees aware that there is a mismatch in beliefs or knowledge bases between interactants, and to alert them that unknown or unexpected information is coming. In order to obtain a database that is rich in emergent common ground, I chose online interactions that deal with a particular culture-specific phenomenon. This phenomenon is not unheard of outside its culture of origin, but it is not at the centre of attention for most people from other cultures. The empirical, data-driven study identifies and describes emergent common ground in an online discussion thread in YouTube. The content of the YouTube video that the discussion is associated with is a short documentary on Hikikomori in Japan. Hikikomori are people who self-isolate by choice, and avoid any contact with the outside world. The topic is culturally sensitive, in the sense that interactants’ knowledge and feelings about it will vary by a large degree. The way people interpret and address the phenomenon depends on their culture of origin and general knowledge and sensitivity with respect to cultural issues. The analysis will identify markers of emergent common ground in selected parts of the discussion thread. Four sources of emergent common ground in online discussions will be discussed and identified in the material. These are collapsing contexts, coherence/adjacency, stance, and uncommon ground. Integrating contemporary research both on common ground and on online communication, I will show that emergent common ground and its markers are powerful notions for the description of the dynamics and the particular communicative style found in online communications. I will also demonstrate that the categorisation and terminology used in the socio-cognitive approach can serve to identify and describe cultural appropriation phenomena in online discussions.

The paper will proceed as follows. Section 2 will outline general pragmatic conditions that apply to online discussions. Section 3 will discuss four phenomena that can be regarded as sources of emergent common ground in online interactions. Section 4 will introduce my empirical study on emergent common ground in online communication. The study examines material from a discussion thread under a YouTube video on Hikikomori people in Japan. Section 5 discusses the results of the study and formulates conclusions.

2 General pragmatic conditions in online discussions

Internet contents like news articles, videos and status updates in social media are generally equipped with a commenting capacity. Online forum discussions give opportunities to ordinary citizens for raising political and societal issues "from below" (Fetzer 2013). Such discussions can be presented alongside the actual news reporting of the professional media, but the media agencies accept no liability for them. The comments appear below the content in chronological order. It is possible to reply to a previous comment, in which case a comment thread with a discussion emerges. People are thus endowed with multiple, easily accessible methods of participation and sharing, and the content liked, shared and tagged the most will have greater chances of spread and consumption (Papacharissi 2010, 2015: 25).

The assessment of levels of shared knowledge and recipient design in online communication turns out to be difficult, as participants remain broadly anonymous. People are joining discussions without introducing themselves and without finding out anything about their interactants. The name and profile information, including an image, may or may not give honest and real life information about the contributor. Generally, the lack of insight into others' backgrounds is accepted as a condition of the interaction and does not lead to inquisitive questions or complaints. The style of communication in online communication and the perspective for learning and sharing insights in this rather recent communication format is generally described in relatively negative terms across the literature. News discussion forums, for example, are not viewed as knowledge-building, democratic discourse, even though they may engage with actual news. The common ground built up here is not necessarily aligned with facts 'in the world', but with sentiments and opinions the participants hold regarding the news report or related issues that they bring into the discussion. News discussion forums have not been found to create spaces of empowerment regarding political participation, given that they enable free speech. Rather, online engagement is described as driven by entertainment and infotainment, and the conversations are characterised by negativity, disconnection, and affect (Johansson 2017; Papacharissi 2010: 19–20). The discussions' "heterogeneous patterns of participation and the mostly face-sensitive topics of political online discussions enhance disagreement, confrontation, derogatory language, deliberate misunderstandings, and provocation." (Johansson, Kleinke, and Lethi 2017: 3).

In terms of the socio-cognitive approach, it seems that egocentrism outranks cooperation in influencing and shaping online interaction. Therefore, online discussion forums are a grand space for emergent common ground to appear. I would like to challenge the rather bleak outlook on online discussion forums as presented from the literature above, even though these observations are certainly not unwarranted. Social networks and online discussion forums are highly popular with people of all ages, so there must be advantages that make people engage in this kind of communication. They revolve around the accessibility and the ease of usage, and certainly include the fact that people remain generally anonymous in the crowd of users. In public online forums, everybody can make their point on a certain topic of interest, get into discussions about it, and engage with other contributants for an unlimited time. Language barriers are not eradicated, but eased: People don't have to worry about addressing others in their respective native language. Contributors don't have to engage with politeness and formal interaction rituals that may be culture specific. No one is expected to e.g. introduce themselves, use culture-specific polite addressing phrases, or explain why they are there, participating (cf. Kecskes 2019 on offline scenarios in which people from different cultures meet for the first time and introduce each other). Everyone with an account is by default invited to join the discussion. Online discussions can be a place to ventilate emotions without being made accountable for it, and as long as participants don't cross certain lines, i.e. attack, insult or discriminate others, that may be relieving and rather harmless. Also, participants may actually take something away from these discussions, even if it is not "knowledge" in the traditional sense, but there may be new insights, new ways of looking at something, a sense of what other people are thinking and feeling about a particular situation or topic. In the example discussed, such new insights may be gained and exchanged regarding life situations like being lonely, being a Hikikomori, being in lockdown. The chaos of this form of interaction affords people new communicative approaches to issues they may find difficult to talk about in real life.

3 Four sources of emergent common ground in online interactions

Given the difficulty to establish, access and maintain common ground through online interactions, it is reasonable to assume that online interactions will involve emergent common ground to a large degree. Because people do not know each other well and do not share a common background, many portions of the information, the code and the overall behaviour they share online will potentially be unexpected and may need explanation. Furthermore, contributions in online interactions appear chronologically, and while some posts may be directed at one particular addressee, or refer to a dialogue established earlier, this will not be obvious unless it is overtly marked. Coherence, reference, turn organisation and adjacency are generally not straightforward and need demarcation. A further source of emergent common ground is the expression of stance, but also its misalignment and misinterpretation that warrants repair efforts. I will also discuss *uncommon ground* (Macagno and Capone 2016) as a source of emergent common ground in online interactions. Uncommon ground includes phenomena like presupposition cancellation, presumption resolution, and the unveiling of dark-side commitments.

The following four sources of emergent common ground in online interactions will be discussed in turn:

1. Collapsing contexts
2. Adjacency/Coherence
3. Stance
4. Uncommon Ground

3.1 Collapsing contexts

In online discussions, the only potentially reliable a priori common ground shared by interactants is the content that the discussion thread is aligned with, and a global real life situation. People generally don't know anything about the background of their interactants, regarding the culture of origin, their interests, or previous knowledge. Context collapse (Boyd 2011; Marwick and Boyd 2011; Androutsopoulos 2014) is a term that describes the case where linguistic and cultural backgrounds collide in an interactive situation online. Discussants may come from different backgrounds and bring very different expectations into the discussion, including "different expectations as to what is appropriate" (Boyd 2011: 30). The fact that the background is not shared and interests are not aligned is generally not addressed unless a challenging situation occurs. From a linguistic perspective, many global interactions resort to English as a Lingua Franca. Language choice and style cannot be taken for granted, however, and metalinguistic negotiations can be expected to occur, including explicit resistance against a particular language style, language policing, and overt references to cultural differences.

3.2 Adjacency/coherence

Bou-Franch, Lorenzo-Dus, and Garcés-Conejos Blitvich (2012) analyse turn management and cohesion in YouTube discussions. Like many other online discussions, YouTube discussions are not moderated, and they do not invite particular individuals, nor do they exclude them or limit the number of participants. While any number of participants can join or exit the conversation at any given time, it is never obvious who is actually following the conversation and will join with a comment. The active interactants are aware of the "distributed recipiency" (Bou-Franch, Lorenzo-Dus, and Garcés-Conejos Blitvich 2012: 503; see also Hutchby 2006). Comments appear chronologically, in real time. It is possible to reply to a comment, in which case a comment thread emerges, whose contributions are again chronological. The chronological appearance may not be consistent with the actual adjacency, i.e. with the turn relations intended by the contributors. Adjacency forms the basis for sequential organisation in interaction and contributes to coherence (Schegloff 1968, 1990). Coherence becomes more difficult to maintain as the number of participants increases. Comment threads can become very long and have hundreds of contributions. According to Bou-Franch, Lorenzo-Dus, and Garcés-Conejos Blitvich (2012: 504–506), "cross-turn addressivity", which means tagging a user name to select the intended addressee, is one of the turn management devices used in online interactions. If the intended addressee is marked by a tag (@) the online software sends a message to this person to inform them that they have been tagged.

Bou-Franch, Lorenzo-Dus, and Garcés-Conejos Blitvich (2012: 515–516) conclude that communication over the YouTube text-commenting facility is not incoherent. YouTube discussions are a space for online interaction rather than a series of disconnected comments. Coherence is created and maintained despite disrupted turn adjacency: linear sequencing may not be as relevant for coherence in some online contexts as it is in oral interaction. Another factor that distinguishes YouTube discussions from face-to-face interactions is that users of online discussion forums have access to a persistent textual record of the interaction, which means that any part of the interaction, even if it was written months ago, can be taken up and addressed in a new contribution at any time.

3.3 Stance

Du Bois (2007: 163) defines stance as follows:

> Stance is a public act by a social actor, achieved dialogically through overt communicative means, of simultaneously evaluating objects, positioning subjects (self and others), and aligning with other subjects, with respect to any salient dimension of the sociocultural field.

The expression of stance is a representation of a social actor's expression of evaluation or self-positioning towards objects of interest in the shared space. It is not a private and individual matter; rather, there is an intersubjective side to it, as other subjects will react to the expression of stance. From both the instigator of the stance expression and the addressee(s), there will be efforts towards an alignment of the stances. Stance is emergent, as it evolves in the intersubjective setting, where viewpoints and opinions of more than one person are present. The expression of stance is also a contributing factor in the assertion and procreation of shared sociocultural values.

> Stance always invokes, explicitly or implicitly, presupposed systems of sociocultural value, while at the same time contributing to the enactment and reproduction of those systems. (Du Bois 2007: 173)

An alignment is a response that calibrates the relationship between two stances. The alignment may be shown by stance markers like verbal expressions of agreement or disagreement, gestures to the same effect or other forms that index alignment. Both the expression of stance and the perceivable alignment efforts are therefore emergent common ground markers, because they contribute to the instigation and intersubjective settlement of new and interactionally shared approaches to a subject matter under discussion.

3.4 Uncommon ground / dark-side commitments

Uncommon ground is a term introduced by Macagno and Capone (2016). It addresses a circumstance where a set of assumptions is treated as shared in a communicative interaction, while it is not actually shared or mutually considered to be true. *Uncommon ground* means the unveiling of presuppositions, presumptions and commitments as *not shared* and therefore, contrary to common expectation, *not common ground.*

The approach is called *polyphonic* in the sense that more than one *voice* is at play. A speaker distinguishes themselves from a set of propositions accepted by others [i.e. the propositions held as common ground]. The voice representing that common ground is in conflict with the speaker's voice. Uncommon ground resembles presupposition suspension, and may therefore be marked by expressions like "in the first place", "actually", "though", "but", or quotation marks that signal that a speaker distances themselves from a particular expression or phrase. I am arguing here that these kinds of expressions are emergent common ground markers, because they mark the fact that alleged common ground turns out to be *not shared* or *not accepted* and requires an update. The emergent common ground markers mark the update, i.e. the thing that the speaker believes to be true in lieu of the alleged common ground, or they demarcate the fact that information updating the rejected common ground is to be expected, generally from the speaker challenging the alleged common ground. In order to reject a proposition that is treated as noncontroversial (the alleged common ground), a reason or argumentation is required (Macagno and Capone 2016: 161, see also Ducrot 1984: 179). The polyphonic approach is based on explicatures. The presuppositions 'hidden' in a given statement or expression are exposed and presented to the interlocutors for re-evaluation.

> The polyphonic approach based on explicatures shifts the analysis of the presuppositions from the epistemic objective level of truth to the dialogical one of commitment. A presupposition is not canceled (or suspended); rather, the use of the predicate triggering it can be contested. (Macagno and Capone 2016: 166)

For example, "stop" and "regret" are presuppositional triggers. If I assert that someone "stopped" doing something or "regrets" something, it always entails that I contend that the thing they gave up or regret has actually been done by them. Using speech acts of either silent acceptance or challenge of presupposed content, an actor in a communicative situation can either consolidate common ground or reject/recreate it (Macagno and Capone 2016: 167–168).

Commitments held by participants towards others or towards a topic are not necessarily "externalised" in terms of explicit concessions. Such "dark-side commitments" are defined by Walton (1993) and Walton and Krabbe (1995) as a participant's deeper or more fundamental commitments that they bring into the dialogue, but that may not be known to the other participants. Like that, the outcome of a dialogue can be determined by factors external to the explicitly shared knowledge that interactants have at the time they are engaging in the dialogue. Non-explicit (dark) commitments have to be inferred by presumption. Dark-side commitments can also be revealed by actions, for example if someone acts in a way that contradicts their alleged principles. In a dialogue, a critic can pull a commitment from the dark side of another participant by aligning it with other light side arguments of that participant. This can result in an *ad hominem* argument (Krabbe 1993: 94–99; Walton and Krabbe 1995: 181–186).

To summarise, the following terms are relevant for the distinction between common ground and uncommon ground. A presupposition is a fact (about the world, an interlocutor, the dialogue) that is taken for granted. "Presupposition is a proposal of common ground" (Kecskes and Zhang 2013: 376). A presumption entails that it is taken for granted that the interlocutor(s) know about a fact (regarding the world, the other interlocutor(s), the speaker, the dialogue) (Macagno 2012: 246–250). A commitment is a speaker's own contention that they bring into the dialogue, concerning a fact or a view. A commitment may not be explicit, but it may resonate in the speaker's actions and communications. Dark-side commitments (Walton and Krabbe 1995; Krabbe 1993) are implicit, non-overt commitments. They remain implicit unless they are revealed as a result of questioning and challenging.

Presupposition is one of the various ways in which common ground can be formed and updated. Efficiency of common ground constructions depends on their "attention-raising quality" that must be adjusted to the actual situational context. Hearers may ignore the available background information activated by a presupposition, and the information updated by an assertion (Kecskes and Zhang 2013: 389). If a proposition does not reach the interlocutor(s) for some reason, it is not part of common ground, as it is not mutually activated as relevant information in this conversation. We will see in the next sections that this is a phenomenon that happens in online discussions: People often do not pay attention to things that were discussed before, even though the thread is visible. As a consequence, they go on to treat some observation or insight as new even though it has been discussed in the same thread before.

Presumptions are effectively assumptions about existing common ground, but they can be challenged and updated if a contributant does not agree with details entailed by them. Such presumption modifications and updates are dialogically achieved and elaborately marked. They are considered as emergent common ground for this analysis. Also, any commitment that is newly shared and any dark-side commitment that is brought to light will be considered as emergent common ground for the remainder of the discussion.

4 Study: Emergent common ground in an online discussion thread in YouTube

In this section, I will outline the small empirical study I conducted with material from an online discussion thread in YouTube, in order to demonstrate the way emergent common ground shows up in an online discussion forum, and how it is dealt with by interactants. I will show that there are formal markers that make interactants aware that new, unexpected information is imminent. The new information may involve updates about a stance or stance alignment, about presumptions and commitments held by either of the participants, or adjustments and explanations about the cultural background. The information considered to be emergent common ground may also have to do with the organisation of coherence and adjacency in the long thread of comments, including direct marking of a specific addressee of a post. The material is a discussion thread under a YouTube clip.[1]

As has been pointed out in the introduction to this chapter, the objective of this study is to analyse material from an original online discussion that contains portions of core and emergent common ground, and markers of the latter. In order to account for the core common ground in a medium that brings together people who do not ostensively share any background knowledge prior to the discourse, I picked a video from the well established and popular platform YouTube, which provides an open and accessible comment section that is not moderated. I assumed that any comments under a given video would treat the contents of the video as core common ground, as the video can be assumed to be consumed by all participants before they post a comment. The video itself was chosen for its contents, which are culturally sensitive. The clip treats a cultural phenomenon that is foreign, but probably not completely unknown, to most (Western) addressees. The comment thread picked for this study includes the first reaction to the video (as visible at the time of observation) and a number of consecutive comments relating to this first reaction. The thread is basically a short controversial

1 This is the link to the video clip (last accessed 19 October 2021): https://www.youtube.com/watch?v=oFgWy2ifX5s

discussion of the initial statement and its wording in relation to the commonly experienced Covid19 lockdown, which is treated as another item of core common ground, because it was a globally shared situation.

In order to provide a thorough analysis of each of the posts including a categorisation with respect to core and emergent common ground and an identification of the mark-up for the latter, the number of posts analysed had to be restricted for space reasons. I am, however, also providing a discussion of a cluster of posts appearing 2 months after the initial thread and relating to one contribution made there.

The video is entitled *Japan's modern-day hermits: The world of Hikikomori.* It was published in YouTube on 18 January 2019, and was produced by France 24 English, which is a French public broadcast service presented in English.

Hikikomori are people of all ages in Japan, who self-isolate by choice and avoid any contact with the outside world. The behaviour has been described in relation with social anxiety and depression. In the video, the English speaking show host and his French interview partner describe aspects of the Hikikomori phenomenon as "shocking", and they assume a culturally distanced viewpoint towards the scenes shown in the video clip. The clip shows interviews with some Hikikomori and their relatives. One longish, rather disturbing scene shows the apartment of an elderly man, who deceased in isolation, being cleaned up by a firm who specialises in cleaning Hikikomori homes after their passing. The following background information about Hikikomori is presented:

The phenomenon Hikikomori was identified in the late 1990s. Japan's post-bubble economic problems affected mainly young people, who were the first ones to retract to an isolated life. Today, the Hikikomori phenomenon is not limited to people from any age, gender or social background. Most Hikikomori, however, are men.

In the video, the sociologist Teppei Sekimizu from Waseda University Tokyo is interviewed on the cultural background that lies behind the Hikikomori phenomenon. He shares some sociocultural insights, like the observation that European countries value the importance of the individual, while the Japanese culture emphasises common rules. In Japan, an individual's value is measured by their ability to conform to the rules. Hikikomori people find themselves unable to do that, and therefore, they feel ashamed and guilty and go into isolation from society.[2] It is pointed out that the social problem in Japan affects everyone, and that

2 This is a summary of Tekimizu's statement, shown with an English translation between minutes 9:50 and 10:20 in the video. Cf. https://www.hofstede-insights.com/country/japan/ for more information about Japan's characteristics of a collectivistic society. I thank Juliane Neumann for pointing out this link to me.

part of the problem is the deterioration of traditional structures, including the family as a resource for support.

Japan has characteristics of a collectivistic society. Gregg (2010: 229) points out that there are "profound psychological differences" between societies that raise children towards loyalty and subordination to parents and peers, and those that encourage their offspring to leave the home and become independent from their parents (see Cross and Gore 2013 for a discussion of these differences). These psychological differences, however, should not be understood to manifest as differences in selves in the sense that the individuals growing up in these kinds of societies can be characterised as "egocentric versus sociocentric" in accordance with the societal outlook. A modern approach to culture and self should acknowledge that individuals adopt features from their distributed cultural heritage selectively, and integrate them into their identity in ways that may be at odds with hegemonic cultural ideals. These processes can create "developmental discontinuities" and "interpersonal tension" (Gregg 2010: 230). See also Bachnik (1994), Rosenberger (1989), Quinn (1994), Shimizu (2001), and Kondo (1990) for an analysis of such processes in the Japanese society.

In the YouTube video, Hikikomori are introduced as a social problem, but also as an interest group who organises action teams to challenge society's obsession with productivity and competition, and who publishes the *Hikipos* magazine to address Hikikomori lifestyle. Towards the end of the broadcast, the show anchor asks his interviewee the obvious question if this kind of lifestyle phenomenon could emerge in the West, and the French interview partner confirms this by saying, yes, it could happen in France as well. This last statement may act as an invitation for Western viewers to reconsider their own lifestyle choices, and it may be the information that triggered the remark by "Alex Radek" that was the first one to appear under the video when I first viewed the material on 23 May 2020. "Alex Radek" has since changed his name to "Mr. Slowpoke". His statement appears as *posted 2 months ago* on 23 May 2020, which dates its original publication to March 2020.

The statement reads "Everyone is a Hikikomori worldwide now". *Now* refers to the globally shared real life situation at the time, which is isolation due to Covid-19-related lockdowns that applied around the world in spring 2020. On 23 May 2020, this statement had 22 replies. On 1 March 2021, I viewed the comment thread again, which had now 41 replies.[3] Parts of the comment thread as it appeared on 1 March 2021 are repeated and analysed here. I will go through the first nine posts

3 The records of these two versions of the thread are available from the author on request.

including the initial statement by “Mr. Slowpoke” and his own replies to others’ statements. After these first nine posts, the original statement gets repeated in variations, initiating more reactions, and time and again, the discussion exhausts itself in more or less nonsensical remarks. However, in some of the later replies, parts of the initial discussion are taken up again. In order to demonstrate an example of how the longevity of comment threads leads to recurrent discussion and facilitates late responses to particular posts, I will discuss a set of posts that appeared 2 months after the first cluster of posts, referring to a statement posted in that first cluster.

The analysis is based on the following questions:

1. Can portions of core and emergent common ground be identified in an online discussion thread?
2. How are these portions identified? Specifically, are there recurrent markers signalling emergent common ground?
3. Can it be confirmed that the portions of emergent common ground found in this material are explainable in terms of the sources of emergent common ground in online interaction, as they were discussed in Section 3?

The analysis of the original material from the YouTube discussion thread is visualised here in the form of a table with four columns. The original individual posts are replicated in individual cells with formal markup for the categories that are relevant for the analysis. The tables have separate columns that explain the categorisation for each cell. Further background information is provided in an additional column. In the columns, we find the following content.

Tables with four columns:

1. Poster nickname and the amount of time passed since the post (material viewed on 1 March 2021).
2. Post in its original wording with markup. Misspellings, use of punctuation and slurs will be represented as they appeared.
3. Classification of core and emergent common ground in the post.
4. Background information on the contents.

Table 1 shows the first part of the discussion thread initiated by Mr. Slowpoke. This first part includes the first nine turns of the conversation that were time-stamped “11 months ago” on 1 March 2021. The last part shown in Table 2 appeared nine months before March 1. It takes up the discussion two months later.

The markup for the analysis identifies portions of core and emergent common ground in the posts. It also identifies portions of text that act as formal demarcations for emergent common ground. The markup is visualised in the second column of each table as follows:

- *Sections of core common ground are in italics.*
- **Emergent common ground appears in bold print.**
- Markers of emergent common ground are underlined.

This thread, initiated by a user who calls himself “Mr. Slowpoke”, contains a lively discussion about Mr. Slowpoke’s initial statement “Everyone is a Hikikomori worldwide now”. This statement summarises a stance that is driven by the Covid experience of lockdown and isolation, and that is potentially not meant in earnest. Other users chime in, and while some applaud Mr. Slowpoke and post variations of his statement (see especially the post by Celz On in Table 1), others challenge this view, maintaining that deliberate isolation should not be confused with forced isolation. For the common ground hinted at in this thread, the shared background can be easily identified as the Covid-related lockdown situation, that affected people globally at the time the thread was written. Other important insights into the background of many sentiments and expressions found here have been obtained through years of observing online interactions (Diedrichsen 2020). The creation and discussion of internet memes, for example, often purports the idea that being a ‘responsible adult’ is an aspiration, but most online-active male youth nowadays feel that they are failing it, acting like Hikikomori themselves, which is probably why the video resonates with them.

In this entire thread, nobody really empathises with the situation of Hikikomori in Japan. Rather, the presumption (presumption 1 in Table 1) shared throughout the largest part of the interaction is that the lives of Hikikomori and withdrawn Western males are comparable. A second presumption, that is initiated by the statement in the first post already, is that Hikikomori lifestyle can be compared to the isolation that is inflicted on everyone due to Covid. Two months after the initial part of the comment thread appeared, a new quarrel ensues about the statement from the user Celz On “nowadays hikikomori means responsible adults. oh the irony”. A user directly addresses Celz On (by tagging) with an attack for their statement concerning the ironic conflation of Hikikomori and “responsible adults”. This last set of posts presented here stems from an author who is most probably Japanese, judging by their name and its spelling in Japanese characters, and also judging by the content. In this contribution, presumption 1 is finally suspended, and the cultural appropriation that is part of this presumption is challenged. The course of the interaction is represented and analysed in Tables 1 and 2.

Table 1: First part of discussion thread, initiated by Mr. Slowpoke.

User nickname (posts marked 11 months ago)	Post content	Classification of core / emergent common ground	Background information, remarks
Mr. Slowpoke	**Everyone is a hikikomori worldwide** *now.*	*Core common ground: now*: makes reference to shared real world situation: Covid, lockdown, experience of loneliness and seclusion **Emergent common ground**: The Hikikomori experience is a shared one, it is the same for everyone (controversial, potentially not meant in earnest)	
metfreak100	I was just thinking about that *now*!!!!	Core common ground: *now*: makes reference to shared real world situation	
Celz On	*nowadays* **hikikomori means responsible adults**. oh the irony	*Core common ground: nowadays*: makes reference to shared real world situation. Presumption 1 (Macagno 2012): The life situations of Hikikomori and withdrawn Western males are comparable Presumption 2 (based on initial post): Hikikomori lifestyle and Covid-related isolation are the same thing. Emergent Common Ground marker: There is irony in the statement, i.e. the author's stance is that Hikikomori lifestyle is contrary to responsible adulthood.	Dark-side commitment (Walton 1993; Walton and Krabbe 1995), based on presumption 1: A responsible adult does not isolate themselves, unless they are forced by Covid, then they do what is required. Background: The idealised notion of a "responsible adult" is a common topic in internet memes: Many internet users live a lonely and withdrawn life and feel guilty for not acting "adult" enough. For these lonely males, being a "responsible adult" who has a family and a social life is the goal,

Table 1 (continued)

User nickname (posts marked 11 months ago)	Post content	Classification of core / emergent common ground	Background information, remarks
		Emergent common ground: Hikikomori lifestyle of isolation is usually the opposite of responsible, grown-up behaviour, but in the current pandemic related lockdown situation it makes one a responsible adult. The author's stance on this is that it is *ironic*, which suspends presumption 2.	a utopian idea. The "irony" is that lonely Western males feel that their own Hikikomori-like lifestyle makes them "responsible adults" in Covid-times, where isolation is required.
Jlex	Disagree with you. **We choose to isolate,** whereas people are *now* being **forced** to. I've been isolated from society and people for nearly my entire life.	*Core common ground: now*: makes reference to shared real world situation Emergent common ground marker: Expression of disagreement that prepares the information update. **Emergent common ground:** Challenging presumption 2 from the previous post and accordingly shattering the hopes hidden in the dark-side commitment: 1. Hikikomori lifestyle and Covid-related isolation are **not** the same thing. 2. Isolating by choice does **not** give you the aspired "responsible adult" status	The author adds a confession that they have been living a life of isolation by choice. By using the pronoun *we*, the author silently identifies their own lifestyle with the one of Hikikomori, which is a dark-side commitment. Presumption 1 is purported, while presumption 2 is challenged. This author completely ignores the expression of irony in the previous statement and therefore fails to acknowledge that presumption 2 "Hikikomori lifestyle and Covid-related isolation are the same thing" has been suspended there already.

Table 1 (continued)

User nickname (posts marked 11 months ago)	Post content	Classification of core / emergent common ground	Background information, remarks
antisocial otaku	**We are simply low-status males,** stop coping being hikikomori is not a choice but **a consequence of being rejected by society**	Emergent common ground markers: *stop* directive, *not. . .but* **Emergent common ground:** New aspect: Hikikomori lifestyle is not a choice, therefore the people are not responsible, rather: **society is to blame**	
Mr. Slowpoke	**Kaku hido** I understand that. But **you can't blame society for your own short comings.** I know this is going to sound all Tony Robbins but **you can always change and better yourself. Society isn't the one holding you back.**	Emergent common ground markers: Maxim of Politeness (Leech 1983: 138): Partial agreement, empathy is expressed as part of a politeness strategy; cognitive disclaimer (Hewitt and Stokes 1975): Both are preventive facework expressions (Guerrero et al. 2018: 95, Cupach and Metts 1994) preceding *but*, which acts as a preparation for a conflicting statement **Emergent common ground:** Addressing phrase (potentially offensive), author challenges addressee to take charge of themselves instead of blaming society	*Kaku hido* is a term for men who believe that they are unpopular with women. *Tony Robbins*: US-American philanthropist, coach for self-help and positive thinking. Stance declaration: 1. People are generally responsible for their own life. 2. Society has no impact on people's quality of life Conflicting Stance: Author states that addressee's coping difficulties are his "own short comings", i.e. flaws that can be conquered with some effort. This is addressee's own responsibility and nobody else's fault

Table 1 (continued)

User nickname (posts marked 11 months ago)	Post content	Classification of core / emergent common ground	Background information, remarks
antisocial otaku	shut up You are free to change your own nature to fit in society but you can not blame me **for being proud of myself** and not doing the same thing Unfortunately people like you are the majority, if you can not fit in society.. simple, change yourself bro Finally, changing his own nature to fit in this society does not mean improving, **often the best people are socially outcast in this pointless world**	Emergent common ground markers: Rude directive *shut up* Acknowledging addressee's stance, counter *but you can not. . .* *Ad hominem* (Walton 1993): *Unfortunately people like you. . .* Marker for stance misalignment: Mocking Mr. S. By rephrasing his opinion ironically: *simple, bro* *Does not mean* (rejecting Mr. S's position) **Emergent Common ground:** Formulating a contradicting stance of his own, claiming that: 1. Author is pround of himself for not fitting in 2. The best people are social outcasts 3. The world is pointless	Antisocial otaku's stance commitment: Society works contrary to people's nature, so it is an achievement to stick to your own nature, in this case: isolate from society. The rephrased quote of Mr. S's statement is ironic because antisocial otaku's own commitment is that fitting in with society's demands is not "simple", but requires 'changing his own nature to fit in society' which means working against one's own personal habits and traits constantly, which would be a betrayal of one's own personality and would not make one a better person ('does not mean improving').
Mr. Slowpoke	kaku hido Hahaha! No, you shut up. Hahaha, no you first. Lol	Emergent common ground markers: Giving back the rude directive to shut up, otherwise mockery of antisocial otaku's rude manner **Emergent common ground:** Refusing the quarrel, checking out	After the face threat received through antisocial otaku's ad hominem attack, Mr. Slowpoke employs corrective facework in terms of aggressive humour (mockery) and the avoidance of further interaction (Guerrero et al. 2018: 95). He is refusing the quarrel (Walton 1993), and checking out of the conversation

Table 1 (continued)

User nickname (posts marked 11 months ago)	Post content	Classification of core / emergent common ground	Background information, remarks
Lvl. 99 Red Chocobo	Hikomoris are *now* **isolation guru the rest of us are trying to imitate.**	*Core common ground: now*: makes reference to the shared real world situation **Emergent Common Ground:** Another take on the idea that being a Hikikomori is comparable with isolating oneself because of Covid (Presumption 2)	It has been discussed in the previous posts that Covid isolation and Hikikomori life are not comparable. This post still treats this as a new insight. This shows that the emergent common ground from previous posts does not reach all participants, even though the thread is fully visible to people who enter the conversation later.

Table 2: Later part of the discussion thread (2 months after thread was initiated).

User nickname (posts marked 9 months ago)	Post content	Classification of core / emergent common ground	Background information, remarks
春人伊藤 **(Haruto Ito)**	@Celz On No it doesn't **all hikikomori are NEET** look it up idiot foreigner.	Emergent common ground markers: actual addressee is tagged (contrary to sequence of posts), negation of addressee's stance expressed in the statement from two months ago (statement is not repeated), directive to look the information up, *ad hominem: idiot foreigner* carries a stance driven by a dark-side commitment.	The post this responds to is NOT the preceding post; the actual addressee is tagged. NEET: Not in education, employment or training. [statement is not factually true, as many Hikikomori work from home.] Dark-side commitment/ stance hinted at in slur: Foreigners (to Japan) should not talk about Hikikomori, as they are culturally foreign to them.

Table 2 (continued)

User nickname (posts marked 9 months ago)	Post content	Classification of core / emergent common ground	Background information, remarks
		Emergent Common Ground: Hikikomori cannot be responsible adults, because they are NEET.	This is a situation where a *context collapse* becomes obvious: A user observes people making remarks about a cultural phenomenon known in Japan, and criticises the way they conflate their own life situation with the Japanese Hikikomori.
春人伊藤 **(Haruto Ito)**	**Only Japanese people are hikikomori** you are not a native Japanese person and were not born and raised in Japan so **you do not understand the problem.**	Emergent common ground markers: Assessing addressee's expertise and concluding (by deductive reasoning) that the addressee does not have the required expertise to comment on the topic. **Emergent common ground:** Isolated people around the world do not compare to Hikikomori, as these only appear in Japan and its particular culture. This statement is emergent common ground, as it suspends presumption 1, which has been held by all other participants throughout this thread.	Author uses deductive reasoning to resolve the dark-side commitment from their previous post: 1. Only Japanese people are Hikikomori 2. Addressee was not born and raised in Japan 3. Therefore, addressee does not understand "the problem" [this reveals another dark-side commitment: Hikikomori are/have a problem]

5 Discussion

The phenomena core and emergent common ground have been analysed in an online discussion thread found in YouTube, under a video on Hikikomori lifestyle, broadcast in English and aimed at European viewers. The classification in terms of core and emergent common ground is facilitated by the fact that the situation that is frequently referred to here (Covid isolation) can indeed be assumed to be shared globally. Other background information, like the shared sentiment that lies behind the use of the term "responsible adult" has been gained from regular insight into internet memes, the interactions accompanying them, and publications on internet memes and online interaction. Generally, references to common ground are relatively scarce in this sort of text. The discussion deviates from what one would generally expect to happen in such a forum. It seems that in the thread analysed here, the participants did not feel compelled to talk about the contents of the video and their feelings about it. There is no reference to anything shown in the video, other than the term *Hikikomori* itself. The cultural backdrop against which Hikikomori are introduced in the video is completely ignored throughout most of the discussion shown here. Therefore, out of the two possible sources of core common ground, which is the shared global situation, on the one hand, and the contents of the video, on the other hand, only the first one actually applies.

In the analysed versions of the original posts shown in Tables 1 and 2, the categories relevant for the analysis are marked up for identification. They comprise core common ground, emergent common ground, and markers of emergent common ground. Part of the working hypothesis was the suggestion that like core common ground, emergent common ground gets *grounded,* by which is meant that formal markers are used to make the interlocutors aware of mismatches or misalignment in common ground and to give them a heads-up, so to say, that new and/or unexpected information is coming.

The following markers of emergent common ground have been found in this analysis:

1. **Negation** appears in the form of lexemes and particles: *it is not, don't, I don't agree*: Negation with respect to previously posted content can signal a common ground or stance misalignment and prepare for a new stance declaration or information update.
2. **Disclaimers:** Expression of consideration for the addressee's stance: *I know this sounds like.* Disclaimers are preventive facework expressions (Guerrero, Andersen, and Afifi 2018: 95). They are used to prepare addressees for an uncomfortable opinion or fact.
3. **But** following an acknowledgement of the addressee's stance or a disclaimer, mostly followed by a counter argument: *But* acts as a preparation for a conflicting utterance.
4. **Directives** appear in the material when the debate gets heated; they address another user directly and tell them to stop talking or to inform themselves. These directives signal a common ground or stance misalignment and prepare for a new stance declaration or information update.

5. **Rude addresses, ad hominem attacks, slurs** are a strong signal of stance misalignment and prepare for a new stance declaration.
6. **Statements and evaluations of expertise,** which may involve the denial of the addressee's expertise and claims to one's own expertise, are frequently found in online discussions. They function as a signal that a statement is to be expected that is in opposition to something posted by the addressee.
7. **Adjacency markers**: These are markers that facilitate the turn organisation and the recognisability of adjacency and coherence in an online conversation. The posts responding to a video or to a previous post show up in the order in which they were posted, such that a discussion with a number of responses will not formally stand out unless the addressee of a contribution is actively marked or tagged in order to signal which post an author refers to with their comment. The tag with an @ serves not only as a visible marker, but also initiates an alert to the user that they have been tagged in a conversation.
8. **Mockery** signals a stance misalignment, and it can be a response to a face threat. It can prepare the interlocutors for a new stance declaration, or mean that a user wants to end the discussion.
9. **Irony** also signals a stance misalignment, and indicates that the users' stance is in opposition to the stance or the fact expressed.
10. **Meta-comments** can express a common ground or stance misalignment regarding somebody else's utterance or an issue stated in a user's own contribution (*oh the irony, stop coping*). They can prepare the readers for a new stance declaration or an information update.

Mockery, irony and meta-comments can act as general distance markers or signals for updates in a participant's role intentions. A user might for example use these as an exit strategy to check out of the conversation.

For the appearance of emergent common ground, four aspects have been suggested to be relevant; these have been explained in Section 3. These general aspects are incidences in communication that will naturally lead to the appearance of emergent common ground. They have been formulated and explained with respect to the challenges of online conversation in particular, but they apply to any kind of communication. This list is not considered to be exhaustive, either in online or offline conversation. In the material, I have identified a fifth aspect that was not suggested earlier. It is noted under E.

A. **Collapsing contexts:** The lack of a priori sociocultural calibration among participants may lead to conflict, which requires active resolution.
B. **Adjacency and coherence** have to be marked explicitly in online communication; confusion may ensue if this is not done.

C. **Stance and its alignment** are a source of emergent common ground, and certainly a source of conflict.
D. **Uncommon ground including presuppositions, presumptions and dark-side commitments** are a source of emergent common ground if they are challenged and/or suspended by interactants. They may be a source of conflict, as well.
E. **Updates on participant role intentions:** This is emergent common ground regarding the intentions a user may express with respect to their own identification and their role in the interaction. A user may make visible efforts to identify themselves or change their participation status. This might entail checking out of the conversation, or ending the discussion.

In the socio-cognitive approach, it is emphasised that natural human communication does not only work on the basis of cooperation, but that there is also egocentrism involved. I have pointed out earlier in this chapter that online discussions in particular exhibit large degrees of egocentrism, because the communication is fast-paced and anonymous, so people cannot be made accountable for their postings. They generally do not know their interactants personally, nor do they take the trouble to find out more about them before they engage with them. In online discussions, we find much idiosyncratic expression of affect and personal opinion. Judging from the material used for this analysis, interactants do not make any effort to check if they are heard and understood. They never ask for feedback on any information or opinion they post. Generally, interactants do not seem to consider if the content of their own post is relevant and takes into account the full information received previously, including the contents of the video, and other people's previous contributions. For example, the idea that Hikikomori isolation and Covid isolation are basically the same thing is presented as a new insight at several points in the discussion thread (only one of these posts is shown here), even though it has been discussed at length and explicitly rejected before.

Despite some very pessimistic takes on online communication discussed earlier, it can be concluded on the basis of the material used for this analysis that there is also a certain degree of cooperation involved in the contributions of the forum discussants. People make the effort to mark coherence and adjacency through tags, to make sure their post is understood as a response to a particular user's previous post. People also use emergent common ground markers to prepare others for unexpected information: Individual takes on a matter or updates in stance and information are not merely blurted out, but properly signified by formal markers that precede the new information. The markers themselves do not always have a cooperative outlook; they show more or less politeness and respect for the other's opinion.

However, even if one concedes that a slur or a rude directive is an example for cooperation, in that it signifies misalignment and prepares for an opposing opinion, there is egocentrism in the way that interactants in this discussion thread address the culturally specific phenomenon of Hikikomori lifestyle, that is mostly foreign to them, but thoroughly explained and discussed in the video material presented. The entire reasoning in the part of the thread analysed here is based on two presumptions shared by Western youths, which are noted as "Presumption 1" and "Presumption 2" in Table 1:

Presumption 1 involves the idea that *the life situations of Hikikomori and withdrawn Western males are comparable.* This presumption seems to be accepted as common ground throughout the interaction. It is not challenged for a long time.

Presumption 2 contains presumption 1, as it is always entailed that Hikikomori lifestyle resembles withdrawn Westerners' lifestyle. Presumption 2 holds that *Hikikomori lifestyle and Covid-related isolation are the same thing.* This presumption is challenged several times, but it is brought up again repeatedly.

The reasoning behind both of these presumptions fails to take into account the cultural, historical and serious mental health implications behind the Hikikomori phenomenon, even though the video has offered information on those aspects. For intercultural pragmatics, this observation is relevant, because it provides us with insights into the ways many people deal with information that concerns cultural phenomena foreign to their own reality. One would assume that people would consume information from other cultures as information updates to their previous knowledge, and also discuss it as such. What we see here, however, is that the people engaging in this thread take the information from another culture and reframe it to fit their own life situation. This may be seen as a case of cultural appropriation, which is what I would suggest, given that the users do not seem to engage with or try to make sense of the background information that is presented to them. As an anonymous reviewer points out, it could also be argued that the interactants in this thread are affected by cognitive dissonance, as the cultural phenomenon discussed in the video is hard to come to terms with against the background of their own culture. However, it is obvious that the people interacting here use the term 'Hikikomori' freely without any visible attempt to understand or to discuss what is actually the cultural background of this phenomenon. Only one discussant, whose posts are shown in Table 2, represents the Japanese perspective, and he seems to be enraged at the lack of insight owned by the other discussants with respect to Hikikomori life and its background.

It has been found that the categorisation and terminology introduced in the socio-cognitive approach is useful for gaining insights into the way foreign cultural phenomena are taken on in an unsupervised, informal online discussion. A number of online interactants' behaviours may seem disappointing from a viewpoint that considers the observance of cooperation principles and the orientation at common ground to be good conduct in conversation. The socio-cognitive approach, however, maintains that core and emergent common ground coexist in natural conversation. They characterise the interplay of cooperation efforts and instances of egocentrism, and the interactive generation and adaptation of new insights that make communicative interaction a highly dynamic activity.

Therefore, while this analysis has only covered a tiny sample of the vast amount of online conversation happening every day, it has showcased sources of emergent common ground that are well known from online and offline communication research, and that have been explained in Section 3. It has also demonstrated that some of the typical behaviours associated with online communication can be identified as markers that signify the appearance of emergent common ground. The reference to the global pandemic has helped to identify portions of core common ground, as well. The intercultural aspect of this piece of conversation has brought out important insights regarding egocentric behaviour with respect to information received: Not only do people feel free to engage with others whose backgrounds are unknown to them, which means that they are effectively holding a conversation mostly devoid of core common ground. They also dismiss core common ground that is actually and arguably available to them, including participants' input available from the thread, and information about the Japanese cultural phenomenon Hikikomori, that is aptly explained in the video. Instead of integrating that available information into their own thoughts and contributions about the matter, they choose to consider, evaluate and discuss the information about Hikikomori only on the basis of their own socio-cultural experience gained in their own home country. It appears therefore that egocentric behaviour that is shared as an attitude acts as a priori available common ground in the form of presumptions, and it overwrites the actually available information that is plain to see for all interactants, but not taken into account for the conversation.

References

Androutsopoulos, Jannis. 2014. Languaging when contexts collapse: Audience design in social networking. *Discourse, Context and Media* 4–5. 62–73.

Bachnik, Jane. 1994. Self, social order and language. In Jane Bachnik and Charles Quinn, Jr. (eds.), *Situated Meaning*, 3–37. Princeton, New Jersey: Princeton University Press.

Barr, Dale J. and Boaz Keysar. 2005. Making sense of how we make sense: The paradox of egocentrism in language use. In Herbert L. Colston and Albert N. Katz (eds.), *Figurative language comprehension: Social and cultural influences*, 21–42. New Jersey: Erlbaum.

Bou-Franch, Patricia, Lorenzo-Dus, Nuria, and Garcés-Conejos Blitvich, Pilar. 2012. Social interaction in YouTube text-based polylogues: A study of coherence. *Journal of computer-mediated communication* 17. 501–521.

Boyd, Danah. 2011. Social network sites as networked publics: affordances, dynamics, and implications. In Zizi A. Papacharissi (ed.), *A Networked Self. Identity, Community, and Culture on Social Network Sites*, 39–58. New York/London: Routledge.

Clark, Eve V. 2015. Common Ground. In *The Handbook of Language Emergence*, Brian MacWhinney, and William O'Grady (eds.), 328–353. Oxford: Wiley and Sons.

Clark, Herbert H. 1996. *Using language.* Cambridge: Cambridge University Press.

Clark, Herbert H. and Catherine R. Marshall. 1981. Definite Reference and Mutual Knowledge. In Aravind K. Joshi, Bonnie L. Webber, and Ivan A. Sag (eds.), *Elements of Discourse Understanding*, 10–63. Cambridge: Cambridge University Press.

Colston, Herbert L. 2008. A new look at common ground: Memory, egocentrism, and joint meaning. In Istvan Kecskes and Jacob L. Mey (eds.), *Intention, common ground and the egocentric speaker-hearer*, 151–187. Berlin, New York: Mouton De Gruyter.

Cross, Susan and Jonathan Gore. 2013. Cultural models of self. In Mark L. Leary and June P. Tangney (eds.), *Handbook of Self and Identity*, 2nd edn., 587–614. New York: Guilford.

Cupach, William R. And Sandra Metts. 1994. *Facework.* Thousand Oaks, CA: Sage.

Diedrichsen, Elke. 2020. On the interaction of core and emergent common ground in internet memes. *Internet Pragmatics* 3 (2). 223–259.

Du Bois, John W. 2007. The stance triangle. In Englebretson, Robert (ed.), *Stancetaking in discourse*, 139–182. Amsterdam/Philadelphia: Benjamins.

Ducrot, Oswald. 1984. *Le dire et le dit.* Paris: Minuit.

Enfield, Nicholas J. 2008. Common ground as a resource for social affiliation. In Istvan Kecskes and Jacob Mey (eds.), *Intention, common ground and the egocentric speaker-hearer*, 223–254. Berlin/New York: Mouton De Gruyter.

Fetzer, Anita (ed.). 2013. *The Pragmatics of Political Discourse: Explorations across Cultures.* Amsterdam and Philadelphia: John Benjamins.

Fetzer, Anita and Fischer, Kerstin (eds.). 2007. *Lexical markers of common ground.* Oxford/Amsterdam: Elsevier.

Gibbs, Raymond W. Jr., and Herbert L. Colston. 2019. The emergence of common ground. In Rachel Giora and Michael Haugh (eds.), *Doing pragmatics interculturally. Cognitive, philosophical, and sociopragmatic perspectives*, 13–29. Berlin/Boston: Mouton De Gruyter.

Gregg, Gary. 2010. Culture and self. In John R. Hall, Laura Grindstaff and Ming-Cheng Lo (eds.), *Handbook of Cultural Sociology*, 223–232. London/New York: Routledge.

Grice, Herbert Paul. 1989. *Studies in the way of words.* Cambridge MA: Harvard University Press.

Guerrero, Laura K., Peter W. Andersen and Walid A. Afifi. 2018. *Close encounters. Communication in relationships.* 5th edn. Los Angeles et al.: Sage.

Hewitt, John P. and Randall Stokes. 1975. Disclaimers. *American Sociological Review* 40. 1–11.

Hutchby, Ian. 2006. *Media talk: Conversation analysis and the study of broadcasting.* Maidenhead: Open University Press.

Johansson, Marjut. 2017. Everyday opinions in news discussion forums: Public vernacular discourse. *Discourse, context and media* 19. 5–12.

Johansson, Marjut, Sonja Kleinke, and Lehti, Lotta. 2017. The digital agora of social media: Introduction. *Discourse, Context & Media* 19. 1–4.

Kecskes, Istvan. 2014. *Intercultural Pragmatics*. New York: Oxford University Press.
Kecskes, Istvan. 2019. The interplay of prior experience and actual situational context in intercultural first encounters. *Pragmatics & Cognition* 26(2). 112–134.
Kecskes, Istvan and Zhang, Fenghui. 2009. Activating, seeking and creating common ground: A socio-cognitive approach. *Pragmatics & Cognition* 17(2). 331–355.
Kecskes, Istvan and Zhang, Fenghui. 2013. On the dynamic relations between common ground and presupposition. In Alessandro Capone, Franco Lo Piparo and Marco Carpapezza (eds.), *Perspectives on linguistic pragmatics*, 375–395. Dordrecht: Springer.
Keysar, Boaz. 2008. Egocentric processes in communication and miscommunication. In Istvan Kecskes and Jacob L. Mey (eds.), *Intention, common ground and the egocentric speaker-hearer*, 277–296. Berlin, New York: Mouton De Gruyter.
Kondo, Dorinne. 1990. *Crafting Selves*. Chicago: University of Chicago Press.
Ladilova, Anna and Ulrike Schröder. 2022. Humor in intercultural interaction: A source for misunderstanding or a common ground builder? A multimodal analysis. *Intercultural Pragmatics* 19(1). 71–101.
Lambrecht, Knud. 1994. *Information structure and sentence form*. Cambridge: Cambridge University Press.
Leech, Geoffrey N. 1983. *Principles of Pragmatics*. London and New York: Longman.
Levinson, Stephen C. 2006. On the human 'Interaction Engine'. In Nicholas J. Enfield, and Stephen C. Levinson (eds.), *Roots of human sociality*, 39–69. Oxford: Berg Publishers.
Macagno, Fabrizio. 2012. Presumptive reasoning in interpretation. Implicatures and conflicts of presumptions. *Argumentation* 26(2). 233–265.
Macagno, Fabrizio and Capone, Alessandro. 2016. Uncommon ground. *Intercultural Pragmatics* 13(2). 151–180.
Marwick, Alice, and Danah Boyd. 2011 "I tweet honestly, I tweet passionately": Twitter users, context collapse, and the imagined audience. *New Media Society* 13. 96–113.
Papacharissi, Zizi A. 2010. *A private sphere. Democracy in a digital age*. New Jersey: Wiley.
Papacharissi, Zizi A. 2014. On networked publics and private spheres in social media. In Theresa M. Senft, and Jeremy Hunsinger (eds.), *The Social Media Handbook*, 109–119. London & New York: Routledge.
Papacharissi, Zizi A. 2015. *Affective publics. Sentiment, technology and politics*. Oxford: Oxford University Press.
Pittner, Karin. 2007. Common Ground in Interaction: The functions of medial *doch* in German. In Anita Fetzer and Kerstin Fischer (eds.), *Lexical markers of common ground*, 67–87. Oxford/ Amsterdam: Elsevier.
Quinn, Charles. 1994. Uchi/soto: Tip of a semiotic iceberg? In Jane Bachnik, and Charles Quinn (eds.), *Situated meanings*, 247–294. Princeton, New Jersey: Princeton University Press.
Rosenberger, Nancy. 1989. Dialectic balance in the polar model of self: The Japanese case. *Ethos* 17(1). 88–113.
Schegloff, Emanuel A. 1968. Sequencing in conversational openings. *American Anthropologist* 70. 1075–1095.
Schegloff, Emanuel A. 1990. On the organization of sequences as a source of "coherence" in talk-in-interaction. In Bruce Dorval (ed.), *Conversational organization and its development*, 51–77. Norwood, NJ: Ablex.
Shimizu, Hidetada. 2001. Beyond individualism and sociocentrism: An ontological analysis of the opposing elements in personal experiences of Japanese adolescents. In Hidetada

Shimizu, and Robert A. LeVine, (eds.), *Japanese Frames of Mind*, 205–227. Cambridge: Cambridge University Press.
Stalnaker, Robert C. 2002. Common ground. *Linguistics and Philosophy* 25. 701–721.
Tenbrink, Thora. 2007. Imposing common ground by using temporal connectives: The pragmatics of *before* and *after*. In Anita Fetzer and Kerstin Fischer (eds.), *Lexical markers of common ground*, 113–139. Oxford/Amsterdam: Elsevier.
Tomasello, Michael. 2008. *Origins of Human Communication*. Cambridge: Massachusetts Institute of Technology Press.
Walton, Douglas. 1993. Commitment, types of dialogue, and fallacies. *Informal logic* 14. 93–103.
Walton, Douglas and Krabbe, Erik. 1995. *Commitment in dialogue*. Albany: State University of New York Press.

Adriana Merino

Co-constructing emergent common ground: The role of the intercultural mediator

Abstract: This research addresses the question of how multilingual interactants interpret and use figurative (or non-literal) language (i.e., formulaic, idiomatic, and metaphoric expressions) in intercultural interactions. Drawing on the socio-cognitive approach to pragmatics (Kecskés 2006, 2008, 2009, 2010, 2014), and focusing on the co-construction of Common Ground (CG), the analysis seeks to explore and explain the reasons underlying misunderstandings, communication breakdowns, and pragmatic missteps among interlocutors when dealing with nonliteral language in intercultural spoken interactions. The datasets come from transcribed conversational exchanges that took place between native (NS) and non-native speakers (NNS), with different linguistic and cultural backgrounds, who were using Spanish as their language in common, or as a lingua franca (SLF). I analyze and characterize the role of the Intercultural Mediator (IM), in transient multi-party, intercultural encounters, and reconceptualize this figure as that interlocutor who contributes to establishing a match between the interactants' private/prior context, and the actual situational context. In doing so, the IM actively, and positively, contributes to the dynamic co-construction of meaning (Kecskés 2008), and the creation of emergent common ground (Kecskés 2014). The IM brings to light correlations between indicators of awareness of potential misunderstandings and figurative language processing. The findings also provide insight into pedagogic interventions for enhancing pragmatic awareness, intercultural social skills, and figurative language use in language learning.

1 Introduction

In today's world, intercultural encounters have become common, and, in some work and academic contexts it is normal for people of different origins, language, and cultures to interact with international interlocutors. Speakers often assume that their interlocutors think, behave, and perceive the world around them in the same way as they do, and of course, this can lead to misunderstandings and unintentional conflict situations, which often has negative effects and may even generate interpersonal conflicts (cf. House 1999; Kaur 2011b; Krippendorff 2009). The way people handle misunderstandings or misinterpretations, or even conflicts in conversations is influenced by individual characteristics, and socio-cultural

https://doi.org/10.1515/9783110766752-007

factors, which are based on who we are, where we come from, how we perceive the world around us, how we perceive others, how we think others perceive us, and what linguistic-communicative experiences we bring to the table when interacting with others (DeVito 2015). In intercultural encounters, misunderstandings (Jandt 2013; Oetzel 2009; Ladilova and Schröder 2022) are complex phenomena and have been explained by either cognitive or socio-cultural perspectives. In recent years, misunderstandings have been studied by new perspectives and theoretical approaches. Istvan Kecskés' Socio-Cognitive Approach to Pragmatics (SCA) integrates social and cognitive factors to explain such phenomenon. It is assumed that the root of the misunderstanding lies in egocentrism, which is both an intrinsic property of verbal communication and a mechanism of individual thought (Kecskés 2008). This is the perspective taken by the present study with which I attempt to explain how interactants establish Common Ground, and how the Intercultural Mediator (IM) emerges in the conversation to mediate the interplay of the interlocutors' prior experience and actual situational contexts, where there is a deficiency in understanding, a pragmatic misstep, or a misunderstanding, especially when dealing with non-literal language. Such a figure, the Intercultural Mediator (IM), which has been previously used in multiple disciplines, will be redefined in the light of this new perspective.

2 Theoretical foundations

This research adopts the notions of core common ground (CG) and emergent Common Ground (ECG), proposed by Kecskés and Zhang (2009) within the framework of the socio-cognitive approach (SCA) in pragmatics, whereby context plays a crucial role in the process of utterance interpretation and production (i.e., meaning construction) by bridging the gap between linguistic meaning and the speaker-hearer's intended meaning. Context is assumed to be "a dynamic construct that appears in different formats in language use both as a repository and/ or trigger of knowledge" (Kecskés 2008). In Kecskés' view, context has both a selective and a constitutive role. In his theory of meaning, Kecskés (2008) argues that the meaning values of words that encode prior contexts of experience are paramount, and their role in meaning construction is as important as the role of situational context, that is, an utterance used in a specific dialogue or discourse. Sociocultural conceptual aspects represent the preferred way of using language within a social and cultural speech community and are present in the conceptual base (Kecskés 2008). According to Kecskés, when people have common or similar prior experiences or contexts, and they have a similar understanding of the actual situational context, they easily build common ground. The main problem with intercultural communication is that interactants have very little common ground (Kecskés 2013).

Core common ground stems from the speaker and hearer's shared knowledge of a previous experience, and emergent common ground arises from the interlocutors' individual knowledge of a previous or current experience. According to Kecskés and Zhang (2009), core common ground consists of systemic knowledge (i.e., knowledge of the language system, or formal sense); world knowledge (or common sense); and knowledge of culture-specific norms, beliefs, and values (or culture sense). Emergent CG is of particular interest to intercultural pragmatics since it is the process of co-construction of common understanding through the interaction of the interlocutors, in their dual role of Speaker-Hearer in a dialectical and sociocultural relationship.

Thus, Kecskés' socio-cognitive approach (SCA) (Kecskés 2009), which recognizes the role of prior experience and actual situational contexts in speakers' linguistic choices accounts for the conversation's situational setting, as well as the interlocutors' common knowledge, individual assumptions, beliefs, culture-specific pragmatic uses and conventional patterns of conversation. Unlike those conversation interactants coming from a relatively similar socio-cultural background who tend to share a high core common ground, intercultural interlocutors in transient encounters only form a temporary speech community (and low core CG), where the prior context represents the "coded" private knowledge based on individual experience (Kecskés and Zhang 2009). By contrast, the emergent situational context represents the cooperative or joint effort of the intercultural interactants to co-create a temporary speaking community. Oftentimes, intercultural hearers and speakers use their individual resources instead of their pre-existing formulas and frameworks tied to the previous context (previous experience linked to the L1 as well as to the target language) to co-construct both the language and conceptual frameworks in the emerging situational context during the process of communication. To illustrate this point, let us examine the following exchange between a Spanish speaker (S1) and an American English speaker (S2), discussing in their common language (English), a student's performance in class.

Excerpt 1

1.	S1: (L1: Spanish)	How's Mary doing (in class)?
2.	S2: (L1: English)	She's an ambitious student.
3.	S1: (L1: Spanish)	Oh! Really? I am so sorry to hear that.
4.	S2: (L1: English)	Why? I think this is amazing! She knows what she wants.

It is obvious that the word "ambitious" has a different meaning value for both speakers: a positive and a negative one, resulting in a mismatch between the speaker's intention and the hearer's interpretation. In Spanish, "*ambicioso*" has a general sense of material ambition, more akin to the idea of acquisitiveness or greed. A person who is "*ambiciosa*" is someone who wants a better car, a bigger house, a better-paid job, and more material possessions. Therefore, in many people's minds, the word has a negative connotation. This materialistic element is also included in the English idea of "ambitious", but more generally, in the English-speaking world, to be ambitious may be regarded as a positive quality – a desire to better oneself, to get somewhere in life, to be motivated and committed. Thus, there is a difference in how the American speaker uses the lexical item "ambitious" and how the Spanish speaker understands it. Though the core sense (i.e., the minimum set of features that we can assume to be shared by interlocutors) of "ambitious" can be described as follows: [having or showing a strong desire and determination to succeed], in intercultural communication, this word has a different culture-specific conceptual property for the native speaker and the nonnative speaker. This is the root of the misunderstanding of the above conversational exchange in Excerpt 1. The Spanish negative cultural load is transferred to the English word. In other words, the misunderstanding arises from differences in the speakers' private contexts or prior experience (familiarity with the word, frequency of exposure, etc.) with the same words, utterances, expressions, etc. The American speaker does not seem to understand the negative attitude of the Spanish speaker, and vice versa.

As we have just seen, finding Common Ground in intercultural settings may be complicated since the interlocutors do not share the same L1, and previous experiences (linguistically, pragmatically, or culturally). Their (individual) private contexts may differ partially or completely (Trbojević Milošević 2019). The application of the Dynamic Model of Meaning (DMM) proposed by Kecskés (2008, 2009, 2010, 2014), which acknowledges the dual role of speaker (S) and hearer (H) in establishing Common Ground (CG) and mutual understanding (Kecskés 2006, 2008, 2009, 2010, 2014), can especially be helpful to explain intercultural communicative situations like the one described in Excerpt 1, since this pragmatic speaker-listener model constructs meaning by bringing together the private inner context and the external situational context (the cognitive and the social), and explains cultural variability and the reasons underlying misunderstandings, and communication breakdowns in intercultural spoken interactions.

2.1 The intercultural mediator (IM)

The concept of mediation has been used across disciplines, mainly in the fields of translation/interpretation, and second language teaching and learning. Only recently has the term been applied to intercultural communication. In these diverse fields, cultural mediation has been broadly outlined as a bridge between two parties, thus favoring the mutual knowledge of cultures, values, pragmatic norms, and socio-cultural systems, in a perspective of exchange, social integration, and mutual understanding.

In the field of translation/ interpretation, the intercultural mediator has often been characterized as someone external to the speech event, usually as the authoritative voice who can act as a problem-solver, or conflict settler. In community interpretation, for instance, this role is preassigned among other participants in the spoken interactions. The job of the translator/ interpreter implies a process of meaning-making, and of re-establishing/ reconstructing meanings in different cultures and interpretive frames (Liddicoat 2016), bringing together complex linguistic and extralinguistic realities in the processes of construction of meanings (Hatim and Mason 1990). Liddicoat (2016) argues that mediation, as an act of interpretation, is not only an interpersonal activity in which meanings are rearticulated into another language for another audience, but it is also an intrapersonal activity, as translators make sense of meanings for themselves (Liddicoat 2016). In other words, translators mediate for themselves as well as for others, and these two processes together are central to the act of translating. According to Liddicoat (2016), mediation for others in intercultural communication is called for when there is some problem in interpretation, and a person external to the problem intervenes to assist in resolving it. Mediation for self involves a process of reflection through which a participant seeks to resolve a problem that s/he identifies in trying to interpret the messages of others. This view of mediation can be seen as an intermediary adopting a position between people with different languages and cultures to work on meaning-making and interpretation. If there is a conflict, the intermediary stands between two (or more) different ways of understanding a particular utterance and acts as a third party to re-express or re-language the meanings of others (Katan 1999, 2004; Pöchhacker 2008; Liddicoat 2016; Van Olmen and Tantucci 2022).

Similarly, the notion of the mediator as an intermediary positioned between participants in communication is also relevant to the field of teaching second and foreign languages, where teachers can be seen as mediating between the linguistic and cultural worlds of their learners and the societies about which they are learning (Kearney 2015; Keating Marshall and Bokhorst-Heng 2018). Byram (1988, 2002) and Barrett et al. (2013) define the concept of intercultural speaker as a mediator within the framework of the Intercultural Communicative Competence (ICC) to form an open-minded intercultural speaker (Byram et al. 2002: 5) The idea behind Byram's view is that the intercultural speaker as a mediator can interact with other speakers of different social identities (Byram et al. 2002: 5) by crossing cultural boundaries or frontiers. Also central to his proposal of the intercultural speaker is the notion of defocusing/ decentering, which involves going outside one's culture to embrace other perspectives (Byram et al. 2002: 7). Again, there is a problem-solving component in this characterization of the intercultural mediator, as someone external to the communication, whose role is to explain meanings to others where miscommunication has occurred (Byram and Zarate 1994).

Recently, the idea of mediation has been applied to intercultural pragmatics (e.g., Liddicoat 2014; McConachy and Liddicoat 2016; McConachy 2018; Liddicoat and McConachy 2019), but the concept seems to be circumscribed in relation to interlanguage pragmatics. In this context, Liddicoat (2014: 276) argues that pragmatics is especially important for intercultural learning "since it represents a fundamental point of interaction between language and culture".

Thus, for Liddicoat (2014: 276), the mediator is required not just to understand meanings but to be aware of and reflect on the process of meaning-making itself. Mediation also involves an intervention into the processes of meaning-making and interpretation in which multiple meanings enable communication across languages and cultures. Intercultural mediation can therefore be understood as a process that involves the ability to understand, through a process of reflection on meanings, the multiple possible interpretations and to use this understanding to facilitate communication across languages and cultural contexts.

In sum, the concept of mediation has frequently been described as a form of action in intercultural communication, and in relation to three dimensions of meaning: in problem-solving, when there is a breakdown in meaning; in meaning-making and interpretation, and in learning-facilitation in language teaching (Liddicoat 2022)

2.2 The role of the IM within the DMM

In this study, I attempt to characterize the role of the IM in spontaneous intercultural transient encounters through the lens of the Dynamic Model of Meaning (DMM), in the process of establishing Common Ground (CG), in co-constructing Emergent Common Ground (ECG), and in disambiguating meanings in the case of misunderstandings, communication breakdowns, and pragmatics missteps. Unlike other views of the IM, like the ones described in the previous section, I will be considering both social factors and cognitive factors in the IM role in arriving at meaning interpretation and meaning making. This new perspective on intercultural mediation and the intercultural mediator, based on the DMM, has theoretical benefits in terms of the specific insights it offers when applied to the analysis of empirical data, providing a solid theoretical framework that unravels the root cause of misunderstandings.

In this view, the IM is an interlocutor with a dual role: as speaker-hearer; as a hearer s/he acts as an interpreter of the speaker's utterance, and as a speaker s/he is that interlocutor who aids with mutual understanding among co-participants by establishing a match between their prior context, and the actual situational context. In so doing, the IM actively, and positively, contributes to the co-construction of meaning, and the creation of emergent common ground (Kecskés 2014) in the dynamic and the complex interplay of private experience (individual trait) and actual situational experiences (social trait), in Kecskés' terms (Kecskés 2010).

The figure of the intercultural mediator emerges in the conversation as that interlocutor – native (NS) or non-native speaker (NNS) – who positions him/herself as the bridge that shortens the distance between the individual and social traits of the interacting participants in a conversation, that is, between the cognitive, the cultural/ social and the situational interpretation/use of language.

The IM is an active co-participant of the spoken interaction, not an outsider as has been previously described (see Section 2.1 of the present study). As an insider of the communicative event, s/he may ask probing questions, s/he may reflect on possible meanings from a plurality of meanings, request utterance (re)elaboration, clarify cultural systems and dynamics, and may contribute his/her own views or opinions to the development of the discussion. In Liddicoat's terms, we may say that s/he is mediating for SELF and for OTHERS (Liddicoat 2014). Although the IM may have the greatest experience with both cultures, that is, a bilingual capacity, and a bicultural perspective regarding speech norms, values, ideologies, and socio-political structures in any given speech community, the IM does not represent an authoritative voice. His/her role is neither pre-assigned nor fixed but rather dynamic and potentially rotating in nature, as it can be played by different interactants (hence, an acting IM) during the conversation, depending on the level and nature of intervention needed at any given time.

The role of the IM is strengthened in cases where there is confusion or misunderstandings, or even non-understanding, for example, when non-literal language occurs. In such cases, the IM is best positioned to identify meaning disparities and resolve the communication breakdown or to take preemptive moves to avoid potential conflicts. Thus, his/her role is crucial in explaining, disambiguating, and processing meanings.

The IM brings to light correlations between indicators of awareness of (potential) misunderstandings and figurative language processing, such as metaphors, or instances of sarcasm. The IM helps to process underlying figurative language (mis)comprehension so that his/her intervention leads to a better understanding of the relationship between figurative meanings and surface linguistic forms, as in the following exchange between an Italian and a French speaker who live in

Buenos Aires, Argentina, and whose common language is Spanish, or Spanish as a lingua franca (SLF). The English participant is the acting IM.

Excerpt 2

5. S1: (Italian) ¡Por supuesto! Cuando estoy en Buenos Aires soy de Boca. No hay otro equipo.
Of course, I am a fan of Boca Juniors. There is no other soccer team.
6. S2. (French) ¿No hay otro equipo?
Isn't there any other soccer team (in Argentina)?
7. S1: (Italian) Claro, ¡no existe otro! **ECG**
Yeah . . . There is no other!
8. S3: (English) Quiere decir que es el mejor. ¡Exagerado! **IM**
He wants to say that it's the very best! An exaggeration.

In this exchange, the French speaker (L1=French) does not understand the sarcasm in the interlocutor's hyperbolic statement (L1=Italian) in line 5. The Italian is using target language framework to refer to his soccer team, "*No existe otro*". "*There is no other x*" (line 7) is in fact a prefabricated expression in the Argentine Spanish dialect to indicate that x is the best there is and cannot be surpassed in importance. The French interlocutor (S2) does not understand the sarcastic underlined meaning, and he misses the point. The third interlocutor (S3), an English speaker, intervenes as an IM to explicitly explain to the French speaker (S2) the pragmatic value of the Italian speaker's statement.

In line 7, the Italian speaker is trying to co-construct ECG with the French speaker by clarifying what he might be understanding right or wrong (due to the potential plurality of meanings). The English speaker (S3), in line 8, explains what the Italian wants to say, "*Quiere decir que es el mejor. ¡Exagerado! He wants to say that it's the very best! An exaggeration.* He distances himself from the usual interpretations of meaning in context and, through a process of evaluation and reassessment of the current situational context, he sees meaning from the perspective of the Italian speaker, grasping the pragmatic value of the utterance, that of an exaggeration.

In the corpus below, I will further explain the dynamics of the conversation, where the interactants try to establish CG, to re-construct ECG, and I will describe the role of the IM in all this process.

3 The study

The study presented here is descriptive in nature and focuses on audio and video recordings of casual conversational exchanges among speakers from different linguistic and cultural backgrounds using Spanish as a medium of communication (NS-NNS). In those cases where there was no native Spanish speaker in the conversational group the participants used Spanish as a lingua franca (SLF).

3.1 Methodology

The data come from a corpus of 30 recorded hours of group conversations among participants from diverse linguistic and cultural backgrounds who met weekly at a Social and Language Exchange Club for a language exchange, in Buenos Aires, Argentina for the purpose of practicing Spanish and/or English. Originally, the recordings would include face-to-face interactions, but due to the COVID pandemic situation of 2020–2021, the Club moved to virtual interaction, and the participants were located at different places, either at their hometowns or at temporary locations. The most recent conversations that are included in the analysis of this study took place over Zoom or other video conference software.

The participants, numbering 23 total, were from 12 different countries (Argentina, Brazil, Canada, Colombia, England, France, Germany, Ireland, Italy, Mexico, Turkey, and the United States) (See Table 1). For all the participants, English or Spanish was a second or foreign language, and in the conversation meetings, they devoted equal amount of time speaking in Spanish and English (15 minutes for each language). One of the organizers acted as a moderator who would remind them to switch languages. In each session, there were always two or three participants of different nationalities who spoke more than one language. The NNS had varying degrees of language proficiency, but most participants had an intermediate (Independent User) or advanced proficiency (Proficient User) in Spanish or English, according to the level assessed by the organizers of the conversation Club using the Common European Framework of Reference for Languages (CEFR) and its standards (See Appendix B). Some NNS speakers of English or Spanish, however, displayed proficiency levels that leaned toward the Independent User Low.

For the purposes of this study, I selected those recordings where there was some misunderstanding, especially in the presence of non-literal language of some sort, and I focused on those sections where Spanish was the medium of communication. Given the varied ethnolinguistic backgrounds of the participants, and the different varieties of Spanish spoken at varying levels of proficiency, the participants had the typical SLF user profile, that is, Spanish spoken as a mother tongue, as a second language, or as hybridized forms (Godenzzi 2006).

To ensure the natural state in which the data were collected, the staff members (organizers) or the participants of the Conversation Club recorded the sessions, without the presence of the researcher. All participants granted permission to the researcher to reproduce their interactions. Informed consent from individual

Table 1: Participants' characteristics in terms of their L1 and L2.

Countries of origin	Number of speakers	L1	L2	Target language proficiency (Spanish)	Target language proficiency (English)
Argentina	5	Spanish	English	N/A	*C1 (3) B2 (2)
Brazil	2	Portuguese	Spanish	C1	B2
Canada	1	French	English	B2	C2
Colombia	1	Spanish	English	N/A	B2
England	1	English	Spanish	B1	N/A
France	1	French	English	B2	C2
Germany	1	German		B2	C2
Ireland	2	English	Spanish	B2	N/A
Italy	2	Italian	English	C1	B2
Mexico	2	Spanish	English	N/A	C1
Turkey	1	Turkish	Spanish	B1	B2
United States	4	English	Spanish	C1	N/A

*C1 (3) B2 (2). Three of the Argentinian speakers self-reported a C1 level of proficiency in English and 2 speakers self-reported a B2 level of proficiency.

participants was obtained by the organizers of these meetings. None of the interactions were artificially staged or acted out for the purpose of the study, nor were the topics pre-assigned; on the contrary, the participants engaged in spontaneous conversations that occurred organically among the members of the group. All the conversations analyzed were first-or-second encounters, and the interlocutors were getting acquainted with one another. The topics ranged from family, country of origin, careers and occupations, housing, sports, entertainment, and health.

The recordings were transcribed using an adapted version of the Vienna Oxford International Corpus of English Transcription Conversations (see Appendix A). The system provides not only the details of what was said but also how it was said. Thus, features of talk like pauses, sound stretches, overlapping speech, cut offs/ interruptions, hesitation markers, and non-lexemes like "uh" and "hmm" are indicated in the transcripts to allow for greater accuracy in the reading of the data. The original transcripts are also time stamped.

For the purpose of this study, the corpus was classified according to a range of different speech events in terms of domain (mainly leisure, educational and/ or professional), function (exchanging intercultural information and finding common ground), and participant roles and relationships (acquainted vs non-acquainted; symmetrical vs asymmetrical).

3.2 Analysis

Data were transcribed and analyzed through a conversation analysis lens using Kecskés and Zhang's socio-cognitive approach to common ground (Kecskés and Zhang 2009). This is a pragma-discursive, or *pragma-dialog* (Kecskés 2012) approach, which considers the speaker's meaning, and the hearer who tries to come to an understanding with the speaker. This approach recognizes the dual function of speaker-hearers both as interlocutors and as dialogic actors who act and react during the conversation (e.g., Weigand 2010a; Kecskés 2012).

The analysis in the present study centers around the co-construction of meaning among interlocutors; their Common Ground, and the cooperative or interactional practices leading to Emergent Common Ground (ECG), mutual understanding, and/or miscommunication, as well as the IM interventions. It should be added that the IM was not officially identified in advance of the conversations but rather, mediation occurred naturally. Various interactional practices emerged through qualitative pragmatic conversation analysis, among which we can mention repetition, paraphrasing, (self-) repair moves in terms of confirmation checks, clarification requests, restatements, understanding checks, all used to establish common ground, and build mutual understanding.

4 Analysis and discussion

4.1 Excerpt 3

Domain: Education. Foreign Degree validation
Function: Co-constructing meaning. Establishing Common Ground (CG) and Emergent Common Ground (ECG).
Participants' roles and relationship: non-acquainted; symmetrical
IM= linguistic (formal sense) and interpersonal facilitator

The interaction below takes place between two native speakers of Spanish (one Argentinian, the other one Mexican), and a non-native speaker of Spanish whose first language is French, a physician, living in the United States. The French speaker had visited Argentina some time ago. The focus of this part of the conversation that I present here depicts how foreign medical doctors can practice medicine in the US. S1: Spanish speaker from Argentina (S1); S2: French speaker, from France (S2), a Spanish speaker from Mexico (S3).

9.	S1 (L1: Spanish)	Ah (.) ¿Estudiaste en Francia? A:h *Ah (.) You did study in France A:h*
10.	S2 (L1: French)	Sí, sí, eso. Estudié en Francia y después a:h tuve ah: mi examen. Exámenes *Yes. Yes. That. I studied in France and then a:h I had a:h my exam. Exams*
11.	S1 (L1: Spanish)	>> EXÁmenes (.) Bien fuerte la a: **IM: language facilitator** *EXAms (.) with the A very strong stress*
12.	S2 (L1: French)	Exámenes, exámenes. *EXAms, EXAms*
13.	S1 (L1: Spanish)	Exámenes. ¡Bien! *EXAms. Good!*
14.	S2 (L1: French)	Tuve exámenes para demostrar que (.) yo sé lo que (.) necesito saber. *I had exams to show that (.) I know what (.) I need to know*
15.	S1 (L1: Spanish)	>>como *convalidar el título* [CG] *Like validating the degree*
16.	S2 (L1: French)	Claro. Bueno . . . Para validar mi diploma. Pero tambi**A**n también . . . hay dos exámenes de ciencia básica y un medicina . . . y también hay una test de un examen de inglés para demostrar que puedes hablar en inglés suficientemente. [ECG] *Of course. Well . . . To validate my diploma. But also . . . there are two basic science exams and one medicine . . . and there is also an English exam to show that you can speak English sufficiently*
17.	S1 (L1: Spanish)	A:: Ah *A:h Ah*
18.	S3 (L1: Spanish)	Me imagino que no debe ser fácil validar el título en Estados Unidos. ¡Qué bien! *I imagine that it must not be easy to validate the degree in the United States. That's great!*
19.	S2 (L1: French)	No . . . porque tuve que revisar todo en inglés. Y.. Y . . . *No . . . because I had to review everything in English. And . . . And . . .*
20.	S3 (L1: Spanish)	>>Y sí: *Yeah*

21.	S1 (L1: Spanish)	@@ Te estaba elogiando Mati, Gabriel.@@. **IM: interpersonal mediator** *@@ She (Mati) was praising you, Gabriel@@.*
22.	S2 (L2: French)	Ah. Gracias. *Ah. Thanks*

In this exchange, the French speaker (S2) explains to his Spanish-speakers audience (S1, S3) the process he had to undergo to be able to practice medicine in the United States. The Argentine speaker (S1) shows pleasant admiration toward this effort when she learns that S2 got his medical degree in France but is practicing in the States. The French speaker starts explaining the process of validating his degree in lines 10–14. S1 acts as an IM in a language-related intervention to correct S1's pronunciation, and orients him to the correct pronunciation of the word "exámenes" (*exams*), with a stress on the second syllable. The French speaker (S2) repeats the word, with a sound stretch, but he then immediately goes back to his own agenda, that is, he continues with the conversation (line 14). The two interlocutors share some CG regarding the process of validating degrees based on their own experiences, so when the French speaker is at a loss for words, he resorts to circumlocution while trying to find the right word. S1 provides him with the correct term *convalidar el título* (*to validate the degree*), in line 15. The native speaker of Argentinian Spanish (S1) is again acting as an Intercultural Mediator (IM as language facilitator). The NNS, the French interlocutor (S2), however, seems to have a different prior linguistic experience in the L2. For him, a "título" (a degree)" is not the same as "diploma" (*diploma*), and he rephrases the term as "validar mi diploma" (*validate my diploma*) and goes on to explain that he also had to take various exams, even a language test. The second native speaker of Spanish (S3) praises the French doctor indirectly in line 18 ("*I can imagine that validating a doctor's degree in the States is not an easy task.*"). S2 missed the compliment altogether, and interprets S3's remarks literally, so he explains why it is not easy to validate a medical degree in the United States "*No (it was not easy), because I had to study everything again, in English*", in line 19. S1, acting as an IM again, clarifies the pragmatic value of S3's remark in line 21. She explains "*Mati* (S3) *was praising you for your achievement*". This time, the IM acts as an Interpersonal facilitator, who intervenes for conversational regulation, highlighting the pragmatic value of S3's remark as a compliment, for which the French speaker is thankful in line 22.

4.2 Excerpt 4

Domain: Society. Socio-cultural practices
Function: Co-constructing meaning. Establishing CG. ECG.
Participants' roles and relationship: acquainted; symmetrical
IM= language facilitator (formal sense). Interpersonal facilitator

A similar situation to the one described above can be seen in the following extract. This time the conversation is between a Canadian (S1) speaker, and two Argentine women (S2, S3). The group discusses sociocultural practices (kissing on the cheek) in France.

23.	S1 (L1: French)	Hay (.) hay una (.)un hábito que no me gusta en Francia (.) Es que los hombres se besan, empiezan <XXX> (.) No me gusta, no me gusta. Pero cuando voy a Francia no puedo evitar. (.) porque no, no quiero ofender, pero no me gusta. Hay muchas, muchas, muchos hombres que tienen un poco de (.) <1> *There is (.) There is a (.) A habit that I do not like in France (.) It is that men kiss, they start <XXX> (.) I don't like it, I don't like it. But when I go to France, I can't help it. (.) because I . . . no, I don't want to offend, but I don't like it. There are many, many, many men who have a little bit of (.) <1>*
24.	S2 (L1: Spanish)	<1> Barba. @ **CG IM1** *<1> Beard.*
25.	S1 (L1: French)	<1> Y un poco de barba (.) Muy corta. Pero es (.) <2> *<1> And a little beard (.) Very short. But it is (.) <2>*
26.	S3 (L1: Spanish)	<2> ¿Te pincha? @@ **IM2** ECG *<2> Does it prick you? @@*
27.	S2 (L1: French)	Nada . . . no es agradable CG *Nothing . . . it's not nice*
28.	S3 (L1: Spanish)	Te pincha la cara. ¡Sí! @@ **IM1** CG *It pricks your face. Yes! @@*
29.	S2 (L1: Spanish)	Lo sabremos nosotras @ *Literally: We will know it @ Cfr: Non-Literally: Tell US about it!*
30.	S1 (L1: French)	¿Qué? ¿Por qué? @@¿Vas a ir a Francia? <3> *What? Why? @@ Are you going to France? <3>*
31.	S2 (L1: Spanish)	<3> No:o: @Quise decir que las mujeres te entendemos@ *Es un modo de*

decir . . . **IM2.**
<3> No: o:: @ I meant to say that women understand you @ It's a way of saying . . . Metalinguistic expression. MPE

The Canadian speaker (S1), whose L1 is French, claims that he does not like the French custom of kissing between men, because he does not like prickly beards (line 23) His statement sets the scene, and creates the actual situational context (cheek kissing). He attempts to explain why he disapproves of this custom, but he does not find the right word maybe due to his limited linguistic repertoire; instead, he gesticulates, pointing at his face (line 23), setting forward an overt appeal for help. One of the Spanish speakers (S2), who immediately understands what he is trying to say (CG), comes to the rescue by prompting the word "beard" (line 24). Acting as an IM (language facilitator), S2 fills the gap between the Canadian speakers' prior experience (encapsulated in lexical items meanings, e.g., facial hair; prickly beard) and the actual situational context, contributing to the dynamic construction of meaning (DMM). More common ground emerges from the other Spanish speaker (S3): she prompts the word "to prick", and agrees with Canadian speaker (S1), by saying "Yes, beard hairs do prick your face" ("*Te pincha la cara. ¡Sí!", that is, beard hairs do prick your face* (line 26). S2 concludes in line 29, "*¡Lo sabremos nosotras!*" (*Yes. Tell us (women) about it!*"), using the future tense (*sabremos*) as concession in a non-literal expression that implies that women are far too familiar with the topic (emergent CG). The Canadian speaker (S1) misses the implied meaning of this last utterance (line 29), he processes it literally, and even though the actual situational context does not support this interpretation, he wrongly assumes that she will go to France, "*What? Why? Are you going to France?*" (line 30). In fact, S1 does not understand the pragmatic value of the verb *saber* in the future tense in this context. The current situational context clashes with S1's prior experience in L2, yielding miscommunication.

The acting IM assists in establishing emergent common ground with its shared sense (i.e., the knowledge, or mutual understanding, that derives from particular personal experiences of communication that is shared with other participants in the conversation, Kecskés and Zhang (2009) by explicitly using a metalinguistic explanation, *"Es un modo de decir" (It's a way of saying)*, in line 31) Thus, IM1 facilitates emergent CG through an action-reaction sequence that helps the two interlocutors work out the misunderstanding.

4.3 Excerpt 5

Domain: Work
Function: Interpreting non-literal language. Clarifying metaphors.
Participants' roles and relationship: non-acquainted; symmetrical
IM= Cultural sense facilitator/ conflict negotiator

The interaction below takes place between two non-native speakers of Spanish, one from the United States and the other one from Ireland, and a native speaker of Spanish, from Argentina, currently living in Mexico. The Irish speaker (S1) works as an English teacher in Buenos Aires, Argentina. The American speaker (S2) lived in Argentina for some time, but now he is back in his country of origin. The conversation takes place over Zoom. This is their first encounter and the conversation centers around what they do for a living and employment payment practices in Latin America

32.	S1 (L1: English):	Sí Sí (.) Eso es lo bueno (.) es que (.) todo el mundo (.) e::r (.) quiere aprender inglés (.)entonces podés ir mudándote por todos lados y siempre va a haber alguien que quiera aprender inglés (.) por suerte (.) pero (.) pero sí (.) *Yes Yes (.) That's the good thing (.) It's that (.) Everyone (.) E:: (.) wants to learn English (.) then you can move around everywhere and there will always be someone who wants to learn English (.) luckily (.) but (.) but yes (.)*
33.	S2 (L1: English):	¿Trabajás en blanco o en negro? *Literally: Do you work in black or white? Idiom: Do you work under the table or it a reported job?*
34.	S1 (L1: English):	No sé . . . puede ser ¿en gris? ¿Puede ser? @ *I don't know . . . could it be in gray? Could it? @*
35.	S3 (L1: Spanish)	Esa pregunta no se hace/ boludo @@ **IM** *That question is not to be asked, dude @@*
36.	S1 (L1: English):	@@ Exa::cto:: @@ *Exactly!*
37.	S2 (L1: English):	Bueno (.) sí (.) Yo quiero preguntar (.) porque no sé (.) si algún día quiero volver a Sudamérica @@@ *Well, (.) Yes (.) I want to ask (.) Because I don't know (.) If one day I want to go back to South America @@@*
38.	S1 (L1: English):	Hay mucha gente que trabaja en negro (.) en general (.) en Argentina

There are many people who work under the table (.) in general (.) in Argentina

39. S3 (L1: Spanish): Sí (.) sí (.)es loco (.) es loco . . . bue . . . pero en todo el mundo . . . se trabaja en negro y en blanco <1>
Yes (.) Yes (.) It's crazy (.) It's crazy . . . well . . . but all over the world . . . people work in black and white <1>

40. S2 (L1: English): <1> ¿Loco?
Crazy?

41. S3 (L1: Spanish): Quiero decir locura (.) es una locura (.) ¡No se puede creer! ¿Sabés que es curioso que en Latinoamérica la mayoría de la gente trabaja más en negro que en blanco (.) o si querés decir trabajo informal . . . es interesante . . . también . . . acá boludo en México . . . es una locura (.) es una locura . . . a menos (.) si trabajás en una fábrica o algo así (.) o una empresa grande (.) Pero la mayoría de la gente trabaja en negro (.) @ Vos, Dick, ¿trabajás en negro o en blanco?
I mean crazy (.) It is crazy (.) Cannot believe it! Do you know that it is curious that in Latin America people work more in black than in white (.) Or if you prefer informal work . . . it's interesting . . . also . . . here dude (boludo), in Mexico . . . it's crazy (.) It's crazy . . . Unless (.) you work in a factory or something (.) or a big company (.) But most people work in black (.) @ And you Dick, do you work in black or white?

42. S2 (L1: English): No: En blanco/ claro (.) Hay que pagar los impuestos. Soy programador así que todo (.) todo en blanco.
No: In white, of course (.) Taxes must be paid. I'm a programmer so everything (.) Everything (.) in white.

The Irish speaker explains why English teachers find jobs easily in other countries, setting the scene for this interaction (line 32). Following this statement, the American interlocutor asks if she is paid "under the table" (line 33) *(¿Trabajás en negro o en blanco?)* Both interlocutors are taken aback by the American speaker's blunt question. The two conversation partners understood the idiom and appear uncomfortable answering it; they do not know how to verbally respond, and they react with puzzled looks, and some giggles, signaling their perplexity. S1 has evidently found the question intrusive, but tries to relieve the tense situation by uttering a playful statement, "*No sé . . . ¿puede ser en gris? I do not know . . . Could it be "in grey"*? (line 34). It is the IM1 (Spanish speaker) who points out the inappropriateness of such a question and says, *Boludo, esta pregunta no se hace . . . (Dude, you shouldn't be asking this question*) (line 35). The Irish speaker (S1) agrees (IM2), "Exactly" (line 36) further contributing to the assumed common ground that is built on the perception of the communicative interaction under way (Kecskés and Zhang 2009). S2 seeks CG, by saying, *Well . . . I just want to ask because I do not know, maybe someday I may want to come back to South America . . .* (line 37). S1 contributes to Emergent Common Ground with an evaluative remark, *There are a lot of workers in the black economy . . . in general . . . in Argentina* (line 38), to which S3 reacts *Yes Yes. It's crazy . . . but . . . well . . . people work under the table everywhere in the world* (line 39)

The exchange exemplifies a pragmatic misstep, some unexpected conflict in communication. Attitude variation toward disclosure of personal matters is something that an Intercultural Mediator must consider, and S3 intervenes to do so performing his role as a cultural facilitator who negotiates a potential conflict, or someone who explicates culturally sensitive topics, or culture-specific norms.

4.4 Excerpt 6

Domain: Place of residence
Function: Disambiguating meanings. Interpreting sarcasm in L2. Working out wrong assumptions.
Participants' roles and relationship: non-acquainted; symmetrical
IM= pragmatic disambiguator and interpersonal facilitator

The following extract illustrates a case of non-literal language use in a sarcastic utterance that the speakers need to disambiguate.

In this exchange, there are three speakers, one from Italy, the other one from the States, and a Spanish speaker who makes a minimal contribution toward the end, for which the exchange can be seen as a case of SLF (Spanish as lingua franca). The Italian and the American speakers are highly proficient in Argentine Spanish since both have lived in Buenos Aires for quite some time.

43.	S1 (L1: Italian):	Y ¿Vivís en un departamento compartido con varios compañeros o cómo es tu [XXX]? *So, you live in an apartment shared with several roommates or how is your . . . [XXX]?*
44.	S2 (L1: English):	Vivo sola. *I live alone*
45.	S1 (L1: Italian):	Ah: Mirá ¿Y? ¿Cómo es tu departamento? Contáme algo del barrio . . ., del edificio. *Oh! And what is your apartment like? And the neighborhood?*

46. S2 (L1: English): Vivo en Recoleta, y sí (.)@@@
I live in Recoleta.

47. S1 (L1: Italian): GUAU (.) Recoleta (.) CG
WOW. Recoleta

48. S2 (L1: English): Sí: (.)@@ Recoleta// Cerca de la Biblioteca Nacional. ¿Conocés? ECG
Yeah. Recoleta. Near the National Library. Do you know it?

49. S1 (L1: Italian): Sí.
Yes

50. S2 (L1: English): Vivo a unas cuadras de ahí (.) Y sí (.) A mí me encanta la zona (.) Muy linda zona (.) Y todo (.). Ehh (.) así que. (.)sí (.) Hace tres años que estoy viviendo en este barrio
I live some blocks away from there. And yes. I love the area. Beautiful area. And everything . . . so, . . . It has been three years living in this neighborhood

51. S1 (L1: Italian): Mira qué bien ECG.
That's great

52. S2 (L1: English): Sí.
Yes

53. S1 (L1: Italian): Un éxito tres años ya. ECG.
Great success. Three years already.

54. S2 (L1: English): Sí . . . Estoy sobreviviendo (.) sobreviviendo. ECG.
Yeah. I am surviving. Surviving

55. S3 (L1: Spanish): Sí/ Sobreviviendo en Recoleta (. . .)
Yeah. Surviving in Recoleta
@@No querés decir eso, ¿no? **IM**
ha! You did not mean that, right?

56. S1 (L1: Italian): @@ Jaja. Sobreviviendo en Recoleta. @@@ Sí. ¡Me imagino!
Ha-ha Surviving in Recoleta. Yeah. I can imagine.

The Italian speaker (S1) makes a false assumption, or miscalculation of the current situational context, at the onset of the conversation in line 43, *You live in a shared apartment with some roommates, right?* S1 seems surprised to learn that S2 lives alone: *Vivo sola. I live alone* (line 44) S1's assumption may be rooted in the speaker's prior experience, for which he assumes that the American girl lives with friends (possibly other international people).

The Italian speaker makes another false assumption: he does not expect S2 to live in the upscale area of Buenos Aires, Recoleta, assuming it is very expensive, and consequently, not a common choice for non-permanent residents. This is shared common ground among the interlocutors so S1 verbalizes his surprise "*Guau . . . Recoleta*" (line 47), which he accompanies with a gesture (from the L2), bringing the index finger to the tip of the nose and pulling it upwards to indicate being posh. This non-verbal gesture is also shared Common Ground among the interlocutors (part of the L2 speech community *collective experience*), *Sí. Recoleta. Cerca de la Biblioteca Nacional. ¿Conocés? Yeah. Recoleta. Near the National Library. Do you know it?* (line 48) and they all laugh, signaling agreement.

It is interesting to see how emergent ground is co-constructed by the interactants in the dynamic flow of the Spanish as lingua franca conversation. The Italian speaker then compliments the American, who is a teacher, for her success living in Buenos Aires, Mirá qué bien*; A great success, three years* already, with an emphatic tone (line 51) to which she jokingly replies "*Sí. Estoy sobreviviendo. Yes. I am surviving*" (line 54)

The third interactant (S3: an NS of Spanish) utters "Oh yes, *Surviving in Recoleta*" (line 55)- a concluding remark, which is meant to be sarcastic. The Spanish speaker wants to make sure that the American indeed understands her sarcasm when she says, *you do not really mean that that you are surviving in your posh neighborhood, right?* in line 55.

In this case, the Intercultural Mediator acts as a pragmatic disambiguator, an interpersonal facilitator that attends to pragmatic meanings, by activating both shared sense and current sense to generate inferencing processes and drawing on contextual knowledge and experiential factors. It is worth noticing here that the Italian Speaker (S1) and the Spanish Speaker (S3) seem to have the same communicative intention, that is, to joke about the word chosen by the American (S2), at which there appears to be a complicit *emergent, co-constructed intention* of sarcasm, as it were.

5 Conclusion

The intercultural conversations analyzed here exemplify various characteristics of the L1- L2 contact and led to important findings in relation to common ground, emergent common ground, and the role of the intercultural mediator in establishing an emergent frame that is co-constructed from elements from prior experience with the target language. The analysis reveals degrees of misalignment between individuals' private experiences, and the current context. By examining the data from a contrastive perspective in the conversations, it became apparent that the speakers' prior contexts (individual trait) in comparison to the actual situational context revealed the nature of the misunderstanding, false assumptions, and pragmatic missteps. In some cases, the dynamic nature of the CG allowed for success in the conversation's (intentional) meaning, often due to the IMs' interventions. It is worth noticing that failure to establish or increment common ground was not necessarily a result of a complete mismatch of the speakers' experiences to the actual context, but rather partial discrepancies in the private contexts of the interlocutors. This is particularly seen in those conversations in which speakers do not have a high proficiency in the L2 (e.g., Excerpts 3 and 4) and where they tend to rely on the L1 by assessing it against the actual situational context. In the case of high proficient speakers of the L2, especially those who have had greater experience in the target language (e.g., Excerpts 5 and 6), the findings suggest that the lingua franca context exerts some influence on the interaction taking place between participants of different cultural groups. To shed further light on the matter, it is necessary to examine in greater detail the sources of misunderstanding in SLF (Spanish as a lingua franca). The more proficient the speaker, the more reliant they are on SLF.

The analysis also exposed the roles of the IMs, whose interventions led to solving "problematic" instances of intercultural (mis)communication. Unlike previous studies on mediation, the perspective adopted in this study allows us to develop accounts of the mediation practices of participants in spontaneous natural conversations beyond the contexts of language learning and translation/ interpretation to investigate practices of language use. Within the framework of SCA to pragmatics and the DMM, the IM role provides an insight into the interactants' internal interpretive process and a link between the social and the private. Within this perspective, at least three types of IM interventions were found, which are linked to the sources of misunderstanding: a. IM as language facilitator: when attending to surface level misunderstanding concerning knowledge of the language system, and linguistic production and interpretation, that is, s/he assists in building "formal sense" (Kecskés and Zhang 2009); b. IM as interpersonal facilitator: acting as a conversational regulator that understands the interests (the communicative agenda) of the dialog partners when there is a lack/or deficiency in pragmatic fluency and socio-pragmatic failures (mainly, pragmatic features and inappropriate language use), as evidenced in Excerpt 5, when the IM points out the inappropriateness of a question about under the table payment. c. IM as a culture-sense facilitator: when attending to culture-specific conceptual properties in interlocutors' utterances as evidenced in the conversational exchange regarding the word "ambitious" in English and in Spanish (Excerpt 1 on this paper).

Thus, the Intercultural Mediator can be defined as that dialogic interactant who increases CG, facilitates emergent CG, and promotes mutual understanding among conversation partners belonging to one or more cultures. Intercultural mediators' task is to bring together language sense (systemic knowledge) and culture-sense (culturally marked verbal terms), or clarification of cultural information and attitudes; and the linguistic system and models of pragmatic interaction (e.g., verbal clarification of non-literal language or verbal clarification of potential conflicts regarding controversial topics (as in Excerpt 5, undeclared work-). We could say that the IMs' tasks such as linguistic interpretation, negotiation in conflicts, and regulation of interactions, converge in the generic activity of verbal clarification that can help facilitate communication among intercultural interactants. These findings regarding the role that the IM has implications in second language pedagogy, where the dynamics of interaction and communication should be oriented towards how multilingual students with different linguistic, sociocultural, and educational backgrounds co-construct meaning and knowledge, trying to find common ground with interlocutors, especially in international settings.

Appendix A: Mark-up transcription conventions

I have adopted a simplified version of VOICE convention for transcribing conversational dialogs. Version 2.1 June 2007.

1. SPEAKER IDs	
S1: S2: . . .	Speakers are numbered in the order they speak. The speaker ID is given at the beginning of each turn.
SS:	Utterances assigned to more than one speaker (e.g., an audience), spoken either in unison or staggered, are marked with a collective speaker.
2. INTONATION	
S1 ¡No me digas! ¿De verdad?	Words spoken with rising intonation are followed by a question mark "?"
S7: No. En absoluto	Words spoken with falling intonation are followed by a full stop "."
3. EMPHASIS	
S2: er travelling abroad is VERY IMPORTANT S3: Estamos en cuarenTEna todaVÍA en Argentina.	If a speaker gives a syllable, word, or phrase particular prominence, this is written in capital letters.

(continued)

4. PAUSES	
Sí (.) una vez	Every brief pause in speech (up to a good half second) is marked with a full stop in parentheses.
5. OVERLAPS	
S1: Sí es lo mejor </1> que te puede pasar <1>. S2: <1> Sí </1> Lo sé. S3: <1>mm </1> ajá	Whenever two or more utterances happen at the same time, the overlaps are marked with numbered tags: <1> <1> . . . Everything that is simultaneous gets the same number. All overlaps are marked in blue.
6. OTHER-CONTINUATION	
S2: No. Aquí la gente no se toca= no se besan=los hombres= las mujeres=quizás(.)	Whenever a speaker continues, completes, or supports another speaker's turn immediately (i.e., without a pause), this is marked by "=".
7. LENGTHENING	
S1: Sí:: En Argentina no pode::mos salir. Extraño: Buenos Aires. Estoy en Buenos Aires pe:ro estoy encerrada	Lengthened sounds are marked with a colon ":". Exceptionally long sounds (i.e., approximating 2 seconds or more) are marked with a double colon ":".
8. REPETITION	
Sí. s-s.me encantaría ir a las Cata-Cataratas.	All repetitions of words and phrases (including self-interruptions and false starts) are transcribed.
9. LAUGHTER	
S1: Sí:: Fue muy cómico <@> S2: {laughing} @@	All laughter and laughter-like sounds are transcribed with the @ symbol, approximating syllable number (e.g., ha ha ha = @@@). Utterances spoken laughingly are put between tags.
10. UNCERTAIN TRANSCRIPTION	
S2: Tenemos muchos (. . .)	Word fragments, words or phrases which cannot be reliably identified are put in parentheses ().
11. TRANSLANGUAGING	
S4: Sí . . . Se abrazan (L2hug).	Utterances in a participant's first language (L1) are put between tags indicating the speaker's L1
10. SPEAKING MODES	
<fast> <slow> <soft> <imitating> <sighing> etc.	Utterances which are spoken in a particular mode (fast, soft, whispered, read, etc.) and are notably different from the speaker's normal speaking style are marked accordingly. The list of speaking modes is an open one.

(continued)

11. NON-VERBAL RESPONSES	
<nods> <shakes head>	Whenever information about it is available, nonverbal feedback is transcribed as part of the running text and put between pointed brackets < >.
12. ANONYMIZATION	
	A guiding principle in this corpus is sensitivity to the appropriate extent of anonymization. As a general rule, names of people, companies, organizations, institutions, locations, etc. are replaced by aliases and these aliases are put into square brackets [ ]. The aliases are numbered consecutively, starting with 1.
13. CONTEXTUAL EVENTS	
{mobile rings} {S7 enters / exits room} {S3 pours coffee (3)}	Contextual information is added between curly brackets { } only if it is relevant to the understanding of the interaction or to the interaction as such. If it is deemed important to indicate the length of the event, this can be done by adding the number of seconds in parentheses. Explanation: The pause in the conversation occurs because of the contextual event.

Appendix B: Global scale – Table 1 (CEFR 3.3): Common reference levels

PROFICIENT USER	C2	Can understand with ease virtually everything heard or read. Can summarize information from different spoken and written sources, reconstructing arguments, and accounts in a coherent presentation. Can express him/herself spontaneously, very fluently and precisely, differentiating finer shades of meaning even in more complex situations.
	C1	Can understand a wide range of demanding, longer texts, and recognize implicit meaning. Can express him/herself fluently and spontaneously without much obvious searching for expressions. Can use language flexibly and effectively for social, academic, and professional purposes. Can produce clear, well-structured, detailed text on complex subjects, showing controlled use of organisational patterns, connectors, and cohesive devices.

(continued)

INDEPENDENT USER	B2	Can understand the main ideas of complex text on both concrete and abstract topics, including technical discussions in his/her field of specialization. Can interact with a degree of fluency and spontaneity that makes regular interaction with native speakers quite possible without strain for either party. Can produce clear, detailed text on a wide range of subjects and explain a viewpoint on a topical issue giving the advantages and disadvantages of various options.
	B1	Can understand the main points of clear standard input on familiar matters regularly encountered in work, school, leisure, etc. Can deal with most situations likely to arise whilst travelling in an area where the language is spoken. Can produce simple connected text on topics which are familiar or of personal interest. Can describe experiences and events, dreams, hopes & ambitions and briefly give reasons and explanations for opinions and plans.
BASIC USER	A2	Can understand sentences and frequently used expressions related to areas of most immediate relevance (e.g., very basic personal and family information, shopping, local geography, employment). Can communicate in simple and routine tasks requiring a simple and direct exchange of information on familiar and routine matters. Can describe in simple terms aspects of his/her background, immediate environment and matters in areas of immediate need.
	A1	Can understand and use familiar everyday expressions and very basic phrases aimed at the satisfaction of needs of a concrete type. Can introduce him/herself and others and can ask and answer questions about personal details such as where he/she lives, people he/she knows and things he/she has. Can interact in a simple way provided the other person talks slowly and clearly and is prepared to help.

References

Barrett, P., Zhang, Y., Moffat, J., & Kobbacy, K.A. 2013. A holistic, multi-level analysis identifying the impact of classroom design on pupils' learning. *Building and Environment*, 59, 678–689.

Byram, M. 1988. Foreign Language Education and Cultural Studies. *Language, Culture and Curriculum*, 1(1), 15–31.

Byram, M. and Zarate, G. 1994. *Définitions, objectifs et évaluation de la compétence socio-culturelle*. Strasbourg: Report for the Council of Europe.

Byram, M., Gribkova, B., & Starkey, H. 2002. *Developing the Intercultural Dimension in Language Teaching: A Practical Introduction for Teachers* [Electronic Version]. Strasbourg: Council of Europe.

Canary, D. J. and Lakey, S. G. 2006. Managing conflict in a competent manner: A mindful look at events that matter. In Oetzel, J. G. and Ting-Toomey (eds.), *The Sage handbook of conflict communication*, 185–210. Thousand Oaks, CA: Sage.
DeVito J. 2015. *Human Communication: The Basic Course*, 13th Edition. Pearson Dialogue. Vol. 2. No. 2: 285–299.
Godenzzi, J. 2006. Spanish as a lingua franca. *Annual Review of Applied Linguistics*, 26, 100–124.
Hatim, B & Mason, I 1990. *Discourse and the Translator*. London: Longman.
House, J. 1999. Misunderstanding in intercultural communication: Interactions in English as a lingua franca and the myth of mutual intelligibility. In Claus Gnutzmann (ed.), *Teaching and learning English as a global language*, 73–89. Tübingen: Stauffenburg.
Jandt, F. E. 2013. *An introduction to intercultural communication: Identities in a global community*. Thousand Oaks, Calif: Sage Publications.
Katan, D. 1999. "What Is It That Is Going on Here?": Mediating Cultural Frames in Translation. *Textus*, 12(2), 409–426.
Katan, D. 2004. *Translating Cultures: An Introduction for Translators, Interpreters and Mediators*. Manchester, UK: St Jerome.
Kaur, Jagdish. 2011b. Intercultural communication in English as a lingua franca: Some sources of misunderstanding. *Intercultural Pragmatics*, 8(1), 93–116.
Kearney, E. 2015. *Intercultural Learning in Modern Language Education: Expanding Meaning-Making Potentials*. Bristol: Multilingual Matters.
Keating Marshall, K. and Bokhorst-Heng, W.D. 2018. "I Wouldn't Want to Impose!" Intercultural Mediation in French Immersion. *Foreign Language Annals*, 51 (2), 290–312.
Kecskés, I. 2003. *Situation-bound utterances in L1 and L2*. Berlin/New York: Mouton de Gruyter.
Kecskés, I. 2006. On my mind: thoughts about salience, context, and figurative language from a second language perspective. *Second Language Research*, 22(2), 219–237.
Kecskés, I. 2007. Formulaic language in English lingua franca. In Kecskés, I. & L. R. Horn (eds.), *Explorations in pragmatics: Linguistic, cognitive, and intercultural aspects*, 191–219. Berlin/New York: Mouton de Gruyter.
Kecskés, I. 2008. Dueling contexts: A dynamic model of meaning. *Journal of Pragmatics*, 40(3), 385–406.
Kecskés, I. 2010a. Situation-Bound Utterances as pragmatic acts. *Journal of Pragmatics*, 42(11), 2889–2897.
Kecskés, I. 2010b. The paradox of communication: A socio-cognitive approach. *Pragmatics and Society*, 1(1), 50–73.
Kecskés, I. 2013. *Intercultural Pragmatics*. Oxford, UK: Oxford University Press.
Kecskés, I. 2015a. Intracultural communication and intercultural communication: Are they different? *International Review of Pragmatics*, 7, 171–194.
Kecskés, I. 2016. Deliberate creativity and formulaic language use. In Allan, K., A. Capone & I. Kecskés (eds.), *Pragmemes and theories of language use (Perspectives in pragmatics, philosophy & psychology)*, 9, 3–20.
Kecskés, I. 2008. Dueling context: A dynamic model of meaning. *Journal of Pragmatics*, 40(3), 385–406.
Kecskés, I., & Zhang, F. 2009. Activating, seeking, and creating common ground: A socio-cognitive approach. *Pragmatics and Cognition*, 17 (2), 331–355.

Kecskés, I. 2010. The paradox of communication: A socio-cognitive approach. *Pragmatics and Society*, 1(1), 50–73.

Kecskés, I. 2012. Is there anyone out there who really is interested in the speaker? *Language and Dialogue*, 2(2), 283–297.

Kecskés, I. 2016. A Dialogic Approach to Pragmatics. *Russian Journal of Linguistics*, 20(4), 26–42.

Kecskés, I. & F. Zhang. 2009. Activating, seeking, and creating common ground: A socio-cognitive

approach. *Pragmatics and Cognition*, 17(2), 331–355.

Krippendorf, K. 2009. *On Communicating: Otherness, Meaning, and Information*. United Kingdom: Routledge.

Ladilova, Anna and Ulrike Schröder. 2022. Humor in intercultural interaction: A source for misunderstanding or a common ground builder? A multimodal analysis. *Intercultural Pragmatics*, 19(1), 71–101.

Liddicoat, A. 2014. Pragmatics and intercultural mediation in intercultural language learning. *Intercultural Pragmatics*, 11(2), 259–277.

Liddicoat, A. 2022. Intercultural Mediation and Intercultural Pragmatics. In Kecskes, I. (ed.), *Cambridge Handbook of Intercultural Pragmatics*. Cambridge: CUP.

Liddicoat, A.J. 2014. Pragmatics and Intercultural Mediation in Intercultural Language Learning. *Intercultural Pragmatics*, 11(2), 259–277.

Liddicoat, A.J. 2015. Intercultural mediation, intercultural communication, and translation. *Perspectives*, 24(3), 354–364.

Liddicoat, A.J. 2016. Translation as intercultural mediation: setting the scene. *Perspectives*, 24(3), 347–353.

Liddicoat, A.J. and McConachy, T. 2019. Meta-Pragmatic Awareness and Agency in Language Learners' Constructions of Politeness. In Szende, T. and G. Alao (eds.), *Pragmatic and Cross-Cultural Competences: Focus on Politeness*, 11–25. New York: Peter Lang.

McConachy, T. 2013. A Place for Pragmatics in Intercultural Teaching and Learning. In F. Dervin and A. J. Liddicoat (eds.), *Linguistics for Intercultural Education*, 71–86. Amsterdam: John Benjamins.

McConachy, T. 2018. *Developing Intercultural Perspectives on Language Use in Foreign Language Learning*. Bristol: Multilingual Matters.

McConachy, T. 2019. L2 Pragmatics as 'Intercultural Pragmatics': Probing Sociopragmatic Aspects of Pragmatic Awareness. *Journal of Pragmatics*, 151, 167–176.

McConachy, T. and Liddicoat, A.J. 2016 Metapragmatic Awareness, and Intercultural Competence: The Role of Reflection and Interpretation in Developing Intercultural Understanding. In F. Dervin and Z. Gross (eds.), *Intercultural Competence: Alternative Approaches for Different Times*, 3–30. New York: Routledge.

Oetzel J. 2009. Effective intercultural workgroup communication theory. In *Encyclopedia of Communication Theory*, 327–328. Sage.

Pöchhacker, F. 2008. Interpreting and Mediation. In Garcés, C. V. and A. Martin (eds.), *Crossing Borders in Community Interpreting: Definitions and Dilemmas*, 9–26. Amsterdam: John Benjamin Publishing Co.

Trbojević Milošević, I. 2019. Skidding on common ground: A socio-cognitive approach to problems in intercultural communicative situations. *Journal of Pragmatics*, 151, 118–127.

Van Olmen, Daniël and Vittorio Tantucci. 2022. Getting attention in different languages: A usage-based approach to parenthetical look in Chinese, Dutch, English, and Italian. *Intercultural Pragmatics*, 19(2), 141–181.

Wright, C. N., & Roloff, M. E. 2013. The influence of type of teasing and outcome on the negative experiences of teasers. *Human Communication: A Publication of the Pacific and Asian Communication Association*, 16(2), 95–107. University Press.

Weigand, E. 2010b. *Dialogue: the mixed game*. Amsterdam/Philadelphia: Benjamins.

Eunhee Kim

The co-construction of common ground through exemplars unique to an ESL classroom

Abstract: Employing sequential analysis with a multimodal orientation, this study closely examines classroom interactions to unpack the construction and negotiation of common ground in the usage of exemplars unique to an English as a Second Language (henceforth, L2) writing classroom. An exemplar in this paper is referred to as a semi-fixed expression (i.e., "I like ice cream", "(my/his grandson) George") which emerges in a particular interactional context in the classroom. Addressing the need for a socio-cognitive view to common ground building, the analysis demonstrates that as ad-hoc expressions take on a symbolic value through the course of a semester, they become bona fide exemplars which do not need any contextual scaffolding for use and eventually function as shared resources for participants to orient to for teaching and learning. Based on the findings, implications are discussed for common ground building in terms of L2 development and the role of humor in L2 teaching and learning.

1 Introduction

This study aims to empirically explore the construction of common ground in the pragmatic development and usage of exemplars unique to an English as a Second Language (henceforth, ESL) writing classroom. An *exemplar* in this paper is referred to as a semi-fixed expression (i.e., "`I like ice cream`", "`(my/his grandson) George`") which emerges in a particular interactional context in the classroom and becomes a shared artifact or resource for interaction among the interlocutors through repeated use in various interactional contexts. Using the data collected in one ESL writing classroom at English language programs (ELP) in a private US university, it aims to understand how certain 'fixed expressions' (i.e., exemplars) are created with meanings and sentiments unique to a particular group of interlocutors in specific sequential contexts. More specifically, it aims to explicate in detail the processes by which the interlocutors co-construct the meanings of the exemplars in an ESL classroom. In so doing, special attention is paid to how common ground is co-constructed among the interlocutors as they develop and negotiate the meaning(s) of the exemplars in local interactional contexts.

https://doi.org/10.1515/9783110766752-008

As Kecskes and Zhang (2009) point out, there is a need for a socio-cognitive view to common ground building, especially in the context of second language teaching and learning. Teaching and learning are bound together in reflexive meaning making processes, and especially in the classroom context, they are together seen as interactional achievements. In particular, an ESL classroom is where language (i.e., English) is both the medium and the object of teaching and learning and is also often a place where people from different sociocultural backgrounds come together for joint meaning making. In this dialectic undertaking, teaching and learning in ESL classrooms are jointly driven by and in turn the outcome of common ground building for successful meaning making. The point I am trying to make here is that common ground building as well as meaning making is not only a socially situated practice but also a cognitive one, in which the social and the individual are bound together (Kecskes 2008; Kecskes and Zhang 2009). In this regard, the socio-cognitive approach, as expounded by Kecskes (2003), warrants special attention, given how the recent scholarship of second language learning has tilted unevenly toward the social aspect of this meaning making process, possibly as a result of the inundation of empirical studies based solely on cognitive theories. (Block 2003; Ortega 2011; Van Olmen and Tantucci 2022). Unfortunately, as the extension and addition of socially oriented theoretical alternatives resulted in focusing solely on social elements of interaction (e.g., Markee 2004; Sert 2015), the scholarship is still left with a one-sided view into the process of language teaching and learning. In other words, this oscillating trend in the scholarship has often completely disregarded both *the social and individual foundations* of the discipline at the same time. As such, in this study I aim to explore the co-construction of common ground during the classroom interactions, paying close attention to not only intention-oriented actions and utterances, operating on the basis of *relevance* and *cooperation* (hence, the social), but also attention-oriented ones, operating on the basis of *salience* and *egocentrism* where speakers' and hearers' rely more on their own knowledge and prior experience than on mutual knowledge and actual situational experience (e.g., Keysar and Bly 1995; Giora 2003; Keysar 2007). Based on these two strands of notions operating together, the framework of the *dynamic model of meaning* (DMM), presented in Kecskes (2008), is applied to the analysis of data. To this end, I aim to explicate, through sequential analysis with a multimodal orientation (e.g., Goodwin 2000; Mondada 2014, 2016), how interlocutors display and negotiate their individual as well as shared knowledge of the exemplars (e.g., "`(grandson) George`", "`ice cream is delicious`") and the dynamic process by which common ground regarding the meanings of the exemplars is mutually constructed.

Notably, the purpose of the study lies in the empirical exploration of the *socio-cognitive approach* to communication (Kecskes 2003, 2008). In particular, the *assumed common ground* aptly captures the dynamic communicative nature of the ESL classroom. According to Kecskes and Zhang (2009), "communication in general is not an ideal transfer of information; instead, it is more like a trial-and-error process that is co-constructed by the participants" (p. 337). This is true in communication in general, and yet, this 'trial-and-error' process arises more often and much more visibly in an ESL classroom as students strive to build common ground in a foreign language to make sense while learning the very language during the process. One important distinction to be made about this speech community is the fact that an ESL classroom often invites students from diverse sociocultural backgrounds. This adds complexity to the affordances that may arise in a classroom as the participants from diverse background negotiate and co-construct their common ground for meaning making. It is also noteworthy that while most intercultural interactions often tend to be short-lived and may not necessarily reoccur with the same interlocutors or in similar local contexts, the ESL classroom offers an environmental constraint under which interlocutors are bound to come together on a regular basis oriented to goals that are specific to their institution-relevant identities (i.e., student, teacher). This unique affordance highlights not only intention-oriented communicative acts (e.g., submitting assignments, giving feedback) but also the emergent property of common ground embedded in fulfilling those intention-oriented goals, which ultimately and yet partially constitute teaching and learning. It is also important to note that for the efficiency and effectiveness of communication within this temporary speech community, a classroom full of participants may come to rely on a set of expectations that they themselves together come to assume and establish. These expectations not only include the unspoken rules or code of conduct that shape (and are shaped by) the institution-relevant identities (e.g., IRF sequence) but also the ones established uniquely through the discursive history shared by the participants within the specific local interactional context. In other words, the expectations also involve a set of actions and expressions that are co-constructed *ad-hoc*, which eventually take on particular meanings through their shared discursive history. While the degree to which they rely on the co-constructed expressions may vary depending on the quality (i.e., interaction) and quantity (i.e., time spent) of the interaction had by the members, it is assumed that as a temporary speech community, a classroom will negotiate and co-construct expressions (e.g., words, phrases) that are uniquely tailored to meet the communicative needs of the classroom members in a given interactional context. These expressions, at first, may be co-constructed ad-hoc to resolve the immediate challenge of communication. Over time, however, when used over and over in similar contexts, these expressions will then become *patterns* that the participants turn to and ultimately rely on as a feature integral to the common ground they share. These expressions, be it word, phrase, or sentence, will be referred to as *exemplars* in this paper to distinguish them from any common expression that may not have gone through such process of negotiation and ad-hoc co-construction of meaning in a particular speech community. To this end, my research questions are as follows: (a) How do instructors and students locally negotiate the meanings of particular exemplars that arise ad-hoc in specific sequential contexts?; (b) Are there any similarities or differences in the way each exemplar develops its meanings through the process of negotiation?; and (c) How does an ad-hoc expression eventually take on a symbolic value and become a bona-fide fixed expression in a temporary speech community? The research questions, respectively, are aimed at 1) explicating the process of negotiation through sequential analysis; 2) investigating the uniqueness of and/or common characteristics between the exemplars in terms of their meaning-negotiation process; and 3) discussing the implications of the findings for the learner's L2 development.

2 Data and methods

2.1 Participants and data collection

The data presented here is part of a larger research project that investigated interactional practices in L2 classrooms from a multimodal perspective aiming at the use of embodied actions, gestures, objectives, and technology for L2 teaching and learning. The data was collected by a team of researchers including myself in an ESL writing classroom (intermediate level) at an English language programs (ELP) in a private US university in which the participants met from Monday through Thursday over the course of seven weeks. The intermediate level was taught by Mr. Kay, who is a U.S.-born male with over 9 years of ESL and EFL teaching experiences in total. The class was diverse in terms of students' nationalities (i.e., China, Saudi Arabia, Kuwait, Colombia, Oman, Japan, Korea). I, as a research team member, observed and video-recorded two class sessions each week (from Monday to Thursday) throughout the six-week course in fall 2017. The data used for this study solely come from the sessions I have attended and observed. The primary data include approximately 24 hours from Mr. Kay's class.

A combination of ethnographic methods (e.g., classroom observation, ethnographic notes, video recording) have been employed in order to manually track all the instances of the exemplars uniquely oriented to local interactional or pedagogical goals. Classroom observation allowed me as the researcher an emic perspective into the dialogic practice in the classroom; taking detailed ethnographic notes while doing the classroom observation and working through the notes later the same day allowed me to have a better focus on notable interactional moments and key expressions emerged in the classroom while my observation was still fresh in my mind. Furthermore, the classroom sessions were videorecorded from start to finish from three distinct points in the classroom, which concertedly allowed a bird eye view on all the participants and interactions happening in the classrooms. More importantly, the videos as well as the notes allowed access to sequences of interest in the classrooms time and again as I studied them in detail for the analysis and discussion of this paper.

2.2 Analytical methods and focal sequences for analysis

As for the selection of data, I take a single case analysis approach (e.g., Schegloff 1987; Waring 2009). In my observation of the classroom interactions, I noticed that certain expressions were created on the spot by the teacher and then later they resurfaced time and again and sometimes adopted by the students later in the semester. As I noted those instances in my notes, there were 5 such semi-fixed expressions that emerged with a number of instances of use. With the goal of a single case analysis, which is to describe a single, complex phenomenon for a deeper and richer understanding of the phenomenon of interest (Schegloff 1987), I selected four excerpts to discuss how two semi-fixed expressions (or as I call them *exemplars*) are used by the class members. By focusing on these selected episodes, I aim to prioritize the in-depth analysis of a small number of sequential moments and describe in detail the actual instances of how the participants negotiate the meaning and function of these exemplars.

Then, to analyze the focal sequences in detail, the study employs sequential analysis (e.g., Sacks, Schegloff, and Jefferson 1974) with particular attention paid to the use of gestures and embodied actions, in order to finely explicate the processes by which the exemplars come to take on different meanings, shared and negotiated in local interactional contexts by the participants. In so doing, I take a multimodal analytical approach (e.g., Goodwin 2000; Mondada 2016) in order to transcribe and analyze in detail the interactional sequences as the negotiation of common ground and meaning making does not discriminate between verbal and non-verbal means of communication. When transcribing data for analysis, I adapted Mondada's (2014) notation system to reveal how embodied, or non-verbal elements are coordinated and synchronized with speech (see Appendix for the transcription notation system). In sum, through the ensemble of the ethnographic methods and the single case analysis approach, four interactional moments were selected for sequential analysis with a multimodal approach as they showcase particular exemplars achieving the status of a temporary norm based on the common ground established, observably and collaboratively, in a given sequential context.

3 Data analysis

The exemplars discussed in this study are 1) "(grandson) George" and 2) "Ice cream is delicious". Both exemplars were initially introduced by the teacher, Mr. Kay, in particular instructional or pedagogical contexts and then later appropriated by both the teacher and students in different interactional contexts with different instructional or pedagogical goals. First, the reason why I call what looks like a nominal reference an exemplar is that through numerous instances,[1] it gradually took on meanings specific to the classroom members, often in particular local interactional contexts fulfilling different interactional goals and social functions. At times, embedded in particular instructional contexts, it became a resource in their shared knowledge that they could draw upon for different pedagogical and/or interactional purposes. For instance, it functioned as a symbol of hope and encouragement[2] (e.g., likening George's learning how to walk to the students' learning how to write); it functioned as a reward for the students' hard work or a symbol of encouragement and comfort (e.g., showing or seeing a picture of George) or provided a ground for punishment (e.g., not recognizing George); sometimes it specifically functioned as a resource for teaching[3] (e.g., introducing a topic). As such, both exemplars, as used in the classroom context, took on multiple meanings beyond what the lexical units simply represent. In this light, I call them *exemplars*, and for analysis, I will analyze four excerpts that involve the exemplars (two excerpts per). In particular, I aim to explicate, turn-by-turn, how the instructor and the students negotiate the meaning of the exemplar as it arises ad-hoc in specific sequential contexts and eventually, if and how it takes on a symbolic value in the classroom community as it continues to surface in their interaction.

1 The first exemplar alone appeared in 44 instances in total in the seven-week semester.

2 Excerpts relevant to this purpose are not included in this paper due to space limit and scope of paper.

3 Excerpts relevant to this purpose are not included in this paper due to space limit and scope of paper.

3.1 Who is George?

Throughout the seven-week semester, Mr. Kay often mentions, "George" – his only grandson, and even shows to class pictures or videos of him. In the following excerpt, the name is brought up again by the teacher, which most students seem to recognize except for Yasmine (YAS), who was absent on the day when Mr. Kay showed George's picture for the first time in class. With an exaggerated expression of surprise, Mr. Kay pokes fun at Yasmine's lack of knowledge of George, or rather what it means not to know what George means in the class. He goes on to tease her that he will deduct points from her quiz for not recognizing who George is. Later, Mr. Kay treats the exemplar as a sign of reward as well as punishment.

Excerpt 1. WHO IS GEORGE? (Sep. 18th).

```
1   TEA: +so I-I got all your drafts, +thank y:ou,(.)
    tea  +GZ at SSS ------------------------------(L2)
2        +u::m I am working on (.) >giving you feedback on them<
3        +so:: (1.0) probably:: +this week on Wednesday or Thursday
    tea  +GZ slightly to left while facing SSS
    Yun                         +GZ at TEA----------------(L4)
4        +you will get your:: draft +back.
    tea  +GZ at SSS
5        +(0.5)
    tea  +push away folder on desk and GZ at computer
6   YAS: +okay.
         +GZ downward
7   TEA: it depends on George.
    tea  +GZ at screen while tapping desk with head jerk--(L8)
    Yas  +GZ at TEA---------------------------------------(L13)
8        (0.5)
9   LAN: +hh ha ha +hh h
    Lan  +GZ at TEA
                   +GZ down
    Kum  +GZ at TEA and then smile with GZ down-----(L11)
10  TEA: +if George visits, that's more important to me.+than
          some(.)STUdents
    tea  +GZ at SSS, palms facing up                   +palms mid air
11  LAN: +phshhh
    Lan  +GZ at TEA and downward--------------------(L12)
    tea  +GZ at pc screen --------------------------(L12)
    amd  +smile at TEA
12       +(2.0)
13  YAS: +who's George?
    Yas  +sit up straight and GZ at TEA
```

```
14  TEA   +WHO'S GEORGE?!
    tea   +GZ at YAS with eyes wide
    Yas   +smile at TEA
    mah   +look surprised; makes "oh" with lips-------(L15)
15  LAN:  +uh- grandson=
    Lan   +point toward TEA while gazing at YAS
    Yas   +GZ at LAN while smiling
    mik   +drop chin while GZ at YAS------------------(L16)
    mng   +smile while GZ at YAS----------------------(L16)
16  YAS:  [=uh (.) yeah yeah]
    Yas   +GZ down while raising LH over forehead
17  TEA:  [+minus +fiv- mi]nus five points.
    tea             +raise arm toward Yas while GZ at SSS
18  LAN:  +yes.
    Lan   +GZ at TEA
    Yas   +smile at TEA
19  TEA:  +what's your quiz.
    tea   +reach for quiz on desk---------------------(L20)
    Yun   +smile while GZ at TEA----------------------(L21)
20  SSS:  ha ha ha h
21  LAN:  +$exactly$
    Lan   +GZ at TEA
22  TEA:  +immediately I have to remove five points
    tea   +shuffle through quizzes
    sss   +laugh
23  SSS:  hh h (.) huh
24  TEA:  +didn't I show you a picture of George?
    tea   +GZ at YAS and around the room
25        +(1.5)
    Lan   +GZ at YAS
26  HEC:  +yeah=
    hec   +GZ at TEA
27  YAS:  =+a picture?
    Yas   +GZ upward
28  LAN:  +yeah
    Lan   +GZ at YAS
29  KUM:  I think she +[(      )]
    Kum   +GZ at TEA --------------------------------->
                      +pointing at YAS
30  PED:              +[(      )]
    ped               +GZ at TEA
31  LAN:              [come o:n]
    Lan               +GZ at YAS
32  TEA:  ↓yeah=
33  LAN:  =+NO! she was absent (.) +the same day (.) yeah.
    Lan   +point toward YAS         + GZ at YAS
```

```
34  TEA:  +so you miss a LOT by being absent=
    tea   +GZ at YAS while nodding slightly
35  LAN:  =+yyeah.
    Lan    +GZ at YAS
36  YAS:  +it's okay
    Yas   +shrugs with arms stretched
    Yun   +smile at TEA
37  MIN:  +ha h h
    min   +smile at YAS
38        +(3.0)
    tea +shuffling through paper on desk
39  TEA:  +>I will show you another picture of George (.) don't worry<
    tea   +collect quizzes from desk
40  TEA:  Maybe maybe (1.0) +if you are good. (1.0) if you behave well
    tea                     +stand up from desk
    Amd   +smile at TEA
41  YAS:  +$Oh thank you so much$
    Yas   +smile at TEA
    Yun   +smile at YAS
```

In lines 1 to 4, Mr. Kay announces his receipt of the students' drafts while offering a cordial acknowledgment ("thank you") and goes on to specify when he will be able to give them his feedback. Then, Mr. Kay predicts their receipt of the drafts (line 4) while gazing at the students. A 0.5 silence follows, where the teacher averts his gaze from the class, thereby communicating a possible end point of the announcement. Yasmine (YAS) takes the next turn by agreeing to this arrangement made ahead of time by saying "okay" (line 6) while gazing downward.

This "okay" (line 6) would be otherwise a sequence closure as Mr. Kay has explained the conditions involved in returning the drafts back to the students, which Yasmine has acknowledged. Then, Mr. Kay announces another condition by saying "it depends on George" (line 7), tapping his fingers on the desk, which could communicate a rather playful demeanor. At the same time, Yasmine and Lana are both gazing at Mr. Kay when he introduces, "George", a rather unexpected condition involved in the timely return of their drafts. Lana breaks the 0.5 silence by laughing while gazing at the teacher and then shifting her gaze downward. Lana's laughing here suggests, at least, her recognition of the reference "George," largely operating on the basis of relevance and cooperation. More importantly, Lana's laughing indicates 1) her knowledge of prior experience involving this particular reference and 2) what that might mean in this situational context where it is said to play a crucial role in the teacher's completion of his work, which in turn could affect the completion of the students' own work. More specifically, Lana's response seems to indicate the process of situational meaning construction which "includes both 'unpacking' (stored private contexts expressed in meaning values of lexical units) and 'constructing' (interplay of private contexts of interlocutors with the actual situational context)" (Kecskes 2008: 391). Prompting this response was the teacher's announcement of the special condition that he might be working under involving "George" (line 7), which later he repairs and expands on (line 9). It is clear that the teacher was operating on what he himself assumed to be *common ground*, seeing as he does not provide any further explanation as to who George is or why it should pertain in any way to the students' timely receipt of their drafts. This explains why the teacher is surprised to hear Yasmine's innocent question later on, "who's George?" (line 13).

Furthermore, in terms of *intention*, the teacher's turn in line 7 seems to have both informative and performative effect, coupled with his tapping gesture and a slight head jerk, to which, quite effectively, Lana responds with a laugh (line 9). The teacher's gestures during his turn seems to aid Lana as she negotiates the meaning of George in that particular sequential context. In line 10, as the teacher follows up with an elaboration as a repair on his previous turn, there is clearly an added emotive effect to the significance of the exemplar "George" as it pertains to the teacher's timely completion of his work, given how "it's more important to me(him)". This emotive intention seems to be the result of the emerging common ground, seeing how Lana, among other students who vaguely smiled, responded with a laugh to the teacher initial inclusion of "George" in the condition he would be working under. This seems to have positively nudged the teacher to go on to add *emotive intention*, which gradually becomes the teacher's primary intention as the conversation unfolds and the participants' shared common ground constantly shifts and emerges, turn by turn. Seeing the teacher's emotive intention unfolds (line 9), Lana provides a token acknowledgment which resembles both a laugh or dismissal ("pshhh") with a subsequent downward gaze. In other words, she treats his emotive intention as non-serious, which aligns with the teacher's playful gestures (line 7, 10) and his implied teasing (line 10). In other words, the function of *George* through these specific sequential exchanges is successfully negotiated to be one of humor. Several other students note the teacher's playfulness and smile back (e.g., Ahmed). Together, they are operating on the ground of *cooperation*, which dynamically shifts as explicated above. This dynamic unfolding of common ground operating on the principle of cooperation is aptly put in Kesckes and Zhang (2009), stating that "intention is not necessarily *a priori* but it can also be generated and changed during the communicative process. This dynamism is reflected in emerging utterances that may be interrupted and started again" (p. 342).

Lana's response is followed by a 2.0 second pause (line 12), where some students shift their gaze downward, signaling a possible ending point of the sequence. However, as a response to the silence, which normally signals trouble, Yasmine rather abruptly utters, "who's George?" (line 13). Yasmine's repair initiation clearly signals her lack of recognition of the reference, *George*, seemingly rejecting its significance for Mr. Kay and in turn for the class and effectively breaking the common ground that the participants all seemed to have assumed that they had mutually established. Her utterance is synchronized with her embodied action – namely, sitting straight up to face the teacher. Yasmine's rather confrontational embodied action sets the sequence off in a new direction. This single turn alone highlights the *dynamism* of the communicative process, in that assumed common ground is constantly shaping and is shaped by the local sequential context. Yasmine's repair initiation pivots the teacher's next turn, when he repeats her question, "WHO'S GEORGE?!" with a much louder volume and pitch while gazing at Yasmine with his eyes wide. Simultaneously, it is worth noting that Lana hand starts to extend toward the teacher (line 14).

Yasmine's question and the teacher's repetition of her question reveal a great deal with regards to what is assumed to be shared knowledge involving the exemplar "George", and together they underscore "the 'untidy' chaotic nature of communication" (Kecskes and Zhang 2019: 347). It turns out, in the turns subsequently unfold, Yasmine is formulating a simple information seeking question, actively seeking common ground (line 13). Her failure to recognize the exemplar and its significance in this local context seems to pertain to the realm of *attention* in common ground building. This clearly displays her failure to summon the most salient meaning of "George" from her prior experience that aligns with the actual situational context. In turn, Yasmine's intention to seek common ground is received with an abject rejection of her request for repair, as seen in the teacher's next turn, "WHO'S GEORGE?!" (see Kitzinger 2013 for discussion on repair). The teacher's apparent disbelief in Yasmine's display of her lack of knowledge and the manner in which his sentiment is expressed (e.g., loud volume, higher pitches, wide eyes) prompts the other interlocutors to come to rescue to help re-build their common ground by actively bringing Yasmine's attention to the exemplar (line 15) and more specifically, its interactional history involving the participants who are assumed to share the knowledge. In lines 14 and 15, several students express their surprise (e.g., chin drop, surprised look), perhaps both at how the common ground that they thought they had just built and shared was contested by Yasmine's question rather unexpectedly and at how the emotive effect previously associated with the exemplar is displayed in full force as the teacher seemingly rejects Yasmine's request for repair. As Lana reminds Yasmine who George is, she shows a sign of recognition by saying "uh (.) yeah yeah" while gazing down with her hand over her forehead. This gesture, presumably displaying a sense of embarrassment, seems to not only spring from her own acknowledgment of her lack of common knowledge (as opposed to her individual knowledge) but also reflects the degree to which the emotive effect of intention that the teacher had previously communicated regarding the exemplar "George" extends.

Now that common ground has been re-established, in an unexpected manner and yet successfully in the end, in lines 17 to 23, Mr. Kay teases Yasmine, possibly orienting to Yasmine's display of embarrassment. The other students play along with the teasing through smile, laughs and a verbal confirmation "$exactly$" (line 21). Notably, Mr. Kay announces that he will take "minus fiv- minus five points" off Yasmine's quiz and goes on to pretend to do so by shuffling through the stack of paper to find her quiz (line 19, 22). In response to the teacher, Lana provides a minimal response "yes." recognizably affiliating with the teacher's act of teasing Yasmine (line 18). Lana's affiliation with the teacher in this sequence seems to highlight the importance of appropriately displaying one's shared knowledge with the group (and *preferably* not one's lack thereof) as it pertains to the core common ground that the class operates upon (on the basis of cooperation) if one were to be deemed as a practical member of the classroom community. This practical sense of membership in the speech community (not the legitimate sense) is constantly put to test and affirmed as the class (re)build their common ground upon their shared prior experience and knowledge through communicative practices (e.g., Schegloff 1972). In that sense, as Yasmine temporarily fails to affirm her membership in the community, the participants join together to affiliate with the teacher's teasing as he pretends to knock off points from her quiz as a form of punishment in a non-serious manner.

Now that common ground has been reestablished and Yasmine has paid the price for her lack of recognition of the exemplar *George* (i.e., teasing), the cause of it unknown at this point, the interlocutors concertedly try to locate this apparent gap in her private knowledge. That is, in line 24, Mr. Kay tries to confirm with his students, "didn't I show you a picture of George?" while gazing at Yasmine in particular and looking around the classroom. His utterance appears to evoke a sense of shared history among the class members specifically with regards to the exemplar *George*. At the same time, it provides a glimpse into the local interactional processes through which this exemplar has taken on various particular meanings and functions among the class members. As the class recollects their prior experiences in one way or another (lines 25 to 31), some of their recollections involve Yasmine's presence in the classroom when *George* was introduced. These recollections accompany gaze shifts toward Yasmine, which appears to prompt her to remember those moments herself (line 27). Probably because Yasmine keeps silent, Lana explicitly urges her to remember by saying, "come o:n" while gazing at her (line 31). Then in line 33, Lana reminds everyone that Yasmine was in fact absent on the day when "`George`" was introduced, by saying, "`NO! she was absent (.) +the same day (.) yeah.`". At the same time, Lana is pointing at Yasmine and gazing at her as if to affirm this very fact not only verbally but also embodically. Building upon Lana's turn, Mr. Kay further teases Yasmine by saying, "`so you miss a LOT by being absent`" (line 34). And then Lana affiliates with his teasing by saying, "`yyeah`", which again indicates the importance of recognizing the exemplar as an important part of their shared knowledge as a member of the class and that attendance is one requisite to the accessibility of that shared knowledge. In line 36, Yasmine plays along with her gestures (i.e., shrugs) along with her utterance, "`it's okay,`" and this leads to more smile from some students (e.g., Ming, Yuan).

In the subsequent turns, while the teacher transitions to what can be seen as curriculum as planned (i.e., handing out drafts), Mr. Kay continues to playfully interact with Yasmine with regards to showing a picture of George, noting, in particular, that he would show his picture only if she behaves well (line 40). With this turn in this sequential context, the exemplar takes on another shade of meaning specific to the classroom community where his picture may be shown as a form of reward. As stated before, the exemplar takes on different meanings, besides what has already been established, through various sequential contexts that are contingent upon the participation of different interlocutors in varying terms and on varying levels, physically (e.g., absence) and/or psychologically (e.g., distraction). These sequential contexts are also contingent upon local instructional contexts (e.g., announcement, introduction of a topic, transition) and interactional phenomena (e.g., teasing, collective recollection).

At the same time, Yasmine's uptake of the teacher's turn is also a non-serious one as she says "`$Oh thank you so much$`" with smile voice, and other students also smile. The use of humor is especially notable here although it is present throughout this excerpt. When common ground is seemingly broken and has to be reestablished among the members, humor plays a key role among the participants as they expertly navigate through the terrain that is both cooperative (as they seek common ground through showing affiliation and responding to each other's intention) and egocentric (individual affect, prior experience). Humor, as an interactional phenomenon, seems to be a resource integral to successful common ground building and in turn teaching and learning (e.g., Bell 2011; Bell and Pomerantz 2016).

3.2 She deserves to see George's picture?

The following excerpt is from the same class session as the first but toward the end of the class. What precedes the excerpt is a pedagogical moment where the class is reading a passage together to learn specific vocabulary (i.e., affect, effect). As the teacher ponders upon the best way for the students to remember the words, Yasmine volunteers an answer, which immediately gains a strong approval from the teacher. In this excerpt, Lana, upon recognizing Yasmine's contribution and the teacher's appreciation of it, asks Mr. Kay whether Yasmine should be redeemed for the apparent mistake she made in the first excerpt.

Excerpt 2. She deserves to see George picture? (Sep. 18th).

```
30  LAN: So: now she deserves to see uh +(.) George picture, ↑yes?
    lan                                  +GZ up at T--------(L25)
31  YAS: +'Course, yeah?=
    yas  +GZ at T with smile--------------------------(L37)
    tea  +GZ shift to left
32  TEA: +=↓No, it only +balances out the mistake she made
    tea                +RH extended toward YAS-------(L26)
33       +(.) by saying who's George.=
    lan  +GZ down-------------------------------------(L35)
34  LAN: +=Okay.=
35  TEA  =So that was +minus five,
    tea               +RH shift to left with GZ at YAS
    lan               +GZ up at T
    sss               +GZ at T while giggling
36  YAS: +And Now?=
    yas  +GZ at T with smile
    sss  +smile at YAS
37  TEA: +=And now she has plus five.
    tea  +GZ shift to class; RH extended back to YAS
    sss  +smile at T
    mng  +smile at YAS
38  YAS: +↓Okay.
    yas  +GZ down with smile
39  TEA: +So zero.
    tea  +turn to face BB
40  YAS: +$↑Thank you$
    yas  +smile at T
    tea  +walk toward center of BB
41  TEA: +She's +back to zero.=
    tea         +turn to face class
    sss  +laugh
    yas         +smile at LAN
    lan         +smile at YAS-------------------------(L42)
42  LAN: =+Yeah
    lan   +LH directed at YAS with palm up
    cha   +smile at YAS
```

In line 30, Lana (LAN) starts a new sequence of talk by volunteering an utterance. After observing Yasmine's contribution to the preceding pedagogical moment, Lana asks Mr. Kay whether Yasmine should be redeemed for the mistake she made earlier by being shown a George's picture. Notably, Lana is drawing upon the collective salience regarding *George* based on what was established earlier in the class: that the exemplar signifies a reward for a good behavior in the classroom. Yasmine displays affiliation by saying "Course, yeah?" while smiling at Mr. Kay. The positive uptake, accompanied by a smile, indicates that Yasmine is actively seeking affiliation from the teacher. In other words, she displays her wish to be acknowledged for the contribution she has just made, not just with a verbal approval (e.g., "*great job*") but also with a more concrete and tangible form of an acknowledgment or a reward. In this case, the reward is seeing a picture of George. In other words, Lana and Yasmine jointly *present* their shared common ground, seeking some evidence of understanding from Mr. Kay (e.g., Clark and Brennan 1991), preferably a positive one. In fact, they seem to be assuming that the common ground they are establishing is positively shared by Mr. Kay and that they just want it to be confirmed, judging by the confirmation-seeking tokens, in line 30 and line 31, respectively (i.e., "↑yes?", "yeah?"). The common ground, however, having been previously established in the previous excerpt and observably assumed by the two students above, is then clearly contested with a firm rejection ("↓No") in line 32. Here, Mr. Kay refers back to Yasmine's "mistake" with a direct quote "who's George?" from the previous excerpt. Most notably, the teacher is not simply accepting or rejecting their presentation of the shared common ground; he is expertly negotiating it, here and now, by making relevant the sequence of talk that happened earlier the same day from the point of *his private context* (e.g., Kecskes 2008). In other words, the assumed common ground is contested and negotiated as Mr. Kay hearably works through the dueling contexts between his private context regarding the previous sequence of talk and the actual situational context here and now.

What *emerges* from this sequential context is a new common ground principally established by Mr. Kay as he dictates the terms upon which Yasmine's contribution is measured against the mistake she made earlier (see line 32 and 33). This, to a certain degree, contradicts what was previously established in Excerpt 1 (see line 39 and 40), in which the teacher stated that he "will show another picture of George.. maybe maybe" if she "behave(s) well". From his strong, positive remarks on Yasmine's contribution ("it's really good," "I like that a lot"), which immediately precedes the excerpt above, both Yasmine and Lana safely assumed that she "deserves" to see George's picture. However, the teacher does not accept this and goes on with a self-initiated, self-repair of his own utterance in line 32 and 33 (see line 35 to line 41 for repair). More specifically, he breaks down for his interlocutors, in arithmetic terms (i.e., "`minus five`," "`plus five`"), his own interpretation of the actual situational context in conjunction with the prior context involving the exemplar. The breakdown essentially showcases a joint common ground building process among the interlocutors as it is sequentially built and confirmed, turn by turn (see from line 35 to line 38).

In line 39, Mr. Kay affirms the common ground that he has just established together with the students, not just through verbal uptakes but also through gaze shifts and smiles, by spelling out what the balancing out amounts to ("`so zero`"). What follows his turn is "`↑Thank you`" from Yasmine (line 40) with a rather highly pitched smile voice. Notice that upon hearing the teacher's initial assessment of her contribution as well as her mistake, Yasmine accepts it, with her gaze down, rather unenthusiastically by saying "`↓Okay`" with a hint of disappointment (line 38). Then, when Mr. Kay affirms the common ground that they have just established (line 39), Yasmine's response is surprisingly a positive one; she thanks the teacher with a big smile. That is, the common ground that they were just operating on has had a dramatic shift as Yasmine attempts to reestablish it with a sense of humor. The teacher does not laugh or deny this shift. He goes on to repair his turn in line 39 by saying "`She's back to zero`," which, on the surface, seems to suggest that they are still operating on the same common ground that he, as the authoritative figure in the classroom, mainly claimed in the previous turns of talk. At the same time, the other participants in the classroom observably affiliate with Yasmine's attempt at humor by laughing or smiling at each other. In other words, by the end of the excerpt, the common ground established regarding the meaning and use of the exemplar *George*, has come to operate not just on the basis of the situationally literal meaning of the exemplar but also the *social function* that it helps to fulfill, which is to poke fun and create an emotional bond among the class members.

Overall, this excerpt shows how the meaning of exemplar evolves and expands as the interlocutors consistently contest and confirm the assumed common ground. First notably, Mr. Kay's utterance in line 32 and 33 alone highlights the notion of *egocentrism* in common ground building, in that it displays his own attentional processing of the actual situational context given his private knowledge of the previous talk. This processing is clearly observed multimodally as Mr. Kay's gaze briefly shifts to his left (line 32 above) as he accesses his private context concerning the sequence of talk from earlier the same day. Another notable moment in the excerpt is the nuanced shift in Yasmine's intention from line 38 to line 40 as she accepts the teacher's technical assessment of her contribution. That is, while her primary intention remains the same (i.e., emotive), in line 40, she clearly pokes fun as she changes her attitude to gladly accept his assessment and express her gratitude ("$↑Thank you$") rather than continuing with her previous reluctant acceptance ("↓Okay."). Such nuanced yet dynamic shift in tone is remarkable because while the common ground that the participants are operating on remains constant, the insertion of humor in Yasmine's remark, which effectively causes the class to laugh or smile, adds a layer of meaning associated with the exemplar *George*. To be more precise, this is not the first time that the exemplar fulfilled a social function. In the previous excerpt, it is also Yasmine who engages in a playful exchange with the teacher as he potentially considers showing her a picture of George on the condition that she behaves well. The dramatic shift in the way that Yasmine renegotiates the terms of the common ground associated with the use of the exemplar perfectly illustrates *dynamism*, a notion central to the assumed common ground.

While the two excerpts above show how an exemplar can develop its meaning and use through classroom discourse and how the common ground associated with it can be built over time, the next two excerpts show how an exemplar takes on a symbolic value in the classroom community to the extent that it reaches a point where it does not require any contextual build-up.

3.3 (According to Kay) Ice cream is delicious

In the following excerpt, which comes from a class session toward the end of the semester, Mr. Kay (TEA) is lecturing how to cite sources in academic writing. As an example, he attempts to (re)introduce the sentence "ice cream is delicious," which he has repeatedly adopted in some form or other (e.g., "I like ice cream") in a similar instructional context. When the teacher is about to share the example sentence, one female student, Lana (LAN), utters, "according to (Kay)" even *before* Mr. Kay says it and goes on to whisper the rest ("ice cream is delicious") to her peer. Lana's turns indicate that she *anticipates* what her teacher would say based on their existing common ground in a similar instructional context. It is argued that this exemplar has been oriented to as a symbol of the common ground shared by the class and used as a source of humor and building an emotional bond among the class members.

What preceded the following sequence was that Mr. Kay was announcing that many students missed citations for their writing assignments and now begin to explain with an example sentence that contains a source.

Excerpt 3. "(According to Kay), Ice cream is delicious" (Oct. 16th).

```
34  TEA:  you +↑must sa::y,
                 +shift GZ back to BB with body toward it
35        (0.8)
36  LAN   +$according to:+[:,$
    lan   +GZ in Yun's direction
    yun                  +shift GZ at LAN while smiling
37  TEA:                  [+according
    tea                    +touch BB with RH while GZ at BB
38        +to:::,
    tea   +write "According to" on BB while facing BB--------------->(L43)
    kum   +shift GZ toward LAN
39  LAN:  +°(?  ?)°
    lan   +whisper with body and GZ toward MIK--------------------->(L40)
40  TEA:  +>you have +two choices,< (.)
    mik             +shift GZ toward LAN with smile
41        <+according (0.8) to:::,>
    lan    +shift GZ back to front
    mik    +shift GZ back to front with smile
    jun    +shift GZ back to TEA
42  S?:   hhhh,=
43  TEA   =and then, +whatever,
    tea              +draw line on BB next to "according to"
44        +the website?
    tea   +point at space above line with GZ at SS to his right
45        +the president?
    tea   +beat at same place while facing SS in front----------------->(L46)
46        +my mothe:r? +(0.6)
    tea                +point toward PS while facing SS and smiling
47        +something,
    tea:  +keep pointing at PS with GZ at BB with smile
48        uh, or- +or u:h,
    tea           +pick BB eraser with RH while facing BB
49        +if it's an author?
    tea   +erase line on BB while facing BB
50        it's a +LAST Name +on- on-ly, (.)
    tea          +quickly shift GZ back at SS while erasing line
    tea                     +shift GZ back to BB
51        +according to Kay,
    tea   +begin writing "Kay" on BB while facing BB
52        +(1.8)
          +keep writing it on BB while facing BB
53  LAN:  +°$ice +cream is +delicious.$°
    lan   +whisper
    lan         +shift GZ to MIK
    lan                    +point in TEA's direction with RHIF--------->(L55)
```

```
54        (0.5)
55  MIK:  +hhh↑
    wan   +smile while facing front
56  LAN:  +haha [haha
    lan   +retract pointing while leaning back
    mik   +shift GZ to LAN with smile
57  TEA:        [u:h,
58        +ice cream is +delicious.=
    tea   +write sentence on BB while facing BB---------------------->(L65)
    lan                 +poke at mik with LHIF while GZ at MIK
59  WAN: =[+ha[h↑
    mik   +face LAN while GZ at her with smile
60  LAN:      [+haha↑
    lan        +point in TEA's direction with LHIF while GZ at MIK
61        +$I +told you,$
    lan  +hold pointing while GZ at MIK
    yun  +start laughing hard
    sss  +begin smiling
    mik      +point at LAN while smiling
62  SSS: hahahaha (.)
63  TEA: +uh- I told you so many times,=
         +keep writing sentence on BB with body toward it------------->
64  SSS: =hahaHAHAHAHA=
```

In line 34, Mr. Kay starts a sentence and implicitly directs the students' attention toward the blackboard as he shifts his gaze back at it. The 0.8 second silence that follows allows an interactional space where students can self-nominate and complete the teacher's utterance (see Koshik 2002 for discussion on designedly incomplete utterance (DIU) for pedagogical purposes). Taking this opportunity to display the most salient piece of information in this particular situational context is Lana, who says, "`according to::,`" with smile voice while gazing in her peer's direction. Yuan affiliates with Lana's turn by smiling back, who seems to have understood the performative intention as well as emotive intention underlying Lana's turn.

Partially overlapped with Lana's turn, Mr. Kay utters and begins to write on the board "`according to`", from line 37 to line 38. This echoing overlap seems to confirm the common ground assumed in Lana's initial turn, and almost simultaneously, Junko (JUN) and Kumi (KUM) displays their recognition of the common ground by shifting their gaze in Lana's direction. While Lana's next turn, in line 39, is not clearly audible, Mr. Kay continues his instruction with the phrase written on the board, which most students orient to through gaze shifts. Now that the common ground established is represented with a tangible referential object on the board (i.e., "`according to`"), the teacher presents a series of candidates that might fit the linguistic interactional context, from line 43 to line 50. In particular, he draws a line on the blackboard right after the phrase and points at the empty space above the line, which visually designates a space for a fitting candidate (see Hazel & Mortensen 2019 for discussion on designedly incomplete objects). Such embodied gestures (i.e., gaze shift, pointing) with the materials involved draws everyone's attention to a tangible space that represents the assumed common ground. At the same time, the tapping, pointing and gaze shift seem to implicitly invite students to fill in the blank space. In addition, the cut off and the hesitation expressed in line 48 indicates that more development would follow in terms of building a context for common ground as the teacher elaborates on a particular type of candidate (i.e., author; see line 49). In line 50, the teacher claims that for an author, it is a last name only, and in line 51, he begins to write his last name, Kay, on the board above the line that he has drawn before while reading the whole phrase "`according to Kay`".

While his act of writing continues to fill the silence that follows, Lana takes advantage of this silence to offer a candidate clause that would follow the phrase (line 53). Notably, as she gazes toward Mika and points toward Mr. Kay, Lana utters the clause with a softer, smile voice, making it hearable only among a few peers rather than the entire class. The two students, especially, Lana and Mika, are seen affiliating with each other more visibly from this point on. That is, they mutually establish and share common ground involving Mr. Kay's re-introduction of the exemplar ("`ice cream is delicious.`") through gaze shifts, whispering, smiling and pointing. In other words, the sharedness of this exemplar is reflexively enacted and confirmed simultaneously by these students who get involved in the process of negotiating common ground. Following a 0.5 second silence, Mika briefly laughs (`hhh↑`), and simultaneously, Wan, who rarely looks up from her desk, also displays her interpretation of Lana's turn as amusing with a smile, which reflexively signifies her participation in the common ground making in this specific sequential context. And then, Lana starts laughing ("`haha haha`") while retracting her pointing at Mr. Kay and leaning back. This turn – particularly retracting her pointing – seems to demonstrate that Lana has achieved an interactional goal (i.e., the emotive intention) amongst her classmates in close proximity, who then are smiling or laughing. By negotiating the meaning and function of the exemplar through the variety of embodied gestures, certain members of the class actively establish and reflexively affirm the common ground that they share.

Overlapped with Lana's laughter, Mr. Kay says "`u:h,`" and completes his turn by saying, "`ice cream is delicious.`" (line 58). During this utterance, Mr. Kay keeps writing the sentence while facing the board. In fact, the teacher's turn confirms that what Lana humorously proffered ("`ice cream is delicious.`") is exactly what he was going to say. At the same time, during Mr. Kay's turn, Lana pokes Mika's arm while gazing at her, which seem to communicate to her that the common ground they were operating on has been confirmed by the teacher. Latched with Mr. Kay, Wan immediately starts laughing (line 59), showing how Mr. Kay's turn coincides with Lana's previous turn and finds the match laughable. At the same time, Mika is smiling at Lana, displaying her affiliation with Lana's emotive intention expressed in previous turns. Lana also starts laughing while pointing in Mr. Kay's direction while maintaining her gaze at Mika (line 60). Then, Lana utters with smile voice, "`I told you,`" directed at Mika. This turn explicitly refers back to the turn when Lana whispered the exemplar to Mika in line 53. Most notably, this turn creates a context that spans two different points in time, evoking the shared knowledge that underpin the common ground that stands relevant in the current situational context. In other words, Lana's reminder and in turn Mika and Yun's uptake (line 61) together signify the reflexive tie between the existing common ground that they already share and the one they continue to establish *in situ*.

In fact, Lana's utterance ("`I told you,`") is followed by the majority of the students' laughing at the same time, including those who are not sitting near Lana. Still, it is important to note that not all students laugh, regardless of whether they are sitting near Lana or not. While most students are displaying their affiliation with Lana's emotive intention through smiles and laughs, some are engaged in diverse actions such as working on their smartphones/computers, choosing not to laugh or smile, or trying to get the teacher's attention in order to ask a question. Arguably, the differences in the students' reactions may depend on both environmental factors (e.g., proximity to Lana) and individual attentional resources (or lack thereof). In this light, the diverse range of (re)actions reflect the dynamic and unpredictable nature of common ground building and its participatory history. Following the joint laughter in line 62, Mr. Kay says, "`I told you so many times,`" while simultaneously writing on the blackboard. Note that the first part of Mr. Kay's utterance is exactly same as Lana's utterance, building upon the linguistic interactional context that Lana has already established. In addition, the use of extreme case formulations (see Pomerantz 1986), which are often used so as to strengthen and legitimize the speaker's claims, suggests that it is the teacher himself that authored the exemplar and that he has played an agentive role in establishing the common ground involving the particular exemplar. At the same time, it also seems to bring to mind, for the class, a sense of history that spans the entire interactional and pedagogical contexts that involved the exemplar, referring back to those moments when the teacher "`told`" the class "`ice cream is delicious.`" In terms of social function of the exemplar, Mr. Kay's utterance, "`I told you so many times,`" invites a loud laughter from the majority of the students (line 64). Their laughter not only affirms their shared common ground but also shows that they find his utterance humorous, which in turn reinforces the social function that the exemplar serves in this particular situational context, namely to build an emotional bond and create a positive atmosphere in the class community.

Finally, it is worth noting that Mr. Kay's last turn, "I told you so many times," indicates that the exemplar can serve as a shared resource among the class members for various purposes, whether to poke fun and build an emotional bond or to explain and understand academic content (i.e., how to do in-text citations in this case). In other words, it can be argued that particular fixed expressions – if they become shared time and again to the point of becoming a bona fide exemplar – become interactional resources for various pedagogical purposes based on the participants' shared knowledge and common ground. In this light, in an ESL classroom, this may enrich or even lead to second language development, the possibility of which rests on the degree and quality of participation of individual members as well as the teacher's awareness and willingness to employ fixed expressions designed for a particular class community. At the same time, different degrees of participation and quality of contribution from individual class members give rise to degrees of the sharedness of an exemplar and ultimately enriching and expanding its potential meaning (or not). Therefore, without closely examining local interactional contexts, such dynamic, reflexive meaning making of particular exemplars and the negotiation of common ground involving them may remain invisible.

3.4 (Because) Ice cream is delicious

The following excerpt illustrates how the same exemplar is animated by a different student in a completely unexpected interactional and sequential context. As seen below, this excerpt is not transcribed fully multimodally as the other excerpts above since I believe that the interaction here does not necessitate the approach in the strictest sense. That said, the context in which the excerpt is imbedded is when the students are finishing up taking the exam and leaving the classroom for good as the semester has come to an end. As Hassan (HAS) walks up to the teacher's desk and submits his work, Mr. Kay acknowledges this and initiates a sequence of talk.

Excerpt 4. "Because Ice cream is delicious" (Oct. 17th).

```
1  TEA:  Okay? You are good?
2  HAS:  Thank you so much
3  TEA:  You are welcome.
4  HAS:  ['cause uh]
```

5 TEA: [When are you leaving?]
6 HAS: Uh?
7 TEA: Are you leaving?
8 HAS: No no:: because because on Saturday I am going to go to
9 (? ? ?). I will stay there
10 six hours from from, from 8 AM=
11 TEA: =Okay
12 HAS: [(? ? ?)]
13 TEA: [Uh huh] I think that I think it's more fun to come to class
14 HAS: hhh. I don't, no no, no of course of course of course
15 class is more fun. Of course. (1.0)
16 Because ice cream is delicious
((GZ and point at BB and smiling at T))
17 TEA: hh. Okay, alright [I will see you later]
18 HAS: [Okay, thank you so much] h h.

Hassan approaches the teacher's desk before he leaves the room. Without directly answering teacher's question in line 01, which most likely means 'Are you all set?' in this particular interactional context, Hassan thanks the teacher (line 2). Before he can tell the teacher why he is thankful (line 4), Mr. Kay says "You are welcome" (line 3). Here, the teacher seems to assume that the student is thanking him for his teaching as the semester has ended instead of expecting a particular reason why he might actually be. In lines 5–12, with the teacher's self-appointed turn ("When are you leaving?"), they start to exchange a casual conversation about Hassan's immediate future whereabouts. This interactional context and the one-on-one participant structure (as opposed to the teacher addressing the whole class) lends more agency to the student to help shape the emergent discourse and hence building common ground with the teacher. In line 13, the teacher turns around the topic of Hassan's whereabouts to poke fun, which is taken up in the subsequent turn by Hassan, who starts by laughing and acknowledging that in fact "class is more fun" as the teacher says so (lines 14 and 15). In line 16, Hassan supplies a reason for why he thinks class is more fun by embedding the exemplar "ice cream is delicious", which is originally authored and brought up by the teacher most of the occasions that it appeared in the class. Especially non-verbally, Hassan says this while smiling, gazing and pointing at the blackboard, which evokes the interactional history involving the exemplar in their shared knowledge. At the same time, the interactional context allowed Hassan to play an agentive role in shaping the emergent discourse, who successfully embeds "Because ice cream is delicious", turning its head toward the author, the teacher, who, historically speaking, had to provide the context for the exemplar almost every time he introduced it. Multimodal in nature (i.e., gazing and pointing at the board), this masterful "head butting" with interactional expectations (Rymes 2009: 184) is not only communicated with the student in the back, who is smiling too, but also with the teacher, who laughs and immediately dismisses the student (line 17). This so-called head butting required no contextual build up whatsoever to make sure that a particular piece of information or knowledge is shared among the participants. In fact, the common ground of the entire exemplar is presupposed in Hassan's turn, which clearly displays that the exemplar, in its entirety with regards to both its form and function, is shared from their mutual experience in the class and activated in this moment. This aligns with Kecskes and Zhang (2009) claim that in common ground building "a frequent ritual occurrence potentially becomes public disposition that belongs to the core part" (p. 349). Again, while the excerpt above comes from the last class session, the exemplar appeared in the class multiple times in various instructional contexts. This frequent occurrence was often initiated by the teacher and necessarily involved the students' participation in making sense of it. At the same time, while the teacher often used the exemplar primarily with informative intention, it started to take on emotive intention as seen in the previous excerpt (Excerpt. 3). As such, the exemplar ultimately serves not only its intended pedagogical function but also social functions. This is clearly demonstrated when the common ground represented in the exemplar is shared and confirmed in the previous excerpt, the use of the exemplar is accompanied by laughs and smiles among the class members, which is seen to build a bond and create a positive atmosphere in the class. What is notable, however, in the above excerpt is that it serves no pedagogical purpose whatsoever; the class has ended, and while the participants roles remain the same (i.e., teacher, student), their conversation does not involve any teaching or learning. Rather, they are socializing. Toward the end of this exchange, the use of the exemplar by the student fulfills social functions only, namely making the participants smile and perhaps creating a bond among them by evoking the sharedness of their mutual knowledge of the exemplar.

4 Discussion

Regarding the first research question, 'How do instructors and students locally negotiate the meanings of particular exemplars that arise ad-hoc in specific sequential contexts?,' the analytic method of the study aptly captures the process of negotiation as it unfolds turn by turn. At the same time, as locally available resources for meaning making are made visible through embodied actions and gestures, which also involves the use of local objects, the participants successfully build and recognize common ground as they construct and make sense of the context for the appropriate use of the exemplars in situ. At the same time, it is also demonstrated that participants make concerted efforts to help one another in the meaning making process as the breakdown of the assumed common ground is seen to interfere, albeit temporarily, with the business of teaching and learning (i.e., Excerpt 1).

With regards to the second research question 'Are there any similarities or differences in the way each exemplar develops its meanings through the process of negotiation?,' the excerpts clearly show that there are both unique and common characteristics between the two exemplars in terms of their meaning-negotiation process. As for common characteristics, while both exemplars are a part of shared knowledge among the class members, they were first created and then often initiated by the teacher in various pedagogical contexts. With both exemplars, in their first respective excerpt, it is the teacher that initiates a sequence of talk involving the exemplar (Excerpt 1) or at least introduce a string of lexical units that are most salient to be followed by the exemplar (Excerpt 3) so that students (i.e., Lana) can correctly predict the exemplar. It is clear that as the author of the exemplar, it is the teacher who seeks to create context for the common ground associated with the exemplar. This point is clearly noted in Kecskes and Zhang (2009), who claim that in order to construct common ground "interlocutors seek information that potentially facilitates communication as mutual knowledge" and that "before the speaker makes the seeking effort, the piece of information is not salient in the hearer as background underlying the upcoming conversation." (p. 350). In other words, with both exemplars, initially, it is the teacher that strives to build context and create frames for common ground so that the students can understand or even expect (see Excerpt 3) the intended use of a given exemplar. In addition, the analysis of the excerpts for both exemplars shows that common ground, reflexively tied with the evolving meaning and function of exemplars, is contingent upon sequential interactional contexts in real time. That is, common ground is not something set in stone – it affects the participants' ongoing interpretation of interaction and at the same it is affected and shifted by it. As Kecskes and Zhang (2009) aptly puts it, common ground is "not something that is already there as a reliable repertoire for interlocutors, nor is it something that comes about as a loose contingent subsequence of the conversation" (p. 346). Furthermore, both exemplars come to fulfill social functions in particular sequential contexts. Most notably, emotive intention (i.e., poking fun, building a bond) takes on more weight than the primary intention that an exemplar is designed to serve, especially as the sharedness of the exemplar gradually increases through repeated use.

The commonalities between the exemplars aside, how the meaning of each exemplar evolves and expands is based on the singularly unique negotiation process of common ground building. In other words, each exemplar develops its meaning and function in different ways. The negotiation process involves an interplay of various factors as they are sequentially realized and layered in different time spans with different participant structures. This unique singularity accounts for various ways in which common ground can be established and negotiated by the members in a temporary speech community as they develop norms unique to their class community. To illustrate differences between the two exemplars more specifically, the analysis of the Excerpts 1 and 2 (regarding the exemplar, "`George`") highlights the notion of *egocentrism* and the *emergent* meaning of exemplar constructed on the basis of dueling contexts between private, individual knowledge and actual situational context. On the other hand, with the Excerpts 3 and 4 (regarding the exemplar, "`Ice cream is delicious`"), the exemplar starts to take on a *symbolic value* as a lexical unit that is more static and stable, rather than emergent and evolving. This is clearly demonstrated in the excerpts as it is the students (i.e., Lana, Hassan) that initiate the exemplar, not the teacher, and it requires little to no negotiation with regards to the meaning and proper usage of the exemplar. Rather, what shines more than the *sense* of the exemplar in the Excerpts 3 and 4 is the *social function* that the use of the exemplar fulfills.

To address the third research question, 'How does an ad-hoc expression eventually take on a symbolic value and become a bona-fide fixed expression in a temporary speech community?,' it is clearly demonstrated that as ad-hoc expression (i.e., exemplar) eventually takes on a symbolic value, it becomes a shared resource for participants to orient to for teaching and learning. For one, it has been argued that humor is positively conducive to teaching and learning in L2 classrooms (e.g., Bell 2011; Bell and Pomerantz 2016). As explicated in the excerpts above, humor is observably present as an underlying interactional phenomenon in common ground building and actively employed and exploited to poke fun and create a bond by the members of the class. Furthermore, for second language (L2) learners, participating in and contributing to the meaning making of the exemplars in the most salient and relevant linguistic interactional contexts can undoubtedly aid in their second language development. While it takes a unique and singular trajectory for a fixed expression to become a bona fide exemplar to be used with as little prior contextual scaffolding as possible, it can be safely assumed that the possibility of enriching or even leading to L2 development relies considerably on the degree and quality of participation from individual learners, not to mention the importance of the teacher's role in supporting the process. As such, it seems important to raise awareness in L2 teachers of the importance of developing shared norms in L2 classrooms and despite the temporary nature of the learning context, seeing how conducive the use of exemplars can be to L2 teaching and learning.

5 Conclusion

The paper clearly demonstrates the ever contingent, shifting nature of common ground and can bridge the gap in the scholarship by bringing the social and individual together. It also demonstrates the compatibility of the sociocognitive approach and sequential analysis with a multimodal approach; even though they may not share the same epistemological roots, the implications of their respective approach are oriented in the same direction. As Kecskes and Zhang (2009) argue, common ground is an assumed enterprise that is not visible to anyone, and yet when communication breaks down, so to speak, interlocutors may go through a process of recalibrating their own vantage point, (re)motivating and communicating their intention while (preferably) effectively allocating sufficient attentional resources. This is in relation to the assumed common ground, which in turn is examined and (re)established through a sequence of talk. "An emergence-through-use view of common ground" (p. 352) can therefore be demonstrated through a sequential, turn-by-turn analysis. In addition to the common procedure of sequential analysis, a detailed explication of embodied actions and gestures, which are at times synchronized with utterances, can effectively show the unfolding of the various interlocutors' understandings of their shared and private knowledge. As such, I believe that the analytic method (i.e., sequential analysis) with a multimodal approach can aptly capture how common ground is built, negotiated and assumed in communication.

Another possible contribution to be noted is that the study can highlight both the selective and constitutive roles of context at the same time in the study of interaction (Kecskes 2008: 378). The sense of reflexivity defines our everyday doings and existence, to which communication is central, and yet perhaps in our attempt to intellectually reconstruct them, we may have chosen to describe only that which can be easily normalized and simplified. In this light, the sociocognitive approach to common ground, expounded in Kecskes & Zhang (2009), is relevant to not only communication in general but also intercultural communication especially in our current times as we strive hard more than ever to seek common ground among people from various sociocultural backgrounds. This does not exclude ESL classrooms. An ESL classroom is a dynamic interactional space with an equal amount of regularity (e.g., institutional setting, frequency of contact) and variability (e.g., diverse sociocultural backgrounds of the interlocutors, levels of linguistic competence). At the same time, the interlocutors share the common goal of sense making in a new language that they are trying to make sense of in the first place. The reflexive nature of communication is again present in this unique learning environment, and I believe it is one that warrants further investigation specifically from the socio-cognitive perspective to common ground building.

Appendix

Transcription conventions

The video-recorded material was transcribed according to the following notation system, whose core was originally developed by Gail Jefferson for the analytic research of conversation. The notation system by Mondada (2014) has also been adopted to some degree in terms of transcribing multimodality.

Symbol	Represents
[	(left bracket) the point of overlap onset
]	(right bracket) the point at which two overlapping utterances end, or the point at which one of them ends in the course of the other
=	latched utterance
(.)	micro pause (±a tenth of a second) within or between utterances
(2.0)	timed (e.g., 2-second) pause
:	(colons) prolongation of the immediately prior sound
.	falling intonation
,	continuing intonation
?	rising intonation
!	animated intonation
↑↓	shift into especially high or low pitch
-	(a dash) cut-off
---------->	action continuing to the end of the line
----------(L#)	action continuing to the end of the line specified
>word<	speech at a pace quicker than the surrounding talk
<word>	speech at a pace slower than the surrounding talk
$	smile voice
Yeah	(underscoring) some form of stress, via pitch and/or amplitude
VERY	(upper case) speech much louder than the surrounding talk
°Um°	speech softer than the surrounding talk
((raise hands))	transcriber's descriptions of details of interactional scene
+	participant's utterance and action that are synchronized
RH	right hand

LH	left hand
IF	index finger
BH	both hands
GZ	gaze
BB	blackboard
PS	projector screen
SSS	multiple students
S?	unidentified student

Additional excerpts (preceding the ones above)

A. "This is George." (Sep. 12th)

01	T:	So we have been talking about, parks and gardens. Has any of you heard of
02		Longwood Gardens?
03	Ss:	Uh-hum
04	T:	Have you been there?
05	Ss:	Uh-hum
06	T:	It's a really great place to go. It's about an hour from here outside of the city.
07		It's a famous garden. The reason why I am telling you is, I went there yesterday.
08	HAS:	Ah
09	T:	So um, I am showing you a picture now. ((bring up the website on PS))
10	T:	But the best part about Longwood Gardens is not the gardens, it's who you
11		go with.
12	SSS:	((laugh))
13	T:	And I went with (2.0) ((T brings up a photo of a woman holding a toddler))
14		these people.
15	SSS:	Whoa ((with a tone of surprise))
16	T:	So this is my wife ((pointing at the woman)) Janet, and this is . . . . .
17	SSS:	George*=
18	T:	= **George, this is George** ((T walks across the room and turns off the lights))
19		So this is at Longwood Gardens. It's it's it's my grandson. He was born on, on
20		April 10th. Why am I showing you this picture? Because you had to do this extra
21		work, this questionnaire. And this is a reward ((pointing at the photo)). So
22		whenever you are feeling. a little bit depressed, it's a rainy day (2.0) you are
23		feeling a little sad (1.0) you can look at a picture of George ((pointing)).
24	SSS:	((laugh))
25	T:	And your life is, sky will be bright, you will feel happier, life will be better.
26		So I hope your life is feeling a little better right now.
27		Now we can do some real work. Um, okay. Does anyone have their book?

* Some students already know who "George" is because some of them took his class before. Others are new to "George".

B. "Ice cream is delicious." (Oct. 10th)

T uses the space in the middle and performs in order to explain what is logical and what is illogical when it comes to counter argument. He uses the ice cream example from the previous class. Central to this explanation is the concept "arguing against. (Notes from Oct. 10, 2017)

01	T:	Um::: I heard some students said something like this (2.0) Um let me see (1.0)
02		Um:: I am trying to give you an example. (5.0) Uh:: Some people like this, they
03		say, let's talk about ice cream again, okay? They say
04	S?:	((giggle))
05	T:	'Some people (1.0) argue', so, I am in favor of ice cream, okay?=
06	S?:	=Okay
07	T:	I like ice cream, okay?=
08	LAN:	=Yea
09	T:	So my thesis is, '*Ice cream* (1.0) *ice cream is::: delicious, cold and healthy*',
10		okay?
11	SSS:	((giggle))
12	T:	Okay, but okay, so but now I am writing this paragraph
13	T:	'*But some people claim that ice cream is not healthy because it is fattening.*'
14	SSS:	Uh hum
15	T:	'*However, it's actually delicious.*'((looking around the room and frowning))
16	SSS:	((giggle))
17	T:	What's wrong with that?
18	SSS:	((giggle))
19	T:	See, that's what I am, that's what I am try ((looking back at the board)), See,
20		that's not, it's not logical, right? ((frowning again))

References

Bell, N. 2011. Humor scholarship and TESOL: Applying findings and establishing a research agenda. *TESOL Quarterly*, 45(1), 134–159.

Bell, N., & Pomerantz, A. 2016. *Humor in the classroom: A guide for language teachers and educational researchers.* New York: Routledge.

Block, D. 2003. *The social turn in second language acquisition*. Edinburgh, United Kingdom: Edinburgh University Press.

Clark, H. H., & Brennan, S. 1991. Grounding in communication. In L. B. Resnick, J. M. Levine and S. D. Teasley (eds.), *Perspectives on socially shared cognition*, 127–149. Washington, DC: American Psychological Association.

Giora, R. 2003. *On Our Mind: Salience, Context and Figurative Language*. Oxford, England: Oxford University Press.

Goodwin, C. 2000. Action and embodiment within situated human interaction. *Journal of Pragmatics*, 32(10), 1489–1522.

Hazel, S., & Mortensen, K. 2019. Designedly Incomplete Objects as Elicitation Tools in Classroom Interaction. In D. Day & J. Wagner (eds.), *Objects, Bodies and Work Practice*, 216–249. Bristol, United Kingdom: Multilingual Matters.

Heritage, J. 2012. The epistemic engine: Sequence organization and territories of knowledge. *Research on Language and Social Interaction*, 45(1), 30–52.

Kecskes, I. 2003. *Situation-Bound Utterances in L1 and L2*. Berlin/New York: Mouton de Gruyter.

Kecskes, I. 2008. Dueling contexts: A dynamic model of meaning. *Journal of Pragmatics*, 40, 385–406.

Kecskes, I., & Zhang, F. 2009. Activating, seeking, and creating common ground: A socio-cognitive approach. *Pragmatics & Cognition*, 17(20), 331–355.

Keysar, B., & Bly, B. 1995. Intuitions of the transparency of idioms: Can one keep a secret by spilling the beans? *Journal of Memory and Language*, 34, 89–109.

Keysar, B. 2007. Communication and miscommunication: The role of egocentric processes. *Intercultural Pragmatics*, 4, 71–84.

Kitzinger, C. 2013. Repair. In J. Sidnell & T. Stivers (eds.), *The Handbook of Conversation Analysis*, 229–256. Chichester, United Kingdom: Wiley-Blackwell.

Koshik, I. 2002. Designed incomplete utterances: A pedagogical practice for eliciting knowledge displays in error correction sequences. *Research on Language and Social Interaction*, 35, 277–309.

Markee, N. (ed.). 2004. Classroom talks [Special issue]. *Modern Language Journal*, 88(4).

Mondada, L. 2014. The local constitution of multimodal resources for social interaction. *Journal of Pragmatics*, 65, 137–156.

Mondada, L. 2016. Multimodal resources and the organization of social interaction. In A. Rocci & L.de Saussure (eds.), *Verbal communication*, 329–350. Berlin: De Gruyter Mouton.

Ortega, L. 2011. SLA after the social turn: Where cognitivism and its alternatives stand. In D. Atkinson (ed.), *Alternative approaches to second language acquisition*, 167–180. Abingdon/New York: Routledge.

Pomerantz, A. 1986. Extreme case formulations: A way of legitimizing claims. *Human Studies*, 9, 219–229.

Rymes, B. 2009. *Classroom Discourse Analysis: A Tool for Critical Reflection*. Cresskill, NJ: Hampton Press.

Sacks, H., Schegloff, E., & Jefferson, G. 1974. A simplest systematics for the organization of turn-taking for conversation. *Language*, 50(4). 693–735.

Schegloff, E. A. 1972. Notes on a conversational practice: Formulating place. In David Sudnow (ed.), *Studies in social interaction*, 75–119. New York: Free Press.

Schegloff, E. 1987. Analyzing Single Episodes of Interaction: An Exercise in Conversation Analysis. *Social Psychology Quarterly*, 50(2), 101–114.

Sert, O. 2015. *Social interaction and L2 classroom discourse*. Edinburgh, United Kingdom: Edinburgh University Press.

Van Olmen, D., & Tantucci, V. 2022. Getting attention in different languages: A usage-based approach to parenthetical look in Chinese, Dutch, English, and Italian. *Intercultural Pragmatics*, 19(2), 141–181.

Waring, H. Z. 2009. Moving Out of IRF (Initiation-response-feedback): A Single Case Analysis. *Language Learning*, 59(4), 796–824.

3 Common ground building

Karsten Senkbeil

Mutual knowledge and the 'hidden common ground': An interdisciplinary perspective on mutual understanding in intercultural communication

Abstract: This chapter argues that there exists a hidden form of common ground which heavily influences intercultural understanding, and which should thus augment existing theories on common ground emergence in Intercultural Pragmatics. It begins with a short recapitulation of the meaning of knowledge in theoretical discussions in linguistics and other humanities, which adds a transdisciplinary perspective on 'mutual knowledge', the key idea in discussions of the common ground. With the aim of a synthesis of current developments in pragmatics, cognitive linguistics and anthropology, this chapter demonstrates that similar trends surrounding terms such as *embodied knowledge* and *empracticism* can be observed across these neighboring disciplines. Combining these ideas into a unified perspective helps reassess what exactly we mean when we discuss 'assumed mutually shared knowledge' among speakers-hearers, particularly in intercultural encounters. Examples from empirical research on intercultural discourse in English as a lingua franca support the theoretical argument. Hence, this chapter intends to show that we need to pay attention to embodied and empractic networks of knowledge that are cognitively and communicatively complex at first glance, but widely shared across cultures, a *hidden common ground* in intercultural communication.

1 Introduction

This chapter explores the meaning of *knowledge*, a term with the highest salience for many philosophical discussions about language and culture. Specifically, it will focus on the role of knowledge in intercultural communication (ICC), to then examine its impact on the *common ground*, one of the key concepts in Intercultural Pragmatics.

As a first step, it discusses the status quo of epistemological theorizing in those two fields that have the highest gravity for ICC studies: linguistics, with a particular focus on pragmatics and cognitive linguistics, and cultural theory in disciplines such as anthropology and cultural studies. It will highlight several trends in

https://doi.org/10.1515/9783110766752-009

knowledge theories in the last decades, particularly those that can be observed in more than one disciplinary (sub-)field. Three of those recurring observations will provide the cornerstones for a reevaluation of our notions of knowledge in communication (intercultural, but also in general), for example, the mostly implicitly held idea that knowledge is only a mental phenomenon.

The second step, and the goal of this transdisciplinary synthesis of ideas is to argue that there exists a 'hidden' transcultural common ground – a mostly sub-conscious pool of shared knowledge among speakers-hearers from different cultures – which may provide a key to explain instances of intercultural understanding when we least expect it. Among others, this argument problematizes the tenor of many ICC studies emphasizing cross-linguistic and cross-cultural differences and/or ensuing misunderstandings, based on different knowledge 'sets', or 'systems'.

As the argument brought forward in this chapter is heavily influenced by advances in cognitive linguistics on the one hand, and by central ideas in functional (pragmatic) theories of language on the other hand, I call this approach *cognitive-functional*. Admittedly, this hardly represents a satisfying (in the sense of unambiguous and precise) label, considering the ongoing debates about both of its components: neither the meaning of *cognitive* (in cognitive linguistics and neighboring disciplines), nor *functional* (in functional approaches to language) is undisputed. This chapter particularly draws on the functionalist school of language theory ("praxeology", see Bühler 2011 [1934]; Habermas 2007 [1981]), which emphasizes the action character of all language in use. The praxeological school has been a sturdy branch in continental European language philosophy and recently gained traction on the international, Anglophone scale (see e.g. Harder 2010). By uniting the cognitive and the social (and sociocultural), the approach proposed in this chapter is adaptable to the 'socio-cognitive approach' to pragmatics outlined by Kecskés et al. (2010, 2009, 2014). Ultimately, my discussion of the nature of knowledge, or rather knowledges that have direct relevance for the common ground, should unite the functional approach to language from a pragmatic perspective with the cognitive and the cultural perspective.

2 Knowledge as a concept across disciplines

ICC studies are intrinsically interdisciplinary. At the same time, defining knowledge has been and still is a transdisciplinary 'problem' in the sense that no single definition of knowledge has reached the status of a universally accepted axiom across the humanities. Any attempt to tackle this complicated concept, and its meaning for ICC, thus needs to look beyond the boundaries of a single discipline. Let me begin with a discussion of knowledge in the most relevant bottom-up and top-down theories in linguistics (Section 2.1), to then summarize what scholars have made of the intersection of knowledge and culture(s) in Section 2.2.

2.1 Knowledge and language

2.1.1 Knowledge in microlinguistics: From bottom-up approaches to the common ground

Language represents and structures human knowledge, so unsurprisingly, linguists have extensively analyzed the knowledge management capacities of syntax, semantics, in texts, and occasionally morphology (particularly in languages other than English). Some of the terminology of linguistic epistemology – for lack of a better umbrella term (but see Busse 2008, who uses the same term slightly differently) – has become common sense among the discipline. *Presupposition*, *implication* and *implicature*, *evidentiality*, *cohesion* and *coherence* in text linguistics, for example, are all terms that ultimately point to language as a tool to manage the distribution of 'new' knowledge vs. 'old' or 'given' knowledge among its users (e.g. Domaneschi et al. 2022). Even classic speech act theory, though it is widely known and appreciated for introducing the interactional dimension to linguistics in the form of the illocutionary act, was and is founded on knowledge: *assertions* and *questions*, two of the main classes of speech acts according to Searle (2008 [1972]) have been defined via a certain piece of knowledge (or lack thereof) of either speaker or hearer.

It is no wonder then, that particularly pragmaticists have made knowledge management in conversations and texts a key concern in their analyses of communication. However, the pragmatic turn has also extended and re-organized linguistic epistemology: on the one hand, pragmatics explicitly reject the idea that authentic language use is *only* a means of distributing knowledge (as in: information) that can be defined and judged by its logical content and its 'truth-value'. Rather, language has many social functions beyond the distribution of information, such as the coordination of actions, cooperation, creating and reaffirming solidarity, expressing identity(ies), and – particularly for those with a 'critical' drift – domination or resistance. And of course, all of these functions are interdependent and recursive. At the same time, however, no pragmaticist would argue that communication is *not* also knowledge distribution, which makes a pragmatic look at knowledge organization not only feasible but an important component of a holistic description of natural communication.

It will not be possible to discuss at length how the pragmatic turn has reformed the study of knowledge in language use on all mentioned microscopic levels. Others have done so comprehensively (e.g. Felder and Gardt 2015; Felder and Müller 2009; van Dijk 2014). Let me instead focus on the term that is of central import to this volume: *common ground.*

The relationship between the common ground and knowledge is simple at first glance: the common ground of two interlocutors is the assumed shared knowledge among them. Successful communication depends on the 'amount' of mutual knowledge, and the correctness of their assumptions about the other person's knowledge (or lack thereof) (Clark 1996). Traditionally, one should think that in an ICC situation, the prior common ground (the amount of shared knowledge when the conversation starts) should by default be much smaller than in an intracultural situation. Thus, assuming or deducing correctly what one's interlocutor may know or not know (including things that oneself takes for granted), to then react appropriately, aptly design one's communcative acts for the recipient, and carefully co-construct a joint, "emergent" common ground (Kecskés and Zhang 2009), becomes the key competence to being a successful intercultural speaker and listener (see also Kecskés 2014).

Clark's ideas have provided workable abstractions of how communication works within the discipline of pragmatics since the 1990s, but need to be reconsidered and revised from several perspectives, Kecskés and Zhang (2009) argue. For one, empirical research has shown that "people turn out to be poor estimators of what others know" (Kecskés and Zhang 2009: 336) – but their communication often functions surprisingly well regardless. This would speak in favor of an emphasis of common ground as an emergent, situational, short-term phenomenon, and de-emphasize the *a priori* knowledge that interlocutors bring to the table before the interaction starts. Secondly, both pragmaticists and cognitive linguists have remarked that knowledge (both of the *a priori* and the emergent type) does not resemble quasi-ontological 'pieces' or 'items' in a repository in our mind (similar to a mental encyclopedia), ready to be taken, compared and exchanged with our interlocutors (Kecskés 2019) – as the early versions of common ground theory (and other trends in pragmatics) implicitly held. Some knowledge is "silent" (Konerding 2015: 64), sub-conscious and can hardly be articulated through language (if at all), but may still be part of the common ground (see Section 2.1.2 of this chapter). Other knowledge may be shared *a priori* by the interlocutors, but useless in the concrete communicative situation, because other topics, problems, and intentions are more salient. It will therefore not contribute to the emergence of relevant common ground in the given situation. This shows that common ground theorizing needs to be more explicit about what types of knowledge it refers to, and how exactly knowledge works in communicative practice.

These questions will return in Section 3. For a well-founded discussion, it first appears necessary to bring to the table a perspective from the philosophy of language, a top-down look at how language (as an observable phenomenon) intersects with knowledge, a fundamentally 'hidden', mental concept.

2.1.2 Knowledge in the philosophy of language: Top-down approaches

In the history of the Philosophy of Language, knowledge has been a key term, and not coincidentally, Epistemology is a philosophical discipline in its own right. Many scholars who have approached knowledge as a language-philosophical subject have tried to tackle its complexity by first and foremost defining subcategories into which to organize it. Scholars' minds, it appears, love dichotomies, and epistemologists in and beyond linguistics are no exception. We find arguments for an organization into *episodic* vs. *generic* knowledge, *implicit* vs. *explicit* knowledge, *autobiographic* vs. *collective* knowledge, *semantic* vs. *encyclopedic* knowledge, *procedural* vs. *declarative* knowledge, *knowledge of acquaintance* vs. *knowledge of description*, and many others (see Konerding's overview 2015). The actual categories, their 'contents' and definitions are sometimes translatable into each other, but sometimes they also differ vastly, depending on the branch of the humanities in which they are rooted. The one recurring element in the mentioned typologies is: the count of two.

The most recent trend in many branches of the humanities has been to question and rethink said dichotomies. To name an example, Kecskés (2019) defines three types of knowledge with relevance for ICC (linguistic knowledge, conceptual knowledge, encyclopedic knowledge), while readily admitting that "the relationship between the three types is much more complicated than just a simple trichotomy" (100). In this and many other cases, epistemology is in a process of thinking beyond dichotomies with occasionally centuries-old traditions.

For the aim of this chapter in particular, let me discuss and problematize one binarism that has had a strong impact on functional (pragmatic) approaches to language: the differentiation of *procedural* vs. *declarative* knowledge. This dichotomy has been relevant for much of what is today considered the 'continental' or 'broad' perspective of pragmatics, as the linguistic sub-discipline with action-theoretical philosophical roots drawing on Hegel, Marx, and more recently Habermas (2007 [1981]). 'Broad' pragmatics is based on the idea that *all* linguistic activity should be analyzed through the prism of (inter-)action, and of human beings using language as an *organon*/tool to solve recurring problems in the real world with other human beings (Bühler 2011 [1934]; Huang 2014). Other branches of linguistics originate in sign-theoretical or system-theoretical philosophical foundations, which leaves the field for pragmatics a much 'narrower' one. Still, even within the narrow, 'component' definition of pragmatics, *procedural* and *declarative* knowledge play central roles.

Procedural knowledge – in the status quo of the current discussion – is usually defined as practical knowledge, a skill, a 'knowledge how to'. Many have identified a 'gap' in the lexicon of the English language here, as English does not provide alternative verbs and nouns for this type of knowledge-as-skill (occasionally called *tacit* knowledge), as opposed to, for example, German *kennen* (and its close relative *können*) vs. *wissen* or French *connaître* vs. *savoir* (see also van Dijk 2014: 18). Procedural knowledge is commonly described as bound to an individual organism and 'pre-symbolic', in that it largely defies being communicated from one human mind and body to another. It is acquired step-by-step and fixated in more or less repetitive exercises in real-world practice. Once fully acquired, it is reactivated and used in purposeful activities without much conscious mental presence of the actual skill, often automatically and with little awareness of the concrete process in a given situation. *Declarative* knowledge, in contrast, is bound to symbolic representation, i.e. language use. It can be articulated in a structured form by using the elaborated systems that language provides: semantics, syntax, modes, tenses, etc.

Traditionally, linguists may have felt that the first of these categories, *procedural* knowledge, is decidedly not their responsibility, as per definition, it defies symbolic, linguistic representability. However, theorists in continental pragmatics tend to object. Language, they point out, has developed as a means to 'fix' or at least mitigate the deficit of procedural knowledge – its impossibility to be transferred to our fellow humans – by creating means to communicate at least fragments, or abstractions of our practical, physical experiences to others. Language is able to symbolically "model" (Konerding 2015: 76, transl. KS) in our minds and communicatively "represent" (Konerding 2015: 76) to others our procedural knowledge, covering a vast spectrum ranging from very simple observations about our immediate surroundings, all the way to highly elaborate abstractions and theories. Therefore, declarative knowledge remains relative to pre-symbolic, physical experiences, routines and behaviors in our life practice, and thus always based on procedural knowledge – if at times very indirectly, depending on the level of abstraction. Bühler's philosophy of language (2011 [1934]) has strongly influenced this working hypothesis for linguistic pragmatics, and recent research on the language acquisition of infants (Tomasello 2008, 2014), and on memory and grounded cognition (Barsalou et al. 2003, 2008) have vindicated it, which hints at an important bridge between pragmatic theory and the cognitive sciences.

If all declarative knowledge directly or indirectly stems from procedural knowledge of some form, then the focus of the philosophy of language shifts away from the modalities of how declarative knowledge is *structured* and *represented* in text and talk (as in much of the 'microscopic' research discussed in Section 2.1.1), towards the modalities of how exactly procedural knowledge *determines* declarative knowledge and language. Thus, one key to illuminating some of the interdependence of said knowledge types turns out to be the human body: as procedural knowledge is primarily acquired through physical activity in the world since early childhood, cognitive scientists have directed their attention to how the human body and mind structure and conceptualize the continued flood of sensori-motor experiences. On the one hand, they highlight *embodied knowledge* (see also the following Section 2.1.3), and variables such as *salience* (a combination of *familiarity*, *frequency* and *conventionality*, Giora 2003) for the creation of mental models. On the other hand, cognitive linguistics asks how language must be organized to communicate said mental model to other human beings. It has developed an extensive (though not unambiguous) vocabulary to describe this process, such as "scripts", "schemas", "frames" etc, which describe the link between the physical groundedness of our experiences, routines and social practices, and the way language systematically enables us to communicate about them. Both pragmalinguists and cognitive linguists (e.g. Harder 2010) have picked up on this perspective and connected it with the intersocial dimension of communication, as for example in the socio-cognitive approach to pragmatics (Kecskés 2014, 2019), but also in discourse analysis (van Dijk 2014).

Meanwhile, as a form of collateral damage, the argument outlined here has also deconstructed the very dichotomy it started out from as a working hypothesis: no 'pure' declarative knowledge exists in human societies in the real world – not because it is unthinkable, but because if a piece of knowledge lacks relevance for anyone's real-life practices it becomes, quite literally, 'use-less', marginal, and sooner or later forgotten. Then, however, we must ask ourselves if this category – an empty set – is of any use for those interested in the authentic usage of language, which is what empirical research on language is ultimately all about.

2.1.3 Knowledge, mind, and body in cognitive linguistics

For a full evaluation of how procedural knowledge influences the common ground in ICC, it helps to take note of another – recently deconstructed – dichotomy with high circulation in Western philosophy: the traditional Cartesian dualism between mind and body. For the sake of an integrated approach to mental activity and language use, Lakoff and Johnson (2010), and Fauconnier and Turner (2003) emphasize that any mind using language does so with reference to a human body in which it is situated. The default of human communication must hence be understood not as an interaction between two minds, but as the interaction between two 'body-mind combinations'. This is more than just a secondary remark for intercultural pragmatics: simply put, 'minds' (however we may define that) are heavily shaped by a person's acculturation and socialization, and hence potentially very different when interlocutors communicate across cultures. The human body, however, is remarkably similar all around the world.

It is interesting that the notion of the general biochemical and physical universality of the human body, but the huge variations in how it is used and represented in culture(s), has also been a recent concern of anthropologists, ethnographers and scholars in cultural studies. This is why a look beyond the linguistic realm helps widening the horizon, particularly for the question at hand: where knowledge originates and how it influences the common ground. This will take place in the next section.

2.2 Knowledge and culture

2.2.1 Praxis and embodiment in current examinations of culture

One of the strengths of the postmodern turn in anthropology and cultural studies in the late 20th century was that it brought to bear the performative dimension of culture. In the status quo of cultural theory, culture is fundamentally defined as shared knowledge among a social group, but it is also the signifying and social practices through which that social group articulates and reinstates this knowledge, i.e.: how it routinely creates awareness about its shared knowledge (so that people become aware that they 'have' or 'are' a culture).

In the mid-20th century, a heated controversy was observable between anthropologists of the Geertz school (1973), emphasizing the practical and the observable, and those with a more cognitivistic approach, emphasizing that everything that has to do with the term 'culture' ultimately boils down to shared knowledge in a group (following, among others, Lévi-Strauss 1963 and Althusser 1971) and is hence situated in the minds of the culture's members. This controversy has largely subsided. Most scholars who take culture seriously will agree that its study needs to strike a balance between the cognitive (i.e. shared knowledge) and the social (i.e. the performative acts of culture, including spaces, materialities, embodied practices, etc.) for a full account of how culture influences humans and vice-versa.

The practical, often physical nature of cultural activity, standing in a dialogic relationship with knowledge, has hence been a salient topic in ICC-related disciplines. Among others, Cohen's definition of an "anthropology of knowledge" (2010: 193) emphasizes the importance of bodily experience for human knowledge and proposes a stronger focus on "embodied anthropological inquiry" (2010: 193). She remarks that all our knowledge depends on our "brains, bodies and environments" (2010: 194), which would appear to be a truism, if it were not for the insightful remark that much of the research in knowledge acquisition and processing has either strongly focused on the first term in this row, "our brains" – the main subject of analysis in the cognitive sciences and neuropsychology – or the third, our (social) "environments" – in disciplines such as discourse analysis, in the sociology of knowledge etc. Much research has largely skipped the body as the third entity that heavily influences what we know, and how we learn. Cohen sketches an 'anthropology of knowledge' as a conscious counterpoint, taking the embodied nature of knowledge into account. Again, this is not dissimilar to, for example, Barsalou's (2008); Lakoff and Johnson's (2010) or Tomasello's (2014) approaches to the development of symbolic (linguistic) competencies on the basis of embodied learning.

So instead of purporting strong arguments for 'radical' cultural relativism, as much anthropological research of the 20th century did, today's arguments tend to de-emphasize cultural difference in the long run (van Dijk 2014: 327–330). The contents of our cultural 'knowledges' vary vastly and observably in different parts of the world, but many have argued that the systems of the acquisition, adaption, and categorization of said knowledge, turn out to be not fundamentally different. Cognitive anthropologists emphasize the cognitive similarities of all humans, rather than the (more superficial) differences of knowledge systems (starting with Lévi-Strauss 1963; later in Greenwood 2009). This thought will return and become relevant in Section 3.

2.2.2 Subcultures and domains of practice

To bring a last player to the table of the proposed synthesis of ideas, let me summarize studies on the knowledge distribution in different (sub-)cultures within the same society (rather than in geographically and culturally distant parts of the world). Discourse studies of professional cultures and their relationship to mainstream society have connected the Foucauldian dynamism of knowledge, discourse, and power with linguistic methods (e.g. Felder and Müller 2009). Again, a binarism has fundamentally structured this field of inquiry: *expert* knowledge vs. *lay* knowledge. Traditionally, *expert* knowledge is largely declarative knowledge in the linguistic definition, i.e. it is mostly explicitly and completely documented in written texts, reflecting and shaping the social practice of members of that particular community of knowledge. *Lay* knowledge is mostly implicit, “silent” (Konerding 2015: 64), often procedural, and usually articulated only in spoken language in private settings, if at all (e.g. when parents teach their children basic knowledge about how to brush their teeth, or tie their shoes). Among other things, the ‘silence’ of lay knowledge is a big methodological challenge for linguists who work empirically.

Wichter (1994) has shown on various examples that expert and lay knowledge closely interact and are often translated into each other: pieces of expert knowledge over time become part of the layperson’s lexicon (though in simplified and occasionally misrepresented versions), including their use as source domains for conventional metaphors and metonymy. Meanwhile, experts must (and usually do) adjust their knowledge representation strategies if they wish to participate in mainstream societal discourses, e.g. public debates on the political stage. Konerding (2015) emphasizes the experiential and thus practical applicability in *both* knowledge transfer processes: experts are not just *communities of knowledge*, but *communities of practice*, too: they do not merely ‘know things’, but they work with their knowledge in practice. And laypeople only acquire fragments of expert knowledge if they feel that it has practical relevance for them. Mental models can hence be readily made compatible or ‘translated’ into a different sub-culture, but only if they have practical applicability, i.e. a form of *knowledge-systematic node*, with which to connect the new knowledge to existing shared practices (i.e. the procedural knowledge that has originally shaped them).

This insight, though originally deduced from expert-laypeople communication has high relevance for all forms of ICC: transcultural knowledge transfer does not necessarily require the same existing knowledge (prior common ground) in both cultures A and B, as a foundation on which to transfer knowledge that is familiar to culture A, but new to culture B – as earlier version of intercultural communication theory have implicitly held. Instead, it requires that similar *domains of practice* and similar recurring activities in said domains exist in both cultures. The concrete practices and the ways of speaking about them may differ vastly, but intercultural communication can still be successful, if members of both cultures note the similarities in terms of *domains of practice* in which a certain piece of knowledge or activity is embedded.

So which domains can be considered both a) based on practice and on procedurally acquired knowledge and b) relatively universal for human beings, independently of their cultural background? Of course, the human body and its abilities come to mind again, which relates to Lakoff and Turner’s central claim of embodied knowledge (2010), as discussed in Section 2.1.3. But transculturally shared domains of practice can be found on further, related, but also more complex levels as well, which I will elaborate on in the following section.

3 Towards a cognitive-functional perspective on knowledge and the common ground

The overview of knowledge typologies and knowledge theoretical approaches to questions of intercultural communication has revealed the following trends. Firstly, the humanities are far from providing a one-size-fits-all definition of knowledge and its sub-types that govern the cognitive, the communicative, and the social dimensions of knowledge. Secondly, at several points in the analysis, I have pointed out an argumentative crisis of the dichotomies that have informed the roots of knowledge theories in many disciplines. Partly, traditional dichotomies have already been controversially attacked and partly debunked by self-reflexive and method-reflexive researchers in the relevant field. In other instances, empirical results have indicated the self-contradictory basis of at least some of the dichotomies in question. This is of high relevance for a linguistic pragmatic perspective as well: in the classic view of conversations as the process of solving a 'knowledge coordination problem' (as proposed in early forms of Relevance Theory and Conversation Analysis) any piece of knowledge needed to be either *prior* knowledge before the utterance in question, or *new* knowledge; it could not be both at the same time. In authentic usage, pieces of knowledge items are developed over time, they combine, build upon and blend into each other, and do many other things (Kecskés 2014; Senkbeil 2017a). In any case, we need to be aware that, here as well, we have destabilized the core of an originally binary typology.

Thirdly, a recurrent topic in many arguments in Sections 2 and 3 was the newfound appreciation and emphasis of the human body as the 'missing link' between the cognitive and the social. Many of the sturdiest branches of today's cognitive linguistics, namely cognitive metaphor theory, blending theory, or mental spaces theory, are rooted in the theory of embodiment, arguing that much of human communication (both literal and figurative) works because it relies on the universal sensorimotor apparatus of human bodies existing in fundamentally very similar environments (including the universal laws of physics, human biology, etc.) (Lakoff and Johnson 2010; Langacker 2008; Dancygier and Sweetser 2014).

The following sections will synthesize these observations to create a hypothesis for an extension of common ground theory.

3.1 The common ground: An empractic, embodied, and non-binary approach

While the common ground is a concept which has been amply discussed in pragmatics (Clark 1996), cognitive linguistics (Giora 2003), and at the intersection of both (Kecskés and Zhang 2009), few studies have paid much attention to how the embodied roots of our semantic systems and the empractic roots of communication influence it, a gap which this chapter intends to fill.

For that matter, Kecskés and Zhang's work (2009) is commendable in its impetus to overcome existing dichotomies. For the authors, communicative action is not either fully cooperation-oriented (as pragmatics has traditionally emphasized), or egocentric (as cognitive linguistic empirical research has shown), but both at the same time. What may appear to be a mutually exclusive binary set – cooperation and egocentrism – turns out to be simultaneous active mindsets when people naturally communicate. The authors develop their model of the common ground from Clark (1996) and fundamentally retain a binary organization into *core* common ground and *emergent* common ground. The core common ground consists of assumed pieces of shared knowledge before a conversation starts. Kecskés and Zhang mention three subcategories or "senses" (2009: 347): *common sense*, *culture sense*, and *formal sense*. The emergent common ground is related to the process of communication itself, and to the individuals who communicate with each other, their shared history, and the situational context. Again, the authors subcategorize into *shared sense* and *current sense* (2009: 347).

Extending Kecskés and Zhang's model, I suggest that for an account of knowledge patterns in authentic communication (particularly in inter- and transcultural communication), we need an embodied and empractic perspective on communication in general, while at the same time avoiding to formulate new dichotomies. That is, I am explicitly *not* arguing that there exists embodied knowledge and then another category including all other (non-embodied) knowledge. Instead I treat embodied knowledge as a core – a core with fuzzy boundaries – to which pieces of knowledge that originate beyond embodied experience, but are readily connectable to it, are able to form networks of compound knowledge. The degree of communicability in intercultural encounters – i.e. the question in how far this knowledge can be considered part of the core common ground for all practical intents and purposes – depends on their proximity or distance to domains of practice that exist in (more or less) all cultures.

What does this 'core' consist of, then? The cognitive sciences have asked similar questions, and remarked on core competencies of the human mind to point out that *image schemas* represent basic units of embodied human perception of objects and activities, structuring large parts of our grammar and semantics (Hampe and Grady 2005). Image schemas can, among other things, be considered proto-metaphors which, if connected to one another, enable us to create a plethora of different conceptual metaphors, mental scripts, and cognitive blends. Kimmel (2008) and Senkbeil (2017b) have shown how compounding image schemas can lead to relatively high degrees of complexity and creativity, forming the "scaffolding" (Senkbeil 2017b) for whole narratives (e.g. novels, films) and discourse genres (e.g. in project management), while remaining a combination of simple, fundamental, embodied set pieces. My argument for compound knowledge, which "scaffolds" large parts of our common ground, works similarly: what we may at first glance consider a complicated piece of knowledge with an accordingly high risk of miscommunication if addressed in ICC, may in fact be a network of simple, embodied or otherwise empractic pieces of knowledge. This would make an utterance relying on this network of knowledge, whether it be literal or figuratively, at the same time complex *and* easily understandable across cultures, due to the *hidden common ground*, to which neither interlocutors themselves, nor scholars analyzing intercultural communication have paid much attention to yet.

The hidden common ground hypothesis augments a key idea in Intercultural Pragmatics (Kecskés 2014, 2019): in an intercultural first encounter, the core common ground is – apparently – much smaller than in an intracultural setting, as the interlocutors 'culture sense', entailing "cultural norms, beliefs and values" (Kecskés and Zhang 2009: 347) is logically not congruent – which is why the term "intercultural" is used. Also, the 'formal sense', i.e. the mutual understanding about which language system (and/or sub-system) should be used in the ensuing interaction, is by no means self-evident in an ICC situation (Kecskés 2014). This would leave 'common sense' (the third subcategory of core common ground) as the place where the hidden common ground is, in fact, 'hidden'. And in part, that is true. I would refrain from emphasizing "natural science" and "cognitive reasoning", as Kecskés and Zhang do in their definition (2009: 347), because embodied and empractic knowledge neither involves a necessary understanding of "science", nor "reasoning" to be available to an individual, but still, the hidden common ground contributes a large portion to our common sense knowledge. This portion is, I argue, surprisingly large, so large in fact that the core common ground is not decidedly smaller than in an intracultural situation after all: according to embodiment theory, the repository of embodied knowledge that all human beings share (because the functioning of their bodies is biologically almost exactly the same independently of their cultural background), is remarkably large.

I argue, moreover, that the hidden common ground is more than merely a component of common sense. Rather, the hidden common ground contributes to our formal sense indirectly, it influences our cultural sense and our cultural values (even when our cultural backgrounds differ), and it even heavily influences the emergent common ground by providing an embodied and empractic scaffolding of available resources and affordances with which we then jointly construct an emergent (and usually growing) common ground for continued communicative interaction.

3.2 Examples of the hidden common ground

These hypotheses about the hidden common ground are due some practical support and, ideally, empirical studies. The latter deserve research projects (and publications) in their own right, so let me bolster my point by quoting two examples from existing research.

Senkbeil (2017b) has shown that very different text genres for different readerships in different cultures make use of the exact same semantic domain to conceptualize a complicated cognitive-emotional state hovering between joy and hope, but potentially also pain and fear: the concept pregnancy. If used as a metaphoric source domain, authors/speakers are able to communicate non-trivial ideas interculturally without much risk of being misunderstood (Senkbeil 2017a, 2017b). The concrete point may be very different in different texts, and, of course, embedded in diverse situational contexts. For example, metaphoric pregnancy conventionally entails the optimistic but also anxious feeling of having to wait for a certain event. But it may also be used to express that there is much more to a certain statement/person/object than visible at first glance, e.g. Polonius‘s exclamation about "How pregnant sometimes his [Hamlet's] replies are. . ." (Shakespeare c1602). Furthermore, Senkbeil (2017b) shows how pregnancy is used to communicate a particular version of body horror, when used in terms of an unwanted 'pregnancy with a monster', as it is used in globally successful science fiction/horror narratives like *Alien* (Scott 1979), *Nemesis* (Roth 2010), *Rosemary's Baby* (Polanski 1968), or *The Matrix* (Wachowski and Wachowski 1999). It is important to note, however, that pregnancy is *not* embodied knowledge in the classic sense: roughly half of the human population has not and will never make the first-hand embodied experience, as opposed to clearly embodied domains such as WARMTH, HUNGER, FALLING etc, which are naturally highly productive source domains across languages and cultures (cf. e.g. Kövesces 2006; Yu 2008). Also, pregnancy is a complicated process to express in terms of image schemas: it represents a compound of various image schemas (the CONTAINER schema, ENTERING and LEAVING as specific cases of the SOURCE-PATH-GOAL schema, GROWTH), a diachronic dimension (pregnancies take quite a lot of time), and, as mentioned, an ambiguous mélange of physical and emotional states (joy and wonder, but also pain and loss of control).

Still, pregnancy – in all its complexity – is a culturally universal concept, as all adult humans (for all practical intents and purposes) understand it and are able to use it literally *and* as a metaphoric domain, when they understand that this – figurative speech – is the context in which it is embedded (cf. Musolff et al. 2014). The key to this argument is twofold: it is based on the combination of its close vicinity to *image schemas* and to a *domain of practice* that is of relevance to all human societies: reproduction. The latter – its embeddedness in a concrete practical domain for a whole culture/society – marks the decisive difference between pregnancy and knowledge about, for example, an appendectomy, a sinusitis, or other medical issues. Though the latter medical conditions are similarly common around the world, culturally near-universal, and even gender-independent, they would hardly qualify as viable source domains for literal or non-literal intercultural communication. Except for a certain professional culture, they lack practical significance on a societal scale, as opposed to pregnancy.

Pregnancy may appear a relatively obvious example for a network of knowledge from the core common ground in an ICC situation, in that it combines a close vicinity to embodied knowledge with a high degree of practical societal significance. Let me therefore mention a less unambiguous example.

Consider the following examples of common ground creation and maintenance in spoken intercultural discourse between scientists from Europe and Africa. They stem from the SeLA corpus which is a collection of intercultural conversation among researchers, who collaborate in a common international research project.[1] All speakers in this research project are non-native speakers, so they use English as a lingua franca. Interestingly, one of the key strategies to create a *discursive interculture* (in the sense of ten Thije et al. 2003, 2006 and Kesckés 2014) in the early stages of this group's collaboration is the use of figurative speech, particularly metaphor.

A naive perspective on figurative language would suggest that metaphoric speech should be particularly unhelpful for ICC: the semantic transfer from one domain to another may seem to a) involve culture- and language-specific conventions and b) be difficult to mentally follow/reconstruct in a foreign language. Recent research on metaphor in ICC has suggested, however, that figurative meaning is

1 The SeLA corpus consists of intercultural discourse that has been recorded between 2012 and 2015 within the framework of the international research collaboration *Scientific e-Lexicography for Africa (SeLA)*, in which lexicographers from Germany, South Africa, and Namibia collaborated to produce electronic dictionaries for native African languages. The project was funded by the German Federal Ministry of Education and Research (*Bundesministerium für Bildung und Forschung, BMBF*) and organized by the German Academic Exchange Service (*Deutscher Akademischer Auslandsdienst, DAAD*).

not per se a hindrance for intercultural understanding (Musolff et al. 2014; Senkbeil 2017a, 2020), depending on those factors that cognitive metaphor theory emphasizes: embodiment and image schemas as 'building blocks' for primary and complex metaphors (as explained in Section 2.1.3).

With this in mind, consider the following statements by three different interlocutors (who stem from different countries and different linguistic backgrounds). Early in their first meeting, one scholar suggests to put into writing what the overall goal or goals of this research project should be:

> S1: And so I thought, ok, we have to do some general planning for *the backbone document* we are contemplating in a very broad outline fashion. (emphasis added)

A few minutes later, one of his colleagues describes a research goal she finds important and concludes:

> S2: [this] is somehow *at the heart* of what we are planning to do

Another few minutes later, a third scholar suggests that an international research project needs to define its theoretical and methodological foundation at an early stage and expresses his opinion:

> S3: I would prefer kind of a hybrid theory. And to get that theory going, one should say I'm taking X from theory Y and I'm taking Z from theory X and *I'm building an animal here* and this animal will be the SeLA animal. It will have the *legs* of the function theory and might have the *ears* of the Wiegand theory and then might have the *belly* of the non-theorists. And in this regard, we are building an animal suited for our specific purposes.

Note how the animal metaphor that is first introduced by S1 (to be precise: a body-part-related entailment: "backbone document") becomes, through repetition and extension, a seminal metaphor for the group's common ground. S3 – a scholar from South Africa – argues for an eclectic, interdisciplinary combination of academic theories into a metaphoric "hybrid animal", functionally combining knowledge from the domain ANIMAL with the embodied knowledge of MANUAL ASSEMBLY ("building"). S3's proposal, and particularly its metaphoric expression are certainly not trivial, but neither complexity nor metaphoricity pose an immediate threat to intercultural communication (see also Senkbeil 2017a).

Note also that this development may serve as a prime example for emergent common ground, not *a priori* common ground: it is highly unlikely that S3 or the other speakers anticipated beforehand that the animal metaphor would become the anchor of how they discuss theories and their combination. The metaphor (USING AN ECLECTIC APPROACH TO ACADEMIC THEORIES IS BUILDING A HYBRID ANIMAL) is far from conventional. It develops and emerges in this discursive interculture. S3 may have been semantically primed by S1 and S2, but either way, he can be sure that he is construing a transculturally understandable conceptual metaphor based on a hidden (but firm) common ground.

The reasons are, in fact, similar to the pregnancy example: MANUAL ASSEMBLY ("building") is a culturally universal concept, as since early childhood, humans learn to (and usually enjoy to) use their hands to build things (cf. Tomasello 2008). Knowledge about animals is *not* embodied, but it is difficult to imagine an adult human with no knowledge about the importance of animals as co-inhabitants of their ecosphere – a *domain of practice* with significance to every human community. The basic knowledge about animals that is necessary to communicate metaphorically as in this case, e.g. that different species exist, that different body parts have different vital functions ("ears", "belly", "backbone" and "heart" are explicitly mentioned by S1 and S3), is cross-culturally shared.

All in all, the concrete communicative event of S3's utterance thus relies on three distinct types of knowledge. Firstly, it can be inferred that all listeners should be familiar with the theoretical concepts that are mentioned, (e.g. "the Wiegand theory"). This has to do with their professional sub-culture: this declarative knowledge is an example for a sub-culture-specific common ground, related to a highly-elaborate, but shared *domain of practice* of those involved in this communicative situation. However, as a case in point for the overarching argument of this chapter, I hold that it is interculturally quite straightforward (for both his listeners and the researcher) to understand what S3 wants and how he tries to persuade his colleagues: the key to reconstructing why this metaphoric mapping 'works' interculturally is based on embodiment, augmented by shared practical knowledge about animals and their body parts.

3.3 The two dimensions of the hidden common ground

So in general, intercultural communicability of knowledge(s) depends on two dimensions: their relative closeness to embodied knowledge, and their adaptability to an existing domain of practice in the target culture. As mentioned, embodied knowledge, what it is, where it comes from, and why cognitive linguists have postulated its relative universality for human cognition is well documented (Lakoff and Johnson 2010). But we might still ask ourselves which *domains of practice* can be considered quasi-universal and hence particularly helpful for all (or at least most) intercultural encounters. This question, interestingly, has been addressed by anthropologists and knowledge sociologists, though usually without referring to the cognitive sciences or linguistics. Van Dijk (2014: 167–169) summarizes and formulates a tentative list of domains that may be considered culturally universal for most intents and purposes (starting out from an anthropological perspective).

Adopting and extending this list, I hypothesize that all cultures have roughly the same basic knowledge about the following topics: death, illness and health, hunger and thirst, sleep, bodily products (feces, sweat etc.), physical reactions to external influences (pain, laughter etc.), childhood and growing up, sexuality and reproduction, sexual arousal, kinship, temperature variation, a fundamental division of life into three categories: plants/animals/humans, weather phenomena, day and night, seasons (with few exceptions), the fundamental laws of physics on planet earth, e.g. ubiquitous unidirectional gravity, water in three aggregate states, and compound knowledge that directly follows from such laws, e.g. that all humans have the potential to learn how to swim, but not how to fly, etc.

This list makes no claim for completeness or even theoretical closed-endedness, based on the 'fuzziness' of both dimensions that are in play here. It should serve as a first approximation of the elements of the hidden common ground.

Many of the knowledges in this list are in fact embodied in a classic Lakoffian sense. For example, the fact that different temperatures are normally experienced in connection to different degrees of physical well-being since early infancy has led to WARMTH, COLD, and HEAT being potent source domains for conceptual metaphors. They are highly productive and similar across cultures and languages, as already remarked in Lakoff and Johnson earliest metaphor-theoretical text (2003 [1980]), and exhaustively shown in later empirical work (e.g. Musolff et al. 2014; Yu 2008). Similarly, childhood is quasi-embodied knowledge in the sense that every adult human has experienced childhood him/herself. But, for example, knowledge about kinship is not embodied. Not everybody has a sibling, and not every person knows and is emotionally attached to both their parents. To rationally understand the concept kinship (and use it in figurative or literal language) we need some non-embodied and non-trivial knowledge, for example about the basic principles of heredity. Still, I hold that communication about (real or metaphorical) kinship is interculturally not just possible, but unproblematic: while the semantics and functions of kinship terminology vary vastly across languages and cultures (Gaby 2017), they do so *within* every culture too, because family and kinship are such important *domains of practice*. Intercultural interlocutors are prepared – and we may say surprisingly sensitive – for shared or different usages of such semantic primitives in ICC practice (Goddard and Wierzbicka 2014; Musolff et al. 2014). Thus, using kinship as a source domain for metaphoric speech in intercultural encounters should lead to fewer misunderstandings than a simple culture-contrastive perspective would indicate. The hidden common ground theory aims to explain why this is the case. Also, it can help explain the opposite scenario: when other expressions or whole semantic domains – i.e. those that have little or no foothold in the hidden common ground – fail to communicate appropriately in ICC.

4 Conclusion

The hidden common ground exists in all (or almost all) human communities and is hence essential to understand intercultural understanding, as opposed to misunderstandings that have been so extensively discussed in other ICC studies. I have argued from the vantage point of three general observations that have gained traction in and beyond linguistics.

Firstly, both cognitive linguistic and anthropological sources have emphasized the importance of being aware of intercultural interlocutors as body-mind-combinations, not just as (culturally different) minds. This renders the human body, or rather the embodiment of much of our language, social practices, and thus culture a much higher stake in ICC than has been the case in prior theories of interculturality.

Secondly, defining the general compatibility of *domains of practice* as a primary concern to answer if and how ICC works is related to the praxeological (or functionalist) approach to language as brought forward by Bühler (2011 [1934]) and Habermas (2007 [1981]), among others. Yet, I have argued with the help of two examples that it may be necessary to extend the traditional definition of empractic communication (in Bühler's sense) by noting that *embodiment* and *domains of practice* are generally separate dimensions of similarity and difference in terms of common ground construction. In the Bühlerian school, they are implicitly defined as congruent.

Thirdly, I hope to have shown that the hidden common ground hypothesis augments rather than contradicts the existing knowledge on common ground at the intersection of pragmatics and cognitive linguistics. I have worked with Kecskés and Zhang's (2009) general distinction between prior and emergent common ground, which encapsulates the dynamics between long-term knowledge that exists independently of the concrete communicative interaction, and the potential for quick and spontaneous adaption and extension, which intercultural interlocutors often show. However, the hidden common ground a) makes the prior common ground larger and more stable, particularly through the implementation of embodiment theory; it b) therefore deemphasizes the importance of cultural knowledge (culture sense) as the source of differences and misunderstandings in ICC, and c) it also has a strong bearing on emergent common ground by remarking on the practical, and the shared *domain of practice* in the concrete situation. Take for example the researchers in Section 3.2, who first come to an understanding of their shared goal (emergent common ground) – writing a "backbone document" – to then develop a strategy of how to do it through a metaphor at the intersection of shared embodied and empractic knowledge. Ultimately, the hidden common ground is situated diagonally to prior and emergent common ground, rather than opposed to, or apart from these categories (Kecskés 2019).

Finally, the cognitive-functionalist approach to Intercultural Pragmatics is loosely related to the praxeologist philosophy in neighboring branches of the humanities, such as Geertzian *thick description* of social and cultural practices (1973), or in the social sciences, in which the Bourdieuian *habitus* (1984) has played a central role. For Intercultural Pragmatics, it remains important to emphasize that ICC takes place linguistically and among multilingual individuals (while neither Geertz nor Bourdieu paid much attention to the affordances and issues of multilingualism), so that ICC research centrally remains a linguistic endeavor. Still, the parallels between anthropology, the social sciences, and cognitive and functionalist linguistics demonstrate the strong influence of the pre-symbolic and the empractic – i.e. procedural or tacit knowledge – on the semiotic system language. In the future, awareness of the hidden common ground may contribute to a reform of at least parts of the difference-based didactics of intercultural communicative competence, which remains common around the world.

References

Althusser, Louis. 1971. *Lenin and philosophy, and other essays*. London: New Left Books.

Barsalou, Lawrence, Paula M Niedenthal, Aron K. Barbey & Jennifer A. Ruppert. 2003. Social embodiment. *The Psychology of Learning and Motivation*, 43–92. New York: Academic Press.

Barsalou, Lawrence W. 2008. Grounded Cognition. *Annual Review of Psychology* 59(1). 617–645.

Bourdieu, Pierre. 1984. *Distinction: A Social Critique of the Judgement of Taste*. London: Routledge and Kegan Paul.

Bühler, Karl. 2011 [1934]. *Theory of language: the representational function of language*. Trans. Donald Fraser Goodwin & Achim Eschbach. Amsterdam: Benjamins.

Busse, Dietrich. 2008. Linguistische Epistemologie. In Heidrun Kämper & Ludwig Eichinger (eds.), *Sprache – Kognition – Kultur: Sprache zwischen mentaler Struktur und kultureller Prägung*, 73–114. Berlin & Boston: De Gruyter.

Clark, Herbert H. 1996. *Using language*. Cambridge: Cambridge University Press.

Cohen, Emma. 2010. Anthropology of knowledge. *The Journal of the Royal Anthropological Institute* 16. 193–202.

Dancygier, Barbara & Eve Sweetser. 2014. *Figurative language*. New York: Cambridge University Press.

Dijk, Teun A. van. 2014. *Discourse and knowledge: a sociocognitive approach*. New York: Cambridge University Press.

Domaneschi, Filippo, Simona Di Paola, and Nausicaa Pouscoulous. 2022. The development of presupposition: Pre-schoolers' understanding of regret and too. *Intercultural Pragmatics* 19(3). 345–379.

Fauconnier, Gilles & Mark Turner. 2003. *The way we think: conceptual blending and the mind's hidden complexities*. New York: Basic Books.

Felder, Ekkehard & Andreas Gardt (eds.). 2015. *Handbuch Sprache und Wissen*. Berlin: De Gruyter.

Felder, Ekkehard & Marcus Müller (eds.). 2009. *Wissen durch Sprache: Theorie, Praxis und Erkenntnisinteresse des Forschungsnetzwerkes "Sprache und Wissen"*. Berlin: De Gruyter.
Gaby, Alice. 2017. Kinship Semantics: Culture in the Lexicon. In Farzad Sharifian (ed.), *Advances in Cultural Linguistics*, 173–188. Singapore: Springer.
Geertz, Clifford. 1973. *The Interpretation of Cultures: Selected Essays*. New York: Basic Books.
Giora, Rachel. 2003. *On our mind: salience, context, and figurative language*. Oxford: Oxford University Press.
Goddard, Cliff & Anna Wierzbicka. 2014. *Words and meanings: lexical semantics across domains, languages, and cultures*. Oxford: Oxford University Press.
Greenwood, Susan. 2009. *The anthropology of magic*. Oxford: Berg.
Habermas, Jürgen 2007 [1981]. *Reason and the Rationalization of Society. The theory of communicative action*. Transl. by Thomas MacCarthy Vol. 1. Boston: Beacon.
Hampe, Beate & Joseph E. Grady (eds.). 2005. *From perception to meaning: image schemas in cognitive linguistics*. Berlin: Mouton de Gruyter.
Harder, Peter. 2010. *Meaning in mind and society: a functional contribution to the social turn in cognitive linguistics*. Boston: De Gruyter Mouton.
Huang, Yan. 2014. *Pragmatics*. Second edition. Oxford: Oxford University Press.
Kecskés, Istvan. 2010. The paradox of communication: Socio-cognitive approach to pragmatics. *Pragmatics and Society* 1(1). 50–73.
Kecskés, István. 2014. *Intercultural pragmatics*. Oxford: Oxford University Press.
Kecskés, István. 2019. *English as a Lingua Franca: The Pragmatic Perspective*. Cambridge: Cambridge University Press.
Kecskés, István & Zhang Fenghui. 2009. Activating, seeking, and creating common ground: A socio-cognitive approach. *Pragmatics & Cognition* 17(2). 331–355.
Kimmel, Michael. 2008. Image schemas in narrative macrostructure: combining cognitive linguistic with psycholinguistic approaches. In Jan Auracher & Willie van Peer (eds.), *New beginnings in literary studies*, 158–184. Newcastle: Cambridge Scholars Pub.
Konerding, Klaus-Peter. 2015. Sprache und Wissen. In Ekkehard Felder & Andreas Gardt (eds.), *Handbuch Sprache und Wissen*, 57–80. Boston: De Gruyter Mouton.
Kövecses, Zoltán. 2007. *Metaphor in culture: universality and variation*. Cambridge: Cambridge University Press.
Lakoff, George & Mark Johnson. 2003 [1980]. *Metaphors we live by*. Chicago: University of Chicago Press.
Lakoff, George & Mark Johnson. 2010. *Philosophy in the flesh: the embodied mind and its challenge to Western thought*. New York, NY: Basic Books.
Langacker, Ronald W. 2008. *Foundations of cognitive grammar. Vol. 1: Theoretical prerequisites*. Stanford: Stanford University Press.
Lévi-Strauss, Claude. 1963. *Structural anthropology*. New York: Basic Books.
Musolff, Andreas, Fiona Macarthur & Giulio Pagani (eds.). 2014. *Metaphor and intercultural communication*. London: Bloomsbury Academic.
Polanski, Roman. 1968. *Rosemarie's Baby*. Paramount Pictures.
Roth, Philip. 2010. *Nemesis*. London: Cape.
Scott, Ridley. 1979. *Alien*. Twentieth Century Fox.
Searle, John R. 2008 [1972]. *Speech acts: an essay in the philosophy of language*. Cambridge: Cambridge University Press.

Senkbeil, Karsten. 2017a. Image schemas across modes and across cultures: communicating horror in Philip Roth's Nemesis and Ridley Scott's Alien. *Language and Literature* 26(4). 323–339.

Senkbeil, Karsten. 2017b. Figurative language in intercultural communication – a case study of German-Southern African international academic discourse. *Intercultural Pragmatics* 14(4). 465–491.

Senkbeil, Karsten. 2020. Idioms in intercultural communication: A cognitive and pragmatic perspective. *International Journal of Language and Culture* 7(1). 38–62.

Shakespeare, William. 1919 [c1602]. *Hamlet, Prince of Denmark.* (Ed.) K. Deighton. London: Macmillan. http://www.shakespeare-online.com/plays/hamlet_2_2.html (26 May, 2020).

ten Thije, Jan D. 2003. The transition from misunderstanding to understanding in intercultural communication. In Laszlo I. Komlosi, Peter Houtlosser & Michiel Leezenberg (eds.), *Communication and Culture: Argumentative, cognitive and linguistic perspectives*, 197–214. Amsterdam: Sic Sac.

ten Thije, Jan D. & Kristin Bührig (eds.). 2006. *Beyond misunderstanding: linguistic analyses of intercultural communication*. Amsterdam: Benjamins.

Tomasello, Michael. 2008. *Origins of human communication*. Cambridge: MIT Press.

Tomasello, Michael (ed.). 2014. *The new psychology of language: cognitive and functional approaches to language structure*. New York: Psychology Press, Taylor & Francis Group.

Wachowski, Lana & Lilly Wachowski. 1999. *The Matrix*. Paramount Pictures.

Wichter, Sigurd. 1994. *Experte- und Laienwortschätze: Umriss einer Lexikologie der Vertikalität.* Tübingen: Niemeyer.

Yu, Ning. 2008. Metaphor from body and culture. In Raymond W. Gibbs (ed.), *The Cambridge handbook of metaphor and thought*, 247–261. Cambridge: Cambridge University Press.

Olga Obdalova, Ludmila Minakova, and Aleksandra Soboleva

The linguistic code as basis for common ground building in English as a foreign language

Abstract: This study was designed to check the validity of two intertwined hypotheses according to which linguistic code plays the role of common ground in L2 use (see Kecskes 2007, 2013) and formulaic language use is an indicator of shared core common ground (Holtgrave 2002). When common ground among participants is high and figurative language is more likely to be understood, and probably more likely to be used, while literal interpretations (linguistic code-based use) tend to be preferred when common ground is low.

In order to check the validity of the hypotheses we organized conversation groups on two levels: intermediate and advanced. On each level there were two groups created. The participating groups received two topics to discuss for 20 minutes on different days. The result was four batches of datasets, each of which was transcribed. The data analysis was based on two measurements: number of formulaic units (idioms, SBUs, speech formulas) and metaphorical density (the number of words used in metaphorical sense divided by the number of words used).

It will be claimed and demonstrated through qualitative and quantitative data that common ground construction in L2 EFL users is highly predetermined by the interplay between the interlocutors' discourse design and salience as a perception quality. It will be argued that speaker's and listener's perspectives are attributable to the linguistic coding by the non-native communicants.

We provide evidence on the role of the linguistic code as a tool of communication in common ground construction and we establish the link between shared core common ground and the nature of communicative means used. The study can deepen our understanding of cognitive processes in interactions between speakers of English as a foreign language at different levels of common ground construction.

Acknowledgment: This study was supported by the Tomsk State University Development Programme ("Priority-2030").

https://doi.org/10.1515/9783110766752-010

1 Introduction

Communication, which is usually called intercultural or cross-cultural, occurs when representatives of different cultures, wishing to achieve mutual understanding, overcome linguo-cultural (and, as in any other type of communication, socio-personal) differences. Using the definition of intercultural communication as "a symbolic, interpretive, transactional, contextual process in which people from different cultures create shared meanings" (Lustig and Koester 2010: 46), we thus focus on its cognitive aspect, that is the creation in its process of common ground as a cognitive basis for communicative success. The interpretive and transactional nature of communication suggests that shared meanings are not just "out there" to be discovered. Rather, meanings are created and understood by groups of people as they participate in the ordinary and everyday activities that form the context for common interpretations. The focus, therefore, must be on the ways that people attempt to "make sense" of their common experiences in the world.

One of the most important findings in pragmatics is that in intercultural communication interlocutors can successfully communicate when they create a common ground, "composed of shared knowledge of prior experience" (Kesckes and Zhang 2009: 333). In classic pragmatics this common ground is considered as a sense shared between participants of communication. Schiffer (1972) called it "mutual knowledge", considered common knowledge within a group or two individuals who presume shared knowledge of word meanings and norms for communication. The same idea was developed by other scientists under different terms. Prince (1981: 232f) suggested the term "assumed familiarity". Following Grice (1981: 190; Grice 1989: 65), Stalnaker (2002) named it "common ground", which he characterized as "presumed background information shared by participants in a conversation" (Stalnaker 2002: 701). According to this view, this notion implies "what speakers [take] for granted – what they [presuppose] when they [use] certain sentences" (Stalnaker 2002: 702).

The dominant pragmatic view (e.g. Stalnaker 1978; Clark and Brennan 1991; Clark 1996) considers common ground as a category of specialized mental representations that exist in the mind before the actual communication process takes place. Over the last few years the traditional approach to common ground (e.g. Clark and Brennan 1991; Clark 1996) has been modified to take into account its complexity. Essentially, modern pragmatic theories attach great importance to cooperation in the process of communication (Barr 2004; Barr and Keysar 2005; Colston and Katz 2005). In these theories, common ground is considered as a distributed form of mental representation adopted as a basis on which successful communication is warranted.

The other approach to common ground is based on the cognitive view, which emerged under the umbrella of recent research in cognitive psychology, linguistic pragmatics, and intercultural communication. Cognitive researchers (Barr 2004; Barr and Keysar 2005; Colston and Katz 2005, Arnseth and Solheim 2002; Koschmann and Le Baron 2003) form a more dynamic view, which conceptualizes common ground as emergence-through-use notion, highlighting an emergent property of ordinary memory processes. The most robust evidence against cooperation and common ground as an a priori mental state derives from empirical cognitive research, which reported the egocentrism of speaker-hearers in mental processing of communication and postulated the emergent property of common ground.

The socio-cognitive approach developed by Kecskes, emphasizes that common ground is a dynamic construct (which complies with other theories) that is mutually constructed by interlocutors throughout the communicative process based both on prior and emergent elements. Findings about the egocentric approach of interlocutors to communication are also confirmed by Giora's (1997, 2003) graded salience hypothesis and Kecskes' (2003, 2008) dynamic model of meaning.

According to current research, if people have common or similar prior experience and participate in similar actions and events, – all that will result in the creation of a common ground. Thus, similar prior contexts, prior experience and similar understanding of the actual situational context will build common ground. But it should be noted that in intercultural communication this common ground exists to a smaller degree than in intracultural encounters. This can be explained as follows. The participants of intercultural communication do not share much of presumed common knowledge and common experience, this leads to a "problem approach" in second language and intercultural communication research. Furthermore, intercultural communication between speakers belonging to different linguistic communities may have difficulty with speaking and interpreting an interlocutor's discourse (Obdalova, Minakova and Soboleva 2017) as they may lack familiar words as a result of a linguistic deficit in intercultural communication. In light of this idea, common ground is directly related to prior context, which constitutes core common ground, and actual situational context considered as emergent common ground. It is also closely connected with cultural models, cultural beliefs and intercultures.

Why is that? Because cultural models make up a set of scenarios that individuals can choose from in any given situation. They provide options for possible plans of action for the individual or possible interpretation of actions of other individuals. The choice is driven by a number of factors including prior experience, the degree of similarity of the given cultural model. Kronenfeld (2008) argued that there is no guarantee that different individuals involved in a given situation will all be working off the same cultural models, in which the participants' cultural norms attached to their first language (core common ground) significantly differ from each other. This is where interculturality and interplay of cooperation and egocentrism become important from the perspective of common ground.

As said above, in intercultural communication the core common ground that participants bring into the interaction is limited. Consequently, relying on limited core common ground interlocutors need to seek, create and co-construct common ground which appears to be emergent common ground in the process of communication. Thus, core common ground refers to the relatively static (diachronically changing) common knowledge and beliefs that usually belong to a certain speech community as a result of prior interactions and experience, whereas emergent common ground refers to the dynamic, particularized knowledge created in the course of communication and conditioned by the actual situational context.

This can be split into three subsets: common sense (generality of the world), cultural sense (which encompasses the social behavior and norms found in society, community or nation), and formal sense (generalized knowledge about the language system) (Kecskes and Zhang 2009). In contrast, the actual contextual part is knowledge that is aroused or evolved as shared enterprises in the particular situational context. This actual contextual part can be split into two subsets: shared sense and current sense (Kecskes and Zhang 2012).

Shared sense entails the particularized knowledge about personal (not of community) experiences that interlocutors share. Current sense entails the emergent perception of the current situation. It constitutes a more private part of common ground.

As Kecskes argues, formulaic language use is a significant indicator of core common ground (Kecskes 2013: 173). Formulaic expressions are usually claimed to be group-identifying since they indicate a speech community's preference in certain interactional situations (Tannen and Oztek 1981; Kecskes 2007; Nowicka 2022). Formulaic language is the part of core common ground that speakers can rely on. High language proficiency contributes to proper and better understanding of these expressions and helps them avoid misunderstandings.

From this perspective the aim of this paper is to figure out what role linguistic code plays in common ground creation in EFL use in a particular communication context.

2 Experimental procedures

This study was designed to check the validity of two intertwined hypotheses. According to Kecskes's view, linguistic code plays the role of common ground in L2 use (see Kecskes 2007, 2013). On the other hand, formulaic language use is an indicator of shared core common ground (Holtgrave 2002).

We assume that when common ground among participants is high, figurative language is more likely to be understood, and probably more likely to be used. While literal interpretations, based on linguistic code use, tend to be preferred when common ground is low.

The main problem in intercultural interactions is that interlocutors do not and cannot have that type of common ground that intracultural speakers sharing one native language and culture (L1 speakers) have because they lack common prior experience. As was proved, non-native speakers lack the socio-cultural background knowledge in the target language being "outsiders", and not members of the given speech community (L2)" (Kecskes et. al. 2018: 221). Consequently, since they have little shared knowledge to activate and seek, they have to create common ground in the course of conversation.

2.1 Research questions

- What is the EFL speakers' preferable linguistic device in building common ground while producing and interpreting the utterance (figurative or literal units)?
- To what extent is common ground dependent on the personal context of EFL learners using non-native language code for communication?
- What type of common ground (core or emergent) contributes more significantly to the EFL interlocutors' mutual understanding in an actual situational context when non-native language code is used?

2.2 Theoretical background

In this study, the process of building common ground will be analyzed by examining the use of formulaic language which serves a shared basis for "coordinating joint communicative actions" (Kesckes 2007: 195).

There are major debates and numerous proposals on how best to define idiomaticity and formulaic language. One definition suggests that formulaic language is "a sequence, continuous or discontinuous, of words or other meaning elements, which is, or appears to be prefabricated: that is, stored and retrieved whole from memory at the time of use, rather than being subject to generation or analysis by the language grammar." (Wray 2000: 465). As it was defined in Kecskes, I. et. al. (2018), formulaic and figurative language is a preferred way of saying things and organizing thoughts in a language when native speakers communicate.

According to Kecskes, collocations, fixed expressions, lexical metaphors, idioms and situation-bound utterances can all be considered as examples of formulaic language (Howarth 1998; Wray 1999, 2005; Kecskes 2000) in which word strings occurring together tend to convey holistic meanings and operate as a single semantic unit. Formulaic language is "the heart and soul of native-like language use" (Kecskes 2008: 194).

In our research we deal with the use of semantically transparent language (literal language) and metaphorical use. We take into account that there is a difference between a metaphor and an idiom, because one can understand a metaphor even with no prior knowledge or context. According to Allerton (1984: 36), a true idiom has a meaning that has no clear relationship to the literal meaning. It is made by an institutionalised combination of words, which is semantically non-compositional and whose syntactic, lexical and phonological form is to a greater and lesser degree fixed. A metaphor expresses an analogy between two objects or ideas that are conveyed by comparing the two unrelated objects with each other. We bear in mind that overarchingcross-domain mappings that influence our thinking refer to conceptual metaphors (Lakoff Johnson 1980), whereas linguistic metaphors are the linguistic realizations of those conceptual metaphors. Conceptual metaphors are a preexisting, fixed part of our conceptual system of knowledge on the basis of which we can make sense of meanings, particularly of novel, imaginative expressions. The degree of transparency of both an idiom and a metaphor is dependent on the degree of analysability, when their internal semantic structure determines understanding of the literal or figurative meaning and their correspondences.

Many words have both literal sense and metaphorical meaning. We bear in mind that idioms are metaphorical units, while some SBUs or speech formulas have no metaphorical meaning. We selected only those words and expressions that have non-literal meaning and referred them to the group of metaphorical units.

> ***e.g SBU:*** *what can I do for you? Thank you for your help. (They have NO metaphorical meaning).*
>
> ***Speech formula:*** *That's OK.; you are right. I agree. (They have no metaphorical senses).*

Note that all SBUs and idiomas are metaphorical, but not all formulaic language units have a metaphorical sense.

Let us demonstrate the choice of linguistic means by the following samples for each category of lexical units taken from the transcripts of the interlocutors' communication:

Speech formulas: *let's begin, first of all, I'm completely agree, can you repeat, I agree with . . ., I believe*
Idioms: *pay attention, do your best, at least, at first sight, body language*
SBU: *I don't get, what about you, it's not the problem, you're welcome, open the doors, it's alright*
Metaphorical: *open the doors, keep the contact, judge at the first sight*

We proceed from Lakoff and Johnson' idea (1980) that the metaphorical use of the word correlates with the degree of abstractness in a word's context. We applied the Abstract-Concrete rule (Turney et al. 2011) to our dataset: considering a concrete concept when used to describe an abstract one as a metaphor. Literary meaning is the most direct or specific meaning of a word or expression (concrete), while metaphorical is the conceptual meaning suggested by the word that goes beyond its literal meaning (abstract).

To construct our data set we introduced two measures, on which the data analysis was based:

measure 1 – **the number of formulaic units** including idioms, situation bound utterances (SBUs), and speech formulas (NFU);
measure 2 – **metaphorical density,** which is the number of words used in a metaphorical sense divided by the number of words used (MD).

2.3 Setting and subjects

The experiment was organized in the natural educational settings of Tomsk State University (Russia) in the frames of the EFL courses for linguistic and non-linguistic students. The context of communication can be described as intercultural communication (Obdalova, Minakova and Soboleva 2016). The participants used English as a foreign language in their interpersonal interaction being themselves representatives of various cultures and speech communities, namely, Russians (N=5), Buryat (N=2), Tuwinian people (N=1), Kazakhs (N=3), Chinese (N=2), Vietnamese (N=1). The core common ground between all of them is that they all are users of English with different levels of proficiency. The English language was employed as a common foreign language by all participants. At the same time, the majority of participants belong to the Russian speech community though some of them are citizens of different countries, Kazakhstan and Russia. Buryat and Tuwinian people are Russian citizens but they constitute different cultural groups. Buryat people come from an ethnic group of Mongols, speaking the Buryat language, historically formed in the area of Lake Baikal and united by a common culture and history. Tuwinian people are the people of the Turkic language group, representatives of the ancient Turkic peoples, constituting the main population of Tuva in Russia. They speak Tuvan, which is part of the Sayan group of Turkic languages. Chinese and Vietnamese relate to a common large group of the South-Eastern culture whose native speech communities are different. This educational environment is formed by the variety of the abovementioned factors and produces a wide socio-cultural context (Obdalova, Minakova and Soboleva 2019).

Participants were 14 individuals, aged 18–22. They were divided into two groups with Intermediate (Group 1, Non-linguistic students of the Institute of Economics and Management, N=6) and Advanced (Group 2, linguistic students of the Faculty of Foreign Languages, N=8) proficiency in English (G1Inter. and G2Adv. correspondingly). All the participants gave written informed consent before the start of the experiment.

Thus, their communication in a foreign language serves as a vehicle for carrying their personal verbal and cultural prior knowledge and experience and constitutes the interlocutors' personal context.

2.4 Data collection

Data were collected in the arranged context oriented communication. The participating groups received 2 topics to discuss for 20 minutes on different days. We assigned participants issues they could be interested to discuss. One talking point topic dealt with the importance of physical appearance in modern society. The second issue related to the role of English as a global language and its impact on people of different cultures.

We assumed that the topic for discussion could be formulated as a question, as a statement, or as a problematic situation. The two tasks representing different actual situational contexts were designed in the following way:

Actual situational context 1 (ASC1)

Please, discuss the following topic:

Does English unify or divide the world?

Talking points:
- What is the role of English for professional development in the modern world?
- What do you think about the "language barrier" and "cultural divide"?
- Do languages separate people from different countries and cause problems?

Support your opinion.

Actual situational context 2 (ASC2)

Please, discuss the following topic:

Do you judge people at first sight?

Talking points:
- How important do you think it is to make a good first impression when you meet a new person?
- What do you judge people on when you first meet them?
- How much do we judge people at first sight?
- Do you think the expression 'Appearances are deceptive' is true? Why?

Support your opinion.

Both discussions were scheduled for different days in the suggested sequence of tasks.

Due to the pandemic outbreak the sessions were hosted via Zoom chosen as a leader in modern enterprise video communications. It provides remote communications services using cloud computing and offers software for video, voice, chat, and content sharing. The process of communication was video recorded and then transcribed into a typed text. The result was four batches of datasets, consisting of 1269 types of words in total used by the interlocutors.

2.5 Data obtained

Thus, we received quantitative data for further analysis. When talking about word count, we distinguish between types and tokens. Types are the distinct words in a text or corpus, whereas tokens are the words, including repeats.

Table 1 shows the number of tokens and types of words used by the participants in the transcripts. Words were counted for each communication group (G1Inter, G2Adv.) and each task (T1, T2) separately with the help of VocabProfile, a software for text vocabulary analysis (Cobb).

Table 1: The number of tokens and types of words.

Words	G1Inter ASC 1	G2Adv. ASC1	G1Inter ASC 2	G2Adv. ASC 2
Tokens	869	1298	1228	1583
Types	281	310	326	352

As we can see from the table, after the fulfillment of two tasks the number of tokens, that is the total number of words in the speech of participants, is calculated as 869 and 1228 for G1Inter and 1298 and 1583 for G2Adv.

When we estimate the types of words in their speech, which refers to different words used, we obtain values 281 and 326 for G1Inter after two tasks and 310 and 352 for G2Adv.

From the next table one can see the results of quantitative analysis we do to evaluate the number of formulaic units and metaphorical density (Table 2). We measured metaphorical density as the number of words used in a metaphorical sense divided by the total number of words used.

Table 2: The results of quantitative analysis according to two measures.

Measure	G1Inter ASC 1	G2Adv. ASC 1	G1Inter ASC 2	G2Adv. ASC 2
NFU	40	76	43	82
MD	0.11	0.20	0.09	0.19

The data obtained were statistically processed according to the student T-test criterion. As can be seen from the table, the differences in the data obtained in the groups are significant. This confirms our hypothesis that interlocutors' personal context has an impact on the building of common ground in each of the actual situational contexts.

The results show that the number of formulaic units for two tasks equals 40 and 43 for G1Inter and 76 and 82 for G2Adv. This fact shows that formulaic language is more likely to be used, and probably to be understood by the participants of communication who are more confident English speakers.

The values of metaphorical density reach approximately 20 and 10 percent of all the words in communication for G2Adv. and G1Inter. correspondingly.

The T-test proved the significance in the difference of the results obtained:

for NFU, $t = 11.2$, the result is significant at $p \leq 0.01$

for MD, $t = 10$, the result is significant at $p \leq 0.01$

3 Analysis and discussion

The first research question focuses on exploring whether the EFL speakers in the actual situational context prefer figurative or literal linguistic units to build a common ground while producing and interpreting the utterance.

The study also attempted to shed some light on the extent the common ground is dependent on the personal context of EFL learners using non-native language code for communication, which is concerned with the second research question.

The third research question relates to the identification of the type of common ground (core or emergent), which contributes more significantly to the EFL interlocutors' mutual understanding in the actual situational context when non-native language code is used.

As we can see, the students of both groups, G1Adv. and G2Inter., mostly rely on the linguistic code of EFL in getting mutual understanding with no regard to any cultural background. This leads to the priority of literal meaning over non-literal (figurative language and formulaic language). The results obtained are consistent with those of Kecskes, who found that ELF language use generally lacks idiomaticity, which is the characteristics of native-native communication (Kecskes 2008).

The findings suggest that EFL speakers strive to convey their ideas and give much attention to expressing themselves, ignoring the grammar rules and other participants' opinions. We assume that this causes the lack of cooperation between the interlocutors. The speakers depend on their limited linguistic experience using various communicative strategies to deliver their message. They employ such discursive techniques as paraphrasing, questioning, probing of words, repetitions, extended explanations, etc.

As an example, we present here 2 excerpts from conversations on Actual situational context 1(ASC1) and Actual situational context 2 (ASC2). The grammar and structure of speech are preserved in the form produced by the participants. Dataset examples below may contain ungrammatical linguistic uses which we ignore as insignificant for the type of analysis we do in our research.

Formulaic language units in focus in these excerpts are underlined.

Let's have a closer look at **ASC1**.

(1) **Student 1 (S1):** . . . *Modern world and English in itself . . . I suppose . . . in today's . . . we can't rid of . . . maybe some kind of knowledge in English . . . That is problem for other people, who would like to speak but they couldn't or can't, it depends, and for my opinion this situation, when we are feeling that barrier – it is not very good. We can overcome it. We're simply to learn, to study, to take part in some any discussion like today. Maybe . . .*

> **Student 2 (S2):** *Can I disagree with you? Well, you know, so we were talking about the percentage of people who can't speak English, saying Russian, and you're talking about so this, you know,* ***English is a tool to unite people. It's impossible.*** *Not many people in our country can speak English.*
>
> **Student 1 (S1):** *Of course, because if we talk about these people who can't speak English – for them it's a really big problem . . .*

A closer inspection of the text of the first conversation reveals that units "*can overcome (a language barrier)*", "*can disagree with you*", and "*of course*" are formulaic language units engaged in common base construction. Out of these three, only '*overcome (a language barrier)*' in the given context can be defined as potentially metaphorical, because its meaning is figurative. For example, of the many senses of 'overcome' listed in the dictionaries, the basic sense is 'to get the better of' as '*overcome* difficulties' or 'to gain the superiority', e.g. to overcome the enemy. In the literal sense the word 'barrier' is a physical object that keeps two areas, people apart. But in the given context '*overcome a language barrier*' the phrase means if you overcome a problem or a feeling, you successfully deal with it and control it.

Our analysis of the linguistic utterances rests on an assumption of common ground that participants bring into interaction based on their prior experience of the use of English. As seen in ASC 1, when S1 points to the necessity of people to speak English, because '*it is not good*' when you cannot, as other people won't understand you, and says "***we can't rid of . . . maybe some kind of knowledge in English..***", the speaker points to a generally accepted fact of the world today that all people try to learn English. S2 openly disagrees, replying ***English is a tool to unite people. It's impossible.*** Here there is an assumption that S2 understands S1' English and the message of the utterance though there are a lot of grammar mistakes in the speech. An important thing is that though S1 uses an idiom '*get rid of something*', which is a part of figurative language, this did not distort the conversation. This speaks to the fact that S1 and S2 built not only a core common ground but also an emergent common ground as in mental processing of communication (Kecskes and Zhang 2009) S2 overcame the linguistic troubles and got the meaning of the utterance. S2 replies that it is impossible for all people to learn English which does not make it ***'a tool to unite',*** inferring the idea that not all people in the world can speak English as a common language which makes it a divide between people and a ***'big problem'***. The achieved mutual understanding can be considered as an act of establishing emergent common ground, because S1 and S2 continued to communicate, and the use of ***'Of course'*** signals that they finally reached not only understanding but also an agreement in the point.

Now let us have a look at the phrase '***saying Russian***'. This is a very interesting case, which we would like to focus on specially. Essentially, in the context of intracultural communication between native speakers of Russian, this phrase sounds like a calque from Russian '*skazhem russkije*', which corresponds to '*let us say, Russians*', '*you know, Russians*', '*say, Russians*'. Russian EFL interlocutors use this calquerized expression from their native tongue which constitutes their shared knowledge implied by this lexical unit. These private contexts incorporate core knowledge (tied to prior experience and common cultural grounding), which is the public part of the private context shared by the other members of the speech community. Due to this, the interlocutors gain understanding of the phrase though it is incorrect in English, and it triggers further discussion between them without any difficulty. On the contrary, for a native speaker of English this strain of words might sound unnatural and cause difficulty in understanding its meaning. Thus, we deal with a core common ground supported by the commonality of linguistic, cultural and personal contexts, as well as with an emergent common ground conditioned by the actual situational context and the use and perception of figurative language. Here, core common ground affords Russian speech community participants to seek for understanding and interact based on commonly presumed shared sense. Thus, we may infer the following finding: the greater personal context is, the greater is the core common ground, which contributes to satisfying an informational exchange.

ASC2

(2) **Student 3:** *...... I think there's no great importance to make a good impression because you just should be yourself, don't try to be better then you are, I mean.*

Student 4: *I am completely agree with Nastya. I think you don't have to impress anyone at first sight. It is not important because you can't be liked by everyone. All people are different. You can't make people love you or like you during the first meeting. So, I don't think it's really that important, but it's important when you work, when you're beginning your work, when you 're at the first interview. And in these situations it's really important to make an influence, a good impression, because it really can help you in future during the work time ...*

Student 3: *OK. Well, I don't know about any situation, but there are different kinds of situation which can be important in your life. For example, when you go to some meeting to impress your employer. So, I think in this situation it's very important to look like very responsible and neat person .....*

ASC2 excerpt contains several formulaic units to construct a common base by the interlocutors. Such units as '*no great importance to make a good impression*', '*I am completely agree with*', '*to make an influence ... a good impression*' refer to formulaic language.

‘*To make a good impression*’ is an idiom, meaning ‘*to impress; to create a good feeling, to give people a good opinion*’, whereas in its literal sense the verb ‘*make*’ will imply something like ‘*form (something) by putting parts together or combining substances*’.

Basically, our special attention is attached to the unit ‘*be yourself*’. Its literal meaning in Russian implies ‘*byt' soboj*’, while its figurative sense is ‘*pridi v sebya, ne glupi*’, which corresponds to the following English meaning ‘*to behave in a natural way, rather than trying to pretend to be different*’. Thus, in Russian, this unit has two senses, literal and metaphorical. As we may assume, in the given situational context the emergent common ground is constructed by Russian speaking participants on the basis of their prior common ground shared by them as members of the same speech community.

Another interesting implication from this excerpt is the following. The interlocutors start speaking about ‘*no great importance*’ of the first impression. S3 expresses this idea and the S4 supports it using the formulaic expression “*I am completely agree with you*’. But, then, S4 develops the idea coming to stating that a first impression is important for a work application, when a person is being interviewed. S4 deliberately seeks to express this idea by using two consecutive phrases ‘*to make an influence*’ and ‘*a good impression*’ to make the point clear. From this we may infer the assumption, that the speaker designs his utterance in such a way that the interlocutor gets a good reason to believe that the addressee can readily understand what was meant on the basis of the utterance along with the rest of their common ground. This appears in the form of a deductive process that contains repairs and adjustments to bring more understanding to the conversation.

In the next conversational turn S3 supports this idea and agrees with S4' utterance. This brings us to an assumption that the emergent common ground between S3 and S4 discussing the question ‘*How important do you think it is to make a good first impression when you meet a new person*?’ has been constructed on the basis of identification of one common sense – if one needs to find a good job, he or she really needs to produce a good impression on the employer.

4 Conclusion

Inspired by research in socio-cognitive pragmatics, we examined the role of linguistic code in building a common ground between EFL interlocutors in an arranged situational context and established the link between shared core common ground and the nature of communicative means used.

In this study, we provide evidence on the prominent role of the linguistic code as a tool of communication in common ground construction. Linguistic code manifests itself within conversational context in the extensive use of words with literal meaning. It facilitates perception and understanding by the interlocutors without hard cognitive efforts. What is more, non-native speaker's and listener's perspectives are highly attributable to the linguistic coding, which serves as a preferred (subconscious) tool of communication in common ground construction. The results demonstrated that this works very well in intracultural communication because interlocutors have communality, relatively common conventions, norms and beliefs, which basically constitute a firm common ground for their interactions. They need to seek and create new common ground to that extent that is immediately connected to the actual situational context in which the interaction occurs.

On the basis of analyzing real language data, we demonstrate that core common ground construction in EFL users is highly predetermined by the interplay between the interlocutors' discourse design and salience as a perception quality. Meanwhile emergent common ground is based on using and understanding formulaic language in order to reach the adequacy in communication.

The data obtained prove that more advanced foreign language proficiency is linked to more confident use of formulaic and metaphorical language. The measures introduced in our study – the number of formulaic units and metaphorical density – were applied for quantitative analysis of the samples produced by Intermediate and Advanced EFL students whose communication was based on non-native language code. The T-test has proved the significance in the difference of the results obtained. Thus, the validity of the hypotheses that linguistic code plays the constructive role for common ground building and formulaic language use is an indicator of shared core common ground has been confirmed. High common ground among EFL participants underlies a higher density of figurative language in speech, while language code-based speech characterizes a low common ground.

A limitation of the analysis of a common ground construction in the present study is determined by the research design, which did not fully explore the socio-cultural personal contexts of the interlocutors. The level of EFL proficiency served a decisive factor for comparing the speech production in the arranged actual situational context. Content analysis performed on the transcribed texts with depersonalized research participants did not allow to consider them as representatives of a particular socio-cultural community.

Another worthwhile topic will encompass a wider range of extralinguistic factors contributing to common ground building.

References

Arnseth, Hans C. & Ivar Solheim. 2002. Making Sense of Shared Knowledge. In Gerry Stahl (ed.), *Proceedings of Computer Supported Cooperative Learning: Foundations for a CSCL Communit*, 102–111.

Barr, Dale J. & Boaz Keysar. 2005. Making sense of how we make sense: The paradox of ego-centrism in language use. In Colston Herbert L. & Albert N. Katz (eds.), *Figurative Language Comprehension: Social and cultural influences*, 21–43. Mahwah, N.J.: Lawrence Erlbaum.

Barr, Dale J. 2004. Establishing conventional communication systems: Is common knowledge necessary? *Cognitive Science*, 28(6). 937–962.

Cieślicka, Anna. 2010. Formulaic language in L2: Storage, retrieval and production of idioms by second language learners. In M. Pütz & L. Sicola (eds.), *Cognitive processing in second language acquisition: Inside the learner's mind*, 149–168. John Benjamins Publishing Company.

Clark, Herbert H. 1996. *Using language*. Cambridge: Cambridge University Press, xi+432.

Clark, Herbert H., & Brennan, S. E. 1991. Grounding in communication. In L. B. Resnick, J. M. Levine, & S. D. Teasley (eds.), *Perspectives on socially shared cognition*, 127–149. American Psychological Association.Cobb, Tom. Web Vocabprofile. [http://www.lextutor.ca/vp/ (accessed 29 May 2021).

Colston, Herbert L., & Katz, Albert N. (eds.). 2005. *Figurative language comprehension: Social and cultural influences*. Mahwah, NJ: Erlbaum

Curtis D. LeBaron, Timothy Koschmann. 2003. Gesture and the transparency of understanding, In Phillip Glenn, Curtis D. LeBaron & Jenny Mandelbaum (eds.), *Studies in Language and Social Interaction: In Honor of Robert Hopper*, 119–132. Mahwah, N.J.: Lawrence Erlbaum.

Gibbs, Raymond W., Jr. 2012. Idioms and Formulaic Language. In Dirk Geeraerts & Hubert Cuyckens (eds.), *The Oxford Handbook of Cognitive Linguistics*, 697–725. New York: Oxford University Press.

Giora, Rachel. 1997. Understanding figurative and literal language: The graded salience hypothesis. *Cognitive Linguistics*, 8(3). 183–206.

Giora, Rachel. 2002. Literal vs. Figurative Language: Different or Equal? *Journal of Pragmatics* 34. 487–506.

Giora, Rachel. 2003. *On Our Mind: Salience context and figurative language*. New York: Oxford University Press.

Grice, Paul. 1981. Presupposition and Conversational Implicature. In P. Cole (ed.), *Radical Pragmatics*, 183–198. New York: Academic Press.

Grice, Paul. 1989. *Studies in the way of words*. Cambridge, MA: Harvard University Press.

Holtgraves, Thomas. 2002. *Language as Social Action: Social Psychology and Language Use*. New York: Routledge.

Howarth, Peter Andrew. 1998. Phraseology and second language proficiency. *Applied Linguistics*, 19(1). 24–44.

Jones, Lara L., & Estes, Zachary. 2005. Metaphor comprehension as attributive categorization. *Journal of Memory and Language*, 53(1). 110–124.

Jones, Lara L., & Estes, Zachary. 2006. Roosters, robins, and alarm clocks: Aptness and conventionality in metaphor comprehension. *Journal of Memory and Language*, 55(1). 18–32.

Kecskes, Istvan. & Zhang, Fenghui. 2009. Activating, seeking and creating common ground: A socio-cognitive approach. *Pragmatics and Cognition*, 17(2). 331–355.

Kecskes, Istvan. 2004. Editorial: Lexical merging, conceptual blending, and cultural crossing. *Intercultural pragmatics*, 1(1). 1–26

Kecskes, Istvan & Zhang, Fenghui. 2012. On the dynamic relations between common ground and presupposition. In Alessandro Capone, Franco Lo Piparo and Marco Carapezza (eds.), *Perspectives on Pragmatics and Philosophy*. Milan: Springer Verlag.

Kecskes, Istvan, Obdalova, Olga, Minakova, Ludmila & Soboleva, Aleksandra. 2018. A study of the perception of situation-bound utterances as culture-specific pragmatic units by Russian learners of English. *System*, 76. 219–232.

Kecskes, Istvan. 2000. Conceptual fluency and the use of situation-bound utterances in L2. *Links and Letters*. 145–161.

Kecskes, Istvan. 2006. On my mind: Thoughts about salience, context and figurative language from a second language perspective. *Second Language Research*, 22(2). 219–237.

Kecskes, Istvan. 2007. Formulaic Language in English Lingua Franca. In Istvan Kecskes & Laurence R. Horn (eds.), *Explorations in Pragmatics: Linguistic, Cognitive and Intercultural Aspects*, 191–219. Berlin/New York: Mouton de Gruyter.

Kecskes, Istvan. 2008. Formulaic language in English Lingua Franca. In Istvan Kecskes & L. Horn (eds.), *Explorations in Pragmatics: Linguistic, Cognitive and Intercultural Aspects*, 191–218. Berlin, New York: De Gruyter Mouton.

Kecskes, Istvan. 2010. The Paradox of Communication: A Socio-Cognitive Approach. *Pragmatics and Society*, 1(1). 50–73.

Kecskes, Istvan. 2013. *Intercultural Pragmatics*. Oxford, UK: Oxford University Press.

Kecskes, Istvan. 2013. Why do we say what we say the way we say it? *Journal of Pragmatics*, 48(1), 71–83.

Kecskes. Istvan. 2003. *Situation-Bound Utterances in L1 and L2*. Berlin/New York: Mouton de Gruyter.

Kronenfeld, David B. 2008. *Culture, society, and cognition: Collective goals, values, action and knowledge*. Berlin: Mouton de Gruyter

Lakoff, George, & Johnson, Mark. 1980. *Metaphors We Live by*. Chicago: University of Chicago Press.

Lustig, Myron W, Jolene Koester. 2010. *Intercultural competence: interpersonal communication across cultures*. 6th edn. Boston, MA: Allyn & Bacon.

Obdalova, Olga A., Minakova, Ludmila & Soboleva, Aleksandra. 2016. The study of the role of context in sociocultural discourse interpretation through the discursive-cognitive approach. *Tomsk State University Journal*, 413. 38–45. (In Rus)

Obdalova, Olga A., Minakova, Ludmila & Soboleva, Aleksandra. 2017. Discourse as a unit of communicative and cognitive processes in interaction between the representatives of different linguocultures. *Yazyk i kul'tura*, 37. 205–228. (In Rus)

Obdalova, Olga A., Minakova, Ludmila Yu., & Soboleva, Aleksandra V. 2019. Indirect Reporting and pragmatically enriched context: A case study into Russian learners of English. *Pragmaticas and Cognition*, 26(1). 85–111.

Nowicka, Agnieszka. 2022. Negotiating religious identity categories in non-professional interviews using English as a lingua franca. *Intercultural Pragmatics*, 19(1). 103–131.

Prince, Ellen. 1981. Toward a taxonomy of given-new information. In Peter Cole (ed.), *Radical Pragmatics*, 223–254. New York: Academic Press.

Schiffer, Stephen. 1972. *Meaning*. Oxford: Oxford University Press.

Sprenger Simone, Willem Levelt & Gerard Kempen. 2006. Lexical access during the production of idiomatic phrases. *Journal of Memory and Language*, 54(2). 161–184.

Stalnaker, Robert C. 1978. Assertion. In Peter Cole (ed.), *Syntax and Semantics Pragmatics*, 315–332. New York: Academic Press.

Stalnaker, Robert C. 2002. Common ground. *Linguistics and Philosophy*, 25. 701–721.

Tannen, Deborah & Pyale C. Oztek. 1981. Health to our mouths: formulaic expressions in Greek and Turkish. In Coulma F. (ed.), *Procedings of the third annual meeting of the Berkeley Linguistic Society*, 516–534.

Tendahl, Markus, Raymond W. Gibbs. 2008. Complementary perspectives on metaphor: Cognitive linguistics and relevance theory. *Journal of Pragmatics*, 40. 1823–1864.

Thibodeau, Paul & Frank H. Durgin. 2008. Productive figurative communication: Conventional metaphors facilitate the comprehension of related novel metaphors. *Journal of Memory and Language*, 58(2). 521–540.

Thompson, Eric C., & Juan Zhang. 2006. Comparative Cultural Salience: Measures using free-List Darta. *Field methods*, 18(4). 398–412.

Turney, Peter D., Yair Neuman, Dan Assaf, Yohai Cohen. 2011. Literal and metaphorical sense identification through concrete and abstract context. *Proceedings of the Conference on the Empirical Methods in Natural Language Processing*. 680–690.

Wray, Alison. 1999. Formulaic language in learners and native speakers. *Language Teaching*, 32. 213–231.

Wray, Alison. 2000. Formulaic sequences in second language teaching: Principle and practice. *Applied Linguistics*, 21(4). 463–489.

Wray, Alison. 2002. *Formulaic language and the lexicon*. Cambridge: Cambridge University Press.

Wray, Alison. 2005. Idiomaticity in an L2: Linguistic processing as a predictor of success. Paper submitted for Proceedings of 2005 IATEFL Conference.

Qing Yang

ELF disagreement as an interactional resource for doing interculturality

Abstract: This study aims to investigate the discourse process of managing cultural differences through the lens of disagreement among speakers with heterogeneous linguacultural backgrounds using English as a lingua franca (ELF). It questions the traditional paradigm of approaching interculturality as a hindrance to intercultural communication and problematizes the social bias in ELF pragmatic research. The focal segment of data analysis was placed on interactional sequences of disagreement in casual ELF conversations, starting from the initial disagreeing turn on an arguable topic and ending with the decay or closure of the topic. The sequential analysis reveals that disagreements are strategically exploited to purport divergences in participants' conceptual knowledge that is structured on their prior linguacultural backgrounds, and to prompt the unfolding sequences for co-creating an *ad hoc* "interculture" (Koole and ten Thije 1994; Kecskes 2013, 2019) as the common conceptual base for mutual understanding. In addition, the lingual analysis is triangulated by retrospective interviews which verify the constructive role of disagreement in pursuit of intercultural understanding. Therefore, it is argued that disagreement is used as an interactional resource for doing interculturality by modifying ELF participants' prior conceptual knowledge and creating common ground in situ. This finding can provide some insights into L2 interactional competence in culturally diverse ELF context by reconsidering the creative use of disagreement as the result of the interplay of societal interaction and individual cognition.

1 Introduction

This study attempts to explore a different route to English as a lingua franca (ELF) communication with an eye on disagreements by which cultural differences are highlighted, negotiated and transformed in pursuit of common understanding. ELF encounters create a "contact zone" (Pratt 1991: 34) for people from diverse linguacultural backgrounds to communicate with each other, using English as "the communicative medium of choice, and often the only option" (Seidlhofer 2011: 7). Although there is limited "self-evident linguacultural commonality" (Widdowson 2015: 364) that interlocutors can rely on, ELF communication always proceeds smoothly as reported in previous literature (e.g. Maura-

https://doi.org/10.1515/9783110766752-011

nen 2006, Kaur 2011). The majority of ELF pragmatic research have shown that ELF interlocutors are "mutually supportive and consensus-oriented" (Seidlhofer 2001: 143) to achieve effective communication. Such findings have provided a "success approach" (Kidwell 2000, cited from Kecskes 2014: 167) to intercultural communication with a focus on convergent practices in ELF conversations employed to pursue common understanding. But does that mean being convergent and affiliative is the only way to common understanding?

Recently, a handful of scholars (e.g., Kecskes and Mey 2008; Ehrenreich 2009) have argued that divergent practices are equally fundamental to understanding ELF communication since individual differences cannot be put aside. Each interlocutor in ELF communication always brings with them heterogeneous linguacultural profiles as *a priori* which can have an effect on actual utterance production and comprehension. In line with this, increasing attention has been paid to "competitive talk" (Ehrenreich 2009: 146), "adversarial aspects" (Konakahara 2017: 315), and "uncooperative interaction" (Jenks 2018: 282) among ELF interlocutors when individual differences are perceived and make relevant to the actual situational context.

Disagreement, a typically divergence-oriented speech act, has been examined in ELF academic discourse (e.g. Björkman 2015; Toomaneejinda and Harding 2018), business negotiation (e.g. Bjørge 2012; Alzahrani 2020) and informal encounters (e.g. Jenks 2018; Konakahara 2016). Disagreement in such contexts is found to be strategically motivated and constructive to suit certain communicative purposes. As to the performative ways of disagreement, the existing ELF studies have tended to be approached through "the lens of interpersonal pragmatics" (Angouri and Locher 2012: 1550) even though they have noticed that face concerns were often decentralized, which consequently leads to inconsistent findings. Furthermore, it is still underexplored how the use of disagreement is interrelated with intercultural elements in ELF context since the cultural dimensions seem to be warded off in most of ELF literature (cf. Baker 2016). Thus, the role that linguacultural backgrounds play in the formulation and interpretation of ELF disagreeing practices remains unaddressed.

In the dataset of this study, disagreement is often used when participants orient to interculturality (or "being culturally different") and deploy the interculturality as a communicative repertoire to drive forward the disagreeing sequences. The interculturality is not a fixed parameter that can be taken for granted but an interactive phenomenon emerging in talk-in-interaction involving "both relatively normative and emergent components" (Kecskes 2014: 18). Following Koole and ten Thije's (2001) discursive approach, this study examines the disagreeing sequences in which interculturality are made relevant, topicalized and reconstructed.

2 Disagreement in ELF communication

Disagreement is universally perceived as a responsive act "to an antecedent verbal (or nonverbal) action" (Kakavá 1993: 36). In the model of conversational analysis, disagreement has been mainly treated as a dispreferred response (Pomerantz 1984; Sacks 1973) that is typically indirect or structurally delayed. The pragmatics-oriented research mainly attributes the structurally dispreferred features of disagreement to "interpersonal concerns" (Angouri and Locher 2012: 1550), and disagreement has always been labeled as a (potentially) "face-threatening act" (Brown and Levinson 1987). Although research has recognized that the ways disagreement is enacted and perceived vary across cultural and contextual settings (Sifianou 2012), the performative ways of disagreement are tended to be associated with certain cultural expectations in many intercultural studies.

The use of disagreement is more complex in ELF context which involves "hybridity" and "inherent fluidity" (Jenkins et al. 2011: 296) of languages and cultures. Recent ELF research found that face concerns were often decentralized in the use of disagreement which is particularly expected in "problem-solving" ELF business talks or "task-oriented" academic ELF interactions. For instance, unmitigated disagreements can often be employed as strategic devices for promoting information clarity and ensuring mutual understanding in ELF business communication (Bjørge 2012). Similar observations have been made in academic settings where disagreement is strategically exploited as a way to defending their own arguments by international students (e.g. Björkman 2015) and jointly accomplishing an instructional task (e.g. House 2008; Toomaneejinda and Harding 2018; Nowicka 2022). Despite being seen as "self-centered practices" (House 2008: 356), direct forms of disagreement have been perceived as politic by ELF interlocutors co-constructing an "intersociety" (House 2008: 356) of local norms. These studies have suggested that interpersonal concerns can be overridden by local communicative needs. However, they do not clarify whether the preferred structure of disagreement is determined by the complexity of the ELF context itself or by the nature of the task-oriented speech activity.[1]

In comparison, disagreement in casual conversations has not received as much attention in ELF research because such settings have been traditionally perceived as creating "ties of union" (Malinowski 1972: 151), that is, disagreement

1 As discussed in the previous literature, disagreement is expected and unmarked in problem-solving and decision-making talk (cf. Angouri and Locher 2012).

is marginalized for being socially disruptive. Of more relevance to the current study is Konakahara's (2016) sequential analysis of unmitigated disagreement in casual conversations between international ELF students, in which it was argued that such unmitigated disagreements were preferred in these types of settings to provide accurate information and ensure mutual understanding. Konakahara's (2016) research implied that it was necessary to reconsider the motivation underlying disagreement in casual ELF settings beyond the interpersonal realm. However, the intercultural issues are not the main focus in her study. Therefore, the association between intercultural elements and disagreement in ELF interactions is as yet unclear and requires further research.

Disagreement identified in the present data of casual ELF conversations is not face-motivated but more related to divergent views that are rooted in ELF participants' "conceptual knowledge" (Kecskes 2014: 66; Kecskes 2019: 94). Individual conceptual knowledge is based on personal experiences and linguacultural backgrounds, which forms a "cognitive predisposition" (Kecskes 2014: 34). Disagreement occurs when ELF participants perceive divergences in their cognitive predispositions regarding the same topic, and relevant conceptual knowledge is exploited to drive the disagreeing sequences towards the joint negotiation of divergences. Therefore, in the current study disagreement is defined as *a way of expressing conceptual divergences among ELF participants regarding the same topic at issue*.

3 Methodology

3.1 Participants

Research data were collected from face-to-face multiparty conversations among two groups of international students who had different L1 language and cultural backgrounds (see table 1). Participants in each group had known each other beforehand and been regularly meeting once a week or twice a month for a casual conversation under uncontrolled conditions.

All participants had had intercultural experiences such as studying, teaching, or even living in other countries. English is their second or foreign language which they had been learning for more than ten years. Given the heterogeneity of their linguacultural backgrounds and the medium role of English in their conversations, the participants in this study were regarded as being typical ELF user representatives.

Table 1: Background details of the participants in the two ELF groups.

Group	Participants	Nationality	First language(s)	Other language(s)
Group1	KA1[2]	Kazakh	Kazakh; Russian	English
	GE2	German	German; Russian	English
	CH3	Chinese	Chinese	English
Group 2	CH1	Chinese	Chinese	English; Japanese
	KO2	Korean	Korean	English
	IN3	Indonesian	Indonesian	English

3.2 Data collection

This study employed two main data subsets: the audio-recordings of the casual conversations between the ELF participants; and retrospective interviews conducted with the individual participants to clarify the observations made from the recording transcriptions.

The core data were two conversation sessions selected from eight hours of audio-recording casual conversations among the two ELF participant groups. Before the data collection, for ethical considerations, the participants signed consent forms; however, the specific research purpose was not explained except for being given a vague description that the study was an investigation into intercultural communication. It was explained that the conversations could be about any topics and could be recorded in any place without the researcher being present to ensure the authenticity and naturalness of the data. Compared with video recording, the use of a voice recorder appeared to be less intrusive and easier to handle. On the other hand, it may fall into what is called "the lingua bias" (Block 2014: 68) for not involving non-verbal features which can provide significant information on the meaning of verbal interactions (Konakahara 2020). Given that, audio-recordings were triangulated by retrospective interviews as a "(re)construction of meanings in data" (Blommaert 2001: 2).

2 To protect their privacy, the speakers in each group are identified by the abbreviations of their countries of origin in the two initial letters with the speaking number based on the order of speaking in the conversation (i.e., KA1, the Kazakh participant who speaks first; GE2, the German participant who speaks second).

The casual conversations mostly took place in public cafés or restaurants selected by the participants. Such space represents a typical place of socialization for international students to discuss current issues, share their daily life and exchange intercultural experiences. As the participants were familiar with each other, the casual conversations tended to go further than just greeting and leaving or talking about "nothing special" (Malinowsky 1972: 151). Hence, casual conversations proffer a unique opportunity to understand the ways ELF participants "do culture with each other" (Holmes and Dervins 2016: 10) by deploying disagreement in a less purposeful setting that has not received much attention in ELF literature.

The other part of the data was retrospective, semi-structured participant interviews to elucidate their orientations towards disagreements in the conversations. After the disagreement focal practices had been preliminarily identified by listening to the data several times, the interviews were conducted via email or face-to-face. The recording fragments identified as the possible focal units were played back to the participants so that they could check and validate the researcher's interpretation of "where to look" and "what to look for" (Stivers 2013: 87). The checking process included mostly open-ended questions about their verbal disagreement behaviors and their perceptions at those moments, such as: "why did you say that at that point in the conversation?;" "do you think the disagreements by your other friends were acceptable or offensive, and why?;" and "what are these disagreements targeted at?." In short, the questions were focused on the essential participant's orientation to the talk details, which was crucial to assess what they were thinking when disagreeing and whether disagreement was destructive or constructive to the conversation progression. But we cannot deny that what the participants actually thought at a given moment in interaction and what they explained in retrospective interviews might not be exactly the same.

3.3 Analytical tools

Conversation analysis (CA) and ethnographic perspectives were adopted for the in-depth qualitative analysis of the casual ELF talk. All recordings were transcribed based on CA conventions (see the Appendix). The disagreement sequences were identified as the analytical focus of the research and qualitatively analyzed to investigate the process of doing interculturality.

The focal data analysis segments were placed on interactional sequences of disagreement, and each episode of disagreeing sequences develops with a clearly identified topic subject, starting with an arguable topic and ending with a coherent topic shift. Based on the dataset, two types of arguable topics (as shown in the Table 2) are likely to invoke divergent stances among ELF participants: B-event topics and AB-event topics.[3] The topic being discussed in conversation reflects the existing relative states of knowledge between interlocutors that operate as a significant determinant in turn design and sequence structure in conversations. The relative states of knowledge between interlocutors can be stratified with their different access to a certain epistemic domain, which can be represented as more knowledgeable (K+) or less knowledgeable (K-) (Heritage 2012a, 2012b).

Within B-event topical type, disagreement from recipient B is elicited as a response to a sequentially initial turn that is designed as a request for confirmation by speaker A who positions themselves as a less knowledgeable (K-) party. Disagreement in such topical sequences is categorized as an other-mobilized response, i.e., a response mobilized by other participants, which affirms the assumption in the initial turn that there is a gap of conceptual knowledge between speaker and recipient. Within AB-event topical sequences, disagreement is self-volunteered from the party B who claims equally unmediated access (K+) to the event at issue and an oppositional stance against the party A. Disagreement in such topical type is categorized as a "volunteered response" (Stivers and Rossano 2010: 23) which is often formulated directly to indicate a clash of conceptual knowledge between speaker and recipient. Twenty-three episodes of disagreeing sequences were identified, and these episodes all took longer than the three-turn sequence structure (cf. Muntigl and Turnbull 1998).

Table 2: Disagreements in two types of topic sequences.

Topics types	Sequential position of disagreements	Examples
B-event topics	*A(K–): a downgraded assessment in a polar question* *B(K+): other-mobilized disagreement*	GE2: but I think the bad words in Chinese is a big deal **right**? You people don't like to use them (.) **right**? (0.5) CH3: →ARE WE? but I use it. GE2: <u>yeah?</u> [but you] CH3: [yea:h] h.h.h. ((laughter)) I use it but. . .

3 Labov and Fanshel (1977) distinguished between A-events (known to speaker A, but not to speaker B) and B-events (known to speaker B, but not to speaker A) to analyze declarative questions which would count as information requests. Also, AB-events refers to event that is known to both parties.

Table 2 (continued)

Topics types	Sequential position of disagreements	Examples
AB-event topics	*A(K+): an unmarked declarative assessment* *B(K+): self-volunteered disagreement*	KO1: it doesn't matter where you live if [you have money] you have an easy life IN3: [you have money] CH2: →no it's not common in China you can have maid (.) like that (.) you know it's = KO1: = no no if you have that money. you can

4 Findings

A key finding from these interactional sequences of disagreement in casual ELF conversations was that the disagreeing turns were used when conceptual divergences are perceived and interculturality is made visible. ELF participants redefine the divergent practice of disagreeing as a divergence in conceptual understandings in situ, and expand the interactional sequence as a way of doing interculturality. Through interactional management of the momentary conceptual divergent, the disagreeing sequence gets to close with explicit or tacit display of understanding and a coherent topic shift. This section takes a close examination of the ways in which disagreements were used as resource of doing interculturality in two types of topic sequences.

4.1 Managing knowledge gaps in B-event topic sequences

When a topic focus drifts to a B-event type, a culturally specific event within the coparticipant's L1 community in particular, cultural identities are raised as locally relevant through the turn-taking patterns that are designed in the polar question-answer pair. A polar question is employed to convey the speaker's mediated access (K–) to the event being assessed, which attributes the authoritative epistemic status (K+) of the coparticipant and mobilizes a conditionally relevant confirming or disconfirming response. The disagreement turn in the second pair part ratifies the knowledge distribution, but rejects the tentative claims expressed in the propositional part of the preceding question. In this way, the cultural identities are implicitly ascribed and reflected through attributed "discourse identities[4]" (Mori 2003: 147) at the particular moment of speaking. That is, the questioner positions themselves as a less knowing (K–) cultural *outsider* and the directed recipient is treated as a cultural *insider* with first-order access to the referent (K+).

The following example is a discourse segment from a casual conversation between the group 1 members. The two participants, KA1 and GE 2, were two international students who had been living in China for nearly 6 months, and CH3 was their mutual friend in China. The perception of using bad language in China was broached as the current topic after GE2 became aware he had just used a bad word in English when elaborating on what KA1 (the Kazakh friend) had attempted to say.

(1) "Is using bad words a big deal in China?" (GE2= German; CH3= Chinese, the Kazakh participant KA1 keeps silent from 01 to 03)

Segment 1

01 GE2: and also I think many English bad words aren't that bad (.) only people think they are bad
02 (.) but in reality words like "shit" and "fuck" are used by almost everyone for those people
03 in Euro so it's not a big deal (.) but <u>I think the bad words in Chinese is a big deal **right?**</u>
04 <u>You people don't like to use them (.) **right**?</u>
05 (0.5)
→06 CH3: ARE WE? but I use it.
((continue to Segment 2))

Regarding the B-event type topic (the situation in China), the German participant (GE2) downgrades his assessment in the form of a tag question (the underlined part of lines 03 and 04) to invite confirmation from the Chinese participant (CH3) who has privileged knowledge access to the referent. After a minimal pause (line 05), CH3 responds with an "opposing question" (Gruber 2001: 1823) in an emphatic way ("ARE WE?" in line 06) to indicate that the questioner's tenta-

---

4 Following Mori (2003:147), the term "discourse identities" refers to "the classifications of the participants' immediate status in ongoing talk-in-interaction, which are ascribed through the sequential development of talk stand in relation to the others present at the site of interaction." For example, in polar question-answer sequences, the participant who delivers a biased polar question casts themselves as the *questioner* and the other participant, who is expected to give the response, is cast as the *respondent* or *recipient* of the question.

tive claim made in the prior turn was problematic. The following counterclaim (Muntigl and Turnbull 1998) initiated by the contrastive conjunction "but" further rejects the questioner's initial assumption, which brings to the fore a divergence in the questioner's and the recipient's conceptual knowledge regarding the event being addressed.

In the discourse segment above, GE2 conveys a "best guess" (Pomerantz and Heritage 2013: 213) based on his personal novice experience as an overseas student in China for just a few months. As dominant types of polar questions are designed to mobilize *yes* or *no* responses, tag questions are commonly used to downgrade the questioner's epistemic access stated in the prior declarative part and to seek confirmation from the coparticipant via the final tag marker using rising intonation. The final-turn tag marker "right" (in lines 03 and 04) signals the speaker's secondary epistemic access to the referent (K–) and distributes the knowing status (K+) to the recipient. Therefore, the initial assessment framed in the first tag question indexes the questioner's predisposition toward the certain answer which is expected yet "putatively secondary access to a referent relative to the coparticipant" (Heritage and Raymond 2005: 20), which subtly categorizes the questioner as a cultural *outsider* (non-Chinese) while the recipient is ascribed as a cultural *insider*. This categorization is more explicit in the follow-up tag question in line 04 by GE2's labeling the recipient's L1 cultural community as "you people".

The function of the disagreeing response here is twofold: (1) to imply the knowledge gap between a cultural *outsider* and a cultural *insider* regarding the event being addressed as the source of conceptual divergence in need of further negotiation; and (2) to advance the sequence expansion from a minimal two-turn sequence to handle the topicalized conceptual divergence.

The ensuing sequence is expanded by using disagreement which shifts the participants' attentional focus to the instant divergence and steers the conversation from the expected trajectory of seeking confirmation and moving on to a new topic. As shown in the continuous segment in the previous example, the original questioner GE2 does not make an immediate concession to the prior disconfirmation even though it is from the knowing recipient. Instead, GE2 expresses doubt by issuing an open question ("yeah?") in the next turn (07 in segment 2) to solicit an account for the preceding "unanticipated or untoward behavior" (Scott and Lyman 1968: 46).

Segment 2

07 GE2: yeah? [but you]
08 CH3: [yea:h] h.h.h. ((laughter)) I use it but uhm when I was like uh a high school student
09 I use it (.) sometimes together with my friends (.) I think it's a mark of my identity

10 to show that I'm not that a good student (.) not [quite a typical good]
11 GE2: [not not super-friendly] girl?
12 CH3: YEAH [yeah yeah yeah]
13 GE2: [yeah yeah yeah] h.h.h. ((laughter)) we like being rebellious
14 CH3: I was that an-and you know one of my teachers called my parents about this problem and
15 my parents thought it's just ok
16 KA1: there's no problem, yeh?
17 CH3: yeahm h.h.h. ((laughter)) but now (.) gradually I don't speak that anymore
18 because people around me they just don't speak
19 GE2: yeah you've in right place [and you know] I was also like that when I'm sixteen
20 CH3: [h.h.h. ((laughter)) YAH]

Monitoring that the original questioner is withholding acceptance, CH3 narrates her personal experience with "a conventional story-prefixed phrase" (Wong and Waring 2010: 128) ("when I was. . ." in line 08) to give a further account that using bad words could meet the psychological needs of youngsters and highlight their individuality in China. The pause for self-repair in CH3's personal experience narration ("not that a good student (.) not quite a typical good" in line 10) offers a conditional entry for an anticipatory completion (Lerner 1996) from GE2 (in line 11) who displays a collaborative involvement and a here-and-now acceptance of the prior turn. In line 12, CH3 ratifies the prior anticipatory completion by a repetitive use of an acknowledgment token with the emphasis put on the first yeah (YEAH) that is echoed by GE2 in the next turn (line 13), which displays an overt alignment. After a burst of laughter, the following statement "we like being rebellious" (also in line 13) indicates that "resonance"[5] (Horton and Gerrig 2005: 10) between the two participants has been invoked by the personal experience narration which upgrades the accessibility of the information provided in the prior account. Also, the use of the "category label" (Zimmerman 2007: 72) "we" here implies that the speaker is resetting himself in a collective community with the coparticipant. Therefore, a shared co-membership has been created and a collectively-shared conceptual base has been constructed by narrating the personal experience which enables the participants to share a reaction to the event at issue. The ensuing conversation proceeds with collaborative moves from the ELF participants who share personal anecdotes of their teenage years (in lines 14–20).

5 Horton and Gerrig (2005: 10) defined "the automatic search of memory involves a memory process" as "resonance." Through a cognitive process of resonance, "a wide range of associated information can potentially become more accessible" (ibid.). It can be utilized as a resource for changing the accessibility of potential information in social interactions.

The second segment showed that the sequential trajectory was reshaped by disagreement to bridge a knowledge gap between a novice member and an insider member about a culture-specific event. Following the disagreement, the third turn from the original questioner was designed as a solicitation for a further account from the disagreeing party, which indicated that the prior disconfirming response was insufficient for the intercultural understanding. Therefore, the recipient took an "explanatory slot" (Antaki 1996: 415) to offer a remedial account to deal with the source of discordance.

As presented in Figure 1, the use of disagreement highlighted the uncommon ground for the B-event topic and set in motion the ensuing account sequence for intercultural understanding. In the initial stage, the less knowing (K–) questioner, who was the novice in the linguacultural community, exploited his second-hand conceptual knowledge as a cognitive basis and communicative repertoire for candidate understanding. After the hypothesis was disconfirmed, the questioner established an explanatory slot and held the directed recipient accountable for the purported conceptual divergence. The knowing (K+) recipient co-ascribed herself as the cultural *insider* by rejecting the prior speaker's assumptions and taking responsibility by giving a further account until sufficient understanding was achieved. Due to the mutual efforts of the two interactional parties, the topic of disagreement was strategically reframed as a common ground link between the initially separated cultural groups. Therefore, the ELF participants co-defined their *ad hoc* "intersociety" (House 2008: 356), which was beyond their own ethnic

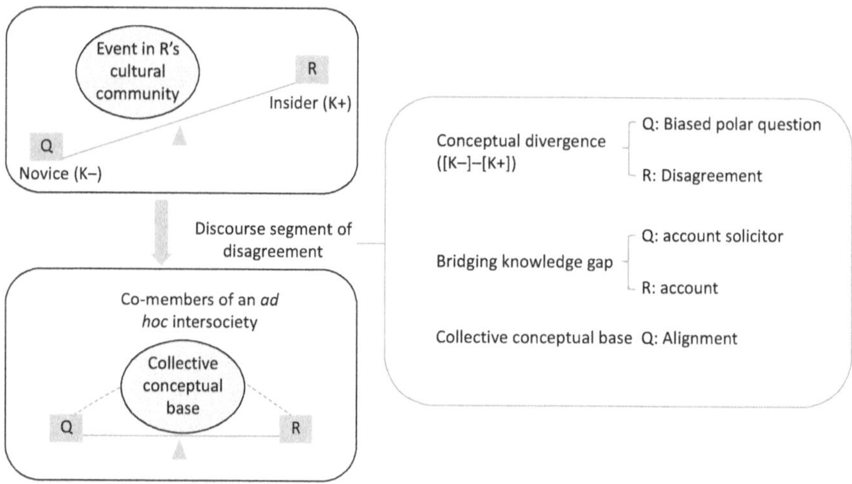

Figure 1: Interactional process for managing the knowledge gap (Q represents questioner, R represents recipient).

boundaries and situated in a collectively-shared conceptual base in the discourse segment of disagreement.

The participants' comments in the retrospective interviews also triangulates the qualitative analysis of the role of disagreement in managing the conceptual divergence between the *insider* understanding and the *outsider* understanding.

The Chinese participant CH3 remarked that disagreement was an integral part of their casual conversations to strive toward intercultural understanding:

> I think disagreements sometimes are quite important when you talking with people from different cultures because you know we may have stereotypical thinking about others and they may have about us. Like some foreigners coming to China always take along their stereotypical beliefs, or even prejudice I can say. I was once shocked by an American saying that he cannot believe that every Chinese are able to afford color TVs. Oh my god! What ages was he still in? So it's not only that you have to clearly tell them the truth but also change their views.

The German participant (GE2) stated their perception of their coparticipant's disagreeing response:

> I think chatting with friends from other cultures can always bring me new insights. And it's meaningful when [CH3] told me that it was not the case that all Chinese took that (using bad words) as misbehavior. Because you know everybody thought Chinese obeyed the Confucianism and we were always told that saying bad words is a big deal in China. {GE2 laughs}. And it's interesting that we found we had common feelings about using bad words in the end.

Therefore, it appears that disagreement in casual ELF conversations is perceived as a favored resource for intercultural understanding. By topicalizing the perceived divergences between the *outsider* understanding and the *insider* understanding, the disagreeing turn prompts follow-up account sequences to deal with the cultural-specific knowledge gaps.

4.2 Managing perspective incongruity in AB-event topic sequences

In the casual ELF conversations, the disagreements could be framed by home culture models to deliver the speaker's self-oriented perspective on an AB-event topic common in the coparticipants' communities. Cultural models are a culturally constructed subclass of knowledge schemas abstracted from a person's cultural experiences and exploited in their communicative repertoire to guide them in interpreting and organizing their current experiences (Kecskes 2014, 2019). Having internalized the cultural model as a conceptual base, when topics focus on intercultural comparisons, culture-specific conceptual knowledge is activated and frames the assessments that ELF interlocutors automatically make in situational interaction. In this case, the direct disagreement is volunteered by a participant to claim equal authoritative status (K+) to the assessable referent in the prior turn, which evokes the division between cultural *self* and cultural *other*.[6]

The example below is a casual conversation episode between three doctoral students (CH1, KO2, IN3) studying in Australia. The topic was focused on the lifestyle of rich people in Asian countries during this episode.

(2) "if you have money, you have an easy life" (CH1= Chinese; KO2=Korean; IN3=Indonesian)

Segment 1

```
  01 KO1: yeah many families are like that they employ people
          ⋮
  11 KO1: it doesn't matter where you live
  12      if [you have money] you have an easy life
  13 IN3:    [you have money]
→14 CH2: no it's not common in China you can have maid (.) like that (.) you know it's =
((continue to Segment 2))
```

In this segment, the Korean participant KO2 delivers an evaluation in line 11 based on a previously-mentioned convention in her own cultural community (line 01); that rich people in Korea can have an easy life because they often employ maids to do the housework. Holding that to be commonly recognized and uncontroversial, KO2 designs the first assessment in an unmarked declarative form that invited a matching second assessment (Heritage and Raymond 2005). Although being supported (line 13) by IN3, the evaluation is denied by CH1 who issues an overtly stated disagreement with the negative particle "no" (line 14). In the following, CH1 elaborates her own cultural model ("not common in China you can have maid like that" in line 14) to further problematize KO2's first assessment.

The forthright disagreement in line 14 is volunteered by CH1 to suspend what was presupposed in the initial assessment, which undermines the knowing status of the prior speaker and implies that the disagreeing party has an equally authoritative knowledge (K+) concerning the assessable referent. Therefore, the

---

6 In this paper, the terms of "self" and "other" here is to display the discourse identities evoked in a given moment of discourse instead of being regarded as a pair of stable categories.

grounding of the prior assessment is framed to be a "speaker-assigned presupposition" (Kecskes and Zhang 2013: 375) (also in tune with the term "individual presupposition" by Fetzer 2001: 452) that is not commonly shared by the co-interlocutors. The incongruity between a *self*-perspective and the *other*-perspective anchored within respective cultural frames of reference is made discernible through the unmitigated form of disagreement. Consequently, the ELF interlocutors are segregated into cultural domains of *self* and *other*, which launches the interactional unfolding to reconcile a momentary "perspectival incongruity" (Shea 1994: 370).

When it was followed by a counteraction or reassertion from the original assessing party in the third position, the disagreement in the second assessment generated an argument sequence in the ensuing talk.

Segment 2

→15 KO1: = no no if you have that money you can
16 IN3: [yeah]
17 CH2: [We:ll] it's=
→18 KO1: = the poor [in Korea]
→19 CH2: [YOU CAN] you can afford it but it gets ANOTHER WAY of doing that (.)
20 °you know° it's [VERY] VERY RARELY but (.) hm (.)
21 KO1: [hh(.) in Korea]
22 KO1: O:h then different from Korea if you have money you employ (.) we don't call them
23 a maid we call them uh
24 IN3: a helper
25 KO1: a helper or assistant

After being rejected, KO1 claims the floor with repeated negation markers to reassert the preceding claim (line 15) before CH2 completes her elaboration in line 14, which turns the current talk into an argument sequence. The counter-disagreement in line 15 is packaged as a blunt interruption that is produced immediately by the first assessor and intrudes in the middle of the prior turn without recognizing the transition relevant places (TRPs) to block the information being transferred by the prior speaker. Thereafter, CH2 makes another attempt in line 17 ("Well it's") to resume what she wants to expand on in line 14 ("you know it's="), yet fails again as KO1 cuts in (line 18) by repeating that the grounding of the first assessment is presumed to be mutually acceptable for co-interlocutors.

The interruption in line 18 is traded upon by KO1 to reiterate the evidential basis for the prior self-claim ("the poor in Korea") from a self-centered perspective and to intercept the information being transferred from the prior speaker CH2. After failing again to resume her clarification, CH2 changes the plan in line 19 by emphatically echoing the focal information that has been conveyed in the preceding turn (line 15) of the counterpart ("YOU CAN you can afford it"). The shift from recycling a self-claim to integrating other information assists CH2 to regain the floor and KO1's attention. Following that, CH2 presents an alternative way of life using the contrastive marker "but" to correct KO1's prior generalized presumption, which is syntactically, prosodically (falling intonation) and pragmatically complete and projects the upcoming possible TRP. Without receiving any substantial response, the current speaker expands the turn by adding an increment with "you know" in a soft voice (line 20). As the upcoming point of possible completion is carefully monitored by the interactants, KO1 prepares to grab the floor at the possible TRP with an audible in-breath (in line 21) serving as a signal for the turn-beginning. Therefore, KO1's repetition to support her own claim ("in Korea") overlaps with the prior speaker's turn-increment (line 20). After further clarification by framing what KO1 presumed to be commonly happening in Korea to be rare in other communities, the overlapping talk is resolved with one party (KO1) withdrawing (line 21) and the argument sequence coming to an end. The following turn (22) is prefaced with a high pitched "oh" from KO1, which serves as a sign of a change in speaker's epistemic state (cf. Heritage 1984). Together with the inferential marker ("then"), KO1's response can be regarded as sequence closure signals (cf. Schegloff 2007). The ensuing talk goes on with the topic focus drifting to what kind of "helper" the rich people often employed.

As demonstrated in the second discourse segment, the two opposing parties made joint efforts to modify the prior presupposition of the first assessment as the information presupposed in the initial assessment ("rich families always employ people" from 01) was unable to obtain a common ground status. With the recognition of the perspective from the opposing party who self-ascribed as a "cultural other", the party who persisted in the self-centered perspective-taking displayed a revised understanding ("then different from Korea"), which was an essential cognitive process to blend the existing cognitive state with the newly acquired information from the coparticipant. The blending of the pre-defined cultural frames and the emerging elements was transformed into an "interculture" (Kecskes 2014: 15) during the interactional sequences of disagreement. These cultural differences that were treated relevant in the disagreeing sequence appeared to be productive for the two opposing parties as they heard the voice of the cultural *other* and were able to adopt a reciprocal perspective for divergence management. In the disagreeing sequence, the prior speaker-assigned presupposition was suspended, modified and transformed until a "collectively shared co-supposition" (Fetzer 2001: 452) (see lines 19, 20, 23) was interactively co-constructed. The interactional process is illustrated in Figure 2.

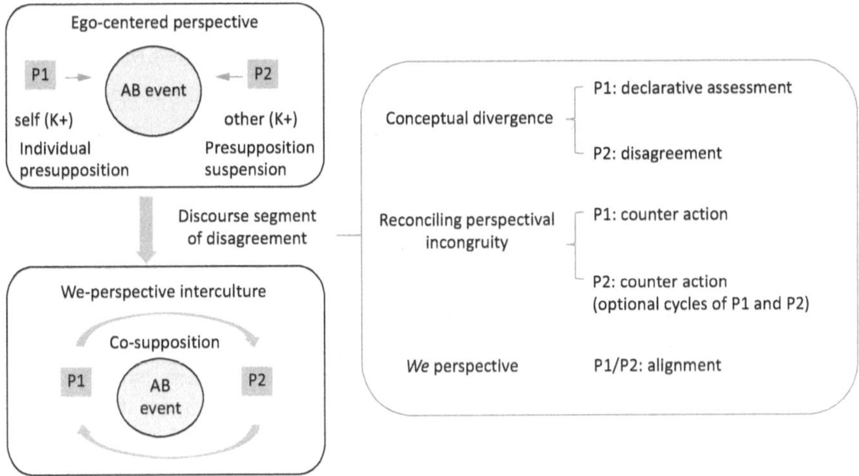

Figure 2: Interactional process for managing perspectival incongruity (P1 and P2 represent the initially opposing parties).

These sequences demonstrate that disagreements in response to prior unmarked assessments can be in explicit and unmitigated forms and can be reacted to by a counteraction to establish a typical "conflict nucleus" (Gruber 1998). The sequential trajectory prompted by disagreement to manage the perspectival incongruity appears to be quite different from managing a perceived knowledge gap (in example 1). Therefore, the participants' perceptions about the use of direct disagreement in such sequential structures are quite critical when interpreting the whole interactional process.

In the retrospective interview, KO1 emphasized the normality of disagreement in their casual conversations, especially when the different cultural frames were relevant.

> People may think Asian people are more tolerant or tend to be more collective. But, actually, we always express different views immediately in our talk and I think it's an efficient way for culture sharing, right? We do think it's quite normal. . .We always take for granted the culture-specific things as generally accepted by others. When [CH2] point out cultural differences in understanding the lifestyle of rich people, I don't think it held back our talk. Instead, that gives me a new understanding.

The Chinese participant (CH2) explained her expression of disagreement as follows:

> I don't think disagreeing with other's opinion in our talk is offensive, and none of us got cross about that. We just shared our views, you know, we had different cultures. So we were open to say our own understandings. And friends are just like that!

Therefore, instead of being considered disruptive to the ELF communication progression, the disagreeing turns were seen as an interactional resource for intercultural understanding. CH2's comments supported the findings in previous studies that unmitigated disagreement in casual conversations displays trust and sincerity among friends (Konakahara 2016).

The conceptual change in KO1's state of knowledge in and through the disagreeing sequence was further verified in their statements, in which it was mentioned that understanding could be achieved even if differences remain.

> We begin to notice the cultural differences when we are told with another voice from another culture. Like here the lifestyle of rich people, I did believe that was common until [CH2] told us there was another way in China. Maybe I will insist my opinion at first, but we're happy to accept differences in the end. You know, we don't need to be the same for understanding each other. Disagreeing with others makes us know more about other cultures since it often brings out more information. It's good we do it like that. So remaining differences is not contradictory with understanding.

5 Discussion

The close analysis of the two interactional sequences combined with participants' comments suggested that disagreeing in casual ELF conversations facilitates rather than disrupts the intercultural understanding.

As demonstrated by the data, disagreements in casual ELF conversations are conditionally relevant when a conceptual divergence is perceived as it frames the prior speaker's understanding as problematic and in need of repair. As can be seen in discourse segment 1 of episode 1, the disagreeing response was issued to reject the common assessment embedded in the preceding question design, which implied there was a knowledge gap between the knowing (K+) recipient and the less knowing (K–) questioner. As shown in discourse segment 1 of episode 2, the disagreeing assessment was self-volunteered by the participant who explicitly rejected the prior speaker's assigned presupposition that was presumed to be commonly shared, which implied that the clash between *self* perspective and *other* perspective was tied to the respective cultural frames of the ELF participants. It was also discernible that the preference structures of disagreement in the two episodes were motivated by the relative states of the interlocutors' conceptual knowledge rather than by face concerns. Disagreement was produced with mitigation in response to the prior polar question in order to project asymmetries in relative states of conceptual knowledge. However, an overt form was chosen to formulate a disagreement without delay in response to an initially unmarked declarative assessment to subvert the knowing status of the intending assessor and to present another cultural perspective.

This paper therefore contends that disagreement can be both interactively motivated and cognitively grounded in ELF interactions. However, these cognitive dimensions in the use of disagreement have been overlooked in previous pragmatic ELF research, most of which has taken an interpersonal pragmatic approach to center on social factors in the communicative process. Without having a "socio-cultural collectivity" (Kecskes 2014: 47), ELF participants tend to rely more on self-centered conceptual knowledge, that is "the individualized reflection of the socio-cultural context" (Kecskes 2014: 159), which forms a cognitive bias and generates an *I-level understanding*. This is in tune with the "self-centered hypothesis" proposed by House (2008: 356) to explain the use of disagreement in her study on ELF group discussions. As exemplified in the two episodes in this study, ELF participants often resort to their own conceptual baggage and linguacultural profiles when engaging in casual conversations from which disagreements arise to bring to the fore the perceived conceptual divergence. It is worth noting that as "the cognitive and the interactional are closely intertwined" (Mauranen 2018: 15) in ELF communication, disagreements can reveal the operational intercultural issues.

This study presented an alternative route to intercultural understanding, which points to the urgent need for ELF scholars to be attentive to both convergent and divergent aspects in the communicative process. This study revealed that intercultural understanding was maintained and enhanced between the ELF participants through the interactional process of disagreeing by orienting to their relative states of conceptual knowledge on a turn-by-turn basis. As shown in the data analysis, the sequential trajectory was generally steered toward handling the conceptual divergence in the unfolding interactions that were prompted by the second turn disagreement. In discourse segment 2 of example 1, this perceived knowledge gap then prompted the ensuing account sequences until the newly-provided discourse information was ratified as being sufficient to address the gap in the relative knowledge states, with the a priori demarcation between the cultural *insider* and the *outsider* being transformed into an *in-group* membership. In discourse segment 2 of example 2, with a focus on the perceived incongruous perspective-taking, it was shown that the argument sequence was propelled until the collective co-suppositions were co-constructed as a shared conceptual base. The perspectival incongruity between the *self* and the *other* was transformed into a collective *we* perspective. Therefore, to maintain intercultural understanding, the ELF interlocutors were cognizant of and oriented to the relative states of their conceptual knowledge, which aligned with the observance in previous literature (Björkman 2015; Konakahara 2016; Komori-Glatz 2018) that face concerns can be set aside in the use of ELF disagreement.

Therefore, interactional sequences of disagreement are socio-cognitive channels for "transcultural flows" (Pennycook 2007: 6) and allow the ELF communicators to exploit their social and cognitive repertoires to handle momentary divergences and restore coordination across linguacultural boundaries. While cultural elements are common in ELF communication, these cultural dimensions are often warded off in a great deal of ELF literature (e.g., House 2008; Kaur 2011, 2016). The reason for this may reside in criticisms of essentialism and the overemphasis on "the need to refrain from making a priori assumption about cultural group membership" (Kaur 2016: 135). However, in contrast with the casual ELF conversations examined in this study, House's and Kaur's data were focused on task-oriented ELF group discussions among international students who had limited freedom in using the language (cf. Cogo and Dewey 2012: 27–29). The findings in this study showed that cultural membership and personal intercultural experiences were often made relevant in the immediate talk and were exploited as communicative repertoires in local discourse, which redefined "interculturality" (see, e.g. Mori 2003: 178; Zimmerman 2007: 71; Kecskes 2014: 15) as a sharedness in the ELF communicative process.

6 Conclusion

This study examined the communicative process of dynamically managing conceptual divergence through disagreeing sequences in casual ELF conversations. To be specific, this paper addressed three main aims. First, it revisited disagreement in casual ELF conversation and found it to be a communicative act that was both interactively motivated and cognitively grounded. Second, the two sequential structures demonstrated that the disagreements were triggered by perceived conceptual divergence regarding the event at issue, and further prompted interactional divergence management. Finally, disagreeing sequences were found to function as socio-cognitive channels through which prior cultural boundaries were crossed and interculturality re-established by transforming an *I-level* understanding into a *we-level* understanding.

This study gives insights into bilingual pragmatic competence in a globalized social reality. The interactional dynamics associated with disagreement and the negotiation of cultural differences demonstrated the agency of the ELF participants, who were found to be willing to break the boundaries of their former knowledge domains to achieve intercultural understanding. The ELF context allowed for the recognition of the multifaceted divergences arising from hybrid linguacultural backgrounds and the multilingual and multicultural assets it can offer. It would therefore be insightful to revisit L2 pragmatic competence in ELF communication to investigate how disagreement is deployed as a socio-cognitive resource for divergence management and intercultural understanding, which could also provide a window for English learners to develop their intercultural awareness and better adapt themselves to the transnational, multicultural world as global citizens.

Future studies need to examine more competent uses of adversarial speech acts in ELF communication, which could inform the current research into L2 pragmatic competence. Also, the cognitive disagreement ELF participant dataset needs to be expanded to reveal more about the intercultural pragmatic characteristics of the use of disagreement in ELF communication rather than relying on interpersonal pragmatic accounts.

Appendix

The transcription notations used in the paper are as follows:

(.)	short pause
(0.5)	time pause (in seconds)
[	the onset of overlap
]	the end of overlapping talk
=	latching
.hh	inhale
h.h.h.	laughter
?	rising intonation indicating a question
.	falling intonation indicating sentence end
wo:rd	elongation
°word	section spoken relatively softer than the surrounding talk
word-	cut-off

References

Angouri, Jo & Miriam A. Locher. 2012. Theorising Disagreement. *Journal of Pragmatics* 44(12). 1549–1553.

Antaki, Charles. 1996. Explanation slots as resources in interaction. *British Journal of Social Psychology* 35(3). 415–432.

Alzahrani, Alaa Ahmed. 2020. Disagreement Strategies used by Speakers of English as a Lingua Franca in Business Meetings. *Advances in Language and Literary Studies* 11(3). 46–56.

Baker, Will. 2016. Culture and Language in Intercultural Communication, English as a Lingua Franca and English Language Teaching: Points of Convergence and Conflict. In Holmes,

Prue & Fred Dervin (eds.), *The cultural and intercultural dimensions of English as a lingua franca*, 70–89. Bristol: Multilingual Matters.

Bjørge, Anne K. 2012. Expressing Disagreement in ELF Business Negotiations: Theory and Practice. *Applied Linguistics* 33(4). 406–427.

Björkman, Beyza. 2015. PhD Supervisor-PhD Student Interactions in an English-medium Higher Education (HE) Setting: Expressing Disagreement. *European Journal of Applied Linguistics* 3(2). 205–229.

Blommaert, Jan. 2001. Context is/as critique. *Critique of Anthropology* 21(1). 13–32.

Brown, Penelope & Stephen Levinson. 1987. *Politeness. Some Universals of Language Use.* Cambridge: Cambridge University Press.

Cogo, Alessia & Martin Dewey (eds.). 2012. *Analysing English as a Lingua Franca: A Corpus-based Investigation*. London: Continuum.

Ehrenreich, Susanne. 2009. English as a Lingua Franca in Multinational Corporations – Exploring Business Communities of Practice. In Anna Mauranen & Elina Ranta (eds.), *English as a Lingua Franca: Studies and Findings*, 126–151. Newcastle: Cambridge Scholars Publishing.

Fetzer, Anita. 2001. Context in Natural-language Communication: Presupposed or Co-supposed? In Varol Akman, Paolo Bouquet, Richmond Thomason & Roger A. Young (eds.), *Modeling and Using Context: Third International and Interdisciplinary Conference, Context 2001 Dundee, UK, July 27–30, 2001 Proceedings*, 449–452. Berlin: Springer.

Gruber, Helmut. 1998. Disagreeing: Sequential Placement and Internal Structure of Disagreements in Conflict Episodes. *Text-Interdisciplinary Journal for the Study of Discourse* 18(4). 467–503.

Heritage, John. 1984. A Change-of-state Token and Aspects of Its Sequential Placement. In J. Maxwell Atkinson & John Heritage (eds.), *Structures of Social Action: Studies in Conversation Analysis*, 299–345. Cambridge: Cambridge University Press.

Heritage, John & Geoffrey Raymond. 2005. The Terms of Agreement: Indexing Epistemic Authority and Subordination in Talk-in-interaction. *Social Psychology Quarterly* 68(1). 15–38.

Heritage, John. 2012a. Epistemics in action: Action formation and territories of knowledge. *Research on Language & Social Interaction* 45(1). 1–29.

Heritage, John. 2012b. The epistemic engine: Sequence organization and territories of knowledge. *Research on Language & Social Interaction* 45(1). 30–52.

Holmes, Prue & Fred Dervin. 2016. Introduction–English as a lingua franca and interculturality: Beyond orthodoxies. In Holmes, Prue & Fred Dervin (eds.), *The cultural and intercultural dimensions of English as a lingua franca*, 1–30. Bristol: Multilingual Matters.

Horton, William S. & Richard J. Gerrig. 2005. The Impact of Memory Demands on Audience Design during Language Production. *Cognition* 96(2). 127–142.

House, Juliane. 2008. (Im)politeness in English as Lingua Franca Discourse. In Locher Miriam A. & Jürg Strässler (eds.), *Standards and Norms in the English Language*, 351–366. Berlin/New York: Mouton de Gruyter.

Jenkins, Jennifer, Alessia Cogo & Martin Dewey. 2011. Review of Developments in Research into English as a Lingua Franca. *Language Teaching* 44(3). 281–315.

Jenks, Christopher. 2018. Uncooperative Lingua Franca Encounters. In Jennifer Jenkins, Will Baker & Martin Dewey (eds.), *The Routledge Handbook of English as a Lingua Franca*, 279–292. London/New York: Routledge.

Kakavá, Christina. 1993. *Negotiation of disagreement by Greeks in conversations and classroom discourse*. Department of Linguistics, Doctoral Thesis, Georgetown University.

Kaur, Jagdish. 2011. Intercultural Communication in English as a Lingua Franca: Some Sources of Misunderstanding. *Intercultural Pragmatics* 8(1). 93–116.

Kecskes, Istvan. 2014. *Intercultural Pragmatics*. Oxford: Oxford University Press.

Kecskes, Istvan. 2019. *English as a Lingua Franca: The Pragmatic Perspective*. Cambridge: Cambridge University Press.

Kecskes, Istvan & Jacob Mey. 2008. *Intention, Common Ground and the Egocentric Speaker-Hear*. Berlin/New York: Mouton de Gruyter.

Kecskes, Istvan & Zhang Fenghui. 2013. On the Dynamic Relations Between Common Ground and Presupposition. In Alessandro Capone, Franco Lo Piparo & Marco Carapezza (eds.), *Perspectives on Linguistic Pragmatics*, 375–395. London/New York: Springer.

Kidwell, Mardi. 2000. Common ground in cross-cultural communication: Sequential and institutional contexts in front desk service encounters. *Issues in Applied Linguistics* 11(1). 17–37.

Komori-Glatz, Miya. 2018. "Cool My Doubt is Erased": Constructive Disagreement and Creating a Psychologically Safe Space in Multicultural Student Teamwork. *Journal of English as a Lingua Franca* 7(2). 285–306.

Konakahara, Mayu. 2016. "The Use of Unmitigated Disagreement in ELF Causal Conversation." In Kumiko Murata (ed.), *Exploring ELF in Japanese Academic and Business Contexts: Conceptualization, Research and Pedagogic Implications*, 70–89. New York: Routledge.

Konakahara, Mayu. 2017. Interactional Management of Face-threatening Acts in Casual ELF Conversation: An Analysis of Third-party Complaint Sequences. *Journal of English as a Lingua Franca* 6(2). 313–343.

Konakahara, Mayu. 2020. Single case analyses of two overlap sequences in casual ELF conversations from a multimodal perspective: Toward the consideration of mutual benefits of ELF and CA. *Journal of Pragmatics* 170. 301–316.

Koole, T. & ten Thije, J. D. 1994. *The construction of intercultural discourse: Team discussions of educational advisers*. Vol. 2. Editions Rodopi.

Labov, William & David Fanshel. 1977. *Therapeutic Discourse: Psychotherapy as Conversation*. New York: Academic Press.

Lerner, Gene H. 1996. On the 'Semi-permeable' Character of Grammatical Units in Conversation: Conditional Entry into the Turn Space of Another Speaker. In Elinor Ochs, Emanuel Schegloff, & Sandra A. Thompson (eds.), *Interaction and Grammar*, 238–276. Cambridge: Cambridge University Press.

Malinowski, Bronislaw. 1972. Phatic Communion. In John Laver & Sandy Hutcheson (eds.), *Communication in face-to-face interaction: Selected readings. Penguin modern linguistics readings*, 146–152. Harmondsworth: Penguin Books.

Mauranen, Anna. 2006. Signaling and Preventing Misunderstanding in English as Lingua Franca. *International Journal of the Sociology of Language* 177. 123–150.

Mauranen, Anna. 2018. Conceptualising ELF. In Jennifer Jenkins, Will Baker & Martin Dewey (eds.), *The Routledge Handbook of English as a Lingua Franca*, 27–44. London/New York: Routledge.

Mori, Junko. 2003. The Construction of Interculturality: A Study of Initial Encounters between Japanese and American Students. *Research on Language and Social Interaction* 36(2). 143–184.

Muntigl, Peter & William Turnbull. 1998. Conversational Structure and Facework in Arguing. *Journal of Pragmatics* 29(3). 225–256.

Nowicka, Agnieszka. 2022. Negotiating religious identity categories in non-professional interviews using English as a lingua franca. *Intercultural Pragmatics* 19(1). 103–131.

Pennycook, Alastair. 2007. *Global Englishes and Transcultural Flows*. London: Routledge.
Pomerantz, Anita. 1984. Agreeing and Disagreeing with Assessments: Some Features of Preferred/Dispreferred Turn Shapes. In J. Maxwell Atkinson & John Heritage (eds.), *Structures of Social Action: Studies in Conversation Analysis*, 57–101. Cambridge: Cambridge University Press.
Pomerantz, Anita & John C. Heritage. 2013. Preference. In J. Sidnell & T. Stivers (ed.), *The Handbook of Conversation Analysis*, 210–228. Oxford: Wiley Blackwell.
Pratt, Mary Louise. 1991. Arts of the contact zone. *Profession*. 33–40.
Sacks, Harvey. 1973. On the Preferences for Agreement and Contiguity in Sequences in Conversation. In Graham Button & John R. E. Lee (eds.), *Talk and Social Organization*, 54–69. Clevedon: Multilingual Matters.
Schegloff, Emanuel. A. 2007. *Sequence Organization in Interaction: A Primer in Conversation Analysis I*. Vol. 1. Cambridge: Cambridge university press.
Scott, Marvin B. & Stanford M. Lyman. 1968. Accounts. *American sociological review* 33(1). 46–62.
Seidlhofer, Barbara. 2001. Closing a Conceptual Gap: The Case for a Description of English as a Lingua Franca. *International Journal of Applied Linguistics* 11(2). 133–158.
Seidlhofer, Barbara. 2011. *Understanding English as a Lingua Franca*. Oxford: Oxford University Press.
Shea, David P. 1994. Perspective and Production: Structuring Conversational Participation across Cultural Borders. *Pragmatics* 4(3). 357–389.
Sifianou, Maria. 2012. Disagreements, Face and Politeness. *Journal of Pragmatics* 44(12). 1554–1564.
Stivers, Tanya. 2013. Sequence Organization. In Jack Sidnell & Tanya Stivers (eds.), *The Handbook of Conversation Analysis*, 191–200. Oxford: Wiley Blackwell.
Stivers, Tanya & Federico Rossano. 2010. Mobilizing Response. *Research on Language and Social Interaction* 43(1). 3–31.
Toomaneejinda, Anuchit & Luke Harding. 2018. Disagreement Practices in ELF Academic Group Discussion: Verbal, Nonverbal and Interactional Strategies. *Journal of English as a Lingua Franca* 7(2). 307–332.
Widdowson, Henry. 2015. ELF and the pragmatics of language variation. *Journal of English as a Lingua Franca* 4(2). 359–372.
Wong, Jean & Hansun Zhang Waring. 2010. *Conversation Analysis and Second Language Pedagogy*. Routledge: New York.
Zimmerman, Erica. 2007. Constructing Korean and Japanese Interculturality in Talk: Ethnic Membership Categorization among Users of Japanese. *Pragmatics* 17(1). 71–94.

4 Common ground in different discourses

Ivana Trbojević Milošević

Working offline: Common ground in written discourse

Abstract: Common ground issues have been and still are dominantly addressed in regard to spoken discourse, such as conversation or other kinds of (more or less) direct interaction. The aim of this paper is to investigate the concept of Common Ground (CG) in the production of written discourse, in particular written discourse intended for international readership. To this end, I have used a parallel corpus compiled of the headlines of articles published in the American edition of the *New York Times* and the articles reprinted (in English) in the supplement to Serbian *Politika* daily in 2006/7. Comparison of the original headlines and articles with the versions published in the supplement showed consistent alterations to suit the overseas (Serbian) audience, which gave rise to the question of differences in construction of CG between spoken and written discourse addressed in this paper. Adhering primarily to the model of CG establishment as proposed in the socio-cognitive approach (Kecskes and Zhang 2009) I shall look into the factors that operate in the construction of CG in written discourse such as recipient design, perspective taking, controlling egocentrism and salience, treatment of and reliance on presupposition and 'cultural knowledge' (van Dijk 2001), preference for explicitness and absence of immediate rapport. The analysis of corpus examples shows that the model of CG establishment in written discourse, although specific and somewhat 'asymmetrical', fits into the framework proposed in the SCA.

1 Introduction

It seems that Common Ground (CG) never ceases to be a thought and debate provoking topic among those scholars who "take pragmatics seriously" (Allan 2013: 286). Even a quick overview of selected relevant work on CG in the past sixty years, from Grice (1981, 1989) and Schiffer (1972) to Stalnaker (2002) on, reveals at least three different, but still closely intertwined streams in attempts to define it, let us name them dominantly philosophical, psycho-linguistic (Clark 1996) and pragmatic (broadly taken, so as to include the latest cognitive and socio-cognitive views, such as neo-Gricean theory, Relevance Theory and the socio-cognitive approach – SCA).

In spite of differences in their viewpoints, scholars agree that CG does play a paramount role in human communication and comprehension. Thus, Allan

https://doi.org/10.1515/9783110766752-012

(2013: 285) states that speakers/writers, when addressing an audience/hearers, are bound to have assumptions about their audience's ability to understand what has been said/written and that those assumptions constitute CG. However, what actually makes the 'fabric' of CG that allows for hearer's recognition of intention and thus her understanding of the utterance became the point of debate among philosophers of language, linguists and psycho-linguistics that lead to a rather confusing set of terms denoting CG. A detailed review and discussion of such terms ('assumed knowledge', 'mutual knowledge' 'background knowledge' 'shared knowledge', 'assumed familiarity' etc. – that Allan (2013: 287) calls 'Common Ground and its Aliases', as well as definitions of CG proposed accordingly) is elaborately given in Lee (1998, 2001).

2 Common ground in written discourse

The distinctions mentioned above do not significantly affect the topic of this paper and neither does the problem of the so-called 'recursive flaw'[1] that surfaced in Schiffer's (1972) definition of 'mutual knowledge*'. What does affect the topic is mentioning the *writer* in the quote from Allan (2013), which evokes applicability of CG in written discourse: on the one hand, we take it for granted that 'language is primarily a form of *interactive* social behavior' (Allan: 2013: 285), and on the other, we may question the nature of interaction when written discourse (such as works of literature, journalistic articles, even in-advance-prepared speeches delivered via media, etc.) is in focus, particularly because the text (or let us still consider it 'utterance') addresses not one or two hearers, but an audience that practically remains virtual throughout the process. Although we regularly speak of writers and authors 'interacting' with 'their audiences', can we still call it 'interaction' in the pragmatic sense that necessarily implies cooperation? Does that mean that the writer (henceforth W) takes a different path in attempting to build CG, if at all, steeped, so to say, in egocentrism? If, however, we take that a huge portion of written language usage is motivated by the *intention to inform* (as is the case with newspaper articles), that means that writers set out to write with audience /readership in mind. Thus, agreeing with Clark et al. (1983: 246) that the speakers formulate their utterances in the manner and with the belief that hearers will be able to construe the utterance meaning without problems and in line with the speaker's intention, I propose that the same applies, *ceteris paribus*, to the writer and

1 'Mutual knowledge*' is infinite, therefore speaker and hearer will be processing the utterance over and over again.

her readership. For that reason, I trust the above questions present a legitimate starting point for investigating the concept of CG building in written discourse.

3 Common ground in written discourse: Previous research

Though research on CG has been dominantly focused on spoken language, written discourse attracted attention of researchers too. Lee (1998) analyzed establishment of CG in interactive written data (correspondence between faculty and students); Allan (2013) uses fictional and non-fictional texts to illustrate and analyze the building of CG between the characters in a detective novel (Chandler's *The Big Sleep*) and *between the author and his readers* in E. P. Abbey's 'Preliminary Notes' to the collection of essays *Down the River* (1982). There are several observations in Allan's analysis that I find crucial for the analysis of data in this paper; those concern egocentricity of the writer ("Abbey was somewhat egocentric in his assumptions about CG with the reader." (2013: 299)) and the commonality of perspective taking ("Linguistic communication in general is a matter of putting oneself into the interlocutor's shoes . . ." (2013: 301)). In spite of the fact that Allan actually argues that the role of egocentricity is overstated in the work of some authors (Keysar 2007, Keysar 2008, Kecskes and Zhang 2009), I believe that the data presented in Section 6 of this paper would confirm its considerable presence in CG dynamics. Finally, although Mey (1998: 12) in the study on literary pragmatics *When Voices Clash* does not explicitly talk about CG, he acknowledges establishment of 'working cooperation' between writers and readers within his definition of literary pragmatics. He recognizes the use of linguistic resources on the part of the writer (author/text producer) and the specific conditions of use of such resources in the establishment of working cooperation with her readers.

Unlike the illustrations from Allan (2013), the written correspondence analyzed by Lee (1998, 2001) represents interactive data; though not unfolding online[2] in the

2 In this paper I use the terms 'online' and 'offline' in the sense they are used when referring to 'mode switching' in the computer-mediated communication (CMC). (Ramirez and Zhang: 2007). Working *online* means that the device is connected to a network, and the processing happens in real time, just as processing in direct human verbal interaction ('meaning is negotiated *online*') does. Offline mode does allow the user to browse cached websites and documents for example. Thus I use the term when referring to writing, and not in the 'face-to-face' sense it has in non-computer mediated communication.

way conversation does, it still allows for all principal phases of CG building (activating, seeking and creating CG) with, to keep to the CMC metaphor, some latency (cf. Sampietro 2022). Written discourse, such as newspaper articles, is created for audiences that are 'out there' in full awareness that they might be very diverse in terms of knowledge, experience and interests. Again, sticking to the CMC metaphor, and aware that immediate rapport in such communication is either missing altogether, or, if it comes, it happens with great latency, we will consider production of such written discourse to be happening *offline*.

4 Modelling CG

I do not intend here to embark on a discussion of critical readings of different CG models proposed by authors from philosophical, pragmatic or socio-cognitive camps – or to discuss 'the recursive flaw': basically, most of the proposed models provide a theoretical framework flexible enough for the intended analysis. Still, a brief outline of two models follows as both, especially taken together, provide an adequate basis for analysis.

Allan (2013: 292) proposes a definition of CG that explicitly introduces speaker and hearer, specifies the grounds of belief (and resolves the issue of 'recursive flaw'):

> Common ground for any community K of two or more people *that include S and H* is that:
> (a) every member, or almost every member, of K knows or believes some fact or set of facts F; and
> (b) a member is presumed to know or believe F by (almost) every other member of K;
> (c) and a member of K knows that both (a) and (b) are true. (Allan 2013)

Once S addresses an utterance (P) to (any) member(s) of K, and the member (H) of K resorts to the knowledge of F in order to interpret P, P becomes part of F and CG gets established. S may address P to any number of members of K who can presume that all other members of K will activate their knowledge of and make P part of F.

The proposed definition of CG recognizes equal importance of both S and H, which is also postulated in the socio-cognitive approach to CG. Besides, (a) and (b) posit the presence of common, or rather, community-owned knowledge and beliefs, that can be understood as *core* common ground in the SC model, inclusive of the three subcategories elaborated by Kecskes and Zhang (2009:347), namely common sense (general knowledge of the world), culture sense (of society, cultural norms, etc.) and formal sense (knowledge of linguistic system).

Kecskes and Zhang's (2009, 2013) socio-cognitive frame further develops the model of CG and sees it as dynamic and integrated concept consisting of core ('mental representation of shared knowledge') and emergent common ground ('shared knowledge that we can seek') that get together during communication to construct a socio-cultural background for communication.

It is particularly important that the socio-cognitive approach to CG acknowledges the interplay between factors such as cooperation and egocentrism (where one does not exclude the other), as well as of intention and attention, accommodating the pragmatic view that communication is intention-directing practice (Kecskes and Zhang 2009), but which shows attention–oriented features. The SCA manages to reconcile pragmatic and cognitive views by acknowledging that both intention and attention are motivated by socio-cultural factors. Kecskes and Zhang (2009) distinguish three types of intention, namely informative, performative and emotive, the first one, informative, being of primary importance when observing construction of CG in written discourse, as writer clearly intends to inform the reader of something. It does not mean that the other two types are not present in written discourse such as newspaper articles, only that the informative intentions lie in the very reason for article writing. An important tenet of the SCA regarding intention is that "[intention] is considered a dynamically changing phenomenon that is the main organizing force in the communicative process" (Kecskes 2010), which will be clearly visible in the examples of written discourse analyzed below. Also, the distinction between core common ground and emergent common ground that get integrated in the assumption of CG (Kecskes and Zhang 2009) provides a fitting framework for a somewhat asymmetrical model of CG constructed in written discourse.

The inevitable problem of presupposition status in and relation to CG needs to be addressed here. Criticizing Stalnaker's (2002) 'mingling presupposition with CG' Allan (2013: 285, 289–291) agrees with Abbot (2008) that although presuppositions are relevant to CG they cannot be equated with it and sees them as preparatory conditions, or requirements on CG that must be met in illocutions.

Kecskes and Zhang (2013) provide a revised view of the relation of presupposition and CG within the SCA, focusing on the dynamic nature of presupposition and pointing to the 'vibrant interaction' between the presupposition and CG:"They enjoy a cross relation in terms of content and manners in which they are formed, and their dynamism is inherently related and explanatory to each other." (2013: 376)

Further on, they state that "presupposition is a joint business in which the speaker and hearer play different roles" (2013: 382). The notion of speaker-assigned presupposition (Zhang 2009) is proposed, in the sense that the speaker forms the background of conversation through presupposition, handing it over for processing to the hearer who may or may not agree. That will naturally either provide for emergence of common ground, or not, challenging further conversation.

When applied to written discourse (where the immediate rapport is missing), the question arises whether and to what extent the writer makes deliberate choices as to what type of presupposition to invest into the establishment of CG. Also, if s/he does, factors that influence such choices should also be considered (such as recipient design). The corpus of examples to be analyzed below should show that the writer assesses the impact different type of presupposition might have on the establishment of CG with the reader.

Leaving differences aside and summing up the converging points, we can conclude that both views of CG recognize:

a. The importance of taking into account the efforts of both the S/W and the H/R;
b. The role of recipient /audience design (Bell 1984);
c. The role of rapport/ feedback as a measure of comprehension;
d. The necessity of perspective taking in the dynamics of CG (co)construction (which may result in controlling egocentrism and salience as consequences of W's prior knowledge);
e. The relation between presupposition and CG (that is not one of equality);
f. The importance of communicative competence as knowledge of linguistic, socio-cultural and discursive rules of communication (Hymes 1972, Canale and Swain 1981, Bachman 1990).

These will provide a basis for the analysis of the corpus of examples presented in the paper, hoping to prove that the dynamic view of CG as elaborated within the SCA accommodates the construction of CG in written discourse, in spite of obvious differences in its dynamics when compared to constructing CG in conversation.

5 About the corpus

In the period 2006–2007, Serbian daily *Politika*, as a host paper, started publishing a Monday supplement featuring the best *New York Times* (henceforth NYT) articles of the week. It brought to the Serbian readership, "globally resonant coverage of ideas and trends, business and politics, science and lifestyles"[3] in the English

3 Wikipedia https://en.wikipedia.org/wiki/The_New_York_Times_International_Edition#The_New_York_Times_International_Weekly.

language. It turned out to be a great resource not only for EFL teaching, but also for teachers who taught linguistics and applied linguistics at our English Department. I also regularly used selected articles for teaching purposes with my students, and among them was an October 2007 article on answering cell phones in public. The article had been inspired by an incident when Rudy Giuliani, then mayor of New York took a call from his wife Judith right in the middle of his address to the National Rifle Association. The headline of the article in the NYT *Politika* supplement was *"Oups . . . Mind if I Take This?"* Being short of enough copies for the students, I tried to find the article in the NYT Archives and I did – it came out on September 30, 2007, but with a different headline: *"Four Score and . . . Mind if I Take This?"* I found it quite intriguing and compared the two versions: besides the changed headline, the article in the *Politika* was slightly shorter (a couple of paragraphs were taken out), but not more than that.

It was the change in the headline that set me thinking: what had motivated the editor's[4] decision? Cropping the article was easily accountable for, as the NYT gives an overview of a week on 16 pages only, but the first part of headline '*Four score and . . . .*' was intriguing. It did resonate as familiar – but I had to consult the Web, where I found it: it was the opening phrase of Abraham Lincoln's Gettysburg Address (Nov 19, 1863, referring to the adoption of Declaration of Independence in 1776: "Four score and seven years ago,[5] our fathers brought forth, upon this continent, a new nation, conceived in liberty . . .". Neither the original NYT article nor the version for international readership made reference to either the Gettysburg address or the Declaration of Independence, but the phrase *must have been there with a reason* – aiming at boosting associative thinking, provoking or exciting certain schemata? Once you read the article and learned that Mr. Giuliani was "smack in the middle of his talk in front of the NRA", i.e. *highly important occasion* that called for an equally highly dedicated and (hopefully) memorable speech, his cell phone rang and he announced he had to take it, because it was his wife calling. Then, the article proceeds to comment on the *appropriateness* of such behavior in public, etc. However, the editors of the NYT *Politika* supplement (as is a well-known fact, the titles are not chosen by authors, but by publishers) decided to change the headline for the international readership (in this case Serbian), to omit the direct association to the Gettysburg Address and to replace

4 All the editing and preparation of the articles was done by the NYT editors in the US. The *Politika* intervened only by adding a short glossary of lexical items assumed to be more difficult for Serbian readers, non-native speakers of English. The *Politika* was (and still is) quite a widely read paper in the region. From the US editors' angle, that could be considered international readership.

5 Score = 20 years, i.e.4 x 20 +7= 87 years.

it with an exclamatory remark '*oups*' (widely used even among the non-English speaking persons) but retained the, so to say, face saving, rhetorical but still perfunctory question *Mind if I take this?* in the newly tailored headline. (Everybody would, no doubt).

This example seems somehow easy to account for: clearly, the editors of the supplement edition *expected* the reference to the Gettysburg address not to be easily grasped by the non-American audiences/readers and consciously looked for an expression that would be at least equally catchy to draw their *attention* to the article but at the same time comprehensible enough. Further down, I shall revisit this example from a critical discourse analysis view point.

However, as it often happens, this accidental finding prompted me to start comparing the articles brought by the NYT *Politika* supplement to the original ones published in the daily American edition. I searched through the NYT *Politika* editions from October 2006 to October 2007 and found their American counterparts in NYT Archives. A random sampling of different rubrics of the newspaper yielded a parallel corpus of 60 pairs of texts. The comparison of articles showed a steady consistency, a regular pattern of change in the headlines. The only type of article that never underwent any change (around 10 percent of the overall sample) were short editorial opinions (op-eds). The articles themselves differed only in length (though not always): those in the *Politika* supplement were more or less cropped,[6] with occasional insertion of 'summary' of the text left out (such as: 'and there many more examples of that, etc.'). But, practically more than ninety percent of headlines had undergone some change: some were completely different, in others only one or a few words were changed.

The examples below present a part of the compiled corpus of headlines that will serve illustrative purposes in this paper.

NYT headline:	NYT *Politika* Headline:
Four Score and . . . Mind If I take this? (Sept 30 2007; KB)	Oups . . . Mind if I take this?
What Kept Russia from Producing Tennis Stars Before Now? (Oct 5 2006, SSch)	In Tennis a Soviet Legacy Lives on
Secrets of Endurance: Eating to Go (and Go and Go) (Aug 24 2006, CSL)	The Secret to Sports Endurance: Eating to Go (and Go and Go)

6 I believe that shortening the articles was due only to the constraints on space, i.e. for practical, not for pragmatic reasons.

Democrats Have Intensity, but G.O.P. Has Machinery (Oct 14 2006; RT)	For Democrats, Passion is on the Rise
Voters Allegiances, Ripe for the Picking (Oct 14 2006; DDK)	For Republicans, a Vote for History
Numbers Are Male, Said Pythagoras, and the Idea Persists (Oct 3 2006; MW)	Pythagoras Thought Numbers Are Male, and Some Still Agree
Vendetta Rapes Continue as Pakistan Resists Change (Oct 14 2006; SM)	Rape as Revenge Persists in Pakistan
Cat Lovers Lining Up for No-Sneeze Kitties (Oct 6 2006; ER)	No-Sneeze Kitties for Cat Lovers with Allergies
Smoking No More Très Chic in France (Oct 6 2006; ES)	France, the Land of Cigarettes, Considers Banishing Smokers
A Bold Little Italian Wine That's Less Polluting (Oct 17 2006; ER)	A Bold Little Italian Wine That's Also Energy-Efficient
Scavullo, Beyond Cosmo: New Appreciation for a Photographer's Work (Sept 29 2006; EW)	Photographing Fashions, With an Artist's Soul

6 Corpus examples analysis

In this section, I shall deal with the following questions:

1. What is the relevance of the findings described in Section 5 for the topic of this paper, i.e. how can the data relate to the issues of CG establishment in written discourse?
2. What is the role of intercultural dimension of the texts?

I shall attempt to do that by looking for the presence/absence of factors listed under a.–f. in Section 4 above.

The findings that came as a result of comparing the NYT article versions inspired reflections on the nature of CG establishment between W and R in written discourse that is intended for virtual audience. As already stated in Section 3 above, the CG issues are dominantly addressed in regard to spoken discourse, such as conversation or other kinds of interaction that (more or less) happens *online*, when *it is possible to monitor* the dynamics of CG co-construction. This talk addresses the question of what happens, in terms of CG construction, if the text is constructed so to say *offline*, when the recipients are readers that constitute a practically virtual audience for the writers who produce written discourse. In other words, the initial communication item (text) is invariably going to be received with a longer or shorter time lapse (between the moment of writing and actual reading) i.e. latency. I particularly have in mind those types of written discourse that practically *exclude the possibility of immediate feedback* and therefore *rapport*, such as newspaper articles. That is the reason why the question of the nature of CG construction between the author and the readers in terms of the models of CG proposed by modern pragmatic theories arose. The approaches and illustrations described in the previous sections allow for a positive answer.

The differences found in the NYT and NYT *Politika* articles actually provide tangible evidence of the construction of CG, with special emphasis on the 'assumed knowledge' or core CG. What is specific for this kind of discourse, and what causes the asymmetry in the model, is the absence of measurable or immediately observable *emergent* CG (especially not in terms of interpersonal dynamics). So, the processing on the R's side again stays unattended to in a way, but actually remains in the assumed domain, though it can be indirectly acknowledged – through the size of circulation/readership or comments and letters to the editor.

The fact that the headlines were consistently changed in the NYT supplement to *Politika* articles prepared for international readership, clearly points to the editors' *awareness* (and thus *intention*, rather of performative type) of the differences and diversity of primarily *socio-cultural knowledge* of the international readership, but also of the readers' (varying) knowledge of English (here definitely functioning as *lingua franca*). The editor (W) is easily recognized as some kind of *intercultural mediator*.[7] That partially answers the question stated under 2. above.

Another thing that surfaces as more than obvious while tracking down the reasons for the alterations in the headlines observed, is that *recipient design* plays an important role – the changes prove that Ws consciously assume possible problems of international readership that might arise if they (Ws) stick to their first choices (salient and therefore egocentric). It is through these assumptions that W, unconsciously though, controls egocentrism expressed through salience. The choices that govern the recipient design therefore derive from the W's *change of perspective* and conscious turning to other available attentional resources (expressed through different linguistic choices, still retaining relevance), which proves that Ws

7 For this reason, I consider these altered headlines/articles instances of intercultural communication. It is the otherness of socio-cultural identities of the international readership that impose the quality of interculturality here.

have assumptions about the average international reader's knowledge of English and opt for attentional resources that they assume would be part of their readership's communal knowledge, therefore their core common ground. Going back to Kecskes' (2007) observation that in intercultural communication *lingua franca* speakers rely more on linguistic means than on CG, it seems reasonable to conclude that they would rely more on linguistic means when processing the text and that Ws have at least correct intuitions about that.

The change of perspective that governs Ws' recipient design is equally strongly motivated by their assumptions about Rs' familiarity with socio-cultural concepts, including those political, with familiarity of discursive practices of American newspapers, etc. True enough, the correctness of such assumptions about Rs' background knowledge, cultural norms and expectations is in a way, at least temporarily, a shot in the dark, again due to the inaccessibility of emergent common ground.

Notice the changes in the headlines of two articles commenting on and analyzing the intensity of the Democrats' and Republicans' voters in the then nearing Congressional elections:

NYT headline:	NYT *Politika* headline:
1. Democrats Have Intensity, but G.O.P. Has Machinery (Oct 14 2006; RT)	1a. For Democrats, Passion is on the Rise
2. Voters Allegiances, Ripe for the Picking (Oct 14 2006; DDK)	2.a. For Republicans, a Vote for History

The W's assumptions about the international readers' lack of familiarity with the abbreviation G.O.P (Grand Old Party for the Republican Party) lead to the decision to omit it in the headline although it was kept in the article itself; just as in the cell-phone article mentioned at the beginning, the W establishes assumed CG with the international reader having changed perspective and 'stepping into the shoes' of the international reader. The change does not have to do with the Rs' knowledge of English, but with the assumed lack of knowledge about socio-political concepts, or, at least lack of familiarity with concepts that are in the Americans' common ground.

In the headline 2. the assumptions have to do with the choice of vocabulary (*allegiances* for *loyalty* or *fidelity*) that need not be salient in the international Rs lexicon. Similar assumptions must have been made about the underlying metaphor VOTE IS FRUIT, which lead the W to omit it in the headline addressed to the international Rs.

Two interesting examples of the W's intervention with *referential expressions* can be found in the following pairs of headlines:

NYT headline:	NYT *Politika* headline:
3. A Scholar is Alive, Actually, and Hungry for Debate (Sep.22 2006, MS)	3a. Despite Rumors, Voice of U.S. Left Is not Deceased
4. Jane We Hardly Knew Ye Died (Sep.24 2006, LA)	4.a American Women, Dying in Battle

The headline 3. introduces an article that comments on the unfortunate blunder made by Hugo Chávez, then president of Venezuela, at a press conference after his speech in the United Nations, when he expressed deep regrets for "not having meet the linguist Noam Chomsky, the icon of American left, before his death". The W decided on rather hefty changes in 3a: notice that the indefinite noun phrase 'A Scholar' referring to Noam Chomsky in the American edition was replaced by 'Voice of U.S. Left' in the NYT *Politika* edition (3,a.). The irony (directed to Mr. Chávez) of referring to one of the world's most distinguished linguists by an indefinite noun phrase was assumed not to be easily recognized by the international R, but the W still did not opt for explicitly naming the referent. S/he rather decided to use the noun phrase 'Voice of U.S. Left', assuming that to the international readership Chomsky was better known as the icon of the American left. The rest of the headline 3.a. is fairly explicit and explanatory, which is in line with the above remark concerning W's expectations about international Rs relying more on linguistic means when processing the text.

The headline 4. comments on the sad fact that too many deaths of American women soldiers in Iraq and Afghanistan passed unnoticed in American public. The W again had to intervene heavily in order to produce a headline that would be more easily understood by international Rs and that would still activate attentional resources that would preserve relevance. The W rightfully assumed that common knowledge of international readership would hardly contain as salient the reference to 'Jane'[8] or the lyrics (*Johnny, I Hardly Knew Ye*).[9] Instead, s/he decides on an explicit reference to American women who lost their lives in combat, keeping the relevance high and requiring less processing effort from the reader.

---

8 John Doe and Jane Doe, any man and woman of unknown name.

9 A traditional Irish song, widely popular in Ireland, UK and US until 1920s, today considered a strong anti-war song; also, the title of a 1972 memoir book about the assassination of John F. Kennedy. (https://en.wikipedia.org/wiki/Johnny_I_Hardly_Knew_Ye).

The attempts at keeping the processing effort as low as possible for the international Rs are also observable in the W's treatment of presupposition in the original and altered headlines. The concept of speaker-assigned presupposition and its dynamic (or, even unstable) nature is valuable for the analysis of the factors that influenced the alterations of the headlines analyzed and compared. In the examples that follow, it is observable that the W of the supplement edition, conscious of all the restrictions (cultural and linguistic included) on the assumed CG of the international Rs, tries to lessen the reliance on the presuppositions that are assumed to activate specific socio-cultural knowledge by making it easier for the R to accommodate them. Since presupposition cannot be omitted altogether, the Ws 'aid' the R either by increasing the explicitness of the headlines or by varying presupposition type:

NYT headline:	NYT *Politika* headline:
5. Cat Lovers Lining Up for No-Sneeze Kitties (Oct 6 2006; ER)	5.a No-Sneeze Kitties for Cat Lovers with Allergies
6. Smoking No More Très Chic in France (Oct 6 2006; ES)	6.a. France, the Land of Cigarettes, Considers Banishing Smokers
7. Islamic Schools at Heart of British Debate on Integration (Oct. 15 2006; AC)	7.a. Islamic Schools Test the Ideal of Integration in Great Britain
8. Vendetta Rapes Continue as Pakistan Resists Change (Oct 14 2006; SM)	8a. Rape as Revenge in Pakistan

For example, the presupposition *p <no-sneeze kittens exist>* in 5. which is retained in 5.a., is made easier to process by adding the presupposition *p1 <there are cat-lovers with allergies>*; the presupposition *s <smoking was très chic in France before>* (6.) is replaced by the presupposition in 6.a. *f< France is the land of cigarettes>* with the new information about the plans for banishing smoking clearly explicated. In 7. presupposition *b<Britain is debating on integration>* is substituted in 7.a. by *t<ideal of integration exists in Great Britain>* and the rest is explicit. The next example is interesting, since the headline 8. completely dismisses the presuppositions *v<rapes out of vengeance have existed in Pakistan for a time>*, *v1< rapes of vengeance have not stopped>* and *r<Pakistan is undergoing change of some kind>* and introduces the topic only relying on existential presuppositions concerning 'rape', 'revenge' and 'Pakistan'. Note that the W's assumption was that the lexeme 'vendetta' (a borrowing from Italian) was changed to English 'revenge', as the W assumes it would be a better choice (in terms of salience in the Rs' CG).

Finally, yet another type of editorial intervention, not immediately observable, regards W's ideological bias. Following Van Dijk's understanding of "ideologies as a special form of social cognition shared by social groups" (Van Dijk 2001) that underlie and influence the social practices of group members, including their discourse as well as the representations of contexts in which members of the group participate, repeated reading of the articles and the headlines revealed rather subtle and sophisticated markers of ideological beliefs. Understanding the tone of the 'cell-phone article' (repeated below as 9.) for example, especially the irony woven into the headline through evoking the Gettysburg Address, requires knowledge of the editorial stance of the New York Times, which is typically liberal,[10] the knowledge that would be part of the core common ground of the author and the addressed readership alike. The choice of the opening words of the Gettysburg Address (also 'shared knowledge' by a large social group of educated Americans) in the context of an important address in front of a prominent and highly conservative organization, easily strikes the right chord in the readership and in a way, guarantees establishment of emergent CG (in spite of the lack in immediate rapport or feedback). The alteration in the headline for the international R indicates the W's assumptions that international Rs do not share the knowledge regarding the political and ideological stance of the NYT and consequently decides on the widely used, so to say neutral exclamation (though still attention-directed and relevant), hoping for easier construction of emergent common ground.

NYT headline:	NYT Politika headline:
9. Four score and . . . Mind If I Take This? (Sep.30, 2007;KB)	9.a. Oups . . ..Mind If I Take This?
10. What Kept Russia from Producing Tennis Stars Before Now? (Oct. 1 2006, SSch)	10.a. In Tennis a Soviet Legacy Lives on

The W, deciding to change the headline 10. from 'What Kept Russia from Producing Tennis Stars Before Now?' to 10.a seems to have had doubts about the strength

10 *The New York Times* has not endorsed a Republican Party member for president since Dwight D. Eisenhower in 1956; since 1960, it has endorsed the Democratic Party nominee in every presidential election. https://en.wikipedia.org/wiki/The_New_York_Times#:~:text=Content-Editorial%20stance,typically%20liberal%20in%20their%20position

of intended ideological undertones in the original headline. The original article expresses bewilderment with the rocket-like success of Russian tennis players after the disintegration of the Soviet Union, given the fact that tennis was never a Russian sport. However, the article did get feedback from a reader, whose letter was published five days after the original one. The reader opposed the author's opinion by stating that tennis 'was always played in the Soviet Union', though in rather humble conditions. The letter was entitled 'Tennis, Soviet Style: When East Hits West' and finishes answering the question put in the original headline: 'All it needed was the collapse of the Soviet system!' The decision to infuse the headline intended for the NYT *Politika* readership with a stronger ideological undertone obviously came from there.

The last example, however, comes just in the right moment to sum up the view I expressed at the beginning of this paper – that the model of dynamic *online* CG construction in conversation as proposed by the SCA also accommodates *offline* CG construction, i.e. in written discourse. The emerging CG gets formed, and the feedback by the intrigued reader clearly shows it. It is true that most of the time it remains inaccessible to the author, in the assumptive domain. If it were not there at all, journalists and writers would probably end up jobless.

7 Concluding remarks

In this paper, I tried to identify the factors influencing the *offline* construction of CG in written discourse which is characterized by absence of interaction and rapport present in the *online* type, such as conversation or (in a way) written correspondence.[11] I compiled a 'parallel' corpus of headlines appearing in the American editions of NYT and its weekly supplements in English, intended for international audience. The headlines in the NYT *Politika* supplement showed consistent changes reflecting the editors' assumptions about the background knowledge of the international readers, as well as of their linguistic and communicative competence. I have attempted to prove that the changes made in the NYT *Politika* supplement headlines present tangible evidence of Ws 'strategies' to create core common ground and activate the construction of emergent common ground, although the latter generally remains without reach, so the

11 In line with the CMC metaphor used in the paper, written correspondence may be an illustrative example of switching between offline and online modes. In other words, the texts themselves are produced offline, but sending them and getting answered (rapport and feedback) make written correspondence similar to the online type, allowing for latency though.

model of constructing CG in written discourse remains asymmetrical or 'open' in a way. Using the corpus which represents a type of *intercultural* communication showed considerable advantages in terms of traceable evidence of W's awareness of socio-cultural, linguistic and ideological differences within the audience of international readers, and that, in turn, enabled me to identify 'strategies' for CG construction which would not be as evident in 'monocultural' written discourse such as journalistic articles.

References

Abbot, B. 2008. Presupposition and common ground. *Linguistics and Philosophy* 21. 523–538.

Allan, K. 2013. What is Common Ground? In Alessandro Capone, Franco Lo Piparo & Marco Carapezza (eds.), *Perspectives on Linguistic Pragmatics*, 285–310. Cham, Switzerland: Springer.

Bachman, L. F. 1990. Fundamental Considerations in Language Testing. Oxford etc.: OUP.

Bell, A. 1984. Language style as audience design. *Language in Society* 13(2). 145–204.

Canale, M., & Swain, M. 1981. A Theoretical Framework for Communicative Competence. In Palmer, A., Groot, P., & Trosper, G. (eds.), *The construct validation of tests of communicative competence*, 31–36. Washington, DC: TESOL.

Clark, H. H. 1996. Using Language. Cambridge: Cambridge University Press.

Clark, H. H., Schreuder, R. and Butterick, S. 1983. Common ground and the understanding of demonstrative reference. *Journal of Verbal Learning and Verbal Behavior* 22. 245–258.

Grice, H. P. 1981. Presupposition and conversational implicature. In C. Peter (ed.), *Radical Pragmatics*, 183–198. New York: Academic Press. [Reprinted in Grice, H.P. 1989. *Studies in the way of words*, 86–116. Cambridge: Harvard University Press.]

Enfield, N. 2008. Common ground as a resource for social affiliation. In Kecskes I. and J. Mey (eds.), *Intention, common ground and the Egocentric Speaker Hearer*, 223–254. Berlin: Mouton de Gruyter.

Hymes, D. H. 1972. On Communicative Competence. In Pride, J. B., & Holmes, J. (eds.), *Sociolinguistics*, 269–293. Baltimore, USA: Penguin Education, Penguin Books Ltd.

Kecskes, I. 2007. Formulaic Language in English Lingua Franca. In I. Kecskes and L. Horn *Explorations in Pragmatics: Linguistic, cognitive and intercultural aspects*, 191–218. Berlin/New York: Mouton de Gruyter.

Kecskes, I. and F. Zhang, F. 2009. Activating, seeking and creating common ground. A Sociocognitive approach. *Pragmatics and cognition* 17(2). 331–355.

Kecskes, I. 2010. The Paradox of Communication: Socio-cognitive approach to pragmatics. *Pragmatics and* Society 1(1). 50–73.

Kecskes, I. and F. Zhang 2013. On the dynamic relations between common ground and presupposition. In Alessandro Capone, Franco Lo Piparo & Marco Carapezza (eds.), *Perspectives on Linguistic Pragmatics*, 375–396. Cham: Springer.

Kecskes, I. 2014. *Intercultural pragmatics*. New York: Oxford University Press.

Keysar, B. 2007. Communication and Miscommunication: The Role of Egocentric Processes. *Intercultural Pragmatics* 4. 71–85.

Keysar, B. 2008. Egocentric processes in communication and miscommunication. In Kecskes I. and J. Mey (eds.), *Intention, common ground and the Egocentric Speaker Hearer*, 277–296. Berlin: Mouton de Gruyter.

Lee, B. P. H. 1998. *Establishing Common Ground in Written Correspondence*. A Dissertation submitted for the degree of Doctor of Philosophy. University of Cambridge. Retrieved from https://www.repository.cam.ac.uk/bitstream/handle/1810/313588/PhD%20Benny%20P%20H%20Lee%201998%20OCR.pdf?sequence=1-40.

Lee, B. P. H. 2001. Mutual knowledge, background knowledge and shared beliefs: Their roles in establishing common ground. *Journal of Pragmatics* 33. 21–44.

Lewis, D. 1969. *Convention*. Cambridge: Harvard University Press

Mey, J. 1998. *When Voices Clash. A study in Literary Pragmatics*. Berlin: Mouton de Gruyter

Ramirez, A. and Zhang S. 2007. When Online Meets Offline: The Effect of Modality Switching on Relational Communication. *Communication Monographs* 74(3). 287–310. DOI:10.1080/03637750701543493

Sampietro, Agnese, Samuel Felder and Beat Siebenhaar. 2022. Do you kiss when you text? Cross-cultural differences in the use of the kissing emojis in three WhatsApp corpora. *Intercultural Pragmatics* 19(2). 183–208.

Schiffer, S. R. 1972. *Meaning*. Oxford: Clarendon Press.

Stalnaker, R. C. 2002. Common Ground. *Linguistics and Philosophy* 25. 701–721.

Van Dijk, T. 2001. Discourse, Ideology and Context. *Folia Linguistica* XXXV/1–2, 11–40. Berlin: Mouton de Gruyter.

Zhang, F. 2009. Speaker-assigned presupposition: A cognitive-pragmatic approach. *Proceedings from The 2nd International Conference on English, Discourse and Intercultural Communication*. Macao: University of Macao.

Ping Liu, Linlin Yang, and Jialiang Chen

Metapragmatic expressions as common ground builders in intercultural business communication

Abstract: Positioned within intercultural pragmatics, particularly the common ground (CG) theory of the Socio-cognitive Approach (SCA) proposed and developed by Kecskes (2008, 2013, 2017 and 2019), this chapter examines the role of metapragmatic expressions (MPEs) in building CG in intercultural business communication (IBC). Drawing on data from 42 recordings (about 7.5 hours in total) of English phone interactions between international customers and Chinese agents of a complaint center of one Chinese airline, we analyze and compare MPEs used by the customers and agents. Data analysis reveals that both agents and customers mainly employ three types of MPEs, namely, situation-oriented, information-oriented and relationship-oriented, to co-build CG for shared physical, cognitive and affective spaces. Under the constraints of institutional rules and regulations, speakers' language proficiency and asymmetrical social-cultural and professional knowledge, the agents employ MPEs to manifest intentions to build CG for shared cognitive and affective spaces; the customers employ MPEs to manifest intentions to build CG for shared physical and affective spaces. Generally, the agents are institutionalized and emotionally detached, whereas the customers are personalized and emotionally involved in CG building. The findings shed light on metapragmatic awareness, intercultural pragmatics and customer service practices in the intercultural business context.

1 Introduction

Metapragmatic expressions (MPEs) are linguistic expressions that explicitly display the speaker's reflexive awareness of language use and his/her intentions to manipulate ongoing interactions to fulfill particular communicative goals and/or needs (Liu and Ran 2016: 463). Positioned within intercultural pragmatics (Kecskes 2008, 2013, 2017 and 2019), this chapter examines the role of MPEs in building common ground (CG) in intercultural business communication (IBC).

Acknowledgments: This paper is part of the research outcome by the "Business Discourse Research Innovation Team" funded by the Department of Education of Guangdong Province, China (No. 2021WCXTD007).

https://doi.org/10.1515/9783110766752-013

Intercultural pragmatics represents a significantly new way of thinking about language use as it investigates how language users from diverse lingua-cultural backgrounds communicate when they cannot count on (or have limited access to) commonalities, conventions, common beliefs, and shared knowledge (Kecskes 2019), which are all parts of the core CG and the collective salience on which intention and cooperation-based pragmatics is built (Kecskes 2013). In IBC, the core CG of the target language appears to be missing or very limited, and hence participants need to (re)negotiate and co-construct CG, at least temporarily, in order to accomplish the task at hand.

It has been documented that a variety of linguistic devices are employed to build, rebuild and co-build CG between participants in intercultural communication, for instance, MPEs (e.g., Liu and Liu 2017a, 2017b, and 2021; Liu and Ran 2016, 2020), indexicals (e.g., Dinh 2019), vague category markers (e.g., Handford 2010), metaphorical expressions (e.g., Macagono and Rossi 2019), argumentation (e.g., Bigi 2018) and specific discursive strategies (Baider 2019). Among these linguistic devices, MPEs are found to express the speaker's intentions to activate, seek and create shared information and knowledge, which construct CG for a new space, referred to as a third space or a third culture in intercultural pragmatics (see Kecskes 2013). Nevertheless, previous studies did little research on actual business interactions, and there were no significant attempts to explore MPEs' functioning as CG builders in IBC in particular. This chapter aims to fill this gap by examining how agents and international customers employ MPEs to activate, seek and create CG throughout complaint settlement in airline telephone interactions.

It is challenging to deal with customer complaints in phone interactions as a complaining act is conflictive by nature. It becomes even more challenging when participants are from different lingua-cultural backgrounds. This is because lack of core CG between participants is likely to prevent them from understanding each other, let alone in voice-to-voice phone interactions where participants do not have access to face-to-face semiotic resources. Previous scholars researched intercultural customer complaints and responses from perspectives of cross-cultural communication (e.g., Li et al. 2016), pragmatics (e.g., Akram and Behnam 2012), and business management (e.g., Filip 2013). In the airline industry, in particular, a few investigated customer satisfaction (e.g., Law 2017) and loyalty (e.g., Dudek et al. 2019). However, insufficient attention has been paid to CG building in complaints and complaint responses, and little attention to the metapragmatic awareness in complaint responses in the airline industry.

Therefore, this chapter delineates how MPEs are chosen to build CG to accomplish communicative tasks in intercultural service encounters. Based on English phone interactions between international customers and Chinese agents of a complaint center of one Chinese airline, it is intended to answer three research questions: 1) what are the major types of MPEs used in complaint responses in intercultural phone interactions? 2) How are these MPEs used as common ground builders in complaint responses in intercultural phone interactions? 3) Is there any difference between the use of MPEs as common ground builders between agents and customers? Drawing on data from 42 recordings (about 7.5 hours in total) of English phone interactions, MPEs used by the customers and agents were identified, categorized, and analyzed to answer these three research questions.

2 Literature review

2.1 Metapragmatics and metapragmatic expressions

The concept metapragmatics has been explored extensively (e.g. Caffi 1994; Cruz 2015; Hübler and Büblitz 2007; Liu and Ran 2016, 2020; Liu and Liu 2017a, 2017b, and 2021; Tanskanen 2007; Verschueren 2000). In essence, metapragmatics is typical of reflexivity and referentiality (Liu and Liu 2021). Reflexivity refers to the fact that some linguistic resources reflect comments and management of discourse to direct the utterance interpretation (Grundy 2002). Caffi's widely cited definition of metapragmatics emphasized reflexivity by stating that metapragmatics refers to "the speaker's competence which reflects the judgments of appropriateness on one's own and other people's communicative behavior" (Caffi 1994: 2461). Referentiality refers to the fact that some linguistic resources point to or refer to something happening within communication (Tanskanen 2007), and it can be further divided into self-referential acts and other-referential acts. For example, the expression "I don't want to be rude but . . ." indicates that the speaker manages to mediate the discourse by reducing the negative effect since he/she realizes that what comes next may be considered offensive, while the expression "You are not telling the truth" is other-referential, operating as an evaluation of other's contribution in the interaction.

Metapragmatic awareness leaves "linguistic traces" at the surface level (Verschueren 2000), which have been named metapragmatic indicators (e.g., Verschueren 2000), metapragmatic utterances (e.g., Tanskanen 2007), metapragmatic comments (e.g., Penz 2007), and metapragmatic expressions (e.g., Smith and Liang 2007). We use metapragmatic expressions (MPEs) in this chapter to name the linguistic expressions that explicitly demonstrate the speaker's reflexive awareness regarding language use and their intentions to manage ongoing interactions for accomplishing interactional goals. Structurally, MPEs are clauses, sentences, fixed and semi-fixed linguistic expressions; semantically, they are not directly related to the propositional meanings of the host clauses; instead, they display the speakers' intentions to comment on the communication they are engaged in. In addition, MPEs could be sub-divided into different types according to their major functions in interactions, including commentaries, message glosses, speech-action descriptions and evidentials, to manipulate information, procedure and relationships development throughout the interactions (e.g., Liu and Liu 2021, 2022; Verschueren 2000)

Previous studies explored MPEs' generic functions, such as the management, negotiation and manipulation of discourse and communicative process, identity construction, problem and conflict resolution as well as rapport management (e.g., Hübler and Büblitz 2007; Liu and Liu 2017a, 2017b, and 2021; Liu and Ran 2020; Sinkeviciute 2017; Su 2019; Verschueren 2000; Yang 2021; Van Olmen and Tantucci 2022). Besides, MPEs used in different discourses were examined to display their diverse functions in specific contexts, for instance, political discourse, legal discourse, media discourse, educational discourse, digital discourse, business discourse, and even in literature (see Hübler and Büblitz 2007: 1–25). In addition, previous studies mainly focused on the fields of theoretical pragmatics (e.g., Caffi 1994), pragmatic competence development (e.g., Cruz 2015), (im)politeness research (e.g., Su 2019) as well as cross-cultural and intercultural studies (e.g., Sinkeviciute 2017).

So far, little research on MPEs has been done from the intercultural pragmatics perspective and their functioning as common ground builders in particular, although some studies have proposed that MPEs can be employed to co-construct and negotiate emergent CG in BELF (English as a Business Lingua Franca) meetings and customer services (Liu and Liu 2017a, 2017b, and 2021; Liu and Ran 2020). Further, as pointed out by Liu and Liu (2021), to delve into the mechanism of MPEs comprehensively and in-depth, it is highly recommended that the analytical framework should take into account layers of contextual factors, including linguistic representations, motivations, communicative events as well as the rights and obligations of the participants, since the functioning process of MPEs is situation-embedded and can only be understood and interpreted in the specific context.

2.2 Common ground

2.2.1 Common ground and its role in communication

Common ground is a fundamental and significant concept in different disciplines, such as psychology, philosophy, linguistics and communication. Within these disciplines, different terms were used to instantiate and highlight the core components and functioning mechanisms of CG, for instance, common knowledge (Stalnaker 1973), shared knowledge and beliefs (Lee 2001), assumed familiarity (Prince 1981), and presumed background information (Stalnaker 2002). In psychology, some researchers called for a perceptual basis and defined CG as "information shared with a conversational partner with that of an emergent property of ordinary memory processes" (Horton and Gerring 2016). In philosophy, it is assumed that certain propositions have "common ground status" (see Grice 1989: 65 and 274). In linguistics and communication studies, particularly from a pragmatic perspective, Stalnaker (1973: 448) defined CG as the background knowledge, beliefs and perceptions purportedly shared among communicators, which "constitute the presuppositions" and in turn "define the context."

It seems that the word 'knowledge' appears most frequently in CG definitions mentioned above (e.g., Lee 2001; Stalnaker 1973). Kreckel (1981, cited in Hinds 1985: 7) made a further distinction between common knowledge and shared knowledge: the former refers to "that knowledge which two or more people have in common as a result of being brought up under similar conditions such as culture, subculture, region and education"; the latter refers to "the negotiated common knowledge based on mutual interaction used for future interaction". The conception of shared knowledge is "temporary structures, created in real-time during human communication, and not maintained permanently" (Wilks 1986: 277).

Regarding the role of CG in communication, a consensus has been reached that the success of communication largely relies on the communal awareness of the shared information regarding and surrounding the communication (e.g., Kecskes 2010, 2013, 2019, and 2021; Stalnaker 2002). It is also argued that CG between interlocutors in discourse is far from static. It is neither absolute nor complete. Instead, it is an interactive and ongoing process in which assumed mutual beliefs and mutual knowledge are accumulated and updated (Clark and Brennan 1991). Furthermore, the negotiation of CG in communication is an attempt for each interlocutor to make their private understanding of the other explicit and to provide and receive feedback to reach some shared premise upon which meaningful communication can take place (Kecskes 2021).

2.2.2 The socio-cognitive approach to common ground

CG has been generally explored both from the pragmatic and cognitive perspectives. The pragmatic view, characterized by centering on the societal quality of CG, focuses on the principle of presupposition, cooperation and recipient design in communication. For instance, Stalnaker's (2002) analysis of CG was based on the information that the communicators assume to be shared. This view is socially-oriented and spelled out in the form of propositional attitudes shared in a speech community. On the other hand, the cognitive view investigates the cognitive structure and mechanism of CG activation and construction throughout the communication process. For instance, Horton and Gerring (2016) revisited the retrieval or formation of CG based on ordinary cognitive mechanisms and claimed that the information offered by the interlocutors in communication enters into the working memory to resonate with that stored in long-term memory, thus guaranteeing an integration between the current situational context and the interlocutors' prior experience.

Kecskes (2010, 2013, and 2019) and Kecskes and Zhang (2013) proposed and developed the Socio-cognitive Approach (SCA), a more dialectic and holistic approach, which fully acknowledges both the social and cognitive properties of CG. SCA holds that CG is a constant effort to integrate the cognitive representation of shared knowledge speakers can activate, seek, and create during the ongoing communication; it contains information and experience that the interlocutors share as human beings as a whole, the realization of local variables concerning the situational context, and the dynamic relationships between the participants (Kecskes 2013: 151). It has been argued that the activation and construction of CG is the essence of a successful and satisfactory communication event (Kecskes 2013).

The issue of CG has turned out to be much more conspicuous and complex in intercultural communication when compared to intracultural communication. Speakers in intercultural communications do not share the same amount of CG that L1 interlocutors are equipped with due to lack of shared previous engagement and embodiment in the same socio-cultural context. In order to get a refined picture of CG in intercultural communication, CG is further categorized into core CG and emergent CG (Kecskes 2013: 160). Core CG refers to the relatively stable, generalized common knowledge, consumption and beliefs, to a large extent, shared by most members of a particular speech community owing to the constant experience within the community. It can be further divided into common sense, cultural sense, and formal sense (Kecskes 2013: 160, 161). On the contrary, emergent CG represents the dynamic, particularized and specialized information and perceptions co-created by the interlocutors in the course of communicative events and usually initiated by the actual situational context, for instance, the new information added, the change of the mental and emotive representation of the interlocutors, and the physical environment as well. Consequently, there are two subcategories of emergent CG: shared sense and current sense. Shared sense refers to the particularized information about the interlocutors' personal (not of the community) experience, belief and attitude activated and co-constructed by the communicators throughout the communication events by different semiotic resources and communicative strategies. On the other hand, the current sense entails the emergent and evolving perception of the current situation (Kecskes 2013: 162).

There is a dialectical interaction between core CG and emergent CG, with core CG operating diachronically, whereas emergent CG functions synchronically. It was also reported that some discursive strategies can be used to confirm core CG or initiate a negotiation between the core CG and the specific statement to be evaluated (Baider 2019). Just as advocated by some researchers (e.g., Kecskes 2019; Liu and Liu 2017a, 2017b; Liu and Ran 2020), it is vital to explore how CG is built and changed at different stages of interactions in different contexts. This chapter is intended to enhance our understanding of the mechanisms of CG building in IBC.

3 Data collection and description

3.1 Data source

The data was obtained from the telephone recordings of English complaints and complaint responses between international customers and the Chinese agents of the complaint center of one Chinese airline, including 42 recordings for about 7.5 hours in total. As the airline provides international air services, the agents working in the complaint center can deal with customer complaints in English, though they are all native Chinese speakers. While the mother tongue of the complainants cannot be determined, many of them are not native speakers of English judging from their intonations and speaking styles, so the phone interactions examined in this chapter can be considered as near BELF interactions (e.g., Pitzl 2015; Kaur and Birlik 2021) and certainly intercultural business communication.

Responding to customer complaints involves managing and adjusting a series of complex issues, such as safeguarding business interests, taking care of consumers' needs, soothing their negative emotions and maintaining harmonious relationships (Liu and Liu 2017b; Liu and Ran 2020). At the same time, the interactive process may be afforded and restricted by multiple contextual factors such as the nature of the complaining issue, different appeals of complainants, and various cultural and language backgrounds of the participants (Liu and Liu 2017b; Liu and Ran 2020). Thus, it is assumed that both the agents and customers choose specific linguistic devices to build CG in order to settle complaints smoothly, MPEs in particular. Besides, since agents and customers have diverse interests and different rights and obligations, it is hypothesized that they would choose different types of MPEs to build CG in different dimensions throughout the interactions.

3.2 Procedure

To answer the first research question, MPEs used in the data were identified first according to the definition given in 2.1 where MPEs were defined as linguistic expressions that explicitly demonstrate the speaker's reflexive awareness regarding language use and their intentions to manage ongoing interactions for accomplishing interactional goals. After that, the referential relationships between MPEs and their host clauses were analyzed and grouped into the main categories according to Verschueren (2000) and Liu and Liu (2021). To test the reliability of the coding scheme, an inter-coder agreement test was conducted on 10% of our data co-coded by the three authors. The result indicated almost perfect agreement in terms of the categories and functions of MPEs with Kappa=0.87.

More specifically, considering the features of IBC and functions of MPEs in interactions, and more relevantly, according to the three components of CG proposed by Kecskes (2013: 151) as reviewed in Section 2.2.2, i.e., information that the participants share, understanding of the situational context, and relationships between the participants, MPEs were classified into three types: information-oriented (to facilitate information sharing), relationship-oriented (to take care of interpersonal relationship), or situation-oriented (to enhance the understanding of the immediate situational context). Besides, new categories were added if emerging from the data during the coding process.

Information-oriented MPEs were classified into four sub-types (see Liu and Liu 2017a, 2017b, and 2021): speech-action descriptions, evidentials, message glosses, and commentaries. Speech-action descriptions contain speech-action and thought-action verbs to manifest the illocutionary forces of the utterances; evidentials contain descriptions of the source of information and message; message glosses contain reformulating or exemplifying expressions; commentaries contain adjectives or negations describing personal judgments, evaluations, and attitudes.

Relationship-oriented MPEs were divided into three sub-types: emotion expressions, rapport indicators, and stance markers. Emotion expressions contain emotive words or feeling descriptions; rapport indicators contain expressions that enhance or challenge self-face, other-face, or rapport, and stance markers contain words and phrases referring to identity, position or stance.

Situation-oriented MPEs contain descriptions of or comments on the immediate communication surroundings and facilities. The classification, coding scheme and examples of each type of MPEs are presented in Table 1.

After coding, the frequency and percentage of each type of MPEs were calculated to get a general picture of their distribution in the data. In addition, to

Table 1: MPEs: Types, coding scheme and examples.

Types	Sub-types	Coding scheme	Examples
Situation-oriented	Non-applicable	MPEs containing descriptions of or comments on the immediate communication surroundings and facilities	Are you talking on a headset or on a telephone?; It's not very clear; I can't hear you
Information-oriented	Message glosses	MPEs containing reformulating, exemplifying expressions, checking, or confirming the understanding of previous or subsequent information or messages	I mean; for example
	Commentaries	MPEs containing adjectives or negations describing personal judgments, evaluations, and attitudes	It is correct; Is that right?
	Evidentials	MPEs containing descriptions of sources of information and messages	As I said; According to the company policy
	Speech-action descriptions	MPEs containing speech-action, thought-action verbs to manifest the illocutionary forces	I tell you this; I ask you a question
Relationship-oriented	Emotion expressions	MPEs containing expressions about feelings or emotive words	I'm happy to hear you say so; It is sad to know this
	Stance markers	MPEs containing words and phrases referring to identity, position, or stance	It is our promise; as your golden member
	Rapport indicators	MPEs containing expressions enhancing or challenging face or rapport	That's what I respect you; I understand how you feel

answer the third research question, Chi-square tests were run to reveal whether there is a significant difference in using each type of MPEs between agents and customers and whether there is a significant difference in using different types of MPEs.

To answer the second research question, CG building of MPEs was illustrated with examples from three dimensions, namely, physical, cognitive and affective. The classification of the three dimensions was inspired by previous studies and empirically supported by our data. As reviewed in Section 2.2.2, Kecskes (2013: 151) distinguishes three components of CG corresponding to physical (understanding the situational context), cognitive (information that the participants share) and affective dimensions (relationships between the participants). Besides, a few studies have distinguished physical, cognitive and affective dimensions in BELF communication to highlight the importance of shared business expertise and interpersonal relationship for effective and efficient BELF communication (e.g., Ehrenreich 2016; Liu and Liu 2017a, 2017b, and 2022; Liu and Ran 2020). Moreover, Fetzer (2021) emphasized the importance of context, provision of background information as well as reception consideration in the co-construction of discourse common ground for computer-mediated communication. Similarly, in Woydack's (2019) linguistic and ethnographic investigation of working scripts and guidance in a multilingual call center in London, she also discovered some standardized operations conducted by call center agents like handling of the immediate situation, provision of adequate information, and the specific use of personal pronouns for rapport management.

4 Findings

4.1 Types of MPEs used by agents and customers

Table 2 presents the types and sub-types of MPEs and their frequency used by agents and customers in the data as well as Chi-square tests results.

Table 2: MPEs used by agents and customers: types, frequency and percentage.

Types	Sub-types	Agents		Customers		P(Chi-square test)
		Frequency	Percentage	Frequency	percentage	
Situation-oriented	Non-applicable	39	8.71%	34	6.16%	$X_2=0.34$, df=1, $p>0.05$
Information-oriented	Message glosses	148	33.04%	58	10.51%	$X_2=39.32$, df=1, $p<0.05$
	Commentaries	44	9.82%	23	4.17%	$X_2=6.58$, df=1, $p<0.05$
	Evidentials	35	7.81%	54	9.78%	$X_2=4.06$, df=1, $p<0.05$
	Speech-action descriptions	116	25.89%	263	47.64%	$X_2=57.02$, df=1, $p<0.05$

Table 2 (continued)

Types	Sub-types	Agents		Customers		P(Chi-square test)
		Frequency	Percentage	Frequency	percentage	
Relationship-oriented	Emotion expressions	27	6.03%	48	8.70%	X_2=5.89, df=1, $p<0.05$
	Stance markers	12	2.68%	22	3.99%	X_2=2.94, df=1, $p<0.05$
	Rapport indicators	27	6.03%	50	9.06%	X_2=6.87, df=1, $p<0.05$
Total		448	100%	552	100%	X_2=10.82, df=1, $p<0.05$
P (Chi-square test)		X_2=295.64, df=7, $p<0.05$		X_2=642.52, df=7, $p<0.05$		

As shown in Table 2, on the whole, the agents and customers demonstrate similarities and differences in using MPEs. First of all, both parties follow the same frequency order in using three types of MPEs: information-oriented MPEs rank the top (agents: 343 occasions, 76.56%; customers: 398 occasions, 72.10%), followed by relationship-oriented MPEs (agents: 66 occasions, 14.73%; customers: 120 occasions, 21.74%) and situation-oriented MPEs with the least frequency (agents: 39 occasions, 8.71%; customers: 34 occasions, 6.16%). However, differences are revealed in terms of each sub-type of MPEs. In the agents' utterances, message glosses (148 occasions, 33.04%) are the highest in frequency and stance markers (12 occasions, 2.68%) are the least, while in the customers' utterances, speech-action descriptions (263 occasions, 47.64%) are the most frequent and stance markers are also the least (22 occasions, 3.99%). Chi-square tests showed that the total number of MPEs between two parties are significantly different (X_2=10.82, df=1, $p<0.05$), and significant differences are also found in the use of each sub-type between two parties, except for the situation-oriented MPEs (X_2=0.34, df=1, $p>0.05$). A within-group comparison showed that the use of these eight sub-types of MPEs is significantly different for both agents and customers. These results demonstrate that both sides employ different types of MPEs to build different types of CG to fulfill different communicative needs.

4.2 Common ground building of MPEs in complaint responses

As mentioned in 3.2, the functioning process of MPEs in CG building for physical, cognitive and affective dimensions was analyzed with examples from the data respectively. There are occasions when the same MPEs served for more than one function in CG building, for example, both for shared cognitive and affective spaces. Nevertheless, the extracts were selected according to the primary communicative intention at a specific stage of the interaction. Next, we will investigate how MPEs contribute to building CG for shared physical, cognitive and affective spaces.

4.2.1 Building CG for shared physical space

Unlike face-to-face communication, the participants in telephone interactions have limited access to each other's physical environment and non-verbal resources (e.g., facial expressions and gestures), which affects the effectiveness and efficiency of communication (Liu and Liu 2021). The data reveal that the speakers often employ situation-oriented MPEs to examine and regulate the interactive process for problem-solving. In addition, due to the nature of international business communication, commentaries and emotion expressions are also chosen to question and comment on the ongoing interactions, which sometimes develops into an additional complaint, as shown in Excerpt 1.

Excerpt 1 (The agent called the customer for changing her flight seat. A: agent; C: customer)

1 C: Hello?
2 A: Hello, excuse me, sir. This is <Company>. ***Are you available to talk now?***
3 C: So-Sorry?
4 A: This is <Company>. (.) ***Are you available to talk now?***
5 C: Yeah, but ***your English is not very good.***
6 A: (Inhale) OK, thank you, sir, because we have done the complaint, because you have a problem in ticket. (Interrupted)
7 C: [No]. [Wait]. ***Your English is really bad***, OK? So if you're on the customer complaints, ***your English needs to be a lot better*** so that ***I can understand it***, because ***at the moment, I don't understand it.***
8 A: OK, because ***we just want to tell you that*** the seat has been changed. (.) But we couldn't help you change it. (Interrupted)
9 C: ***Say again?***

In Excerpt 1, the agent called the customer for a seat change. Being aware of the possible time differences, the agent uses the situation-oriented MPE "are you available to talk now" twice to check whether it is an appropriate time to make this phone call. The construction of a current sense of temporal availability for shared physical space is further modified by the customer's comment on the agent's English proficiency. Several commentaries like "but your English is not very good", "Your English is really bad", "your English needs to be a lot better", "I don't understand it" are employed in sequence to mediate the effectiveness of the interaction. The speech-action description "we just want to tell you that" is intended to arouse the customer's attention to the following new information in order to construct a shared sense regarding the solution for the complaint, namely, the changed seat, whereas the speech-action description "say again" is employed for a new round of CG building due to the failure of the previous CG construction.

This excerpt demonstrates how MPEs can be used to build CG in temporal and spatial spaces by constantly checking the smoothness of the communication (Kolozsvari 2015). Sometimes, situation-oriented MPEs are also employed particularly by the customers to build up the current sense of their negative evaluation on the present communicative quality to underscore their impatience and anger. By doing this, the customers try to seek for both physical attunement and affective comfort from the agents, but illustrations are omitted due to space limitations.

4.2.2 Building CG for shared cognitive space

The agents and customers have limited sharing of core CG (Kecskes 2013: 160), owing to the epistemic discrepancies in terms of the industry regulations and business practices of the airline as well as their diverse socio-cultural backgrounds. Further, the customers and agents are strangers without any previous contacts, and thus they are bound to have a limited shared sense of previous personal experiences. What is more, interactions via phone lines make it more difficult for the co-construction of the current sense of the communicative situation. Finally, the participants' different cultural backgrounds and English proficiency tend to increase the difficulties of information sharing and understanding, requiring more effort for CG building. Considering all these factors, the speakers are motivated to employ different types of MPEs as both pre-emptive and repairing strategies to build CG for cognitive alignment. Excerpt 2 shows how MPEs contribute to efficient message delivery and information sharing.

Excerpt 2 (The agent called the customer for a ticket refund issue.)

1 A: Hello, <Company>. My agent number is XXX. ***It's still about the (choosing?) ticket refund problem***. We have delivered to the (related department?) ***They said that*** when booking a ticket, for the ticket condition we have showed on website, (Interrupted)

2 C: [Sorry]. ***I can't hear anything you said***. ***I'm sorry***. ***Just give me one minute***. OK?

3 A: OK.

4 C: Sorry. ***Can you said that again***?

5 A: Yeah. ***They said that*** (-) for the ticket condition when we make a booking on the website, we need to keep to the related document and then to make all successfully. So through that way we still cannot use (???) ***I mean that*** whether have you

considered to keep this ticket for further change? Because this ticket (.) can be change paid to (???) price differences ***according to this ticket condition. I mean*** you can still give back a few of the taxes. ***We are so sorry.***

The interaction goes directly into the ticket refund issue. The message gloss "It's still about the (choosing?) ticket refund problem" is intended to activate a shared sense of the previously mentioned information, so both parties can be positioned in the same cognitive frame. Next, the evidential "They said that" is used twice to create a current sense of the feedback provided by the relevant department to enhance the credibility of the message and seek to update the customer's mental state regarding the complaint. During this process, the customer uses two situation-oriented MPEs "I can't hear anything you said" and "Just give me one minute", one speech-action description "can you said that again" as well as one emotion expression "I am sorry" to build a current sense of the immediate communicative context. These MPEs indicate a failure of shared sense construction and therefore a new round of CG building for both shared physical and cognitive space is required. Later, the message gloss "I mean (that)" is used twice to arouse attention for the subsequent message. In this way, the message becomes more salient and is further negotiated and mediated to reach the current sense of the agent's suggestion (followed by the first "I mean that") and ticket condition provided by the airline (followed by the second one). Finally, the evidential "according to this ticket condition" is employed to enhance the shared sense of the professional explanation offered by the agent by resorting to the airline's policy to upgrade the persuasiveness of the explanation. The emotion expression "We are so sorry" is further employed to build up the current sense of the agent's empathy for the inconvenience caused to the customer, hence seeking to reach both a cognitive and affective attunement with the customer.

The use of these MPEs in this excerpt reveals the speaker's metacognitive awareness (Culpeper and Haugh 2014) to dynamically and deliberately co-construct and enrich the emergent CG by consciously negotiating meaning and monitoring information flow. As a result, the shared cognitive space can be enlarged. Besides, the speakers' choice of these MPEs demonstrates the principle of recipient design since both participants purposefully provide adequate and relevant information for CG building to reduce the cognitive loading of meaning processing.

4.2.3 Building CG for shared affective space

One of the most challenging aspects of customer complaint responses is that the customers are usually overwhelmed with negative emotions such as worries, remorse, irritation, anger, depression and frustration. Therefore, it is of vital importance for the call center agents to comfort the customers while protecting institutional interests. These types of MPEs, such as emotion expressions, stance markers, rapport indicators and message glosses are regularly employed to create current senses, hence taking care of interpersonal relationships. In other words, MPEs serve the function of co-constructing CG to reach a shared affective space between the interlocutors to solve the conflicts more humanely. In this way, the seemingly unfavorable customer complaints could be reversed into a valuable opportunity to rebuild the corporate identity as a considerate corporate citizen caring for customers' emotional needs (Khan et al. 2021).

Excerpt 3 (The customer was worried about the order of his name on the ticket.)

1 A: Yes. Because ***I don't think that is a problem*** without your middle name of your schedule, because ***you mean that*** some might cut that is result of middle name either the example to visa and maybe it's the same, so ***I don't think so this is the problem because you mean that*** you had take any time for the flight without middle name. So for ***the next information is matched, so I don't think so this is a problem***.

2 C: Well, ***I'm happy to hear you say so***. But ***I'm very surprised*** I had such an issue with that for the last four days.

3 A: Yes. ***I mean that*** because ***I was just afraid that*** because your passport there is no middle name, but in our ticket, so maybe ***I'm afraid that*** the ***information is not matched***.

4 C: Sure. Sure. ***I mean like I said I know*** about the A names, and I actually know people names, ***that is***, Thailand, and ***that is, you know, I mean***, so similar, ***you know***, I (???) go on in another country because of this middle name thing, so ***I understand, you know***, western names are short, ***I guess it is what I want to say***.

5 A: Yes. Of course. Because ***another information is matched, for example***, the passport number, the passenger team, ***for example***, the expire date, even the certain name, ***all information is matched***, so ***I told you this is not a problem***.

6 C: ***So, which the same thing is you firmly believe that*** when I check in on September, I will not have any problems.

7 A: ***Correct***.

8 C: OK. ***That is good to hear. I wish I would, this is you say, but I will believe you*** and look forward to it.

The customer was worried about her name order on the ticket. The agent uses the commentaries "I don't think", "so I don't think so", the message gloss "you mean that", and the commentary "the next information is matched" to interfere with the understanding of this issue and relieve the customer's worries. These MPEs are intended to provide convincing explanations and create a current sense of the agent's professional judgment and epistemic authority over the name order issue. Besides, the message gloss "you mean that" and commentary "the next information is matched" are intended to activate a shared sense of the customer's previous experiences with the name order issue. The agent's professionalism and consideration are fully appreciated, as indicated in the customer's emotion expression "I'm happy to hear you say so". In this way, the problem is not only resolved, but the customer's affective state is upheld, leading to building emergent CG for shared affective space.

Although partly reassured, the customer continues to elaborate on his problem by telling his confusion about different answers offered by the same Company with the emotion expression "I'm very surprised", which indicates communication dynamics. The agent uses the message gloss "I mean that" and emotion expression "I was just afraid that" twice to heighten the shared sense of the Company's explanation. The customer shows complete understanding and appreciation of the Company's efforts by using a series of MPEs, including the message glosses "I mean", "you know" and "that is", the evidential "I said" as well as speech-action descriptions "I understand" and "I guess it is what I want to say". The frequent use of MPEs is intended to highlight the cultural sense of different name systems in Thailand and Western countries. As a positive response, the agent uses the commentaries "another information is matched" twice and "correct", the message gloss "for example" and evidential "I told you" to confirm further the shared sense of their previous discussion on the solution provided by the airline and further comfort the customer. Finally, the customer employs the speech-action description "you firmly believe that", "I wish I would", the evidential "that is you say", the emotion expression "that's good to hear" and rapport indicator "I will believe you" to confirm the shared sense of their settlement and reconstruct the current sense of customer's trust on the agent. In this way, both emotional and cognitive alignment are reached for a supportive interpersonal relationship between the participants.

This excerpt clearly illustrates how various MPEs work together to build both a shared affective and cognitive space to degrade the salience of the seriousness of the problem. By showing understanding of and timely response to the customer's emotional needs, the agent discursively constructs his professional identity of being competent, considerate and trustworthy. The agent's effort is rewarded by the customer's satisfaction and even trust revealed by the use of MPEs.

5 Discussion

To provide a more comprehensive understanding of metapragmatics in IBC from the intercultural pragmatics perspective, this chapter has identified a taxonomy of three types of MPEs, including eight sub-types in complaint responses in a call center of one Chinese airline. These metapragmatic awareness indicators (see Verschueren 2000) play a distinct and constructive role in facilitating complaint settlement by building CG for shared physical, cognitive and affective spaces. In addition, the use of these MPEs reveals the speaker's reflexive awareness of language use and meta-cognitive representations in this particular setting (Liu and Liu 2017a, 2017b). For instance, our data demonstrate that both customers and agents are motivated to employ different types of MPEs as CG builders to fulfill their communicative intentions, indicating the speaker's metapragmatic awareness of intersubjectivity construction (Jiang 2019). Besides, to advance the reflexivity of MPEs on pragmatic manipulation in the interactions, which was fully discussed in previous studies (e.g., Liu and Liu 2017a, 2017b), we have found that MPEs are also employed to facilitate the ongoing communicative quality and identity construction during the whole interactive process. Therefore, we could conclude that the use of MPEs in the IBC context of telephone complaint responses is much more complex compared with daily face-to-face communication. In this way, this study has enhanced our understanding of the working mechanism of MPEs characterized by reflexivity, multi-functionality and context-dependence.

Previous classifications of MPEs highlighted the function of information sharing and rapport management (e.g., Liu and Liu 2017a, 2017b). In order to draw a more comprehensive picture of MPEs family, our study has enriched the taxonomy of MPEs by adding situation-oriented MPEs. The three-dimension division of MPEs neatly integrates the situation, information and relationship dimensions generally intertwined in any communicative process, hence empowering us to explore the dynamics of MPEs as CG builders more thoroughly.

Our study has delved into the concept of 'a third space', which refers to a new opening site between interlocutors in intercultural communications (Kecskes 2013). However, as Vivien and Nick (2019) pointed out, the fuzziness of the concept 'a third space' has laid it open to skepticism. Therefore, we stratified this abstract concept into physical, cognitive and affective spaces to depict the dynamic and evolving mechanism of MPEs in CG building. In this way, we can explore the functioning mechanism of the third space constructed by agents and customers jointly during complaint responses via telephone.

To be specific, information-oriented MPEs are mainly used to build CG for shared cognitive space between participants. Since both parties use information-oriented MPEs most frequently (agents: 76.56%; customers: 72.10%), we may infer that the construction of CG for shared cognitive space plays a more prominent role in IBC telephone complaint responses in order to identify and solve the problems more effectively and efficiently. Besides, the result that the agents employ more information-oriented MPEs than customers implies that agents, with more epistemic authority, are more information-oriented, spending more effort in reaching cognitive alignment with the customers. In addition, our data reveal that when two parties reach a cognitive alignment, it is easier for them to be emotionally connected. Situation-oriented MPEs, to a large extent, are used to co-construct and enrich the current sense (Kecskes 2013: 162) of their present situational context for a shared physical space. However, different from the claim made by Hart and Secil (2021) that the construction of current sense is not quite an observable discursive act in its nature, quite a number of instances of current sense for a shared physical space were found in our data. Our data also show that agents use slightly more situation-oriented MPEs (agents, 8.71%; customers, 6.16%) to build CG for shared physical space to ensure that they are in the same temporal and physical environment. On the customers' side, they often integrate situation-oriented MPEs with commentaries and emotion expressions to construct CG for both shared physical and affective space (e.g., expressing customers' negative evaluation on the poor quality of telephone lines). These differences indicate that the construction of different types of CG is mainly triggered and conditioned by both prior and emergent intentions. In addition, most situation-oriented MPEs are situation-bound utterances with features of pragmatic regularity, situational conventions and predictability (Kecskes 2013). They can activate the most salient contextual factors to participate in the ongoing interactions so that the speakers can monitor and regulate the communicative process and negotiate meanings more resourcefully and with less cognitive effort.

In terms of the relationship-oriented MPEs, the analysis has revealed that more often the customers express other-condemning emotions to seek empathy from the agents or press psychological pressure on the agents. For example, when the customers are overwhelmed by extreme anger, the complaint is made against the agent, upgrading the issue from business-related to person-related. Customers usually use negative emotion-loaded MPEs to construct shared affective space strategically to appeal to pathos, seeking both psychological and economic compensations from the airline. In addition, a closer look at the data reveals that customers employ significantly more relationship-oriented MPEs than agents (agents, 14.73%; customers, 21.74%) to unfold their affective situations and call for attention and responses from the agents. On the other hand, the agents are more institutionalized in the construction of CG for affective alignment with the customers. This indicates that the agents could pay more attention to taking good care of the customers' affective needs in IBC telephone complaints.

Therefore, our analysis has manifested more intricate properties and functioning mechanisms of CG building for three spaces by MPEs in IBC, and it has strengthened and deepened our understanding of CG building and IBC practices. First, both agents and customers employ MPEs for CG building during the interactions to fulfill their seemingly conflicting communicative goals. From the side of customers, they manage to legitimize their requirements by using MPEs to build up the CG that can upgrade the transgressions of the airline and the inconvenience caused. Regarding the agents, they spare no effort for CG building to satisfy the customers' cognitive and affective needs and protect the institutional interests. During this dynamic and evolving process of CG building, contextual factors across these three spaces play an eminent and decisive role. For instance, situational factors like long-distance communication and English as a lingua franca, cognitive factors like epistemic authority over professional knowledge, and affective factors initiated by the conflict of interest and emotional disturbance all motivate both parties to jointly construct different types of CG for physical, cognitive and affective alignment by using MPEs.

Our study also has demonstrated that CG building by MPEs for these three spaces in IBC may emerge, evolve, be enhanced, or break down at any communication time. During this communicative process, sincere attentiveness plays a pivotal role in managing the interaction of previous and emergent intentions as well as updating the mental and affective state (Fukushima 2020). For instance, in response to the customers' negative emotions, the agents often use "regular metapragmatic act" (Büblitz and Hübler 2007: 13) like "I am so sorry to hear this" to comfort the customer. However, just as confirmed by (Lutzky 2021), the customers were always not satisfied with the repeated expression like "sorry" offered by the airlines, considering it insincerity and shielding of responsibility. Our data also reveal that sometimes the customers respond to the agents' saying sorry negatively by using MPEs like "That doesn't mean anything". Therefore, we recommend that customer service employees use more situational, personalized and emotional expressions when handling customer complaints.

Finally, findings of this chapter have shed light on English language education and research as well as professional training. The creativity, practicability and cultural diversity of BELF (Louhiala-Salminen et al., 2005) display that BELF users do not draw their attention to nativelikeness but efficient use of language resources, like MPEs, to achieve interactional goals under the communicative affordance and constraints, as illustrated in the excerpts above. Therefore, our study calls for more attention to the metapragmatic awareness and intercultural competence of language learning and professional training. Likewise, this study could invite more discussions on the unique linguistic resources employed and communicative norms negotiated by English users in various contexts.

6 Conclusion

Building on Kecskes' (2010, 2013, 2019 and 2021) theoretical construction of CG as well as the relevant studies of MPEs, this chapter explored the role of MPEs in building CG for shared physical, cognitive and affective spaces in complaint responses via phone from the intercultural pragmatics perspective. Our study revealed how agents and customers employ MPEs to co-build CG in complaint responses to facilitate complaint settlement and rapport management. It demonstrated the dynamics, self-regulation, emergence and co-construction of IBC characterized by the dialectical interaction of three types of MPEs and three spaces built throughout interactions. The contextual factors such as professional roles, different types of complaints and speakers' pragmatic competence may constrain the use of MPEs and their functioning process. Therefore, the findings can enhance our understanding of the mechanism of metapragmatic awareness and CG building in achieving mutual understanding, problem-solving and relational work in intercultural business communication. However, since the data analysis was based on telephone complaint responses and from an etic perspective, which may, to a certain extent, limit the generalization of the findings. Therefore, future studies can integrate both etic and emic perspectives to provide a more comprehensive picture of the mechanism of MPEs for CG building in other IBC contexts. For example, one significant future direction is to incorporate linguistic analysis of interactions with analysis of company guidelines and training materials, surveys and interviews with professionals and customers to gain a clear picture of the motivations behind their use of MPEs and a better understanding of their conscious use of CG building strategies.

References

Akram, Azarmi, Behnam, Biook, 2012. The pragmatic knowledge of Iranian EFL learners in using face keeping strategies in reaction to complaints at two different levels. English Language Teaching 5(2), 78–92.

Baider, Fabienne, 2019. Double speech act: Negotiating inter-cultural beliefs and intra-cultural hate speech. Journal of Pragmatics 151, 155–166.

Bigi, Sarah. 2018. The role of argumentative strategies in the construction of emergent common ground in a patient-centered approach to the medical encounter. *Journal of Argumentation in Context* 7(2). 141–156.

Caffi, Claudia. 1994. Metapragmatics. In: *Encyclopedia of Language and Linguistics*, 2461–2466. Amsterdam: Elsevier.

Clark, Herbert H., Brennan, Sussan, E. 1991. Grounding in communication. In: Resnick, L.B., Levine, J.M., Behrend, S.D. (eds.), *Socially Shared Cognition*, 127–149. Columbia.

Cruz, Manuel. 2015. Fostering EF/SL learners' meta-pragmatic awareness of complaints and their interactive effects. *Language Awareness* 24(2). 123–137.

Culpeper, Jonathan, Haugh, Michael. 2014. *Pragmatics and the English language*.Basingstoke: Palgrave Macmillan.

Dinh, Hanh. 2019. The use of indexicals to co-construct common ground on the continuum of intra- and intercultural communicative contexts. *Pragmatics & Cognition* 26(1). 135–165.

Dudek, Andrzej, Jaremen, D.E., Michalska-Dudek, L., Walesiak, M. 2019. Loyalty Model Proposal of Travel Agency Customers. *Sustainability* 11(13). 3702.

Ehrenreich, Sebastian. 2016. English as a lingua franca (ELF) in international business contexts: key issues and future perspectives. In Murata, K. (ed.), *Exploring ELF in Japanese Academic and Business Contexts: Conceptualization, research and pedagogic implications*, 135–155. New York: Routledge.

Fetzer, Anita. 2021. Computer-mediated discourse in context: Pluralism of communicative action and discourse common ground. In: Xie, C., Yus, F, Habeland, H. (eds.), *Approaches to Internet Pragmatics: Theory and practice*, 47–74. Philadelphia: John Benjamins Publishing Company.

Filip, Alina. 2013. Complaint management: a customer satisfaction learning process. *Procedia-Social and Behavioral Sciences* 93. 271–275.

Fukushima, Saeko. 2020. *Metapragmatics of Attentiveness A Study in Interpersonal and Cross-cultural Pragmatics*. Sheffield: Equinox Publishing.

Grice, Herbert Paul. 1989. *Studies in the Way of Words*. Cambridge, MA: Harvard University Press.

Grundy, Peter. 2002. Reflexive language. In: Trappes-Lomax, H.R., Ferguson, G. (eds.), *Language in Language Teacher Education*, 83–94.Admsterdam/Philadelphia: John Benjamins Publishing Company.

Handford, Michael. 2010. *The Language of Business Meetings*.Cambridge: Cambridge University Press.

Hinds, John. 1985. Misinterpretations and common knowledge in Japanese. *Journal of Pragmatics* 9(1). 7–19.

Horton, William S., Gerring, Richard J. 2016. Revisiting the memory-based processing approach to common ground. *Topics in Cognition Science* 8(4). 780–795.

Hübler, Axel, Büblitz, Wolfram. 2007. Introducing metapragmatics in use. In: Büblitz, W., Hübler, A. (eds.), *Metapragmatics in Use*, 1–26.Philadelphia: John Benjamins Publishing Company.

Hart, Deniz, Ortaçtepe, Seçil, Okkali. 2021. Common ground and positioning in teacher-student interactions: Second language socialization in EFL classrooms. *Intercultural Pragmatics* 18(1). 53–82.

Kaur, Jagdish, Birlik, Seval. 2021. Communicative effectiveness in BELF (English as a Business Lingua Franca) meetings: 'Explaining' as a pragmatic strategy. *The Modern Language Journal* 105(3). 623–638.

Kecskes, Istvan. 2010. The paradox of communication: Socio-cognitive approach to pragmatics. *Pragmatics and Society* 1(1). 50–73.

Kecskes, Istvan. 2013. *Intercultural Pragmatics*.New York/Oxford: Oxford University Press.

Kecskes, Istvan. 2019. The interplay of prior experience and actual situational context in intercultural first encounters. *Pragmatics & Cognition* 26(1). 112–134.

Kecskes, Istvan. 2021. Intercultural communication and our understanding of language. *Langages* 222(2). 25–42.

Kecskes, Istvan, Zhang, Fenghui. 2013. On the dynamic relations between common ground and presupposition. In: Capone, A, Piparo, F.L., Carapezza, M. (eds.), *Perspectives on Linguistic Pragmatics*, 285–310.Berlin: Springer Science & Business Media.
Khan, Muhammad, S., Du, Jianguo, Farooq, Anwar. 2021. Corporate social responsibility and the reciprocity between employee perception, perceived external prestige, and employees' emotional labor. *Psychology Research and Behavior Management* 14. 61.
Kolozsvari, Orsolya. 2015. "Physically We Are Apart, Mentally We Are Not." Creating a shared space and a sense of belonging in long-distance relationships. *Qualitative Sociology Review* 11(4). 102–115.
Kreckel, Marga. 1981. *Communicative Acts and Shared Knowledge in Natural Discourse*. New York: Academic Press.
Law, Colin. 2017. The study of customer relationship management in Thai airline industry: A case of Thai travellers in Thailand. *Journal of Airline and Airport Management* 7(1). 13–42.
Lee, Benny P.H. 2001. Mutual knowledge, background knowledge and shared beliefs: Their roles in establishing common ground. *Journal of Pragmatics* 33(1). 21–44.
Li, Mimi, Qiu, Shangzhi, Liu, Zhaoping. 2016. The Chinese way of response to hospitality service failure: the effects of face and guanxi. *International Journal of Hospitality Management* 57. 18–29.
Jiang, Hui. 2019. Concept, application and trends on metapragmatic research. *Journal of Tianjin Foreign Studies University* 26(4). 138–150.
Liu, Ping, Liu, Huiying. 2017a. Creating common ground: The role of metapragmatic expressions in BELF meeting interactions. *Journal of Pragmatics* 107. 1–15.
Liu, Ping, Liu, Huiying. 2017b. Responding to direct complaints: The role of MPEs in common ground construction in institutional telephone interactions. *Pragmatics & Cognition* 24(1). 4–32.
Liu, Ping, Liu, Huiying. 2021. Salience adjusting: Metapragmatic expressions in complaint responses. *Journal of Pragmatics* 176. 150–163.
Liu, Ping, Liu, Huiying. 2022. Pragmatic manipulation of metapragmatic expressions in BELF meetings. *Applied Pragmatics* 4(1). 92–118.
Liu, Ping, Ran, Yongping. 2016. Creating meso-contexts: The functions of metapragmatic expressions in argumentative TV talk shows. *Intercultural Pragmatics* 13(2). 283–307.
Liu, Ping, Ran, Yongping. 2020. Complaint Responses: Metapragmatic Utterances and Negotiation Awareness. *Foreign Languages and Teaching* 313. 11–24.
Louhiala-Salminen, Leena, Kankaanranta, Anne. 2012. Language as an issue in international internal communication: English or local language? If English, what English? *Public Relations Review* 38(2). 262–269.
Lutzky, Ursula. 2021. "You keep saying you are sorry". Exploring the use of sorry in customer communication on Twitter. *Discourse, Context & Media* 39. 1–8.
Macagno, Fabrizio, Rossi, Grazia. 2019. Metaphors and problematic understanding in chronic care communication. *Journal of Pragmatics* 151. 103–117.
Penz, Hermine. 2007. Building common ground through metapragmatic comments in international project work. In: Büblitz, W., Hübler, A. (eds.), *Metapragmatics in Use*, 263–292.Philadelphia: John Benjamins Publishing Company.
Pitzl, Maria-Luise. 2015. Understanding and misunderstanding in the Common European Framework of Reference: What we can learn from research on BELF and Intercultural Communication. *Journal of English as a Lingua Franca* 4(1). 91–124.

Prince, Ellen F. 1981. *Towards a Taxonomy of Given-new Information. Radical Pragmatics*. New York: Academic Press.

Sinkeviciute, Valeria. 2017. Funniness and "the preferred reaction" to jocularity in Australian and British English: an analysis of interviewees' metapragmatic comments. *Language & Communication* 55. 41–54.

Smith, Sara W., Liang, Xiaoping. 2007. Metapragmatic expressions in physics lectures. In: Büblitz, W., Hübler, A. (eds.), *Metapragmatics in Use*, 167–197.Philadelphia: John Benjamins Publishing Company.

Stalnaker, Robert. 1973. Presuppositions. *Journal of Philosophical Logic* 2(4). 447–457.

Stalnaker, Robert. 2002. Common ground. *Linguistics and Philosophy* 25(5/6). 701–721.

Su, Hsi-Yao. 2019. The metapragmatics of Taiwanese (im)politeness: Conceptualization and evaluation of limao. *Journal of Pragmatics* 148. 26–43.

Tanskanen, Sanna-Kaisa. 2007. Metapragmatic utterances in computer-mediated interaction. In: Büblitz, W., Hübler, A. (eds.), *Metapragmatics in Use*, 87–106.Philadelphia: John Benjamins Publishing Company.

Van Olmen, Daniël, Tantucci, Vittorio. 2022. Getting attention in different languages: A usage-based approach to parenthetical look in Chinese, Dutch, English, and Italian. *Intercultural Pragmatics* 19(2). 141–181.

Verschueren, Jef. 2000. Notes on the role of metapragmatic awareness in language use. *Pragmatics* 10(4). 439–456.

Vivien Xiaowei, Zhou, Nick, Pilcher. 2019. Revisiting the 'third space' in language and intercultural studies. *Language and Intercultural Communication* 19(1). 1–8.

Wilks, Yorick. 1986. Default reasoning and self-knowledge. *Proceedings of the IEEE 74* (10). 1399–1404.

Woydack, Johanna. 2019. *Linguistic ethnography of a multilingual call center: London calling*. Berlin: Springer.

Yang, Kun. 2021. Disclaimer as a metapragmatic device in Chinese: A corpus-based study. *Journal of Pragmatics* 173. 167–176.

Greet Angèle De Baets and Ellen Van Praet

Harmony and common ground: Aikido principles for intercultural training

Abstract: This paper investigates the added value of aikido, a martial art, as an embodied pedagogy for intercultural communication training: what is the potential of bringing the physical practice of aikido into the intercultural communication classroom, emphasizing experiential discovery instead of traditional didactic explanations?

To this end, we conducted a benchmarking study identifying the core principles of aikido. We interviewed twenty aikido experts worldwide and performed a qualitative content analysis of the transcribed interview data relying on NVivo software. First, and foremost, our findings show fundamental similarities between aikido interaction and intercultural interaction. They reveal a shared significance of focused interaction by consciously seeking harmony and co-creating common ground. Second, we demonstrate that the aikido pedagogy teaches harmony and common ground through (i) multisensory learning practice and (ii) somatic discovery by training physiological and mental tranquility. Our conclusion is that aikido has potential as an embodied pedagogy for intercultural communication training.

1 Introduction

Aikido is one of the martial arts practiced globally. Most martial arts stand for combat. However, aikido typically stands for protecting the self, avoiding serious injury to the other and seeking harmony (Friedman 2005; Kong 2016). Aikido has the reputation of being a martial art with a philosophy of harmony. Moreover, aikido practitioners see how they use the body in aikido practice "as a metaphor to make sense of non-martial challenges in their everyday lives" (Foster 2015). Experiencing your body and your self in physical practice is called embodied practice.

Not much research is available on a possible link between intercultural communication and aikido. Bannister (2018) stated that aikido is a field of practice

Acknowledgment: The authors wish to thank the participants in this research and the reviewer who contributed significant suggestions for revising the original manuscript.

https://doi.org/10.1515/9783110766752-014

with valuable insights for ethical guidance in ethnobiological research involving cross-cultural work. Salih et al. (2022) observed and interviewed six aikido practitioners in Dubai to study the influence of aikido practice on their professional communication in multicultural teams. They concluded that aikido could play a role in both leadership training and cultural intelligence training. In his master's dissertation, Husak (2012) examined how the qualities that arise from the practice of zen meditation and aikido might be effectively applied to interpersonal and intercultural interactions.

Much research has been conducted on cultures, cultural intelligence, intercultural communication and intercultural training. Gudykunst and Hammer (1998) introduced a typology of intercultural training design in 1983 in which they distinguished between didactic expository and experiential discovery. Didactic expository focuses on explanations to transfer knowledge whereas experiential discovery approaches develop the emotional and behavioral dimensions of an individual's intercultural competence by e.g. discussing case studies and participating in role plays (Graf 2004) or ethnographic inquiry (Díaz and Moore 2018). Scholars who reviewed intercultural training designs argue the need for training methods with experiential discovery rather than conventional didactic explanations (Díaz and Moore 2018; Graf 2004; Treven 2003; Waxin and Panaccio 2005).

Didactic expository divides mind and body into a dichotomy that regards the body as little more than a subordinate instrument in service to the mind. Contrarily, pedagogy that joins body and mind in a physical and mental act of knowledge construction "entails thoughtful awareness of body, space, and social context" (Nguyen and Larson 2015: 332). This pedagogy is called embodied pedagogy and draws on discovery through bodily and mental experience. Embodied pedagogy is, therefore, an example of an experiential training method.

Considering the need for more experiential intercultural training and the embodied practice of aikido, we examined the potential of bringing the physical practice of aikido into the intercultural communication classroom, emphasizing experiential discovery instead of traditional didactic explanations. To investigate aikido's potential, we determined what principles of aikido serve intercultural communication training by conducting a benchmarking study. Twenty semistructured in-depth interviews with aikido experts from all over the world provided an understanding of aikido's core principles from a global and contemporary perspective. Previous research on aikido and its possible applications originated from one aikido expert, one aikido school, one aikido style, one part of the world or the twentieth century. The analysis of the twenty interviews showed what aikido experts from different parts of the world deem essential today. Moreover, the interview findings opened avenues to link aikido interaction with intercultural interaction.

The validation of the benchmarking study's findings is beyond the scope of this paper. A subsequent study will explore the efficiency and effectiveness of aikido-based intercultural business communication training. Before presenting the methodology and the findings of this study, we deal with the theoretical background and key concepts of aikido as a martial art of harmony, common ground in intercultural interaction and embodied pedagogy.

2 Theoretical background and key concepts

2.1 Aikido, the martial art of harmony

Many publications on aikido as a martial art and its philosophy are outside academia, some are within academia. They often refer to the time of the founder of aikido, Ueshiba Morihei, who passed away in 1969. John Stevens assembled and translated the secret teachings of Ueshiba. In *Budo, Teachings of the Founder of Aikido* (2013), Stevens wrote how Ueshiba stated that establishing harmony is the purpose of true budō, which roughly translated means martial art. "True budo is not for the sole purpose of destroying an opponent; it is far better to defeat an opponent spiritually [by making him realize the folly of his actions] and then he will gladly abandon his attack" (Ueshiba 2013: 35). Kenji Shimizu, one of Ueshiba's direct disciples, described in his book, The heavenly road (1994), that "one day, he [Ueshiba] realized that 'Aikido exists beyond all those techniques and apart from the settlement of victory or defeat.' He understood that 'Aikido is the way of harmony.' Thus he established today's Aikido" (Shimizu 1994: 6). Consequently, many aikido practitioners call aikido the martial art of harmony.

Aikido is a martial art that emerged in the first half of the twentieth century from a longstanding martial culture which had transformed a system of fighting arts, devised to inflict injury and death, into martial arts, dedicated to developing self-perfection by integrating mind, body, and spirit (Faggianelli and Lukoff 2006). Aikido is a primarily weaponless, noncompetitive martial art characterized by circular movements, throws and locks applied to the joints (grappling techniques involving the manipulation of an opponent's joints, Figure 1). Today it is practiced globally as self-defense, as a recreational activity, as a meditative technique, as a social activity, or indeed for some as a ritual act (Niehaus 2019). Aikido's elaborate and effective fighting techniques and its claim to self-defense are subordinate to the path of nonviolence (Wagner 1999). It is for this reason that in aikido an attack is not blocked but redirected. It is the principle of nonresistance that distinguishes aikido from other martial arts (Wagner 2015). Aikido aims to turn opponents into partners, to build bridges even when the odds are against harmony (Ueshiba and Stevens 1993).

Figure 1: A wrist lock in aikido (Stein 2012a).
Note. The image shows Annette and Markus Röllig from Aikido Zentrum Offenbach e.V. Copyright by Dirk Stein, www.lichtwanderer.de, used with permission.

The physical creation of harmony in conflictual encounters is the essence of aikido practice. It is reached by the blending of movements and breathing (Faggianelli and Lukoff 2006). Wagner (2015) described this creation of harmony and called it attunement. First, the aikido practitioner under attack, the attackee, adjusts to the intensity and rhythm of the attack. Then the attackee converts it gradually either in the direction of deceleration to decrease the excitation and tension level (to calm down) or in the direction of acceleration (to disperse the tension and arousal level). It is a strategy of pacing, leading and building rapport (Tosey and Mathison 2010). Wagner saw similarities between this strategy and Beebe and Lachmann's strategy (2013). Their impressive body of work explained the nature of co-constructing interactions between adults and infants, and between therapists and patients:

- Joining, to blend in terms of timing, rhythm, coordination and synchronization.
- Altering, to transform the other person's state.
- Complementing, to reciprocally complete the behavior of the other.

"Thus, if we consider that the practice of aikido (and the practices of all other martial arts as well) is a social fact, and if we want to understand how practitioners find common ground on which to tactilely communicate, then martial art studies will do well to explore further the insights afforded by observing naturally-occurring interactions" (Lefebvre 2016: 107). Lefebvre used finding common ground to refer to the harmony in aikido practice or to what Wagner (2015) called attunement.

Common ground is not readily found in the challenge of an aikido interaction. It is the result of conscious, deliberate action. Beebe and Lachmann (2013) called it conscious involvement. Goffman (1966) called it focused interaction. Both Wagner (2015) and Lefebvre (2016) linked the respective co-constructing and focused interactions with aikido interactions because aikido practitioners focus their attention on seeking harmony in each aikido interaction.

2.2 Common ground in intercultural interaction

In intercultural interaction, the micro-level of intercultural communication, people with different cultural norms and values may have a heightened chance of misunderstanding, miscommunication and mismanagement (Blommaert 1998). When understanding troubles that occur in intercultural interactions, analysts typically search macro-level cultural differences for a cause, without considering other factors, or more importantly, without examining what interlocutors might be doing to overcome them (Kecskés 2018).

Interestingly, the use of semantically transparent language results in fewer misunderstandings and communication breakdowns than expected (Kecskés 2020). Although we do not have exact figures, it is similar to what many researchers found: cultural differences do not necessarily lead to misunderstandings. In most instances, no damage is done, on the contrary (Blommaert 1998). Therefore, the emphasis on communication breakdowns in intercultural interaction is no longer considered to be a relevant approach. The fewer communication breakdowns do not mean that intercultural communication is not challenging. Intercultural communication deals with challenging interactions in which a macro-level intercultural conflict does not necessarily result in a micro-level conflict with communication breakdown. Cultures should even not be considered as conflicts that differentiate people. People do not have a culture; they create and recreate it through text and talk (Piller 2017). Kecskés (2014), referring to Bulcean and Blommaert's (Hinnenkamp 1996) and Rampton's (Rampton 1995) data, adds to the definitions that culture cannot be seen as something that is "carved" in every member of a particular society or community. In fact, culture is a manifestation that can be changed, manipulated and dropped in interaction.

When interlocutors in an intercultural situation interact, there is limited common ground. They need to co-create it in the interactional context in which they are functioning at that moment. The interlocutors in intercultural interaction are common ground creators rather than just common ground seekers and activators as is the case in intracultural interaction when members of the same culture interact (Kecskés 2018). Kecskés (2018) explained that intercultural interaction relies more on emergent common ground because of the limited availability of core common ground resulting from little or no mutual prior experience. Co-construction, which is the co-creation of emergent common ground, builds not only on actual situational needs and context but also existing shared knowledge and information.

For dealing with the challenge of intercultural interaction, Kecskés (2018) defined co-created common ground as a critical component. He added a second critical component: conscious recipient design. "Humans have a remarkable capacity for tuning their communicative behaviors to different addressees, a phenomenon also known as recipient design" (Blokpoel et al. 2012: 1). Because interlocutors in intercultural interaction pay more attention to what is said and how it is said, recipient design in intercultural interaction is more conscious (Kecskés 2018).

Francisco Varela, who was a renowned cognitive scientist and neuroscientist, expressed the phenomenon of conscious recipient design and co-created common ground in the following words: "Circulation in the sense of the highly complex dialogue and reciprocal influence between two disparate communities that share a new common ground" (Varela 1989: 15). Varela and other scholars such as Charles Briggs (Briggs and Hallin 2016) used circulation for the dialogue between two domains, fields or communities. The new common ground in Varela's definition is what Kecskés called emergent or co-created common ground. The complex dialogue and reciprocal influence in Varela's definition resemble Kecskés' conscious recipient design in the interaction between members of two cultures. The term circulation could thus denote the conscious acts of co-creating common ground and fostering recipient design in challenging interaction.

2.3 Embodied pedagogy

Involving physical discovery in a learning environment is referred to as embodiment, embodied learning or embodied pedagogy (Brown et al. 2011; Dixon and Senior 2011; Gordon 2019; Nguyen and Larson 2015; Stolz 2015). Embodied learning is educationally significant because it treats the person as a whole being, permitting the person to experience themselves "as a holistic and synthesised acting, feeling, thinking being-in-the-world, rather than as separate physical and mental qualities which bear no relation to each other" (Stolz 2015: 474). Wendy Palmer, a renowned aikido expert, applies aikido in leadership training: "I have found the body to be the most revealing and rewarding focal point for exploring" (Palmer and Kornfield 2010: 5). Explicitly involving the aikido practice in the learning process contributes to both multisensory learning and somatic discovery.

Multisensory learning involves learning stimuli of multiple sensory modalities (Shams and Seitz 2008), e.g. visual, auditory, olfactory, gustatory and kinesthetic (bodily, physical and tactile) stimuli. Learning mechanisms operate optimally under multisensory conditions. One of the main arguments in research is that the perceptual and cognitive mechanisms of the brain have evolved for, and are tuned to, processing multisensory signals. Training with multiple meaningful congruent stimuli has better learning effects, engages learners with different learning styles, benefits later performance and facilitates memory (Shams and Seitz 2008).

Somatic discovery refers to all things related to the soma, the own body in Ancient Greek. Hanna (1988) stated that everything we experience in our lives is a bodily experience. Somatics deals with the voluntary nervous system, i.e. the mind's control of movement, flexibility and health. If an aikido curriculum comprises exercises to train tranquility, it uses somatic exercises: breathing and movement techniques resulting in physiological and mental changes. Medical, biological, neurological and behavioral researchers (Porges 2007; Porges 2021; Swinnen 2020; Swinnen 2021; Park and Thayer 2014) referred to a practical link between the voluntary nervous system and the autonomic nervous system. In simple terms, somatic exercises can create changes in the autonomic nervous system that influence behavior positively: resilience, creativity and empathy. Medical, biological and behavioral research findings, therefore, emphasize the importance of training tranquility.

3 Methodology: Benchmarking study

Considering the aim of this research, we embarked upon a study to benchmark the principles of contemporary aikido. Many sources on aikido's principles trace back to the time of aikido's founder, Morihei Ueshiba (1883–1969). Ueshiba hardly wrote anything down himself. His son, his grandson, his disciples, translators and practitioners wrote about aikido. Most written sources on aikido are non-academic and come from one specific aikido school. This study aimed to learn about aikido by benchmarking aikido principles from various aikido schools around the world in 2020, more than fifty years after the passing of Ueshiba. We conducted twenty semistructured expert interviews, transcribed them and performed a qualitative content analysis.

3.1 Expert interviews

Expert interviews are a valuable and legitimate empirical research method to reveal insider knowledge (Bogner et al. 2009; Van Audenhove and Donders 2019). However, the concepts of expert and expertise are difficult to define. Bogner et al. (2009) stated that simply possessing specific knowledge does not suffice to determine who constitutes an expert. Van Audenhove and Donders (2019) distinguished types of expert knowledge based on the knowledge types of Kaiser (2014) and Bogner et al. (2009):
- Technical knowledge – data, facts, technical information, business facts, statistics, etc.
- Process knowledge – knowledge about processes, interactions, organizational constellations or routines in the field.
- Context knowledge – knowledge about the context, power and interest structure interfering in solving societal conflicts.
- Explanatory knowledge – knowledge with subjective relevance, points of view, interpretations, meanings and explanations held by the expert.

Van Audenhove and Donders (2019) and Bogner et al. (2009) do not recommend expert interviews to find technical knowledge only. Technical knowledge is often available in other sources. Expert interviews are an appropriate method for gathering process, context or explanatory knowledge. Expert knowledge then has less to do with knowledge in the classical sense but is due to the position a person holds. People should only be referred to as experts if they also have a certain degree of power (Bogner et al. 2009). Next to power and position, an expert's knowledge is enriched by their reflection. Blommaert and Jie (2010: 2–3) referred to the degree of reflection and stated that participants "are not a catalogue of their culture or language. However, it is possible to talk about it, because they have reflected."

For this benchmarking study, we focused on a selection of experts involved with teaching aikido, holding aikido examinations and organizing aikido schools or federations. They provided explanatory knowledge by explaining what is at the heart of aikido. The semistructured nature of the interviews invited the experts to give process (e.g. aikido pedagogy) and contextual knowledge (e.g. aikido evolution) as well. Even when some answers in the interviews seemed irrelevant, they helped determine whether the interviewee was indeed an expert. Moreover, experts are not easily influenced and are used to defending their position (Van Audenhove and Donders 2019), contributing to the authenticity of experts' input during the interviews.

3.2 Participants and data selection

The selected experts in this research came from all over the world, which made sense since people practice aikido globally and this research involves intercultural communication. The experts who participated were, therefore, not randomly sampled. They were purposively selected due to qualities they possess (Etikan 2016): technical, process, contextual and explanatory knowledge. The sample needed to meet identifiable qualities. The sampled experts all teach aikido. This implies that they master the art of aikido and have reflected and communicated about it, at least for the purpose of teaching it. Most of them manage a dojo (*dōjō*), a training hall or club for Japanese martial arts. Some have their aikido school or have a prominent position in a national or an international aikido federation.

Typically, the aikido grade is an indicator that the interviewee is an expert. Aikido practitioners do examinations and receive grades, often expressed in belts. A grade or a belt makes the status of a martial artist visible. It usually takes ten years to obtain a first-degree black belt. In simple terms, the higher the grade, the higher the expertise. However, this is not an absolute system. First-degree black belts may be, or not, outstanding experts. An eighth-degree black belt should be. The black belt grades are called *dan* grades (Figure 2). Although there is a curriculum and a system for the examinations in most aikido federations and schools, the evaluation standard is influenced by the people who administer the dan grades and sometimes by the role the aikido practitioner plays in the dojo or the aikido community (Westbrook and Ratti 2001). An aikido teacher may have a low dan grade compared to their position in the aikido community and the other way around. It often depends on the particular aikido school's old or recent history in a region or country.

The sample consisted of aikido experts that were purposely linked to a variety of aikido styles. Aikido is a martial art with many variations. Although most schools of aikido in the west teach gentle, nonviolent, soft forms of self-defense, others teach hard combat techniques (Friedman 2005). Husak (2012: 15) referred to "the continuous debate between practitioners who experience aikido as Ueshiba [the founder of aikido] intended, an art of peace, and those who take advantage of the profound power of the techniques to simply dominate opponents by inflicting pain or injury, as in most other martial arts." The sample in this research represents aikido styles of different positions in the continuum between soft and hard styles.

The sample was homogeneous in knowledge, expertise and era. It was heterogeneous in geographical spread. The deliberate choice for geographical spread meant that the respondents needed to come from different countries and continents. The sample contained at least one expert from each inhabited continent. Figure 3 shows the countries the experts resided in at the moment of the interview: Algeria,

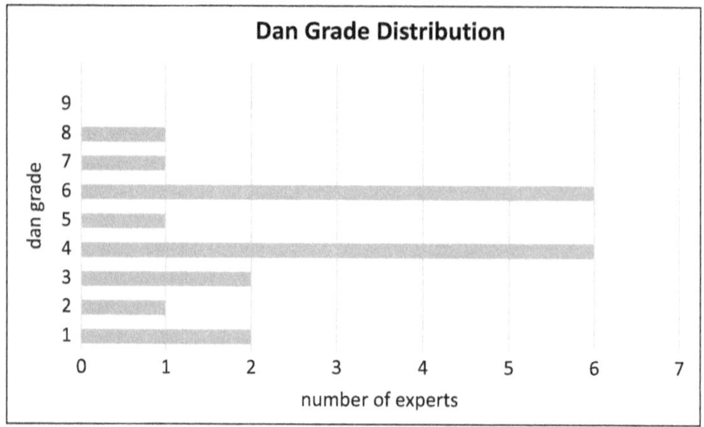

Figure 2: The dan grade distribution of the 20 interviewed aikido experts.

Australia, Belgium, Brazil, East-Africa, France, Germany, Israel, Japan, Malaysia, South Africa, Taiwan, Thailand, The Netherlands, UAE and USA. Figure 4 shows their nationalities: Algerian, American, Australian, Belgian, Brazilian, Dutch, French, German, Iraqi, Israeli, Japanese, Kenyan, South African and Taiwanese. The dark and light color shades do not refer to the number of experts. The shades denote the different countries.

Figure 3: The regional spread of the 20 interviewed aikido experts.

Figure 4: The nationality of the 20 interviewed aikido experts.

3.3 Ethics

The interviewees agreed to informed consent and knew that the interviews would be anonymized except for their aikido grade, martial biography, nationality, current country of residence and gender. The study used pseudonyms with a Japanese influence: a number and the Japanese *san*-suffix. San can mean both Mr. and Ms., both formal and informal, regardless of a person's gender. Moreover, it is common in Japanese to add the san suffix to other nouns and turn them into proper nouns. I have thus interviewed One-san, Two-san, Three-san etc.

3.4 Data collection

I conducted twenty semistructured interviews with open-ended questions, which gave each expert room to articulate their responses fully (Aberbach and Rockman 2002). Therefore, the interview was more a conversation than a list of questions to be answered (Berry 2002). The major common denominators were these six topics (see Figure 8 in the appendix): aikido principles, the relationship between a martial art and harmony, aikido critique, aikido outside the dojo, demographic and intercultural experience, and the intangible aspect of aikido (e.g. spirituality).

Open-ended questions provided a greater opportunity for the interviewees to organize their answers within their frameworks. It increased the validity of the responses and was best for the kind of exploratory and in-depth work we were doing, but it made the analysis more challenging (Aberbach and Rockman 2002). We transcribed 1,520 minutes (25.33 hours) of interview data using EasyTranscript and performed a qualitative content analysis in NVivo. EasyTranscript did not automatically transcribe the audio file, the researcher transcribed word for word. Although time consuming, it was an opportunity to get familiar with the interview data and start reflecting on the data analysis.

3.5 Data analysis

To identify relevant information in the interview data, we labeled or coded the contents in NVivo. Content-coding or coding involved careful reading of the interview transcripts and identifying chunks of text relevant for one of the codes, several of the codes and the research altogether. The coding addressed the research question and showed what twenty aikido experts worldwide identified as aikido principles in an interview in 2020. The codes in this research were more analytic than descriptive. The analysis generated categories, themes, subthemes and patterns. The terms that refer to the interview findings are taken from general English, no aikido jargon, so as to be understood by any researcher or any person who is not involved in the practice of aikido. Therefore, the terminology is not in vivo, i.e. used by the interviewees, but analyst-constructed (Gibbs and Flick 2018).

Whereas coding in quantitative analysis is for the explicit purpose of reducing the data to a few types in order that they can be counted, coding in qualitative analysis is a way of organizing or managing the data. All the original data are preserved. Codes add interpretation and theory to the data. In fact, typically, text may be densely coded; not only will most text be assigned a code, but much will have more than one code attached to it (Gibbs and Flick 2018). Figure 5 shows the hierarchy chart of the coded data that led to the findings discussed in this paper. A hierarchy chart is a diagram that shows data as a set of nested rectangles of varying sizes. In this case, the size represents the amount of coding references in the interview data. Larger areas display at the top left of the chart; smaller rectangles display toward the bottom right.

The findings of the qualitative content analysis explained what aikido experts have in common, or not. Would a researcher who reproduces the research in the same way as it was done originally come up with the same results? This question refers to research reliability. To improve reliability, we meticulously prepared a codebook and involved two senior researchers in coding a sample of the data.

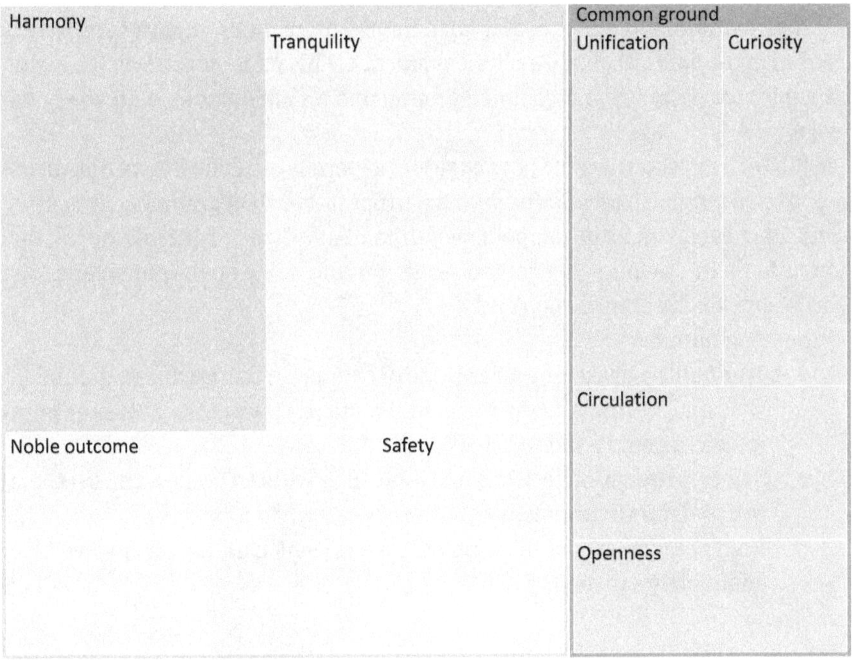

Figure 5: Hierarchy chart of the aikido principles of harmony and common ground.

One researcher was familiar with qualitative content-coding and is the second author of this paper. The second researcher was familiar with the contents, i.e. martial arts studies, aikido in particular.

4 Findings

The benchmarking study provided twenty sets of answers to the same questions (see Appendix). The answers came from experts who represented various manifestations of aikido from places all over the world in 2020. Each answer was a product of the expert and the expert's individual, aikido, social, cultural and demographic contexts. When the interviewed experts talked about aikido interaction, they referred to aikido principles with the same core meaning, however, with local or individual nuances. Some experts saw added value in the combat effectiveness and others in the philosophy of aikido. Interestingly, the analysis of the interview data revealed that the way they learn, teach, understand and perceive aikido has fundamental similarities.

Next to the aikido principles for challenging interactions, many of the experts referred to the value of aikido's physical practice. This paper reports on the aikido principles for harmony and common ground and on aikido as an embodied pedagogy.

What all experts share is knowledge and expertise in aikido interaction on the mat. Aikido emphasizes working with a partner rather than grappling or fighting against an opponent as in competitive tournaments. Typically, an aikido interaction unfolds in the following components from the point of view of an aikidoist who is attacked by another person:[1]

- Seeking harmony
  - Tranquility: to assume an attitude of calmness, centeredness, groundedness and alertness in the moment. Practicing tranquility alters the physiological and the mental state.
  - Safety: to behave effectively and efficiently without doing harm to others, self and the environment.
  - Noble outcome: to achieve an outcome in which all people involved feel adequately satisfied.

1 Aikido practitioners generally refer to the principles with jargon or Japanese terms. The experts in this study used their preferred terms, either in their mother tongue, in a lingua franca or in Japanese. The following list refers to the experts' words. It is non-exhaustive and translated into English. Moreover, the terms do not necessarily cover the principle completely and may overlap with other principles:

- Seeking harmony
  - Tranquility: calm, vertical posture, centered, grounded, alert and in the moment, empty mind, a beginner's mind (*mushin*).
  - Safety: harmlessness, nonviolence, social contract, protecting and respecting life, preserving life, without hurting, lack of injury to the other and the self, *la noblesse de l'échec* (the nobility of failure).
  - Noble outcome: win-win outcome, zero-sum outcome, mutually beneficial outcome, harmony, peace and *masagatsu agatsu katsuhayabi* (true victory is victory over self).
- Building common ground
  - Openness: nonresistance, letting go of tension, muscular force and ego.
  - Curiosity: positive attitude, sensitivity towards the other and action-orientation.
  - Unification: blending, joining, connecting, merging, uniting, awase (harmonizing with, blending and matching) and musubi (tying together; the physical, mental, and spiritual connection).
  - Circulation: circularity, sphericity, tenkan, turning, cooperating and adding the other person's perspective.

- Building common ground
  - Openness: to take an inviting attitude of observation, positivity and flexibility, with a focus on the moment, not on prior assumptions, judgments or thoughts.
  - Curiosity: to have the motivation to interact, discover and learn.
  - Unification: to blend with the other person by fostering physical closeness, sensitivity and a willingness to build common ground.
  - Circulation: to take the perspective of the other and to cooperate.

The components are not entirely sequential, they flow into one another, and some, e.g. safety, are present throughout the interaction. What aikido practitioners physically discover in an aikido interaction resembles what expert interviewee, Ten-san, described in example (1).

[associated audio-1-DeBaets.MP3 with example (1)][2]

(1) *When we make this blending movement, by not opposing, moving in and turning, all of a sudden, we're side by side with this person and we're side-by-side in this amazing, rather brilliant, transformative movement that puts us in the middle of the action. All of a sudden, the person who was coming at us and we're like this [shows a slight tenkan movement, a turn of almost 180°] is on the periphery of a circle that we're in the center of. And from there we can leave the action, we can guide the action. There is no more attack. The attack, magically almost, although rationally, disappears in the act of the blend. In the very action of making that joining movement, there's no more attack. That is why people sometimes look at aikido and think it's fake or that we are just cooperating or we're just putting up dancing. Because you don't see the attack anymore because it vanished, it disappeared by not opposing it. And then, all of a sudden we're moving harmoniously and it looks like dancing or it looks like we're just cooperating or it looks like we're just being nice.* (From the interview with Ten-san)

4.1 The principles for seeking harmony

Harmony was a topic in each interview. Many expert interviewees linked tranquility, safety and noble outcome with aikido being the martial art of harmony. Thirteen-san mentioned in (2) some prerequisites for harmony in aikido:

2 The corresponding audio files are available for download here: https://www.degruyter.com/document/isbn/9783110766752/html

[associated audio-2-DeBaets.MP3 with example (2)]

(2) *Well, of course maintaining calm among people is important, but without the centering, without being mindful of of what I'm doing, how I'm doing it, how correctly I'm doing, how noble I'm doing it, is, without that nothing can happen.* (From the interview with Thirteen-san)

Thirteen-san referred to centering, i.e. aligning the body's center (lower abdomen or *hara* in Japanese) with the vertical posture line. It is one of several ways to train tranquility, see (2). Training physiological tranquility reinforces mental tranquility. Five-san (3) referred to aikido's tranquility as a physical and mental attitude. He explained it when referring to the soft power of aikido in contrast to the muscle fighting power of some people.

[associated audio-3-DeBaets.MP3 with example (3)]

(3) *Et l'aïkido, c'est tout le contraire. L'aïkido, c'est la victoire par la paix. C'est c'est . . . C'est la force tranquille . . . C'est . . . C'est une discipline euh . . . zen attitude, voilà.*

[And aikido is quite the opposite. Aikido is victory through peace. It's . . . It's the tranquil force . . . It's . . . It's a discipline uh . . . zen attitude, that's it.] (From the interview with Five-san.)

Not all of the interviewed experts compare aikido's tranquility with zen. Four-san (4) stressed that his strong, quick, highly martial style of aikido was quite different from most aikido styles practiced in Europe. Even so, he highlighted the importance of avoiding direct confrontation, centering and tranquility. Moreover, he mentioned the usefulness in daily life while at the same time downplaying it by referring to the similar usefulness of practicing other sports.

[associated audio-4-DeBaets.MP3 with example (4)]

(4) *Voor mij als principe in aikido is ten eerste de . . . het . . . weggaan van directe confrontatie in een beweging. En voor mij persoonlijk het bewaren van jouw . . . center.*
(. . .)
Het was een zeer sterke . . . euhm een zeer sterke stijl die wij hebben gedaan.
(. . .)

En natuurlijk je neemt het mee in jouw dagelijks leven ook en alleen door het feit dat je anders beweegt bijvoorbeeld . . . dat je door aikido of andere gevechtskunsten te bestuderen . . . ook rustiger bent denk ik, of rustiger wordt. Andere sporten hebben natuurlijk hetzelfde effect op je lichaam, maar bon (lacht). . . . Dat zijn allemaal dingen die denk ik bijdragen tot een soort van anders in het leven staan.

[For me as a principle in aikido, first of all, the . . . the . . . moving away from direct confrontation in a movement. And for me personally keeping your . . . center.
(. . .)
It was a very strong . . . uhm a very strong style that we have done.
(. . .)
And of course you take it into your daily life as well and only by the fact that you move differently for example . . . that by studying aikido or other martial arts . . . also calmer I think, or become calmer. Other sports have the same effect on your body, of course, but well (laughs). . . . Those are all things that I think contribute to a kind of being different in life.]
(From the interview with Four-san.)

Whatever style of aikido, the concept of safety plays an important role. It refers to safe behavior, i.e. behaving effectively and efficiently without doing harm to other and self.

[associated audio-5-DeBaets.MP3 with example (5)]

(5) *Being self-responsible is the principle. Being self-responsible, having a . . . a mind of non-dissension . . . euh learning how to center yourself so that you can handle more of life's up and downs, (sniffs) euhm . . . yeah, looking to protect all life, protect and honor all life.* (From the interview with Eleven-san.)

Even though not every expert calls the counter-intuitive approach in aikido's self-defense non-dissension (5), they agree that aikido does not cultivate violence and aggression.

(6) 放眼世界上各家武術，無不鑽研如何打擊、摧毀、致人於死傷的強力破壞之法；而合氣道的追求，在於化解攻擊、止息紛爭、將對方置於可控制卻不至於傷害的境地。這並非消極地躲避或不作為，反而是在不傷害任何人的狀況下，得到的最大的勝利、最好的結果。這是為何道祖 植芝盛平先生 所開創的合氣道是『愛與和平』的武術，而非製造傷害的武術了

[Looking at various types of martial arts in the world, they all study how to powerfully strike, destroy, and cause injury and death; however, aikido seeks to resolve attacks, stop disputes, and place the other party under control but does not hurt them. This is not passive avoidance or inaction, but oppositely, it secures the greatest victory and best result without harming anyone. This is why the aikido, which was founded by Ueshiba Morihei, is a martial art of "love and peace", rather than a martial art of harm.]
(Translated from the text Sixteen-san sent as a preparation for her interview.)

Because of its aim, some call aikido the martial art of harmony, other peace or even love (6). Harmony, peace and love have many interpretations and connotations. Therefore, this study uses a term understandable for aikido practitioners and non-aikido practitioners: noble outcome.

[associated audio-7-DeBaets.MP3 with example (7)]

(7) *Un: beaucoup de calme. OK? De pas r . . . Pas des réactions: j'aime, j'aime pas. . . . OK? Ça, voilà. Euh . . . Et en même temps, ça permet de. . . d'observer.*

[One: a lot of calmness. OK? Not r . . . No reactions: I like this, I dislike this. . . . OK? That's it. Uh . . . And at the same time, it allows you to . . . to observe.]
(From the interview with Six-san.)

A noble outcome does not appear by merely being tranquil and acting safely. However important a tranquil state is (7), aikido practitioners soon consciously involve the attacker(s), the other person(s) in the situation.

4.2 The principles for co-creating common ground

Because aikido interaction is challenging interaction, seeking harmony in an aikido interaction is not obvious. Therefore, the aikido practitioner adopts an open and curious attitude from the onset of an interaction. It is a necessary first phase of assessing information and signs that quickly transitions into a phase of constructing common ground. The interviewees did not use common ground as a term. Instead, they referred to the importance of joining, blending, cooperating, attuning, connecting, circulating and unifying (1). Some experts called it connection. Nine-san (8) explained three main principles: centering, connection and creativity.

[associated audio-8-DeBaets.MP3 with example (8)]

(8) *And then and and then I would say the other the third principle is, is like a creative response, which is, when the first and the second principle are happening. And you allow yourself to stay open and channel the energy of yourself and the other through the system, then it automatically begins to move towards resolution, automatically begins to move towards wholeness.* (From the interview with Nine-san.)

Nine-san (8) claimed that connection cannot happen without centering, a tranquility technique. He then explained connection automatically evolves into a resolution. He called it wholeness, yet another word for what the study calls noble outcome. Connection in aikido comes in many forms. Some techniques involve circular movements while connecting with the other person (Figure 6), other techniques involve immediate closeness (9). Whatever the technique, the purpose is to unify your movements with the other persons movements without hitting, knocking or punching. Interestingly, by circulating and unifying you shift your position and sense the other person's position (1). Three-san (9) explained it in much detail.

[associated audio-9-DeBaets.MP3 with example (9)]

(9) *In face of of a problem . . . in aikido, it's physical danger, but in face of a problem, we shrunk, we turn our head, we skip. So first: face it. Then enter in it. So this is very difficult. So euhm, and and then blend. Euh, so try to, so euh, using the, so the attack comes and and you, you take contact, you enter. Next, you make one step and you, you blend. So you see what the other guy is seeing. You can see his point of view, you can blend. You touch him, you you you feel him, you you, and then, you help him going the direction he wants until you you can take control of the movement and return it in the way you want. If you have the margin, you can return it gently. Or you can just (makes a whistling sound) euh, let him go his way and go yours, so there is nothing but a stroll.* (From the interview with Three-san.)

What Three-san (9) called facing and entering, is called openness and curiosity in this study. What he called contact and blending, is the study's unification principle. He did not explicitly refer to circulation. However, an aikido practitioner would associate physical circulation with Three-san's description of blending to see the other person's point of view.

[associated audio-10-DeBaets.MP3 with example (10)]

(10) *Another thing, it's about the circularity of aikido, so, the essential movements it's based on circular power and movement, and when she started to practice and she started practicing during the doshu Kisshomaru Ueshiba (the son of aikido's founder, 1921–1999), and he used to say, and he used to have a very circular aikido and he used to say that his naming maru, it's circle. And maru is circle. So, that's why he's very circular. And the technique he used to practice was very, very simple.*

(From the interview with Twelve-san: first Twelve-san speaks in Portuguese (not transcribed) and then the interpreter says it in English.)

The principles of openness, curiosity, unification and circulation sum up the idea of common ground in aikido interactions. Circulation, sphericity or circularity (10) characterize (Figure 6) most aikido strategies of self-defense, regardless of how slight or barely noticeable that circularity may be when advanced practitioners perform techniques at great speed (Westbrook and Ratti 2001). Unification and circulation are entwined, not sequential, and denote movement that facilitates perception and interpretation of the other(s) to fit, match, meet and co-create a new relationship.

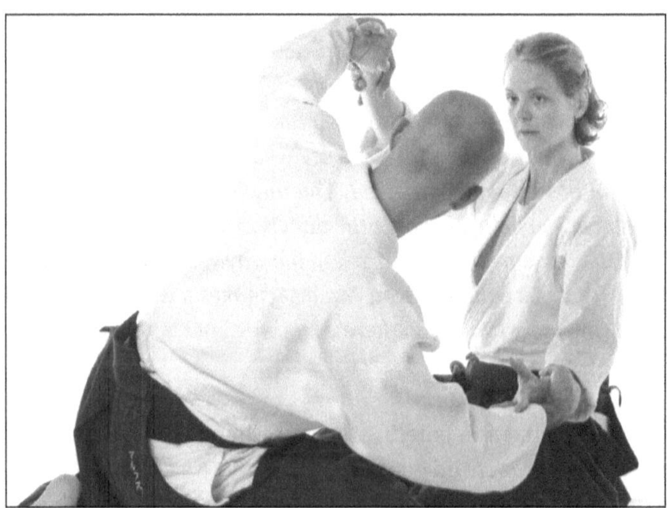

Figure 6: A circular movement in aikido (Stein 2012b).
Note. The image shows Annette and Markus Röllig from Aikido Zentrum Offenbach e.V. Copyright by Dirk Stein, www.lichtwanderer.de, used with permission.

5 Discussion

This paper investigates the added value of aikido, a martial art, as an embodied pedagogy in the intercultural communication classroom. Intercultural communication training aims to develop skills for dealing with challenges and achieving appropriate outcomes in intercultural interaction (Deardorff 2020). The findings of the benchmarking study show fundamental similarities between aikido interaction and intercultural interaction: focus, skills and embodied learning.

The road to a noble outcome in a challenging interaction requires focus, whether it is an aikido or an intercultural interaction. Thirteen-san in (1) referred to this focus using the word mindful. Because the odds seem to be against at the very beginning of the interactions between disparate communities, common ground does not emerge haphazardly, and focus is the way towards a noble outcome. When aikido practitioners deliberately seek harmony and circulate to build common ground, they are in a focused aikido interaction. When interlocutors from different cultures consciously foster recipient design and co-create common ground (Kecskés 2014), they are in a focused interaction. The circulation, typical of aikido interaction (Figure 6), is similar to Varela's definition of circulation (Varela 1989). Circulation in aikido and circulation in intercultural communication refer to the capacity and sensitivity for tuning behavior to interaction partners.

Intercultural interaction that does not end up in a communication breakdown has many similarities with aikido interaction that ends with a noble outcome. Taken together, aikido practitioners start an aikido interaction by assuming an attitude of calmness, centeredness, groundedness and alertness in the moment. This tranquility alters the physiological and the mental state and remains throughout the interaction. They behave effectively and efficiently without doing harm to others, self and the environment. They intend to achieve a noble outcome, i.e. an outcome in which all people involved feel adequately satisfied. They are open. They take an inviting attitude of observation, positivity and flexibility, focusing on the moment, not on prior assumptions, judgments or thoughts. At the same time, they are curious. They have the motivation to interact, discover and learn. They see their attacker as a partner in an aikido interaction. They move, then blend with their partner by fostering physical closeness, sensitivity and a willingness to build or co-create common ground: they unify. They circulate physically to take the perspective of the other and to cooperate. The result is a noble outcome.

A model with seven core principles emerged from the study's analysis (Figure 7). It visualizes the course of an interaction and shows the relationship between the seven core principles. This interaction model stems from aikido,

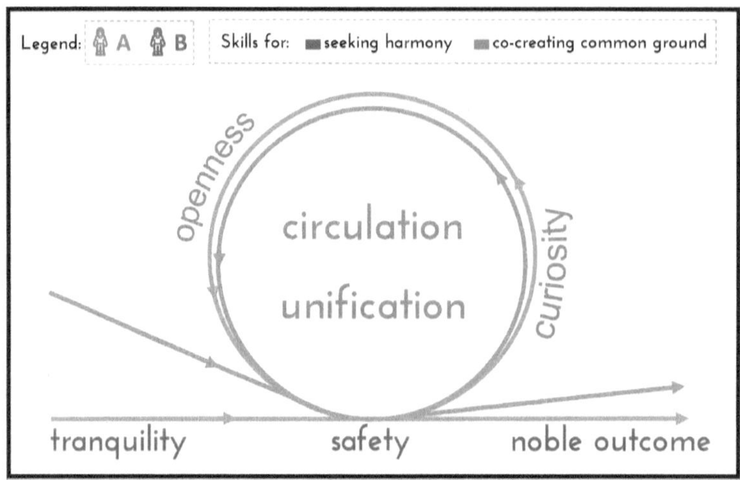

Figure 7: Aikido interaction model of harmony and common ground.

which can explain each principle with physical techniques and bodily movements. The principles thus shift into physical, mental and interactional skills. The seven principles in the model present two interwoven sets of skills that revolve around harmony and common ground. Figure 7 shows persons A and B in an intercultural interaction based on the two skill sets. Person A is motivated to seek harmony and adopts mental and physiological tranquility. Person A assures safety throughout the interaction by not sending signals of unsafety and not taking any unsafety signals of person B personally. The safety effort creates a welcoming, inviting and cooperative atmosphere for person B. To achieve a noble outcome that is appropriate and acceptable for both persons A and B, person A focuses on co-creating common ground. Person A takes an open, inviting attitude of observation, positivity and flexibility, focusing on the moment, not on prior assumptions, judgments or thoughts. The openness goes hand in hand with curiosity, i.e. the motivation to interact, discover and learn. Person A's openness and curiosity result in active circulation: to take the perspective of the other and to cooperate. The more person A succeeds in circulating, the more persons A and B unify. They blend and co-create common ground. The interaction has a high probability of achieving a noble outcome.

Aikido moves and exercises turn principles into skills for interaction. From participants' point of view in an intercultural training course, they discover the physical activities as a multisensory message. The physical discovery gains meaning by linking moves to the main principles for harmony (tranquility, safety and noble outcome) and common ground (openness, curiosity, circulation and unification). If an intercultural communication course applied the physical discovery of an aikido interaction, it would alternate aikido movements with discussion moments. In the discussions, the course participants give meaning to what they discover in the aikido movements. Both the movement and the discussion parts of the training course serve as an example of experiential discovery. The trainer guides the translation process from aikido interaction into intercultural interaction.

Introducing the physical practice of aikido into an intercultural communication training course adds the kinesthetic stimulus to other obvious stimuli such as visual (slides, whiteboard and pictures) and auditory (explanations and stories) stimuli. Such a multisensory learning environment benefits "encoding, storing and retrieving perceptual information" (Shams and Seitz 2008: 5). After all, learning is acquiring knowledge and skills, and having them readily available from memory to make sense of future problems and opportunities (Brown 2014). Although easy aikido movements will suffice to learn about applying aikido principles in intercultural interaction, it will take some effort from the learners to do aikido. The effort is an advantage: learning is deeper and more durable when effortful. Learning that is easy is like writing in sand, here today and gone tomorrow (Brown 2014).

Aikido exercises teach interactional skills. In addition, some of the aikido exercises offer somatic (Hanna 1988) learning: techniques resulting in internal physiological and mental changes. Practicing tranquility involves breathing, posture and movement exercises to become calm, centered, grounded and alert in the moment. Somatic exercises can create changes in the autonomic nervous system that influence behavior positively: resilience, creativity and empathy (Porges 2007; Porges 2021; Swinnen 2020; Swinnen 2021; Park and Thayer 2014). Positive behavior, empathy and creativity (Kecskés 2020) are critical factors in intercultural interaction and the development of intercultural competence (Deardorff 2020).

6 Conclusion

Intercultural communication training that relies on conventional didactic explanations results in knowledge about intercultural communication, not in competence in intercultural interaction. Competence is the result of experiential discovery, of learning through experience. Intercultural communication training can bring experiential discovery into its classroom by introducing the embodied pedagogy of aikido. Firstly, aikido interaction and intercultural interaction share the significance of focused interaction in which participants consciously seek harmony and co-create common ground. Secondly, aikido's embodied pedagogy provides the classroom with multisensory learning practice and somatic discovery.

Harmony and common ground in challenging interaction, such as in aikido, result from focused action. Aikido practitioners consciously seek harmony by practicing tranquility, creating safety and pursuing a noble outcome, i.e. an outcome in which all people involved feel adequately satisfied. They build or co-create common ground on an attitude of openness and curiosity on the one hand and by unifying and circulating with any person involved in the interaction on the other hand.

We found similarities between seeking harmony and building common ground in aikido interaction and conscious recipient design and co-created common ground in intercultural interaction. The way interlocutors in intercultural interaction consciously foster recipient design is similar to how aikido practitioners seek harmony in aikido interaction. Interlocutors in intercultural interaction do not readily find common ground. Instead, they co-create it with the same focus aikido practitioners have when building common ground in aikido interaction. In sum, focused interactions in intercultural and aikido situations achieve a noble outcome by seeking harmony and co-creating common ground.

The embodied pedagogy of aikido comprises multisensory learning and somatic discovery. Pedagogical and educational research showed the benefits of multisensory learning, of combining visual, auditory and physical stimuli in the learning process. To train physiological and mental tranquility, aikido involves somatic exercises. Medical, biological and behavioral research showed that the somatic practice of tranquility creates changes in the autonomic nervous system that influence behavior positively: resilience, creativity and empathy. These advantages in behavior are favorable for seeking harmony and co-creating common ground in challenging interactions. Participants in an intercultural communication training course that relies on aikido discover conscious recipient design by physical contact and movements. They train tranquility and feel how it creates conditions for seeking harmony and co-creating common ground. The trainer facilitates the embodied discovery process and the translation from aikido interaction into intercultural interaction. We, therefore, conclude that aikido has potential as an embodied pedagogy for intercultural communication training.

7 Limitations and future research

Research participants were limited to twenty aikido experts. They were primarily selected on the basis of their expertise. To study various aikido practices and thus have an acceptable degree of representation of the aikido world, the research sampled different aikido styles and aimed for a global geographical spread. Although the sample was varied, it did not cover every possible manifestation of aikido in the world. Furthermore, to make the research results intelligible for everyone, we referred to the found principles with general English words instead of aikido jargon. Because of the differences in aikido practice and vocabulary, we cannot assume that the terms used in this research mean the same things to every aikido expert or practitioner.

Using aikido principles in intercultural communication does not remove other intercultural principles. The embodied pedagogy of aikido does not intend to replace other intercultural communication training approaches. It complements it. Rew and Ferns (2005: 232) wrote about the complementary value of applying aikido in conflict resolution practice: “The use of eastern philosophies and techniques, such as aikido, have been used successfully in conflict resolution and are worth considering as an alternative method to complement such teaching methods as good communication skills.” Moreover, the link between aikido and intercultural communication explored in this research may be useful for individuals who seek to investigate any link between communication and a traditional eastern art they practice, such as hapkido, iaido, kendo, tai chi chuan, kyudo, chado and shodo. Aikido practitioners and scholars are invited to explore any link between aikido and intercultural communication. It would be interesting to compare their version with the version presented in this paper.

Future research should consider investigating the efficiency and effectiveness of an intercultural training course based on the embodied pedagogy of aikido. This requires the development of a pedagogical framework. The study of applied aikido for intercultural communication training and intercultural interaction may contribute to existing research on applied aikido in target domains such as nonviolent communication, conflict resolution and psychotherapy. It may also contribute to pedagogical studies and to specific aspects of intercultural communication studies such as experiential discovery methods and pedagogical frameworks for intercultural competence building.

Appendix

Preparation for expert interviews: An investigation of the potential of aikido, a Japanese martial art, for intercultural encounters and communication

Greet De Baets – Ghent University – Department of Translating, Interpreting and Communication

Version of 31 January 2020

1. Disclaimer
   Informed consent:
   - in writing
   - on recording

2. Purpose
   My name is Greet De Baets, I am a researcher at Ghent University and I am conducting academic/doctoral research on aikido-based intercultural communication training.

   The purpose is to learn what you consider to be principles of aikido on and off the mat. It is important to know this from you, an expert in aikido, in [location] in [year].

3. Topic list
   A semistructured interview:

Section	Topic	Question	Probing	Internal comment
A. Martial biography	Lineage	Which school of aikido do you belong to?		Lineage is the line of teachers tracing back to the founder of aikido, o'sensei, Ueshiba Morihei.
	Expertise	What is your grade?		Dan grades (black belt grades) and status grades in the Japanese martial schools' system.

(continued)

Section	Topic	Question	Probing	Internal comment
	Broadness	What other martial arts do/did you practice?	So why aikido?	
B. Aikido principles	Facts	What are the key principles of aikido?		Important for the terminology and coding categories.
	Opinions	How do you interpret them?		
	Challenge for completeness	What are the inconsistencies or shortages in the aikido principles, if any?		
	Peace	How come a martial art can be an art of harmony?	What does fighting mean in aikido? What does winning mean in aikido?	
	Target domain	How have you used aikido off the mat?	[If the experience was a physical self-defense] Has aikido inspired you in other ways?	To test a possible link to communication and behavior.
	Intangible aspect	What intangible/ spiritual value does aikido have for you?		
C. Demography	Whereabouts now and before	Where have you lived?	What is your experience with intercultural encounters?	To test a possible link to intercultural communication and behavior.
	[If no intercultural experience] a case-based question	If [I present an intercultural case] you suddenly need to complete a two-year assignment on another continent where you don't know the language, what would you do?	What is the link between an aikido blackbelt and a communication blackbelt?	

(continued)

Section	Topic	Question	Probing	Internal comment
D. Conclusion	Uniqueness?	Some say that aikido is unique: what are your thoughts on that?		
	Anything else?	Is there anything else you consider important or relevant?		

4. The end of the interview
   Leaving with a bridge towards future communication: e.g. to ask for a second interview, to give feedback on the results (a short report).
   Snowballing . . .

References

Aberbach, Joel D. & Bert A. Rockman. 2002. Conducting and Coding Elite Interviews. *Political Science & Politics* 35(04). 673–676. https://doi.org/10.1017/S1049096502001142. http://www.journals.cambridge.org/abstract_S1049096502001142 (accessed 2 November 2019).

Bannister, Kelly. 2018. From Ethical Codes to Ethics as Praxis: An Invitation. *Ethnobiology Letters* 9(1). 13–26. https://doi.org/10.14237/ebl.9.1.2018.1060. https://ojs.ethnobiology.org/index.php/ebl/article/view/1060 (accessed 11 October 2021).

Beebe, Beatrice & Frank M. Lachmann. 2005. *Infant Research and Adult Treatment*. 1st edn. New York, NY: Routledge. https://doi.org/10.4324/9780203767498. https://www.taylorfrancis.com/books/9781135060411 (accessed 14 June 2021).

Berry, Jeffrey M. 2002. Validity and Reliability Issues In Elite Interviewing. *Political Science & Politics* 35(04). 679–682. https://doi.org/10.1017/S1049096502001166. http://www.journals.cambridge.org/abstract_S1049096502001166 (accessed 2 November 2019).

Blokpoel, Mark, Marlieke van Kesteren, Arjen Stolk, Pim Haselager, Ivan Toni & Iris van Rooij. 2012. Recipient design in human communication: simple heuristics or perspective taking? *Frontiers in Human Neuroscience* 6(253). 1–13. https://doi.org/10.3389/fnhum.2012.00253. http://journal.frontiersin.org/article/10.3389/fnhum.2012.00253/abstract (accessed 7 November 2020).

Blommaert, Jan. 1998. Approaches to intercultural communication: A critical survey. Presented at the Expertentagung über Lernen und Arbeiten in einer international vernetzten und multikulturellen Gesellschaft, Universität Bremen, Germany, 27–28 February 1998. http://rgdoi.net/10.13140/2.1.1052.0324 (accessed 25 October 2020).

Blommaert, Jan & Dong Jie. 2010. *Ethnographic fieldwork: a beginner's guide*. Bristol, United Kingdom: Multilingual Matters.

Bogner, Alexander, Beate Littig & Wolfgang Menz (eds.). 2009. *Interviewing Experts*. London, UK: Palgrave Macmillan UK. https://doi.org/10.1057/9780230244276. http://link.springer.com/10.1057/9780230244276 (accessed 2 November 2019).

Briggs, Charles L. & Daniel C. Hallin. 2016. *Making health public: how news coverage is remaking media, medicine, and contemporary life*. New York, NY: Routledge.

Brown, Peter C. 2014. *Make it stick: the science of successful learning*. Cambridge, MA: The Belknap Press of Harvard University Press.

Brown, Steven D., John Cromby, David J. Harper, Katherine Johnson & Paula Reavey. 2011. Researching "experience": Embodiment, methodology, process. *Theory & Psychology* 21(4). 493–515. https://doi.org/10.1177/0959354310377543. http://journals.sagepub.com/doi/10.1177/0959354310377543 (accessed 2 July 2021).

Deardorff, Darla K. 2020. *Manual for developing intercultural competencies: story circles* (Routledge Focus on Environment and Sustainability). London; New York: Routledge, Taylor & Francis Group.

Díaz, Adriana Raquel & Paul J Moore. 2018. (Re)imagining a course in intercultural communication for the 21st century. *Intercultural Communication Education* 1(3). 84–99. https://dx.doi.org/10.29140/ice.v1n3.84.

Dixon, Mary & Kim Senior. 2011. Appearing pedagogy: from embodied learning and teaching to embodied pedagogy. *Pedagogy, Culture & Society* 19(3). 473–484. https://doi.org/10.1080/14681366.2011.632514. http://www.tandfonline.com/doi/abs/10.1080/14681366.2011.632514 (accessed 23 May 2021).

Etikan, Ilker. 2016. Comparison of Convenience Sampling and Purposive Sampling. *American Journal of Theoretical and Applied Statistics* 5(1). 1–4. https://doi.org/10.11648/j.ajtas.20160501.11. http://www.sciencepublishinggroup.com/journal/paperinfo?journalid=146&doi=10.11648/j.ajtas.20160501.11 (accessed 2 November 2019).

Faggianelli, Patrick & David Lukoff. 2006. Aikido and psychotherapy: a study of psychotherapists who are aikido practitioners. *The Journal of Transpersonal Psychology* 38(2). 159–178.

Foster, Drew. 2015. Fighters who Don't Fight: The Case of Aikido and Somatic Metaphorism. *Qualitative Sociology* 38(2). 165–183. https://doi.org/10.1007/s11133-015-9305-4. http://link.springer.com/10.1007/s11133-015-9305-4 (accessed 13 October 2021).

Friedman, Harris. 2005. Problems of Romanticism in Transpersonal Psychology: A Case Study of Aikido. *The Humanistic Psychologist* 33(1). 3–24. https://doi.org/10.1207/s15473333thp3301_2. https://citeseerx.ist.psu.edu/viewdoc/download?doi=10.1.1.542.9741&rep=rep1&type=pdf (accessed 18 December 2020).

Gibbs, Graham & Uwe Flick. 2018. *Analyzing qualitative data* (The SAGE Qualitative Research Kit). 2nd edn. Los Angeles & London: SAGE.

Goffman, Erving. 1966. *Behavior in public places: notes on the social organization of gatherings*. Paperback. New York & London: The Free Press Collier Macmillan.

Gordon, Michael A. 2019. *Aikido as Transformative and Embodied Pedagogy: Teacher as Healer*. Cham, Switzerland: Springer International Publishing. https://doi.org/10.1007/978-3-030-23953-4. http://link.springer.com/10.1007/978-3-030-23953-4 (accessed 1 April 2021).

Graf, Andrea. 2004. Assessing intercultural training designs. *Journal of European Industrial Training* 28(2/3/4). 199–214. https://doi.org/10.1108/03090590410527618. https://www.emerald.com/insight/content/doi/10.1108/03090590410527618/full/html (accessed 18 May 2020).

Gudykunst, W.B. & M.R. Hammer. 1998. Basic training design: approaches to intercultural training. In D. Landis & R.W. Brislin (eds.), *Handbook of Intercultural Training*. (Issues in Theory and Design 1), 118–154. New York, NY: Elmsfield.

Hanna, Thomas. 1988. *Somatics: reawakening the mind's control of movement, flexibility, and health*. Cambridge, MA: Da Capo Life Long.

Hinnenkamp, Volker. 1996. Intercultural communication. In Jef Verschueren, Jan-Ola Östman, Jan Blommaert & Chris Bulcaen (eds.), *Handbook of Pragmatics*, 1–20. Amsterdam, The Netherlands: John Benjamins Publishing Company. https://doi.org/10.1075/hop.1.int9. https://benjamins.com/online/hop/articles/int9 (accessed 23 October 2021).

Husak, Gregory. 2012. *Zen Communication – A Cross Cultural Approach to Mindfulness, Appropriate Response, and Flow in Dyadic Interactions*. Mankato, MN: Minnesota State University MA thesis.

Kaiser, Robert. 2014. *Qualitative Experteninterviews: Konzeptionelle Grundlagen und praktische Durchführung*. Wiesbaden: Springer-Verlag.

Kecskés, István. 2014. *Intercultural pragmatics*. Oxford: Oxford University Press.

Kecskés, István. 2018. How does intercultural communication differ from intracultural communication? In Andy Curtis & Roland Sussex (eds.), *Intercultural Communication in Asia: Education, Language and Values*, 115–135. Cham, Switzerland: Springer.

Kecskés, István. 2020. Interculturality and intercultural pragmatics. In *The Routledge Handbook of Language and Intercultural Communication*, 138–155. London: Routledge.

Kong, Jieyoung. 2016. Moving beyond the anthropos and reclaiming the geo in intercultural communication: The transculturation of the martial art practice of Aikido. *Journal of International and Intercultural Communication* 9(2). 179–197. https://doi.org/10.1080/17513057.2016.1142599. http://www.tandfonline.com/doi/full/10.1080/17513057.2016.1142599 (accessed 2 November 2019).

Lefebvre, Augustin. 2016. The pacific philosophy of aikido: an interactional approach. *Martial Arts Studies* 0(2). 91. https://doi.org/10.18573/j.2016.10066. https://mas.cardiffuniversitypress.org/article/10.18573/j.2016.10066/ (accessed 2 November 2019).

Nguyen, David J. & Jay B. Larson. 2015. Don't Forget About the Body: Exploring the Curricular Possibilities of Embodied Pedagogy. *Innovative Higher Education* 40(4). 331–344. https://doi.org/10.1007/s10755-015-9319-6. http://link.springer.com/10.1007/s10755-015-9319-6 (accessed 2 July 2021).

Niehaus, Andreas. 2019. The Aikido of Ueshiba Morihei as Ritual Practice to Reconstruct the World. Presented at the Workshop: Sport and Religion in Japan, Western Michigan University, Kalamazoo, MI, 2 March 2019.

Palmer, Wendy & Jack Kornfield. 2010. *The practice of freedom: Aikido principles as a spiritual guide*. Berkeley, CA: Rodmell Press. http://site.ebrary.com/id/10395342 (accessed 14 June 2021).

Park, Gewnhi & Julian F. Thayer. 2014. From the heart to the mind: cardiac vagal tone modulates top-down and bottom-up visual perception and attention to emotional stimuli. *Frontiers in Psychology* 5(278). 1–8. https://doi.org/10.3389/fpsyg.2014.00278. http://journal.frontiersin.org/article/10.3389/fpsyg.2014.00278/abstract (accessed 12 September 2021).

Piller, Ingrid. 2017. *Intercultural Communication: A Critical Introduction*. 2nd edn. Edinburgh, UK: Edinburgh University Press.

Porges, Stephen W. 2007. The polyvagal perspective. *Biological Psychology* 74(2). 116–143. https://doi.org/10.1016/j.biopsycho.2006.06.009. https://linkinghub.elsevier.com/retrieve/pii/S0301051106001761 (accessed 23 May 2021).

Porges, Stephen W. 2021. Polyvagal Theory: A biobehavioral journey to sociality. *Comprehensive Psychoneuroendocrinology* 7(100069). 1–7. https://doi.org/10.1016/j.cpnec.2021.100069. https://linkinghub.elsevier.com/retrieve/pii/S2666497621000436 (accessed 12 September 2021).

Rampton, Ben. 1995. *Crossing: language and ethnicity among adolescents* (Real Language Series). London & New York: Longman.

Rew, Maggie & Terry Ferns. 2005. A balanced approach to dealing with violence and aggression at work. *British Journal of Nursing* 14(4). 227–232. https://doi.org/10.12968/bjon.2005.14.4.17609. http://www.magonlinelibrary.com/doi/10.12968/bjon.2005.14.4.17609 (accessed 16 October 2021).

Salih, Ahmad Muhamad, Wilko Vriesman & Uday Saul. 2022. The Role of Aikido and Cultural Intelligence in Harmonising Leaders-Followers Relationship. In Taran Patel & Ahmad Muhamad Salih (eds.), *Cultural spaces in international business: theories and applications*. Routledge.

Shams, Ladan & Aaron R. Seitz. 2008. Benefits of multisensory learning. *Trends in Cognitive Sciences* 12(11). 411–417. https://doi.org/10.1016/j.tics.2008.07.006. https://linkinghub.elsevier.com/retrieve/pii/S1364661308002180 (accessed 2 November 2019).

Shimizu, Kenji. 1994. *Aikido, the heavenly road*. Carol Stream, IL: Edition Q.

Stein, Dirk. 2012a. *A wrist lock in aikido*. Photograph. https://www.aikido-zentrum-offenbach.de/aikido/ (accessed 5 May 2020).

Stein, Dirk. 2012b. *A circular movement in aikido*. Photograph. https://www.aikido-zentrum-offenbach.de/aikido/ (accessed 7 November 2021).

Stolz, Steven A. 2015. Embodied Learning. *Educational Philosophy and Theory* 47(5). 474–487. https://doi.org/10.1080/00131857.2013.879694. https://www.tandfonline.com/doi/full/10.1080/00131857.2013.879694 (accessed 23 May 2021).

Swinnen, Luc. 2020. *Rust voor je brein: train je offlinebrein en versterk je veerkracht, creativiteit en empathie* [Rest for your brain: train your offline brain and strengthen your resilience, creativity and empathy]. Tielt, Belgium: Lannoo.

Swinnen, Luc. 2021. *Activeer je nervus vagus: een revolutionair antwoord op stress- en angstklachten, trauma en een verminderde immuniteit* [Activate your nervus vagus: a revolutionary answer to stress and anxiety complaints, trauma and reduced immunity]. Tielt, Belgium: Lannoo.

Tosey, Paul & Jane Mathison. 2010. Neuro-linguistic programming as an innovation in education and teaching. *Innovations in Education and Teaching International* 47(3). 317–326. https://doi.org/10.1080/14703297.2010.498183. http://www.tandfonline.com/doi/abs/10.1080/14703297.2010.498183 (accessed 21 March 2021).

Treven, Sonja. 2003. International training: the training of managers for assignment abroad. *Education + Training* 45(8/9). 550–557. doi.org/10.1108.

Ueshiba, Morihei. 2013. *Budo, Teachings of the Founder of Aikido*. (Trans.) John Stevens. 2nd edn. New York, NY: Kodansha USA.

Ueshiba, Morihei & John Stevens. 1993. *The Essence of Aikido, Spiritual Teachings of Morihei Ueshiba, compiled by John Stevens*. Japan: Kodansha International.

Van Audenhove, L. & K. Donders. 2019. Expert interviews and elite interviews. In M. Van den Bulck, K. Puppis, K. Donders & L. Van Audenhove (eds.), *Handbook of Media Policy Methods*, 179–197. London, United Kingdom: Palgrave MacMillan.

Varela, Francisco J. 1989. Reflections on the Circulation of Concepts between a Biology of Cognition and Systemic Family Therapy. *Family Process* 28(1). 15–24. https://

doi.org/10.1111/j.1545-5300.1989.00015.x. http://doi.wiley.com/10.1111/j.1545-5300.1989.00015.x (accessed 19 November 2020).

Wagner, Winfried. 1999. *AIKI-DO und wir: Atem, Bewegung und spirituelle Entwicklung*. Petersberg, Germany: Via Nova. https://www.amazon.com/AIKI-DO-wir-Winfried-Wagner/dp/3928632507.

Wagner, Winfried (ed.). 2015. *AiKiDô: the Trinity of Conflict Transformation*. Innsbruck, Austria: Wolfgang Dietrich, UNESCO Chair for Peace Studies.

Waxin, Marie-France & Alexandra Panaccio. 2005. Cross-cultural training to facilitate expatriate adjustment: it works! (Ed.) Chris Brewster. *Personnel Review* 34(1). 51–67. https://doi.org/10.1108/00483480510571879. https://www.emerald.com/insight/content/doi/10.1108/00483480510571879/full/html (accessed 12 May 2020).

Westbrook, Adele & Oscar Ratti. 2001. *Aikido and the Dynamic Sphere: An Illustrated Introduction*. North Clarendon, VT: Tuttle Publishing.

Contributors to this volume

Keith Allan, Emeritus Professor, Monash University, Melbourne, Australia.

Greet Angèle De Baets, PhD researcher, Department of Translation, Interpreting and Communication, Ghent University, Belgium.

Jialiang Chen, postgraduate student at School of English for International Business, Guangdong University of Foreign Studies, Guangzhou, P.R. China.

Elke Diedrichsen, Researcher, Member of Computational and Functional Linguistics Research Group at Technological University Dublin, Ireland.

Istvan Kecskes, Distinguished Professor, State University of New York, Albany, USA.

Eunhee Kim, PhD student in the Department of Educational Theory and Practice of the Graduate School of Education at State University of New York, Albany, USA.

Ping Liu, Professor at The Center for Linguistics and Applied Linguistics and School of English for International Business, Guangdong University of Foreign Studies, Guangzhou, P.R. China.

Fabrizio Macagno, Assistant Professor in the Department of Philosophy and Communication at the Universidade Nova de Lisboa, Portugal.

Adriana Merino, Lecturer, Department of Spanish and Portuguese, Princeton University, USA.

Ludmila Yu. Minakova, Associated Professor at Tomsk State University. She is a Senior Research Fellow of the Laboratory of Socio-cognitive Linguistics and Teaching Foreign Language Discourse.

Arto Mustajoki, Emeritus Professor, University of Helsinki, Finland.

Brian Nolan, Head of Informatics and Creative Digital Media (retired) at the Technological University, Dublin, in Ireland.

Olga A. Obdalova, Professor at Tomsk State University, Russia. She is the Head of the Laboratory of Socio-cognitive Linguistics and Foreign Language Teaching as well as the Acting Head of the Department of Foreign Languages, Tomsk Scientific Center, Siberian Branch, Russian Academy of Sciences.

Karsten Senkbeil, Post-doc researcher at the Department of Intercultural Communication, University of Hildesheim, Germany.

Aleksandra V. Soboleva, Associate Professor of the Faculty of Foreign Languages and a Senior Research Fellow of the Laboratory of Socio-cognitive Linguistics and Teaching Foreign Language Discourse at Tomsk State University.

https://doi.org/10.1515/9783110766752-015

Ivana Trbojević Milošević, Associate Professor at the English Department, Faculty of Philology at Belgrade University, Serbia.

Ellen Van Praet, Professor, Department of Translation, Interpreting and Communication, Ghent University, Belgium.

Linlin Yang, PhD student at School of English for International Business, Guangdong University of Foreign Studies, Guangzhou, P.R. China.

Qing Yang, Lecturer at Guangdong Ocean University, Zhanjiang, P.R. China.

Index

https://doi.org/10.1515/9783110766752-016

www.ingramcontent.com/pod-product-compliance
Lightning Source LLC
Chambersburg PA
CBHW020220170426
43201CB00007B/273

* 9 7 8 3 1 1 1 6 1 9 6 2 0 *